Statue of Liberty–Ellis Island Centennial Series

Books in the
Statue of Liberty–Ellis Island Series

*A Century of European Migrations,
1830–1930*

A Century of European Migrations, 1830–1930

EDITED BY

Rudolph J. Vecoli

AND

Suzanne M. Sinke

UNIVERSITY OF ILLINOIS PRESS
Urbana and Chicago

The preparation of this volume was made possible in part by grants from the Northwest Area Foundation and the Division of Research Programs of the National Endowment for the Humanities, an independent federal agency. Publication was made possible in part by a grant from the Statue of Liberty–Ellis Island Foundation.

This book is printed on acid-free paper.

Library of Congress Cataloging-in-Publication Data

A Century of European migrations, 1830-1930 / edited by Rudolph J.
Vecoli and Suzanne Sinke.
    p. cm.–(Statue of Liberty–Ellis Island Centennial series)
    Papers chiefly from a symposium held at the Spring Hill Center,
Wayzata, Minn., Nov. 6-9, 1986.
    Includes bibliographical references.
    ISBN 0-252-10796-X (cl)
    1. United States—Emigration and immigration—History—Congresses.
    2. Europe—Emigration and immigration—History—Congresses.
    3. America—Emigration and immigration—History—Congresses.
    I. Vecoli, Rudolph J. II. Sinke, Suzanne. III. Series.
JV6450.C46 1991
325'.24'0973—dc20
                                                    90-20301
                                                         CIP

Contents

Introduction

RUDOLPH J. VECOLI

This volume is the outcome of a symposium held at the Spring Hill Center, Wayzata, Minnesota, November 6-9, 1986 to mark the centennial of the Statue of Liberty and the twentieth anniversary of the Immigration History Research Center at the University of Minnesota. The objective was to bring together leading practitioners of migration history to assess the state of the field, to explore new perspectives and new methodologies, and to promote transnational cooperative and comparative studies. Forty-three scholars participated, twenty-four from the United States and nineteen representing nine other countries. As Frank Thistlethwaite subsequently observed: "This was more than a conference: it was a coming together of a multi- and trans-national group of migration historians, all working on related subjects and communicating on the same high frequency wavelengths." That such a meeting could take place was itself an indication of the dynamic and cosmopolitan state of migration history.

The past quarter century has witnessed an unparalleled outpouring of studies of the transoceanic migrations which over the course of a century carried some fifty-five million Europeans to the four corners of the earth, some thirty-three million of whom came to the United States. The study of immigration history has been an established field of scholarship in this country since the 1920s, but a quantum leap in the quantity and quality of work by Americans has occurred since the sixties. Equally striking is the parallel development in other countries of scholarly interest in immigration and emigration. It is interesting to speculate on the reasons for this contemporary emergence of migration history, not only in the United States and Europe, but in Canada, Australia, and South America as well.

During the nation-building stage, neither emigration nor immigration were appealing historical themes, because the former was shameful abandonment of the fatherland and the latter the intrusion of often unwelcome aliens. In the climate of the post-World War II

1

decades, revulsion from nationalistic historiography opened the way for the consideration of this transnational phenomenon. Another shift in historical thinking, reflective of the populist upheavals of the 1960s, was the new interest in the history of common people rather than the traditional focus on elites. This "history from the bottom up" approach informed the new social history which turned to the study of the ordinary lives of peasants, workers, women, and migrants. Meanwhile, a fascination (if not always affection) for all things American among Europeans fed a growing curiosity about what had happened to their American cousins as Americans in turn became absorbed with tracing their "roots" to the "Old Country." Moreover, the dramatic population movements from the third world to the developed countries (former countries of emigration now became countries of immigration) created more than academic interest in the historic experience of the United States with ethnic diversity, assimilation, and nativism. All of these conditions have made migration history an international "growth industry."

Migration history by its very nature demands a transnational perspective. However, it was only as scholars working independently in a dozen different countries gradually became aware of each other's work that they discovered that they shared a common subject. Like the five blind men, we realized that we all had been examining different parts of the elephant. As a result of conferences, exchanges of publications, correspondence, and visits, the field has become international, and the symposium and this volume are some of its fruits.

The catalyst for these exciting developments clearly had been Frank Thistlethwaite's essay "Migration from Europe Overseas in the Nineteenth and Twentieth Century," presented at the Eleventh International Congress of Historical Sciences in Stockholm in 1960. That essay is reprinted in its entirety in this volume, along with a "Postscript" by Thistlethwaite in which he reflects on its origins. Within the span of twenty-five pages, he presented a cogently argued thesis which placed the Atlantic migrations at the very center of European history. "The great overseas migration," he observed, "is in a very broad sense to be treated as a major, but subordinate, aspect of European population growth and European industrialization." Moreover, he delineated the multidirectional and complex patterns of population movements within Europe as well as overseas, of which the immigration to the United States was but one, if major, expression. In his words, "we are a long way from a simple case of 'America fever.' " The concept of the Atlantic economy as an integrated system in which European capital and labor exploited first the grasslands, and then the iron and coal deposits of North America, provided an encompassing explanation.

Thistlethwaite admonished students of migration to abandon stereotypes of "an undifferentiated, mass movement of 'peasants' or indeed 'artisans' thronging toward immigrant ports from vaguely conceived 'countries of origin' " in favor of an analysis of the "honeycomb of innumerable particular cells, districts, villages, towns, each with an individual reaction or lack of it to the pull of migration." In the context of the economic opportunities created by the unleashed forces of capitalism, he suggested that migration was an aspect of social mobility. Scattered throughout the essay in a profligate manner are provocative questions intended to stimulate curiosity and research: What of the remigration of perhaps a third of those who immigrated to the United States? What of the comparative impact of the immigration of greater intensity to South America? What of the relationships between local/regional intra-European migrations and overseas migrations? What of the migration of skilled craftsmen and technicians within the international labor markets? What of the great majority who did not leave Europe? Thistlethwaite advised his colleagues "to think neither of emigrants nor immigrants, but of migrants, and to treat the process of migration as a complete sequence of experiences whereby the individual moves from one social identity to another."

Thistlethwaite's compelling paradigm evoked a widespread response among both European and American scholars. As one who first read the essay in the early sixties, I can testify to the exhilarating effect of its broad vision which opened new vistas of research. It helped to liberate my generation of historians from the stultifying straits of consensus and nationalist history. As this volume attests, the Thistlethwaite thesis set the agenda for this generation of American migration scholars. In Europe, Swedish scholars were the first to embrace this new paradigm under the aegis of the "Uppsala Project" and with typical methodicalness produced some twenty-five dissertations and other studies culminating in the summary volume *From Sweden to America* (1976).[1] Subsequently, other migration history projects were initiated in Finland, West Germany, Italy, and in a number of East European countries (Poland, Hungary, Yugoslavia, and Czechoslovakia).

Frank Thistlethwaite, then Hill Visiting Professor at the University of Minnesota, participated in the 1986 symposium. His presence added a particular aura to the meeting. If, however, as was said, "we are all Thistlethwaitians," it was evident that the conferees had not gathered simply to pay adulation to their mentor. Rather, as these essays demonstrate, the common purpose was to test and challenge Thistle-thwaite's paradigm as he had those of his predecessors. Selected from the twenty-five papers presented at the symposium, the chapters in-cluded in this volume range from those which offer macroperspectives on the Atlantic migration to those which report on meticulous micro-studies of particular migratory phenomena.

This volume opens as did the symposium with a challenge to im-migration history from the perspective of American colonial history. Lamenting the division between colonialists and immigration scholars, Russell Menard maintains that both have much to learn from each other. Menard stresses the ethnic and racial diversity of the population of colonial America. The "re-peopling" of North America, however, resulted in a holocaust for the Indians and in slavery for the trans-ported Africans. Citing the alleged failure to encompass these racial experiences, Menard charges immigration history with "profound Eurocentrism." (Since as Thistlethwaite points out, immigration his-tory had earlier been guilty of "American-centredness," there perhaps has been some progress.) He analyzes the processes of migration resulting from the operation of an Atlantic labor market and the availability of land which brought people from various parts of Europe to British North America. Yet Menard concludes that by 1776 the population of the new republic had realized a high degree of homo-geneity due to Anglicization and the emergence of "creole cultures." The new United States was pluralistic, but it was a pluralism based on race rather than Old World origins.

Taking the Thistlethwaite thesis as his point of departure, Dirk Hoerder develops a theoretical framework for considering migration in the Atlantic economies in terms of the operation of international labor markets. Because migrants responded to demands for their labor, Hoerder argues that labor markets, not nation-states, should be the focus of migration studies. However, migrations might be traditional, seasonal, temporary, permanent, regional, intra-European, or trans-oceanic, depending on the stages of development, pressures, and op-portunities in both the sending and receiving areas. Modern migra-tions have been characteristically from the rural periphery to the industrializing, urban core. Hoerder, however, does not subscribe to a simple "push-pull" migration model. He seeks to combine a world-systems approach with a "from the bottom up" perspective which views men and women making decisions based on personal and familial considerations. Chain migrations grounded in kinship and neighborly ties were, therefore, basic to initiating, directing, and sustaining migrations. Because they often moved from their village to a predetermined ethnic enclave and job, migrants were not "uprooted."

Hoerder is also concerned with whether the labor migrants who moved within the Atlantic economies constituted an international proletariat sharing a class consciousness or were fragmented by differences of skill, culture, language, and religion. While citing contradictory findings, he concludes that class solidarity and mutual aid did transcend ethnic boundaries. Women, Hoerder maintains, played a particularly important role in knitting such social networks. A common experience of exploitation among migrant workers of diverse ethnic origins elicited a shared consciousness and commitment to struggle for social justice.

Thistlethwaite's injunction to examine as through a magnifying glass the "honeycomb of innumerable particular cells, districts, villages, towns, each with an individual reaction or lack of it to the pull of migration" has been particularly taken to heart by a younger generation of scholars. Armed with computer technology, perseverance, and curiosity, they have abstracted individual-level data from a wide range of records for their microanalyses of migration processes. Several of the chapters in this volume exemplify this approach and methodology.

Migration traditions which channeled population flows between places of origin and destination over a period of decades are analyzed for the Finnish case by Reino Kero. Drawing upon passport registers, passenger lists, and church records, he is able to trace in minute detail the development and persistence of such traditions between specific localities in Finland and the United States. Once established by recruiters or pioneers, traditions were sustained and reinforced by remigrants, letters, and, especially, prepaid tickets. Traditions could wither if opportunities dried up, and new ones born. Kero finds that any given Finnish locality might have a number of migration traditions with quite different destinations.

Robert Swierenga also identifies migration traditions which were long-lived and powerful between specific Dutch and American places. The small group and excellent records for them permit Swierenga to subject all sixty-two thousand Dutch emigrants from 1835 to 1880 to scrutiny, tracing their places of origin, socioeconomic status, family condition, and paths of migration. This comprehensive profile is the basis for an analysis which particularizes the causes of Dutch emigration by province and even to the village level. Conservative in character, seeking to avoid change through emigration, the Dutch in America clung to their village loyalties and cultures, kinship groups, and churches in their highly concentrated settlements.

Jon Gjerde attributes the same characteristics of solidarity and insularity to the Norwegian "kinship colonies" in the Upper Midwest. Chain migrations created these clustered settlements of relatives and neighbors from the same localities where Old Country customs and beliefs could be maintained. Such communities were characterized by a high degree of social and economic interdependence and a slow rate of cultural change. Gjerde, however, cautions against the reification of the concept of chain migration, reminding us that what we perceive as patterns was created by a myriad of decisions by historical actors. He demonstrates his contention through a microanalysis of the complex chain migrations from two regions on the west coast of Norway. Gjerde also observes that seldom was the entire population of a settlement drawn from just one place of origin. Rather, multiple chains often brought several nationalities as well as subgroups of the same nationality together. The interaction, including the potential for conflict, among these groups was an important feature in the life of such communities.

The chain migration of an atypical group of Norwegians is the subject of Odd Lovoll's essay. Many migrants from the district of Voss settled in Chicago, unlike the majority of their countrymen who chose rural settings. Voss was a center of cottage industry, peddling, and horsetrading, and Vossings were reputed to have a bent for business. Lovoll describes their decisions to emigrate as considered and realistic, motivated by a fear of downward mobility and a desire for improved well-being. Although farmers and artisans, they possessed skills valued in the emerging city, and many of them became well-to-do. The Chicago Vossings created a society to refute negative reports circulating in Norway regarding the condition of Norwegians in the United States. They also formed the Vossing Emigration Society to provide assistance to their poor countrymen who wished to emigrate. Lovoll remarks on the class consciousness and bitterness toward the official class of Voss which animated these activities, sentiments he traces to the resentments engendered by social abuses suffered in Norway.

Secondary migrations within the United States are interpreted by June Alexander as an integral part of the larger chain migration process which initially brought Slovaks to Pittsburgh. The same logic shaped both forms of migration: movements to locations where one's townspeople were living, whether from overseas or from one city to another in the United States, guaranteed a degree of material and emotional support. Alexander uses fraternal lodge and church records to trace the complex chains based on village ties of Slovaks as they moved in and about Pittsburgh in response to changing working and living conditions. She concludes that these migrants were not behaving like a "floating proletariat," but were acting in a purposive manner within networks of personal relationships.

In a study, based primarily on oral sources, of migrants from the village of Szamosszeg, Julianna Puskás confirms Alexander's contention of the continuation of chain migrations within the United States. Through extensive interviews, she compiled the life histories of almost three hundred individuals who comprised the total emigration from this one village in Hungary. Their common motivation, she found, was to make money in America in order to improve their families' condition in Szamosszeg, primarily through the acquisition of land. Although all intended to return, only half did, which points up Ewa Morawska's admonition regarding the need to study shifts in the immigrants' attitudes toward repatriation. The mining camps of West Virginia were the first destination of the Szamosszegeans, but in time most of them chain migrated to industrial cities, especially Detroit and New Brunswick, New Jersey. Puskás observes that although family and friendship bonds largely held the villagers together during the first generation, the immigrants' children married non-Szamosszegeans, and their grandchildren married non-Hungarians. She concludes that microanalysis in this case confirms the findings of macroanalysis regarding the character of the Hungarian immigration.

Several of the chapters herein deal with the paradox that a country or region could simultaneously be an area of emigration and immigration. Bruno Ramirez offers a case study of the province of Quebec, which at the turn of the century was the recipient of large numbers of southern and eastern Europeans at the same time that Quebecers were emigrating en masse to New England. Ramirez attributes this to the regional disparities within the province between the marginal, overpopulated rural areas and the rapidly industrializing city of Montreal. He contends that a segmented labor market attracted Italian sojourners to fill unskilled, temporary jobs which were shunned by rural French Canadian migrants, who preferred the better-paid and more diversified opportunities in the United States. Emphasizing the mediating roles of family and community, Ramirez contends that we need to view migration in terms of an interaction between economic and cultural influences rather than as a mechanical response to impersonal market forces.

The chapter by Franco Ramella on emigration from northwestern Italy complements that of Ramirez because it too deals with an area of simultaneous emigration and immigration. Ramella also agrees on the need to set aside the "push-pull" model and to focus on the strategies of persons who chose to migrate. In northwestern Italy, the years of most intense industrialization also witnessed an increase in emigration. Ramella dismisses as too simplistic the explanation that industrial development was simply unable to absorb surplus rural labor. Rather, he identifies several types of migration with causes and consequences particular to themselves. Some were traditional and seasonal, such as the migration of skilled workers from the mountainous areas; others were responses to the intrusion of modern capitalism, such as peasant proprietors fleeing the descent into the ranks of the landless or protoindustrial workers displaced by changing production methods. Ramella suggests that traditional social strategies of peasant families, which had long viewed temporary migration and separation not as deviant behavior but as normal and essential for survival, could readily accommodate the fact of mass migration.

Another topic to which Thistlethwaite called attention and which subsequently has been the subject of considerable study was the phenomenon of massive repatriation. Ewa Morawska sets forth a theoretical and research agenda for the study of return migrations. Viewed within the context of recent thinking about migration, repatriation need not be interpreted as unusual, deviant, or a sign of failure. Rather, the global system of core and periphery, Morawska maintains, accommodates the remigration of workers in response to personal and social factors as well as structural forces. Decisions to migrate and remigrate were not governed by the push-pull of economics or demographics, but were the products of collectivist strategies. Neither the fluctuations of economic cycles nor the original intent of the sojourner are adequate explanations Morawska insists, calling for analyses of specific situations stimulating or inhibiting repatriation. For example, while the volume of migration and remigration varied with the fluctuations of the American economy, we do not know what effects ethnic concentrations in particular industries or conditions in the countries of origin had on differential rates of return. Morawska suggests that the degree of "social imbeddedness" in family and community in the United States also influenced decisions to stay or leave. What effects did remigration have on the societies of origin? Studies suggest that neither the dollars nor the ideas of the repatriates served as agents of change, because of the conservative character of both the migrants and their home villages. Morawska, however, calls for further comparative study of these issues.

Walter Kamphoefner challenges the off-the-cuff estimate that a third of all immigrants to the United States remigrated, because that generalization, based on twentieth-century statistics, simply has been projected back into the nineteenth century, for which comparable data do not exist. Analyzing mid-nineteenth-century German return migration using German state figures, Kamphoefner concludes that the rate of repatriation was much lower than had been previously estimated. He also questions the equation of remigration with disenchantment, that is, failure, citing his findings that repatriates had double the financial resources of emigrants.

The final section of the volume consists of essays devoted to a consideration of the role of ideology in shaping, justifying, and controlling migrations. Hartmut Keil is concerned with the German socialist immigration to the United States in the second half of the nineteenth century. This migration was not simply one of persons, but also involved the transfer of ideas and institutions which laid the basis for a German-American socialist movement. In addition to those socialist activists who fled repression in Bismarckian Germany, Keil identifies a large segment of the German immigration (artisans and skilled workers) who were most likely sympathetic to socialist ideas. The prominent role of Germans in the socialist labor movements in the United States in the late nineteenth century testified to their presence. Keil describes the intricate communications network between German-speaking socialists in Germany and America which helped sustain the ideological and cultural traditions within the immigrant communities. Not surprisingly, the German-American labor movement modeled its institutions after the successful German example. Following the end of German mass emigration, however, Keil finds that the intimate relationship between socialist ideology and ethnic culture began to fade as German socialists aspired to become part of an "Americanized" movement.

If Keil's socialists posed a threat to the ruling establishment of Germany and thus were encouraged to emigrate, the Irish emigrants posed an ideological dilemma for the dominant Catholic social classes and Catholic church of Ireland. According to Kerby Miller, the vast majority of Irish who emigrated did so for economic and social reasons similar to those of other European emigrants. Further, it was the Irish Catholic bourgeoisie and strong farmers who bore a major responsibility for the post-famine exodus. Yet only radical changes in Irish society, which would have undermined the position of the Irish Catholic middle class, could have addressed the causes of this mass emigration. Given the existing social structure, emigration was a necessity to relieve the social conflicts and tensions resulting from the presence of a great number of landless agricultural laborers and disinherited children. The interpretation of emigration as exile thus served as an ideological resolution of the contradiction between the reality of a fragmented, exploitative Irish society and the ideal of a harmonious, organic "holy Ireland." Miller applies the Gramscian concept of cultural hegemony to explain how this view of emigration as involuntary expatriation caused by British oppression was used by the Catholic middle class and clergy to defuse the resentments of the Irish masses and to reconcile them to their fate. Miller cites the dedication and contributions to the cause of "holy Ireland" on the part of Irish Americans as evidence of the persistence of this hegemonic ideology.

Arnold Alanen presents a different effort to establish cultural hegemony and social control over the immigrant workers in the Lake Superior mining region. Welfare capitalism was an ideology and policy designed to win the loyalty and compliance of employees to managerial goals of productivity, discipline, and orderliness. Alanen describes these programs as they were implemented in the raw mining settlements of northern Michigan and Minnesota. Operating in isolated wilderness settings, the mining companies had to create physical as well as social environments for their polyglot work forces. Using maps, town plans, and photographs, Alanen portrays how these company towns, including "model villages," were constructed. But like other welfare provisions such as educational and recreational programs, medical services, and pensions, company housing was assigned in a preferential manner. The best quality was reserved for mining supervisors, captains, and foremen, who also tended to be native Americans or "old stock" immigrants; the middling was assigned to skilled workers of similar ethnic background; and the poorest lodgings were consigned to the unskilled laborers, mostly recent immigrants, Finnish, Slavic, and Italian. Thus the administration of the welfare programs accentuated the hierarchial and segmented character of the work force. High rates of labor turnover, strikes, and the appeal of radicalism among the new immigrants suggest that welfare capitalism failed as a system of cultural hegemony as far as they were concerned, but it may have succeeded in winning the loyalty of the higher echelons of employees and thus in splitting the workers along lines of skill and ethnicity.

The portrait of the migrant that emerges from the following chapters is that of a social being deeply embedded in a matrix of familial and village relationships. Decisions to emigrate are interpreted not as expressions of individual will or ambition, but as collective strategies designed to realize the optimum good for the kinship group. Such decisions were made not in desperation or in the delirium of "America fever," but through calculated, informed judgments. Thus prospective migrants were themselves historical actors who chose among options: to go or to remain; to migrate to Argentina or the United States; to the Ruhr or to Pittsburgh. The idea of migration was neither new nor frightening because sojourning had long been an established pattern in many villages. Rather than seeking freedom from traditional constraints to make new lives in the New World, a more common motive was to resist adverse changes, to fend off descent into the landless on the part of peasants or the loss of skills on the part of craftsmen. As Thistlethwaite observes, migration was one aspect of a heightened social mobility, but the betterment of one's family status and well-being could be achieved by some through permanent settlement and by others by remigration. Repatriation in this view becomes for many the normal, expected behavior. What has to be explained is not the decision to return, but the decision to remain.

Several contributors go to pains to distinguish the concept of chain migration from the push-pull model based on economic rationality in which migrants responded mechanically to changing labor markets. Chain migration rather implies that networks, based on kin and kith, of information, mutual help, and emotional and material resources provided guidance and sustenance to those undertaking the trip. Such networks determined timing and destinations, promised lodgings and jobs, and insured social integration into a community. Migration traditions are preferred by some to indicate that decisions were not made on a tabula rasa, but were the result of an accretion of knowledge, experience, and social bonds which in effect created bridges between two places thousands of miles apart. Migrants can be thought of as traveling across these bridges with a sense of familiarity and comfort knowing that there would be a warm welcome at the end of the journey. As a consequence, clustered settlements of kinship groups were formed in urban as well as rural areas, settlements characterized by a high degree of cultural homogeneity and social solidarity.

This portrait of self-determined, free-willed migrants who established cohesive communities is troubled, however, by a number of discordant thoughts expressed at the symposium and represented in this volume. Having rescued the migrants from the caricature of uprooted, oppressed, traumatized victims, have we exaggerated the degree of autonomy which they enjoyed? The nation-state with its sovereign power over migrations was a reality, as was the established church in most countries, as was the class structure, as was the developing capitalist system. The constraints imposed by these institutions upon the sphere of choice allowed to common people, including decisions regarding migration, were often severe, and have perhaps not been taken sufficiently into account in recent migration history. Hoerder, for example, describes how the contrasting policies of Germany and France prescribed quite different statuses and prospects for immigrants. He also reveals how the functioning of various labor markets predetermined the fortunes of migrants depending on skill level and ethnicity. Miller and Alanen demonstrate how dominant classes sought to control the thoughts and behavior of migrant workers through ideologies and programs. The concept of cultural hegemony as Miller explicates in the case of Ireland might profitably be applied to help explain the acquiescence by other migrants in mass expulsion from their native lands. Perhaps they did acquiesce but left with bitterness and hatred in their hearts. Hoerder and Lovoll suggest that at least some migrants nourished class antagonisms if not full-blown class-consciousness. Hoerder concludes that, having suffered exploitation in common, the migrants did develop a transnational proletarian identity. However, more studies are needed of the influence of political ideologies on migrants' thinking to determine the extent to which they were under the sway of hegemonic creeds and to what extent they subscribed to oppositional beliefs, as did Keil's German socialists.

One observation by Thistlethwaite that appears to have been largely overlooked is his identification of the "Dissenter" as the archetypal emigrant personality, and his call for comparative study of the "Dissenting element." The Dutch Seceders, the German socialists, and the Vossing pietists fit this category; however, all of the others appear to have migrated for familial reasons unrelated to larger social movements in their societies. Political and religious persecution have received little attention as causes of emigration in recent studies, perhaps because they are incompatible with the portrait of the self-determined migrant. However, the predominance among the world's migrants today of refugees should cause us to recall the not-inconsiderable number who were involuntary migrants in the past. Menard, of course, reminds us that the vast majority of the first immigration came in a condition of servitude, either as servants from Europe or as slaves from Africa. In a symposium paper, which unfortunately is not included in this volume, Peter Shergold discussed the nineteenth-century migrations of convicts and indentured servants within the imperial British, French, and Dutch labor markets.[2] Was this century of European migrations exceptional in the history of migration because it was largely "free"?

To charge this volume and the symposium which spawned it with "Eurocentrism" is a tautology. Yet is was the sense of the discussion as it is of certain essays that we need to move beyond the framework of the "Atlantic Migration." Certainly that conception as introduced by Marcus Lee Hansen and elaborated by Thistlethwaite has stimulated an enormous amount of important work. However, as Shergold observed, it also blinkered us to the global nature of the phenomenon. For this reason, the massive imperial migrations to which he called our attention could remain outside our field of vision. We also could neglect the colonial period of migration history and particularly the experience of African migrants. And as Morawska points out, we need to incorporate the most recent episode in our scheme of migration history, the vast influx of peoples from the third world into the United States and other developed countries over the past quarter century. Certainly our portrait of the migrant will change considerably if we include the experiences of the African brought over in chains and the Hmong fleeing from genocide.

The quarter century since the publication of Thistlethwaite's essay has been productive of much original historical writing on migrations. The authors of some of the best of it are represented in this volume. The objective of the symposium and of this volume, however, is not to celebrate current scholarship, but to help define a fresh agenda for the field. If we have not emerged with a fully defined agenda, I believe we can distinguish the salient lineaments of one. We need to think of a global system of migrations which are expressive of the disparities of wealth and power within as well as among the many nation-states. In addition to human beings, we need to include in our conception of migration the totality of transactions and exchanges among societies, including capital, raw materials, technology, and ideologies. The disequilibrium within societies which always precedes migrations can be the result of either political, demographic, and economic internal dynamics or of military as well as commercial and technological external disruptions. Labor migrations within an international labor market are themselves subject to the imperatives of capitalist development and state policies. But our conception must be inclusive of other types of migration, including forced labor and refugees. Massive expulsions and transfers of population have been more characteristic of the migrations of our time than has the classic nineteenth-century "free" migration. This is admittedly an ambitious holistic vision of migration history, but the only one, I believe, that will do justice to its subject.

NOTES

1. Harald Runblom and Hans Norman, eds., *From Sweden to America: A History of the Migration* (Minneapolis, 1976).

2. "The Convict as Migrant: An Australian Perspective," A Century of European Migrations 1830-1930, Symposium, November 9, 1986.

PART ONE

Macroperspectives

1

Migration from Europe Overseas in the Nineteenth and Twentieth Centuries

FRANK THISTLETHWAITE

A generation has elapsed since the late Marcus Lee Hansen, the father of modern historical scholarship in migration, first set the field for meaningful investigation.[1] The questions posed by Hansen in his famous article published in 1927 largely remain unanswered and continue to haunt the student of migration. Five years after the Hansen paper a committee of the American Historical Association merely re-phrased them;[2] and as recently as 1956 the latest commentator has little further progress to report. Dr. Richard Haskett's "introductory" bibliography for the history of American immigration (1607–1955), to which will not be possible to do justice in this *rapport,* runs to about two hundred pages of close print: yet in his prefatory essay he can hardly do more than proliferate the questions which are implicit in Hansen's seminal paper, and he concludes that "the chief effect of a generation of professional study has been a recognition of the awesome task confronting anyone who attempts to master the subject of emigration."[3] As candid students we must endorse both the awesome character of the job before us and the inconclusive nature of the results hitherto achieved.

Why is this so? An attempt to answer this question is relevant not only to historiography but also to the present state of migration studies.

The study of modern migration has its origin not in Europe, the continent of emigration, but in what came to be overwhelmingly the most important country of immigration, the United States. This is scarcely suprising in view of the intimate connection which exists between migration and the American experience. Migration is central to American national tradition. The influx of diverse European, African and Asiatic strains induced a self-consciousness about ethnic origins, the juxtaposition of minorities and concern for the effect of ethnic mixture upon the national character and institutions which is

17

unique in modern history. The attitude of American publicists and scholars towards this controversial subject at the turn of the 20th century when the inpouring of millions of "new" immigrants presented urgent social problems was contentious and in part wildly ethnocentric; yet it was in a true sense sociological. It is no accident that the adopted home of the struggling science of sociology came to be the United States, and its chief stimulus has been the immigrant problem.[4]

One must also bear in mind that the study of migration originated with the social scientists, as more narrowly defined, and not with the historians. Investigations resulting from the concern of social reformers at the "new" immigration provided the first comprehensive and systematic evidence for historical research into immigration. The publication of the forty-one volumes of the United States Immigration Commission Report in 1911 was accompanied and followed by a spate of studies of different ethnic, immigrant groups. Only later did historians like McMaster and Channing begin to show that the historical craft had assimilated both the subject matter and the disciplined approach of social science in this respect.

Some of this literature is of limited use as historical evidence owing to the partisan spirit in which it was written. This is particularly the case with the highly-coloured pseudo-historical writing of the filio-pietists, usually of the older immigrant stocks, who were quick to assert the positive contribution of their Scotch-Irish, German, Irish or Scandinavian fellow-citizens to American culture.[5] More useful, though often pessimistic enough to provide ammunition for the restrictionists, were studies of a more sociological nature, usually of the new immigrants, such as that by Foerster on the Italians and those by Fairchild and Burgess on the Greeks, which, together with that by Babcock on the Scandinavians, are of continuing usefulness.[6] Between the Wars filio-pietist and sociological approaches each resulted in a flood of periodical literature of mixed quality, and in a few major works of scholarship of which Blegen's work on the Norwegian migration might be allowed to represent the filio-pietist tradition and Handlin's work on Boston's immigrants, the sociological.[7] Each is the end-product of a long process of refinement and sophistication peculiar to American scholarship in which the sociological and the narrative-historical have grown closer to mutual advantage. In particular the Handlin achievement represents a blending of the historical and the sociological approaches of immense value to the study of migration. I shall return to this later.

There are, however, limitations to the American achievement. Naturally enough, in view of the original impetus to migration studies in the United States, American scholars have been overwhelmingly pre-occupied with one phase, and one phase only, of the migration process: that of immigration. The term "immigrant" is said to have been coined in 1789 by Samuel Morse as an Americanism essential to describe someone whom language had hitherto universally described as an "emigrant";[8] and it was in the nature of things that American tradition and, when it came to recognize migration as a legitimate field of study, American historical scholarship should assume the same point of view and, taking the migrant's departure very much for granted, should concentrate upon his destination. Settlement, assimilation and, more recently, acculturation: these have been the central, urgent issues for American historians and sociologists alike.

As a result it has been the consequences and not the causes of migration which have received most attention; and, moreover, the consequences in the receiving, not the sending country. The causes, if not exactly taken for granted, have been given more perfunctory investigation. It is a long time since a scholar could assert that the reason why the French did not emigrate was because they had liberal institutions and leave it at that;[9] and American scholars are no longer guilty of succumbing to what the State Department demographer calls "the American stereotype of the hungry denizen of the old world casting an envious eye on the wealth and opportunities of the new";[10] yet there are few with the detachment to ask the question posed of immigrants long ago by Foerster: "Has the game for them been worth the candle?"[11]

One of the few is Professor Oscar Handlin whose powerfully written study of *The Uprooted* manages to communicate a much deeper insight into immigrant experience than anyone has hitherto achieved.[12] To convey the immigrant experience as tragic as well as epic has exalted rather than diminished the moral experience of migration and has forced it upon the attention of general historians as one of the great historical themes. Yet even Professor Handlin is not entirely innocent of the American limitations. It has been pointed out that "what emerges is a mystical projection of the 'peasant' conditioned through fifteen hundred years in Europe to passive and pathetic acceptance of his unhappy lot" before being uprooted and transplanted willy-nilly to the American scene.[13] I shall return later to this characteristically American stereotype of "the peasant" which, along with "feudalism" and "the customary society," makes a romantic backdrop to the realistic drama of immigrant adjustment in America. Suffice it here to say that this touch of unreality in Handlin's work derives from the immigrant—or American—centredness of it. Europe is given, so to speak, taken for granted as necessary background: only the immigrant is real; and the result is that the historic experience of migration, as a totality from the first intimations of dislodgement at home to ultimate reconciliation or defeat abroad, is frustrated. Recent American scholarship has wonderfully enriched our knowledge of immigrant adjustment; but there still appears to be a salt-water curtain inhibiting understanding of European origins.

The great, though not the only, exception to this judgement is Marcus Lee Hansen himself. Hansen's work[14] was the result not only of painstaking researches in European archives and newspapers but of long brooding upon the complete process of migration; and the discerning reader may find in his closely woven writing not merely all the important questions but suggestive leads of the kind that Americans delight to call "insights." For Hansen the history of emigration had almost universal implications and it is regrettable that he did not live long enough to complete a general history of the subject.[15] He could have made it the central theme for a history of the American people which would have been more lasting, because more profound, that that of Frederick Jackson Turner; for settlers were emigrants before they settled and migration has more than the wilderness to do with American character and institutions. Yet in the search for a history of migration Hansen was destined to be a Moses not because he died young, but because, despite his masterly diagnosis of the emigration fever as it touched neighbourhood after neighbourhood across Europe, he only concerned himself with migrants who had one special destination: the United States. His history would have been American, not universal. This is the final limitation of American scholarship in migration. Even in so fine a mind as Hansen's there is always the presumption that the ultimate objective of overseas migration from Europe is North America and even, because so much Canadian immigration was transient, the United States. "During the century, therefore, it may be said that America was a huge magnet of varying intensity, drawing the people of Europe from those regions where conditions made them mobile and from which transportation provided a path. American conditions determined the duration and height of the waves, European, the particular source."[16]

Now one must face the fact that of the fifty-five million Europeans who emigrated overseas between 1821 and 1924 thirty-three million or three-fifths went to the United States:[17] and yet an argument of this paper is that to treat 19th, and still more, 20th-century overseas migration as an essay in the peopling of the United States may provide a false perspective. As will be argued below the process was much more complex than the transatlantic movement would imply. Viewing the phenomenon of migration as a whole the United States destination, though a powerful "magnet," may be a less significant factor than American scholars have assumed; and it may be that in concentrating so much upon the "America fever" we have got off on the wrong foot and that this may be one reason for the slow progress of scholarship in the migration field.

Should this hypothesis prove correct, Europeans have themselves, not the Americans, to blame for it. If American efforts have been limited largely to "domestic" aspects of the subject European efforts have hardly had any results at all, even in those aspects of the subject which are domestic to us. We see mere flashes of welcome light in an otherwise dark continent.

The treatment of modern migration by European historians is a remarkable example of the blinkers which traditional ways of looking at the past impose on the historical imagination. The removal overseas of some fifty-five million Europeans in the century before American restriction is one of the more remarkable phenomena of modern times; and yet it appears to have made little if any impact upon the writers of general European history. The reasons for this are no doubt bound up with the fact that European history has been the history of nations and, from this point of view, overseas migration is essentially negative. Supra-national in manifestation, it represents a drain or loss to the nation which cannot easily be assessed. For example, the British Isles contributed by far the largest proportion of emigrants, about 19 million;[18] yet even taking into account the fact that this includes an important proportion of Irish, it is surprising how little notice English historians take of the fact. The volume of the standard Oxford History of England which covers the 1880's, a decade when the rate of British (and largely English) emigration, at six persons per thousand population, was almost as high as that of Scandinavia, contains two laconic references to the figures without interpretation;[19] and a few general and meagre references to emigration in the standard social history of England, where, if anywhere, one would expect the subject to be properly handled, give the totally erroneous impression that most British emigrants in the 19th century went to the British colonies.[20] To the national historian emigration appears to be an embarrassing subject, best ignored.

Yet, if it is plausible, by concentrating upon the phenomena of agrarian upheaval, industrialization and urbanization, to by-pass the *causes* of emigration and to dismiss emigrants as so much inconsequential wastage, one might think that the *consequences* of an important bloodletting of population through emigration would not be so easy to ignore. It was once again an American W. R. Shepherd who, in a famous article as long ago as 1919, asserted that "the possibilities of investigation suggested by a survey of the process by which the world at large has become Europeanized are neither so moral nor so interesting and important as those involved in a study of the reaction of its expansion upon the life and thought of Europe itself."[21] But in 1932 that Committee of the American Historical Association was still touting the field as virgin territory,[22] and as recently as 1952 a United Nations report lamented the paucity of studies of the social effects of emigration on the home country.[23] In particular the effects of emigration on a country where the *rate* of emigration to total population has been as high as, say, in Scandinavia (700 per 100,000) must have been so great as to determine to a degree the course of national development. Indeed, as long ago as 1913 the great Swedish demographer Sundbärg said, "To discuss 'Swedish emigration' is the same as to discuss 'Sweden'; there is hardly a single political, social or economic problem in our country which has not been conditioned, directly or indirectly, by the phenomenon of emigration."[24] Yet this does not yet appear to have been attempted;[25] and, despite the brilliant efforts of Professor Koht and Mrs. Semmingsen this would also appear to be the case in Norway.[26]

This is not to imply that there has not been good, even brilliant monographic work of recent years: the point I am making is that it is still a comparatively neglected field, that it is a field dominated by American, not European, scholarship and that the best hope of a new advance is to take a new look at the subject *as a whole* from a different point of view; from neither the continent of origin nor from the principal country of reception; we should try to think neither of emigrants nor immigrants, but of migrants, and to treat the process of migration as a complete sequence of experiences whereby the individual moves from one social identity to another. This paper attempts to suggest ways of re-directing inquiries along these lines.

One group of students who have habitually studied migrants rather than immigrants or emigrants are the demographers. I have already referred to the extent to which the historical study of migration has in the past leant upon the social scientists. The findings of demographers, economists and sociologists are no substitute for historical research; yet it is once again the case, as it was fifty years ago, that the social scientists are setting the pace and historians have much to learn from the advances they have made. One reason for this is the elusiveness of the usually anonymous individual migrant compared with other subjects of historical research, so that special reliance must be placed upon the evidence of the statistics.

The first point to be made is that their handling of statistics has at last given us the orders of magnitude of the problems concerned. Migration statistics have been a notoriously intractable problem, discussed at conference after conference of the International Statistical Institute since 1891, at the International Conference on Emigration and Immigration at Rome (1924), and the International Parliamentary Commercial Conference at Rio in 1927. The International Labour Organization in 1947 considered migration statistics "still very imperfect and incapable of serving as a basis for international comparisons,"[27] an opinion re-iterated by the United Nations Department of Social Affairs and the World Population Conference of 1954.[28]

The gaps and discrepancies between the various types of statistical evidence—from ports, frontiers, passenger lists and passports—each of which vary from country to country and in time-scale are notorious;[29] it has sometimes been more convenient to make up rough estimates of migration based upon natural increase rather than rely on the emigration statistics and much historical research still remains to be done.[30] Yet the famous survey undertaken on American initiative for the International Labour Office by Ferenczi and Willcox in 1931 did, as the authors claimed, enable the historical study of migration to be "taken up on new bases."[31] Since 1931 historians have had at their disposal at least the broad orders of magnitude of overseas migration between continents, countries and even districts, of return migration, and of cyclical fluctuations; and in relation to particular countries such as Sweden and the United States, where population statistics have been especially well developed, there is buried away a wealth of occupational and other information about migrants which demographers are beginning to bring to light but which historians have hardly yet taken into account.[32] In short, the demographers have given us a sense of proportion which makes some of the earlier narrative writing, revealing as it is, often obsolescent. We know statistics are dangerous; the contributors to *World Migrations* for instance, were quick to point out that figures cannot determine motives;[33] but at least they are a guide to the sensitive areas of investigation.

The statistical evidence would on the surface appear to justify the "American-centredness" of the older historians. In the century before restriction 33 million of the 55 million emigrants from Europe went to the United States; and the power of Hansen's magnet is revealed by the attraction thither rather than to the British Empire of perhaps 60% of British emigrants.[34] Surely this is justification for the assumption that the history of migration is virtually the history of American immigration? Yet the more one qualifies this crude figure the more complex does the picture begin to look and the less prominent, in many respects, does the United States begin to appear.

In the first place, it is estimated that perhaps a third of United States immigrants re-emigrated, thereby considerably reducing the intensity of the immigrant impact;[35] yet between the First and the Second World Wars, the residue of the great trans-oceanic migration left some twenty million persons in overseas countries who were born in Europe, of whom about 12 million were to be found in the United States, the same proportion as the crude figure.[36]

In the second place there were other receiving countries in the Western hemisphere with a volume of immigration *relatively* more significant than the United States: Argentina with 5.4 million, Brazil with 3.8 million and Canada with 4.5 million.[37] If one takes *intensity* of immigration, a more significant criterion that the crude absolute figure, one finds that Argentina has had the largest number of immigrants in proportion to population and that Canada occupies as a rule a higher place than the United States. In the decade 1901–1910 the rates per hundred thousand were: United States just over 1000, Canada 1500, Argentina 3000.[38] It would seem, therefore, from these proportions that the South American countries, and especially Argentina, might be of even greater importance than the United States to one concerned strictly with the impact of immigrants upon the receiving country. Further, the South American differs from the North American experience in the comparatively limited number of ethnic groups from whom the immigrants were recruited. Before 1900, when more Italians went to Brazil than to the United States;[39] they provided up to 70% of immigrants into Argentina and up to 63% into Brazil;[40] in the generation after 1895 one eighth of the population of Argentina was Italian;[41] and in 1910 they comprised a third of the population of the Brazilian State of Sao Paulo.[42] Such a concentration of one culture group presents an interesing contrast from the situation in North America; for example, by dominating both the building trade and the profession of architecture the Italians have given an Italian character to the cities of South America, an immigrant influence without parallel in the United States. Certainly the South American, as well as the Canadian, experience is of the greatest importance for any comparative study of migration and here, also, is a field ripe for research. We need to know very much more, not only about the relation, sometimes oscillating, between migrant flows to South and to North America but about the different ways immigrants from the same ethnic stock adjusted to their respective communities.

However, even this appears a formal and limited problem as one explores further the implications of the statistics. For instance, I have mentioned that the repatriation rate for the United States may have been over 30%; for Argentina it was as high as 53%.[43] It is clear that in South, even more than in North, America and for an important fraction of individuals, migration was temporary and transitory. We know that this proportion varied greatly between periods—it was at its greatest during the height of the "new" industrial immigration to the United States—and between ethnic groups—between 1908 and 1923 the repatriation rate was as high as 86–89% for Balkan peoples and as low as 11% for the Irish and 5% for Jews.[44] The rate of naturalization was equally variable: for example, for the southern Italians who had qualified for United States citizenship less than a sixth had become citizens at the time of the U.S. Immigration Commission.[45] Whatever else the experience may have meant, migration often did not mean settlement and "acculturation."

Unfortunately, we know comparatively little about this important aspect of the history of oceanic migration.[46] What was the rate of velocity of re-migration? What was the proportion of "repeaters" moving to and from the country of emigration, the proportion of "wanderers" moving from one receiving country to another? What was the experience of re-migrants who returned permanently to their country of birth? These areas of exploration are almost the further face of the moon; but what we can glean from qualitative sources suggests a configuration of great interest and complexity.

To begin with, it is clear that a significant proportion of the re-migrants were "repeaters," who made a regular practice of temporary migration. In 1904, ten percent of Italian immigrants entering the U.S. had been there before.[47] Migrants in several of the important ethnic groups were seasonal workers who hired themselves out on alternate shores of the ocean. The *golondrina* (swallow) was a peasant who left Italy in November after harvest for the flax and wheat fields of northern Cordoba and Santa Fé; between December and April he harvested corn in southern Cordoba and Buenos Aires, and in May he returned to Piedmont for the spring planting. This great seasonal movement differed only in the remarkable ocean ferry from the flux of Mexican harvesters through the wheat fields of Montana and California.[48] The building workers who departed from Venetia for the United States each March and returned in October to repeat their migration the following spring, had further to travel but a less complicated routine than the English house-painters who pursued their trade to the United States in the spring, to Scotland in the summer before English families went north and to England in the autumn while the shooting season was still in progress.[49] The miner who returned to Scotland to idle the winter through on dollars earned in summer in an Appalachian coal-seam, risked finding his underground pitch queered by a peasant earning dollars to buy land in his native Polish village.[50] The mule-spinner who shuttled between Bolton, Lancashire, and Fall River, Massachusetts, found himself replaced by a French-Canadian who hoped to return with a little laid by to the Province of Quebec.[51] This restlessness sometimes impelled the migrant to travel from one receiving country to another, like the Italian cobbler in Pennsylvania who had worked for several years in Brazil, or the father of Charles Forte, the London-born caterer, who had been an Italian steel worker in Pittsburgh where he had understood the importance of the soda fountain.[52] Before the First World War between five and ten thousand Italian immigrants entered the United States each year from other countries than Italy.[53] Such birds of passage provide as yet only partial information concerning the complex migration patterns of the Atlantic in the 19th and early 20th centuries. Yet as one authority puts it: "It is possible that if records of such movements were to be gathered they would reveal an amazing frequency of proletariat globe-trotting, a frequency unequalled by the upper-class traveller of the richer countries."[54]

If, like good ornithologists, we persevere in "ringing" birds of passage, we begin to find that the migration pattern is even more complicated. It has to take into account, not merely a one-way movement from Europe overseas nor a reciprocal movement between country of origin and country of reception, nor even between countries of reception, but an extensive migration within the Mediterranean basin and Europe itself.

The British potter in East Liverpool, Ohio, who had worked for years at a time in Holland and France before reaching the United States, the Irish immigrant in a Rhode Island spinning mill who had learnt his trade in Lancashire, the Jewish tailor or cigar-maker who had learnt *his* trade in the East End of London as a bird of passage from Russian Poland,[55] all these are tell-tale evidence that the movements of 19th-century migration may have been powerfully attracted to the New World but acquired momentum within Europe itself. The waves of migration surging across to the Americas in ever-widening circles were formed by impulses which were local and had originally quite neighbourly affects. Take the Mediterranean for instance. The Italian *mediero* or *arrendatio* who pioneered the wheatfields of Argentina and the coffee plantations of Brazil was the compatriot of the Sicilian or Calabrian colonist on a less remote wheat frontier only six hours journey from Palermo in Tunis.[56] The Greeks who, after having tried the Transvaal, followed the Italians to both South and North America, had already provided Bulgaria and Rumania with general labourers and Turkey and Egypt with merchants and petty traders.[57] Italians helped build the Panama Canal; but their compatriots had already worked on its Suez exemplar.[58] In the early stages most of this Italian emigration had Europe or North Africa as its destination, though the proportions shifted from 82% to Europe and North Africa in 1876 to 36% in 1913; between 1876 and 1926, whereas 8.9 million Italians went to the Americas, as many as 7.5 were content to move within Europe and the Mediterranean.[59]

As the foregoing figures imply, we are dealing with an intra-European as well as a trans-oceanic phenomenon. While Calabrian labourers were working on the Suez Canal, artisans from Lombardy and Piedmont were building tunnels and railways in Switzerland and France. There were over a quarter of a million Italians in France by 1886 and nearly half a million in 1911, roughly a third of the Italian-born population in the United States.[60] The emergence of France as one of the major countries of immigration is a neglected fact of migration history. France's slow and lagging industrialization attracted not only Italian labourers, but Poles, Belgians and, later, Spaniards to the extent of about two million by the 1920s when France became the second most important and, after the United States Restriction Acts, *the* most important country of immigration in the world.[61] By 1931 there were in France over 900,000 Italians, over 500,000 Poles, over 330,000 Spaniards and over 300,000 Belgians. German industrialization attracted an even more intensive, though shorter-lived immigration after 1890, chiefly from Austria-Hungary and Italy.[62]

Again, it is difficult to distinguish emigration from migration within countries. Speaking of the southern Italians who moved north in such large numbers, Foerster wrote: "Emigration is in some respects more of a kind with the extraordinary internal migration of Italy than with the transoceanic movement,"[63] and the experience of the Irish who migrated to Lancashire, the Scots to Birmingham and the South Welsh to London differed only in degree from that of their neighbours who migrated to Boston, Toronto and Scranton respectively. Each move involved uprooting and in varying degrees the development of the migrant mentality.

In short, trans-oceanic migration was only one aspect of a bewil-deringly complex pattern of tidal currents which carried not merely Norwegian settlers to Minnesota homesteads and Irish immigrants to New York tenements, but Polish peasants to *and from* East German estates, Appalachian coal mines and Silesian steelworks, Italian la-bourers to and from Chicago, Illinois, and Homécourt, France, Italian hotel workers to and from Lausanne, Nice and Rio de Janeiro, Scots-men to and from London and Buenos Aires and Spaniards to and from Marseilles and Santos. We are a long way from a simple case of "America fever."[64]

Next, if we look more closely at the *origins* of migrants, we do not discover what both the gross statistics and the stereotypes of the older historiography might lead one to expect, that is to say, an undiffer-entiated, mass movement of "peasants" or indeed "artisans" throng-ing towards immigrant ports from vaguely conceived "countries of origin" like "Italy," "Germany," or even "Poland" or "Ireland." Even discounting the obvious fact that such terms were, for most of the period, inept labels for geographical expressions or political provinces, the picture is false. Seen through a magnifying glass, this undiffer-entiated mass surface breaks down into a honeycomb of innumerable particular cells, districts, villages, towns, each with an individual re-action or lack of it to the pull of migration. This is not simply a question of Scottish Highlanders emigrating in a body to Upper Can-ada, Rhinelanders to Wisconsin, Swedes to Montana, northern Italians to France and Argentina, southern Italians to the United States, though these elementary distinctions are important. We only come to the secret sources of the movement if we work to a finer tolerance. We must talk, not of Wales, but of Portmadoc or Swansea, not of North or South Italy, but of Venetia Guilia, Friuli, Basilicata and Calabria, not of Greece, or even the Peloponnese, but of Tripolis, Sparta and Megalopolis, not of Lancashire but of Darwin or Blackburn, not of Norway but of Kristian and North Bergenhus. There were villages in the Peloponnese, Basilicata and Friuli where boys grew up expecting to emigrate:[65] there were sections of New York where immigrants from individual Italian districts occupied separate streets, with often mutual hostility.[66] Only when we examine such districts and townships, and trace the fortunes of their native sons, do we begin to understand the true anatomy of migration. As Hansen well recognised, "at any given moment the phenomenon of emigration is characterized, not by the nation as a whole, but by a comparatively restricted part of it, and when again it makes its appearance, though the participants are still listed as Germans or Italians, their origin was distinct."[67]

Intimately connected with particular districts are particular occupations, an acquaintance with which will dispose once and for all of the stereotype of an undifferentiated "peasant" mass. One of the most striking features of successive analyses of the foreign-born in the United States since 1911 is the extent to which different ethnic groups have adhered to particular trades.[68] Although this was partly the consequence of job opportunities, it was often related to work conditions in the home country. Thus unskilled southern Italians worked on construction and heavy industry in the United States; but they also congregated in certain specific, self-employed occupations. The Italians, and after them the Greeks, who followed a similar pattern, established their first "toe-hold," so to speak, in American cities as bootblacks. A few dollars earned in this way on the street permitted an outlay on a fruit or ice cream barrow and ultimately an opening by way of ice cream parlours and florists into the restaurant and hotel trade.[69] Four-fifths of the emigrants from Laurenzana, in Basilicata, became bootblacks in America.[70]

Such a concentration was partly due to a follow-the-leader instinct which was exploited by the Italian or Greek *padroni* who recruited youths from their home districts under informal and often sweated-labour contracts. However, the *padroni* in the United States were able to do this because the system was already well established, both in southern Italy and in Greece. It was the practice in the poverty-stricken pastoral district of the Peloponnese to send a boy of ten or twelve away to the cities of Greece or Turkey to earn money for his parents, often in brutal conditions, as a bootblack or in a coffeehouse or grocery store; and it was from here that the *padroni* often recruited them for the United States.[71]

This was low-grade work which anyone from the fields could do. However, "peasant" emigrants were not limited to such occupations. The Italian was the largest of such migrations; yet of those who settled in Argentina during the wheat boom of 1876 to 1897, at least a third were not farmers but craftsmen, including those masons, carpenters, quarrymen, gardeners, brick workers and plasterers who gave South American cities their Italian manner, and the Genoese shipmasters, navigators and sailors who ran the coastal shipping of the River Plate.[72] And there was a similar concentration of craftsmen in the United States.[73] Here too the pattern was set before migrants crossed the Atlantic in any numbers. An important element in the Italian migration to Switzerland, France and later to Germany were skilled tradesmen especially from Friuli, the greatest single source of Italian emigrants, where the élite of the population came increasingly to think in terms of temporary migration. Scores of thousands of workmen kept a winter habitat in Venetia who could not have found permanent work there and who had never expected to be other than emigrants.[74] Boys in Friuli were deliberately trained as stonecutters or carpenters to take advantage of the demand for these skills in France, just as boys in Caserta or Basilicata were recruited by direct arrangement with their fathers for the Lyons glass industry.[75] The connection between migration and a trade was often close, and it was, moreover, already well established in Europe before the attraction of America began to be felt.

In discussing the skilled migrant we have so far been concerned with the village craftsman who was easily absorbed into the comparatively primitive economies of an agricultural frontier. The subject acquires a heightened significance when one examines the role of the migrant technician in the industrialization of countries of immigration. The dissemination of technology through the migration of technicians is an aspect of migration history which deserves a great deal of further study, and it is here that the student of British emigration has a special contribution to make. British industrial leadership, capital, commerce and trade routes combined to encourage an unprecedented emigration of British technicans who, in country after country, provided the essential *cadre* of skills for industrialization. In the case of new countries, such as the United States in the 19th and Canada or Australia in the 20th century, the role of the British technician was so important that industrialization itself may be conceived as an aspect of migration history. However, even in old, established economies that role was considerable; and although there is a temptation to concentrate on the spectacular case of the United States, here, as in other aspects of migration history, we are dealing with a phenomenon which is best treated internationally. Men used to practising a specialized trade took advantage of demand and cheaper transport to pursue it all over the world. Cornish miners hired themselves out wherever there was a need for their skill and provided the first, aristocratic generation of mine captains in the lead, tin and copper mines not only of Illinois and Michigan, but of Bolivia, the Rand and Broken Hill, sometimes moving from continent to continent in the single-minded pursuit of their esoteric craft.[76] Textile operatives from the Pennines built and worked the looms of France and Belgium at the time when Slater, the Scholfields and their successors were building and working the mills of New England; Welsh and English foundrymen and furnacemen performed a similar office for the iron trade not only in Pennsylvania but in France and Russia;[77] Staffordshire potters also worked in France and Russia as well as mastering the problems of New World clays;[78] English and Scots engineers built and operated railways in almost every quarter of the globe *except* the United States, from Belgium to New Zealand, India to Argentina; and so on, throughout most of the range of 19th-century industrial technique; and if we knew more about them, it is possible that the resulting British communities in Fall River, Massachusetts, or East Liverpool, Ohio, would be found to bear more relation to the British communities in, say, Buenos Aires, Charenton and Montreal, than to other hyphenated American communities in the United States.[79]

The study of the migration of technicians in fact often provides a clue to identifiable communities (and through communities to individuals) which is often lacking in the study of the inchoate ethnic mass, but which is essential if we are to learn anything worth while about motives, causes, adjustment, indeed anything at all about the true nature of the migrant *experience*. Skill acts, as it were, as a radioactive tracer in the blood stream of migration and, as I have argued elsewhere, we would do well to develop the study of it as an instrumental technique.[80] Enough is known, for example, about British technicians in the United States, for the student with the right kind of eye to suggest answers to most of the big questions.

The migration of British technicians has a distinctive character. One can discern successive phases: first the migration of the carriers, of creative innovators, in textiles, iron and steel, pottery and mining, who introduced the new technology; then, on their heels the scores and hundreds of skilled operatives who were to provide the mule spinners, machine makers, foundrymen and miners, some only seasonal migrants, some settling into communities of British folk ways and craft loyalties and organizing labour unions; then there was the third phase when improved machinery and American production methods reduced the scope for skilled labour and increased the number of jobs which could be handled by cheaper, unskilled and more docile workers recruited from more recent immigrant stocks from Ireland, French Canada and eastern Europe. As this happened the British element moved upwards into supervisory or managerial positions, and apart from an occasional specialist, the migration of technicians came to an end. The many illuminated facets of this sequence would take us far beyond the limits of this paper.[81] Suffice it to state that it had characteristics which were repeated in industry after industry from the Lancashire cotton spinners of 1800 to the Welsh tinplaters of the 1890s; and although one would like to be able to compare such migration to the United States with that to, say, Canada or Australia, both of which are still in progress, the evidence at hand already provides important clues about the wider implications of transatlantic migration.

The migration of tradesmen calls attention to the economic aspects of the subject. Although it is a truism that 19th-century emigration was predominantly economic in motivation, in the older conceptual framework the actual economic determinants were very vaguely formulated. One was presented with a laundry list of "push" and "pull" factors which were then left in the background owing to a preoccupation with the cultural and political considerations involved in assimilation. A knowledge of artisan migration is a good way to achieve a greater definition. In the first place, it was determined by trade routes and, as far as North America was concerned, trade routes from the British Isles. The fact that emigrants were essentially valuable bulk cargo for unused shipping space in raw cotton or timber ships on the return voyage is a basic fact which is only beginning to receive the attention it deserves.[82] The fortunes of shipping companies from Cunard and Austro-American to the modern Greek lines have been based upon emigrants; the trade remained long in British hands and to some extent continued to pass through British ports long after the recruiting grounds had moved to central and eastern Europe. The trade in emigrants was a development of that largely Anglo-American trade which brought America and northwest Europe together into a single Atlantic economy.

The concept of an Atlantic economy, like that of an Atlantic history itself, is of comparatively recent origin;[83] but is of first importance in understanding Western history in the 19th century. The term is justified because it describes, not merely a condition of international trade, but one in which there was such freedom of movement for the factors of production that we can hardly distinguish the two principal countries concerned, Britain and the United States, as separate, closed economies. The Atlantic economy was concerned with exploiting the grasslands of North America by means of European capital and labour in the interests of cheaper cotton and wheat for Europe and overseas markets for European manufactures. The migration of the twin factors of capital investment and labour was the key to it and emigrants were essential to its operation.[84] The precise way in which this mechanism worked is still a matter for research and controversy. As far as emigration is concerned, the first attempt to refine the old crude assumptions about the push mechanism of overpopulation and exploitation in Europe and the pull mechanism of American opportunity was made by American economists—and here again one must notice the initiative of Americans and of nonhistorians—as a by-product of research into the operations of the business cycle some thirty years ago. Jerome found a direct correlation between fluctuations in immigration into the United States and the short-term American business cycle, and, later, Kuznets and Rubin established three long swings in net immigration between 1870 and 1945 which tended to follow swings in income per head.[85]

These statistical estimates are, however, of only limited usefulness to historians of migration; the emphasis on "pull" factors leaves much out of account and is open to the suspicion of American-centredness. However, a more ambitious, but in the long run, more satisfactory attempt at a theory relating the flow of migration to other economic activity is that recently put forward by Brinley Thomas.[86] In his study of Great Britain and the Atlantic economy Thomas set out to show that the rhythms of economic growth in the United States and the United Kingdom were closely related to the course of migration between the two countries. Briefly he found that there was an inverse relation between home investment and the level of income in Britain, on the one hand, and emigration and capital exports, on the other; a positive relationship between immigration, investment and income in the United States and, correspondingly, disharmony between the rates of economic growth on the eastern and the western sides of the Atlantic. Despite the controversial nature of some of Thomas's statistical data, his work represents a major advance for the student of emigration. In the first place he found no simple correlation between upswings in American business and in immigration: before about 1870 the upswing in business activity tended to come after an upswing in immigration, the inference being that, at least for this period, migration was impelled more by "push" factors in Europe than "pull" factors in the United States; but more important, in concentrating upon the Atlantic economy he develops a two-country theory which is more complex but more helpful to the historian than the single-country theories of American-centredness which had preceded it. He demonstrates that the mechanism is at least a two-way process and can only be understood by taking into account conditions in both country of origin and country of destination, as well as the whole complex of interacting factors, of which labour was only one, contributing to the economic development of the North Atlantic basin.[87]

The Thomas approach opens possibilities of relating emigration to the dynamics of economic growth on a more universal scale: for though he produces valuable corroborative evidence for Sweden and the British Dominions, the United Kingdom and the United States remain the focus of his interest. One can conceive a time when a development of his technique will enable us to understand much that is obscure about the mechanisms of migration, not merely in the North Atlantic basin but in other theatres, as well as the complex of connections among them.

Thomas also sharpens our focus about problems of phasing. The Atlantic economy was only a phase of economic development and carried within itself the seeds of its dissolution. The ease of movement which brought farmers to grow wheat on the prairies brought artisans to exploit minerals and markets and establish modern industry on the western shores of the Atlantic. As it developed from colonial to metropolitan status, the American economy ceased to be dependent upon European capital, labour or skills. The difficult adjustments facing the Atlantic basin as a result of the emergence of the United States as a great Power are a logical consequence of the transcendence of the old Atlantic economy: and there is no doubt that the difficulty of those adjustments has been enhanced, as Thomas points out, by the inadequacy of United States policies between the two Wars, compared with the British attitude towards the emigration of capital and labour in the great liberal era of the 19th century. As far as the labour side of the question is concerned, it may be that the drastic restrictionist policies of the United States between 1917 and 1924, together with those of South America, had important effects on the course of events in the late 1920's and 1930's. The contribution of restriction to the "stagnation" of the American economy during the depression of the 1930s, a widely held conviction among economists at the time, needs further investigation; as well as its alleged effects on over-crowding in Europe such as the deflection of Italian emigration to Mussolini's North African empire. The investigation of the effects of large-scale emigration upon European countries is a difficult historical problem, though even here an American scholar like Dr. Schrier has done pioneer work for Ireland on the basis of the materials of the Irish Folklore Commission;[88] but it might be illuminated by studies of the effects of restriction and this is one of the many problems hitherto neglected by European students.

However, it seems clear that whatever the short-term problems of restriction, the long cycle of mass emigration from Europe was coming to an end between the Wars.[89] That cycle was determined by the settlement of the great unoccupied grasslands outside Europe, part of a greater cycle which colonized, not merely Australia, Argentina and North America, but the Indus Valley, Siberia, Inner Mongolia and Manchukuo.[90] By 1930 the limits of effective settlement were approaching even in Australia where so much of the interior, by known agricultural standards, remains desert. Already by the turn of the twentieth century the centrifugal tendencies of European migration were counterbalanced by centripetal tendencies.

The greatest migrations were not to the grasslands, but to the concentrations of coal and iron where industries were being established. Between 1870 and 1914 there was a net migration of even American natives from the farms to the mines, factories and cities of Appalachia and the Rockies; and more European immigrants found a living in American industry than on prairie homesteads. The peak of the great cycle, the so-called "new" immigration, may profitably be thought of as a rural-urban migration which happened to be trans-oceanic rather than local in character; and while some Italians, Poles and Ukrainians were moving to Pittsburgh or Chicago, others were swelling the immigrant populations of France and Germany in Le Creuzot, the Ruhr and Silesia. By 1927 European migrants to European destinations outnumbered those to trans-oceanic destinations;[91] and France had become the most important country of immigration in the world. In the 1930's for the first time in modern history Europe gained population through net in-migration.[92]

Moreover, there are signs that this trans-oceanic migration was slackening even before American restriction. For example, the intensity of emigration — or the international mobility of labour — that is to say, migrants per thousand of population, had declined well before 1914 both in countries of emigration and in the United States;[93] and the shutting down on the United States intake did not lead to any corresponding diversion to other countries.[94]

In fact at the outbreak of the second World War it already looked as if the great cycle had come to an end and students of emigration would have to deal with a purely historical problem with little contemporary relevance. "The peopling of other continents from Europe is probably a passing phenomenon."[95] Postwar experience has not seriously modified this view. Europe still has its black spots for rural overpopulation, notably southern Italy and Greece and no doubt other Balkan countries; and there has been an interesting case of emigration fever in the Netherlands;[96] but in general there is no great pressure to emigrate in Europe; and while rates of economic growth in some of the traditional receiving countries, especially Australia and Canada, have been accompanied by a demand for immigrants, and although Australia was for a time absorbing them at a record rate, the movement has settled down to more modest and selective proportions. An international conference of economists was in fairly general agreement in 1955 that a renewal of large-scale emigration was neither likely nor relevant to the problems of the underdeveloped countries of the mid-twentieth century which, unlike the virgin grasslands of the 19th, are already overpopulated.[97]

In short, a consideration of the phasing of overseas migration both places it within a limited time-scale and reduces its significance in relation to intra-European migration. These proportions are foreshortened still further if one examines the orders of magnitude of European population as a whole. At the same time as Europe was providing up to sixty million emigrants for overseas countries, the Continent was increasing its own numbers so greatly that its proportion of world population rose from 20.7% in 1802 to 25.2%:[98] and it is as well to remember that in no decade has emigration drawn off more than 40% of Europe's natural increase.[99] In other words, the centripetal tendencies which kept people at home were at least as strong as the centrifugal tendencies which sent them abroad. If we accept this fact and look at "the great dispersion," not as the dominant demographic factor of the 19th century, but as a subordinate feature of demographic trends within Europe, a very different and more interesting picture begins to emerge. Instead of Europeans taking flight to the Americas and Australia we see Europeans themselves colonizing. By using their labour, capital and know-how to exploit the foodstuffs and raw materials of virgin lands, Europeans made it possible not only to feed an ever-growing population at home, but to industrialise their continent; as population emigrated so did it multiply and concentrate at home in the regions of coal and iron. Moreover once the outward movement of population had gone far enough to ensure adequate supplies of essential raw materials, it began to slacken and the mobile element in the population migrated, not overseas, but into the urban-industrial complex of western Europe itself. In the end this tendency became the dominant one and, as Forsyth put it, the "areas of concentration" replaced the "great open spaces" as magnets of migration.[100] The great overseas migration, therefore, is in a very broad sense to be treated as a major, but subordinate, aspect of European population growth and European industrialization. We are, again, a long way from the America fever.

In other words, this new angle of vision for which I am arguing shifts the focus from frontier to metropolis, from "pull" to "push" factors, and especially to those demographic influences which Brinley Thomas suggests may have been the dynamic element in Atlantic growth.[101] The inner secrets of emigration are to be sought in the working of those two "revolutions" which are so interconnected, the demographic and the industrial.[102]

There is no space to enter into the notorious complexities of the demographic revolution. It looks, however, as if a reduction in death rates without a compensating reduction in birth rates led to a rise in the rate of natural increase, beginning in north-west Europe and moving east and south, as communities became affected by medical and dietary advances. This increase, though compensated for by new and nutritious foods, especially the potato, brought the rural population to the margin of subsistence.[103] The result was a latent propensity to emigrate which transformed itself sometimes, though by no means invariably, into actual emigration, not only at times of catastrophe caused by the failure of the potato crop, but as transport and communication to the ports and overseas made this possible. In country after country, beginning with Ireland and ending with Italy and Greece, there is a direct correlation between rates of emigration and rates of natural increase twenty years previously, which represents the migration of the surplus proportion of a larger age group at the point when it was ready to enter the labour market. In the case of Norway, for example, two major upward swings in emigration, in the late 1830's and the late 1860's, occurred when there was a disproportionately large age group between 20 and 30.[104] This is confirmed by the overwhelmingly youthful character of emigrants; between 86 and 95% of immigrants into the United States during the period for which figures are available were under forty years; and in the early 20th century two-thirds of British emigrants were under thirty-one.[105] Manifestations of the Mathusian devil appeared in country after country across Europe irrespective of rural social structure, laws of inheritance, land tenure, the condition of agriculture or the policies of landlords.[106]

However, rural overcrowding did not in itself result in mass emigration as the condition of Ireland in the 1830's or Greece in the 1890's showed. There had to be three further conditions which Hansen defines as *freedom, desire* and *means* to move;[107] and it is in the operation of these conditions that the ultimate secrets of migration are to be found.

The *means* to move are easiest to define; but the roads and railways, canals and steamships, posts and telegraphs, banks and travel agencies, by means of which the emigrant travelled were themselves the products of forces which were breaking up the self-contained existence of rural Europe, and providing the peasant with both the *freedom* to move, negative as in the abolition of serfdom, positive as in opportunities for employment, and the *desire* to move resulting from widening horizons, and contracting opportunities at home. Emigration was, in fact, intimately connected with that quickening of communications, markets, commerce and capital which, in the 1840's and 1850's in Scandinavia, the 1880's and 1890's in Italy, was the first phase of the establishment of a modern economy.[108] This erosion of the customary community by commercial forces was an essential precondition to migration; it caused a revolutionary increase in social mobility which both job and travel opportunities transformed into a propensity to migrate. Migration was, in fact, an aspect of social mobility.

This propensity had differing effects in different periods and countrysides. It might, as in the case of the Irish in 1846, result in a catastrophic, direct, oceanic emigration; or, with the Poles in Germany, it might be largely European in its ramifications or even, as with the London Welsh, internal and local. The point is that overseas migration was only one, though the most important, result of a revolutionary increase in social mobility which had the effect of creating large numbers prepared to travel in search of jobs. In the first instance it was only where there were no suitable jobs close at hand that the young man was impelled to look overseas and take what appeared to be the once-for-all step of alienation and become an emigrant. Later, when the habit became established by emirgrant letters and remittances, it might persist long after there were jobs at home; but despite such lags, all the evidence goes to show that Europeans in general emigrated in large numbers while there were no opportunities in the home country and ceased to do so when opportunities once again existed. For some people those opportunities were never to come again, as in the case of those Jewish traders and clothing workers who lost their function in Tzarist Russia and had to seek an outlet in New York,[109] or the Scottish handloom weavers, or the southern Italians and Greeks, whose emigration was shut off at its height by American restriction and who were to contribute to the rural underemployment or concealed unemployment of the present times. But in the principal countries of western and central Europe those opportunities did come, in the form of work in mines, factories and offices.

The connection of migration with industrialization and urbanization (the two cannot be separated) was as close as with the Malthusian devil. Now it is true that Lombard peasants farmed in Argentina and Swedish *statare* in Montana; and that a growing proportion of British emigrants to the United States in the 1880's and 1890's were skilled technicans moving from one industrial area to another. But, by and large, the great migrations after 1890 were from farm to factory, from village to city, whether this meant from Iowa to Chicago, Silesia to Pittsburgh or Piedmont to Buenos Aires.[110] To the country people of the Norwegian fjords a fellow countryman on his way to embark was already an "American";[111] and even after the second World War "Americanization" was a synonym for "urbanization" in an immigrant Norwegian community which was attempting to preserve its Lutheran integrity in rural Wisconsin.[112]

However, the dynamic forces which created the propensity to emigrate in time fostered those industries which, by providing employment, made emigration no longer imperative. At this point oceanic migration began to diminish. Industrial Britain was already absorbing most of the potential yeoman emigrants of England by 1850 and many potential Irish emigrants to America from 1900. Norwegian timber and Swedish mining began in the 1870's to make inroads into Scandinavian emigration, the course of which was thenceforward determined by the pulls of American employment and the uneven progress of Scandinavian industrialization, until it petered out on the eve of the first World War.[113] The most spectacular case is that of Germany, where the emigration peak had already been passed for the west and south-west by the 1850's and for the country as a whole by the mid-1880's with the onset of heavy industrialization in that decade.[114] Nor was employment the only aspect of industrialization-urbanization to lessen the attractiveness of emigration. Cheap meats and grains from overseas increased real wages; with the growing number of white-collar occupations, urban life became more attractive; the emergence of the concept of State welfare, with public education, unemployment and old-age insurance offset the old fear of military service; a new sense of nationalism, which was the ultimate and potent compensation for the peasant's loss of identity in his village, led to State action against emigration; and finally, the reduction in the birth rate, the absence of which alongside low death rates had started the demographic revolution, reduced that pressure on population which had been the latent condition of emigration and eventually was to depress population rates below the level of replacement.[115] Thus the great oceanic migrations of the 19th and early 20th centuries occurred in a transitional phase of European development between the breakdown of the old rural societies and the onset of modern industrialism.[116]

Economically, that phase was concerned with the widening of markets, commerce and finance; but I am not trying to suggest that the resulting social mobility, of which emigration was only one aspect, was a simple effect of economic causes. Only in the impossible world of economic abstractions could Hansen's *desire* to move be conceived of as mere economic opportunity; commercialization, like an enhanced social mobility, was a result as well as a cause of the dissolution of the customary rural community; and the search for the inner secrets of emigration, as of population growth, leads to a consideration of the many unknowns which hedge round this breakdown.[117] It is beyond the scope of this paper to do more than indicate the rough dimensions of this, the penultimate problem in the field of emigration.

The gulf which may exist between *freedom* and *means*, on the one hand, and *desire*, on the other, is strikingly illustrated by the Netherlands. Even in 1870 the rate of increase of the Dutch population was greater than that of any other country in north-west Europe and unlike those other countries showed hardly any decline down to the present. Yet there was very little emigration until the end of the second World War. The increase was absorbed at home into a society which was resistant to change. As one Netherlands authority puts it: "The 19th Century ended only in 1930 in the Netherlands."[118] The efforts of the Netherlands Government since 1945 to encourage systematic emigration to Canada in order to syphon off an expected surplus population have met with least response precisely in those parts of the south-east where the cumulative effects of population growth had produced heavy and chronic rural underemployment; this is a district of small family farms, orthodox and conservative in religion and politics, with strong ties binding the individual to his family and to the local community which he only reluctantly leaves. "Evidently, where judging the need for emigration, the demographers and economists aply standards whose validity the agrarian population has not yet recognised."[119]

This is an extreme example, chosen because of its full modern documentation, of almost total resistance on the part of a community to emigration, even where the economic inducements are apparently overwhelming. It is not suggested that this is typical, but the degrees of cohesion, of homogeneity and the comparative rigidities in the structure in the local community which it illustrates are important to understanding the great 19th-century migrations. Where there was no emigration, it looks as if there was probably a highly stable social situation, whatever its comparative lack of prosperity. Where there was emigration, there was likely to be a degree of social instability which prompted elements in the population to take steps to protect or better their status. Emigrants, more concerned with status than job opportunity, were driven to seek it abroad because of despair at preserving or improving it at home. We might expect to find causes of emigration, therefore, in a social situation which was unstable, but contained rigidities threatening inherited status or impending advancement.

With present knowledge it is impossible to substantiate so general a hypothesis. Certainly the study of social history has not reached a point in my country where much that is useful may be said in its favour. However, the evidence for Scandinavia seems more promising, because it is less complex, because of the excellence of demographic statistics, especially for Sweden, and their use by authorities like Professors Dorothy Thomas and Arne Skaug, and because of the outstanding work of historians like Professor Blegen and Professor Semmingsen.[120]

To begin with, emigrants were overwhelmingly youthful; a very high proportion were young men of the landless and labouring classes whom one would expect to form the surplus population; and in addition they included an important contribution from the independent land-owning class in the persons of younger sons denied an inheritance by the process of overpopulation and subdivision. But the situation was characterized by a spirit of revolt which went far beyond the natural consequences of rural underemployment and restless youth. "A transformation of values had taken place among the country youth," wrote Mrs. Semmingsen of the Norwegians: "Many of them refused to remain in the home community any longer."[121] "Forth will I! Forth," sang Björnson, "I will be crushed and consumed if I stay."[122]

Here at last, the cautiously statistical approach of this paper enters upon that more familiar historical country concerned with individual values and motives. This spirit of revolt was more than the frustration of lack-land youth; it infected others who were beginning to chafe at a situation in which a small privileged class kept a tight hold on government, the church, and the professions and resisted or neglected demands and opportunities for a broader social order. In Mrs. Semmingsen's words, there was a "more conscious self-assertion," instead of a "dull hopeless spirit."[123]

It was no accident of history that the "Sloopers" whose voyage in the *Restauration* in 1825 heralded the large-scale Norwegian emigration to America, were Dissenters seeking refuge from an intolerant State Church; nor that they should have been members of the Society of Friends, converted by Quaker missionaries from England. For the emigrant stream to the United States from Norway and Sweden, as from England, contained a marked Dissenting element disproportionately great both in numbers and in leadership. The phenomenon deserves comparative study.[124]

Moreover, it was not simply a matter of Janssonists or Haugeans fleeing their respective Conventicle Acts or English Nonconformist farmers fleeing religious tithes, still less of Mormons from all three countries seeking the promised land. Dissenters of whatever persuasion from Evangelical "enthusiasts" to Unitarians developed towards institutional orthodoxy an attitude of criticism and withdrawal which led them to resist not merely the church Establishment but what in England has been recently called the governing "establishment" of politics and the professions. This made them natural leaders for emigrants, who, in Blegen's words, were "always non-conformist in some sense."[125] Among emigrants, in fact, the Dissenter was the archetypal personality. The affinity of Dissent with emigration was especially marked in relation to the United States, where republican institutions and the separation of church from state exerted a positive influence not only on emigrants but on European domestic politics.[126] For, where it did not culminate in emigration, this dissenting spirit found expression in radical politics, as in the case of the Haugeans who "sharpened the issue of the *bønder* with officialdom" and "blazed the trail of popular agitation" in Norway.[127] If universal suffrage had been granted in Sweden in 1880, many subsequent emigrants might not have left.[128] Radicals were ultimately to reform those institutions and practices from which emigration was a reaction and even to throw their weight in favour of emigrant restriction. The relation of the labour movement to emigration in its various phases, in Scandinavia as in Britain, was an aspect of these changing tensions.

With Dissent in this broad sense we are dealing with a phenomenon which, ubiquitous in its 19th-century form, almost transcends social history. The ultimate problem of emigration is one of individual psychology. Not all oppressed *bønder*, landless sons, workless labourers or Evangelical clergy chose the emigrant course. The choice, or the line of least resistance, for many was to stay at home, to adjust, to conform, even though this might mean bearing the strains of radical politics. The contrast in temperament between he for whom the moral choice is to stay put and he for whom it is "to get out from under" or, as the Americans say "to go someplace else," is central to the study of emigration, just as it is to an understanding of the perennial tensions between American and European cultures. With the emigrant we are studying the effects on the human being of choosing the one rather than the other of these two alternatives. Emigration is undoubtedly the more momentous. One does not have to be familiar with the harrowing conditions of 19th-century emigration to be aware that it was a disturbing experience even where little was at stake; and where, as in the characteristic case, it meant uprooting from a traditional rural culture and transplanting thousands of ocean miles to a modern, urban, industrial community, it could be traumatic. The effects of such an experience upon the human psyche lie perhaps beyond the powers of the historian to assess and fully to understand. Yet Oscar Handlin has made a not unsuccessful attempt to do so and Florian Znaniecki, in his phenomenal study of the Polish peasant in Europe and America, based upon his work for the Emigrants Protective Society in Warsaw between 1911 and 1914, has provided historians with an enormous volume of pertinently chosen evidence bearing upon what this paper defined earlier as the "complete sequence of experiences whereby the individual moves from one social identity to another."[129] Znaniecki's work is sociological, not historical; but we need more scholars both prepared to assemble emigrant letters and other data on a comprehensive scale, and with the mental power to address themselves to this, the ultimate problem of emigration.[130] Only by such means will it be possible to achieve, what this paper set out to discuss, namely, an understanding not merely of uprooting as profound as that which American scholarship has given us of acculturation, but of the complete experience of migration from one society to another such as Hansen set out to achieve for the North Atlantic. It will be an achievement of the highest order; no less than a study of liberty in a modern setting.

NOTES

This chapter was originally delivered at the Eleventh International Congress of Historical Sciences, Stockholm, 1960, and is reprinted from XIe Congrès International des Sciences Historiques, *Rapports* (Uppsala, 1960), 5:32-60.

1. Marcus Lee Hansen, "A History of American Immigration as a Field for Research," *American Historical Review* 32 (April 1927): 500-518.

2. American Historical Association, Committee on Planning and Research, *Historical Scholarship in America: Needs and Opportunities* (New York, 1932).

3. Richard C. Haskett, "Problems and Prospects in the History of American Immigration," in George Washington University, *A Report on World Population Migrations as Related to the United States of America* (Washington, D.C., 1956), 48.

4. See C. Wright Mills, *The Sociological Imagination* (New York, 1959), 90-91.

5. Notorious examples are Henry J. Ford, *The Scotch-Irish in America* (Princeton, 1915); Albert B. Faust, *The German Element in the United States* (Boston, 1909); Alfred O. Fonkalsrud, *Scandinavians as a Social Force in America* (Brooklyn, 1913); George T. Flom, *A History of Norwegian Immigration to the United States from the Earliest Beginning Down to the Year 1848* (Iowa City, 1909). In this connection see the comments of Edward N. Saveth, *American Historians and European Immigrants* (New York, 1948), 216.

6. Robert F. Foerster, *Italian Emigration of Our Times* (Cambridge, 1919); Henry P. Fairchild, *Greek Immigration to the United States* (New Haven, 1911); Thomas Burgess, *Greeks in America* (Boston, 1913); Kenneth C. Babcock, *The Scandinavian Element in the United States* (Urbana, 1914).

7. Theodore C. Blegen, *Norwegian Migration to America 1820-1860* (Northfield, 1931); Oscar Handlin, *Boston's Immigrants* (London, 1941).

8. Mitford M. Mathews, *A Dictionary of Americanisms on Historical Principles* (Chicago, 1951), 1:863.

9. Thomas W. Page, "The Causes of the Earlier European Immigration to the United States," *Journal of Political Economy* 119 (October 1911): 676-700.

10. Dudley Kirk, "Demographic Trends in Europe," *Annals of the American Academy of Political and Social Science* 262 (March 1949): 46.

11. Foerster, *Italian Emigration of Our Times*, 374.

12. Oscar Handlin, *The Uprooted: The Epic Study of the Great Migrations that Made the American People* (Boston, 1951); an autobiographical study, equally valid and powerful, is Alfred Kazin's *A Walker in the City* (New York, 1951).

13. Vera Shlakman, review of Handlin, *The Uprooted, Journal of Economic History* 13 (1953): 242-43.

14. Marcus Lee Hansen, *The Atlantic Migration, 1607-1860: A History of the Continuing Settlement of the United States*, ed. Arthur M. Schlesinger (Cambridge, 1940); Hansen, *The Immigrant in American History*, ed. Arthur M. Schlesinger (Cambridge, 1941); Hansen, *The Mingling of the Canadian and American Peoples* (New Haven, 1940).

15. Saveth, *American Historians and European Immigrants*, 222-23.

16. Hansen, *The Immigrant in American History*, 192.

17. Imre Ferenczi, "An Historical Study of Migration Statistics," *International Labour Review* 20 (1929): 356-84.

18. Walter F. Willcox, ed., *International Migrations* (New York, 1931), 1:85.

19. Robert C. K. Ensor, *England 1870-1914* (Oxford, 1936), 271, 500.

20. George M. Trevelyan, *English Social History* (London, 1942), for example, 473-75, 547.

21. William R. Shepherd, "The Expansion of Europe," *Political Science Quarterly* 34 (1919): 210-25.

22. American Historical Association, *Historical Scholarship in America*, 76.

23. United Nations, *Determinants and Consequences of Population Trends* (New York, 1952), 299.

24. *Emigrationsutredningen: Betänkande i Utvandringsfragen* (Stockholm, 1913), 660.

25. Brynjolf J. Hovde, "Effects of Emigration upon Scandinavia," *Journal of Modern History* 6 (1934): 254.

26. See Blegen, *Norwegian Migration to America,* 326, for the failure to understand the importance of emigration on the Thrane movement.

27. International Labour Office, *First Report of the International Labour Organization to the United Nations* (Geneva, 1947), "Reports," 1, chapter 11.

28. United Nations, Department of Social Affairs, *Problems of Migration Statistics* (New York, 1949), 41; *Proceedings of the World Population Conference* (1954), "Papers," 2:761.

29. Ferenczi, "An Historical Study of Migration Statistics," 359.

30. United Nations, *Problems of Migration Statistics,* 3.

31. Ferenczi, "An Historical Study of Migration Statistics," 384.

32. See especially the work of Edward P. Hutchinson, Simon Kuznets, and Dorothy Thomas of the United States, and Brinley Thomas of the United Kingdom.

33. Willcox, ed., *International Migrations,* 2:291, 341.

34. Ibid., 1:101; the British percentage to the United States excludes migration into Canada, much of it transient, on its way south. In the second half of the nineteenth century between 61 percent and 72 percent of British emigrants sailed for the United States. W. A. Carrothers, *Emigration from the British Isles* (London, 1929), Appendix 2, 308.

35. The estimate is a projection backward from figures for the period after 1907 when returns for reemigration first became available; Willcox, ed., *International Migrations,* 2:89, table 17; Alexander M. Carr-Saunders, *World Population* (Oxford, 1936), 49; Julius Isaac, "International Migration and European Trends," *International Labour Review* 66 (September 1952): 188.

36. Dudley Kirk, *Europe's Population in the Interwar Years* (Princeton, 1946), 90.

37. Each country with a comparative remigration; the figures cover the period from 1821 to 1924. Ferenczi, "An Historical Study of Migration Statistics," 374-75.

38. Willcox, ed., *International Migrations,* 1:210; Dorothy S. Thomas, "International Migration," in *Population and World Politics,* ed. Philip H. Hauser (Glencoe, 1958), 141.

39. Foerster, *Italian Emigration of Our Times,* 279, 320.

40. Ferenczi, "An Historical Study of Migration Statistics," 379.

41. Foerster, *Italian Emigration of Our Times,* 229, 275.

42. Ibid., 289.

43. Ferenczi, "An Historical Study of Migration Statistics," 380; whereas the U.S. figure is an estimate projected backward from 1907, the first year of repatriation returns, the Argentina figure is based upon returns over the entire period from 1857 to 1924.

44. Ibid., 380; there is a rough correlation between repatriation rates and the proportion of males to females, for example, a high proportion of 96 percent males among the Greeks and a low proportion (52 percent) among Jews. Fairchild, *Greek Immigration to the United States,* 112; Willcox, ed., *International Migrations,* 2:506-7.

45. Foerster, *Italian Emigration of Our Times,* 273, 400.

46. The term *oceanic migration* is used to exclude migration across the Mediterranean Sea.

47. Foerster, *Italian Emigration of Our Times,* 36.

48. Ibid., 47, 243-44.

49. Ibid., 37; Rowland T. Berthoff, *British Immigrants in Industrial America* (Cambridge, 1955), 82.

50. Berthoff, *British Immigrants in Industrial America,* 52; Andrew Roy, *A History of the Coal Miners of the United States,* 41-42; William I. Thomas and Florian W. Znaniecki, *The Polish Peasant in Europe and America* (Chicago, 1918-20), 1:192.

51. Hansen, *The Mingling of the Canadian and American Peoples,* 165-66.

52. Foerster, *Italian Emigration of Our Times,* 21; *Observer,* August 3, 1959.

53. Foerster, *Italian Emigration of Our Times,* 21.

54. Ibid., 37.

55. Frank Thistlethwaite, "The Atlantic Migration of the Pottery Industry," *Economic History Review* 2d series, 11 (1958): 270; Berthoff, *British Immigrants in Industrial America,* 33.

56. Foerster, *Italian Emigration of Our Times,* 215-16.

57. Fairchild, *Greek Immigration to the United States,* 75-78.

58. Foerster, *Italian Emigration of Our Times,* 21.

59. Willcox, ed., *International Migrations,* 2:450; 1876 marks the first attempt, by Capri, at a statistical coverage.

60. Foerster, *Italian Emigration of Our Times,* 129-30.

61. Kirk, *Europe's Population in the Interwar Years,* 100, 105.

62. Ibid., 97-104.

63. Foerster, *Italian Emigration of Our Times,* 19.

64. Thomas and Znaniecki, *The Polish Peasant in Europe and America,* 1:168; Foerster, *Italian Emigration of Our Times,* 21.

65. Fairchild, *Greek Immigration to the United States,* 87; Foerster, *Italian Emigration of Our Times,* 123-24, 145.

66. Ibid., 393.

67. Hansen, *The Immigrant in American History,* 191-92.

68. See Edward P. Hutchinson, *Immigrants and Their Children 1850-1950* (New York, 1956), passim.

69. Hutchinson, *Immigrants and Their Children,* 338-39, Appendix, Table A, 2a; Fairchild, *Greek Immigration to the United States,* 127, 165, and Appendix, Table 15; Foerster, *Italian Emigration of Our Times,* 147.

70. Ibid., 417.

71. Fairchild, *Greek Immigration to the United States,* 174-75.

72. Foerster, *Italian Emigration of Our Times*, 255.

73. Hutchinson, *Immigrants and Their Children*, 338-39.

74. Foerster, *Italian Emigration of Our Times*, 123-24.

75. Ibid., 145.

76. Berthoff, *British Immigrants in Industrial America*, chapter 4; John Rowe, "Cornish Emigrants and America," *Bulletin of the British Association for American Studies*, no. 8 (1950).

77. William O. Henderson, *Britain and Industrial Europe 1750-1870* (Liverpool, 1954), chapters 2, 3; Berthoff, *British Immigrants in Industrial America*, chapter 5.

78. Thistlethwaite, "The Atlantic Migration of the Pottery Industry," 270.

79. Unfortunately, owing to a surprising absence of British filiopietists, very little is known about the British communities abroad, even in the United States, where, contrary to the normal assumption, "hyphenated" American communities were as characteristic of the British as of other ethnic groups; an exceptional study is Lloyd G. Reynolds, *The British Immigrant: His Economic and Social Adjustment in Canada* (Toronto, 1935).

80. Thistlethwaite, "The Atlantic Migration of the Pottery Industry," 270; see also Oscar Handlin, "International Migration and the Acquisition of New Skills," in *The Progress of Underdeveloped Areas*, ed. Berthold F. Hoselitz (Chicago, 1952).

81. Frank Thistlethwaite, *The Anglo-American Connection in the Early Nineteenth Century* (Philadelphia, 1959), 29-33.

82. See Maldwyn A. Jones, "The Role of the United Kingdom in the Transatlantic Emigrant Trade 1815-1875," Ph.D. diss., Oxford University, 1956.

83. See Brinley Thomas, *Migration and Economic Growth: A Study of Great Britain and the Atlantic Economy* (Cambridge, 1954); H. Hale Bellott, "Atlantic History," *History* 31 (March 1946): 56-63.

84. For a sketch of the system as it affected emigration see Thistlethwaite, *The Anglo-American Connection in the Early Nineteenth Century*, chapter 1.

85. Harry Jerome, *Migration and Business Cycles* (New York, 1926); Simon Kuznets and Ernest Rubin, *Immigration and the Foreign Born*, Occasional Paper 46 (Washington, D.C., 1954).

86. Thomas, *Migration and Economic Growth*, passim.

87. See also Dorothy Thomas in *Population and World Politics*, ed. Hauser, 159.

88. Arnold Schrier, *Ireland and the American Emigration, 1850-1900* (Minneapolis, 1958), passim.

89. William D. Forsyth, *The Myth of Open Spaces* (Melbourne, 1942), passim.

90. Isaiah Bowman, *The Limits of Land Settlement* (New York, 1937), passim; Forsyth, *The Myth of Open Spaces*, 13.

91. Ibid., 14-16.

92. Kirk, *Europe's Population in the Interwar Years*, 85-88.

93. Willcox, ed., *International Migrations*, 2:244, 290, 355; Henning Ravnholt, "A Quantitative Concept of the International Mobility of Population and its Application to certain European Countries in the Period 1851-1935," in International Population Congress, *Proceedings* (Paris, 1937); Forsyth, *The Myth of Open Spaces*, 7, 8.

94. Kirk, *Europe's Population in the Interwar Years*, 86.

95. Kirk, "Demographic Trends in Europe," 96; see Forsyth, *The Myth of Open Spaces*, passim.

96. See pages 134-55 of this volume.

97. Brinley Thomas, ed., *Economics of International Migration* (London, 1958), passim.

98. Carr-Saunders, *World Population*, 42.

99. Dudley Kirk, "Survey of Recent Overseas Migration," in *Proceedings, World Population Conference* (1954), 2:97.

100. Forsyth, *The Myth of Open Spaces*, 16-17; Isaac, "International Migration and European Trends," 186-191.

101. Thomas, *Economics of International Migration*.

102. Kirk, "Demographic Trends in Europe," 48.

103. This increase came at a time when, in some instances, labor-saving techniques were cutting the demand for farm laborers.

104. Ravnholt, "A Quantitative Concept of the International Mobility of Population"; United Nations, *Population Trends*, 117-18; Blegen, *Norwegian Migration to America*, 1:165-66.

105. Forsyth, *The Myth of Open Spaces*, 45; the preponderance of males is also marked.

106. Kirk, *Europe's Population in the Interwar Years*, 148-49.

107. Hansen, *The Immigrant in American History*, 192.

108. For Norway, see Blegen, *Norwegian Migration to America*, 1:345; for Sweden, Dorothy Thomas, *Social and Economic Aspects of Swedish Migration 1750 to 1930* (New York, 1941), passim.

109. Willcox, ed., *International Migrations*, 2:515-17.

110. Even the later urban emigrants from Norway were very largely rural migrants who had sojourned awhile in the towns. Ingrid Gaustad Semmingsen, "Norwegian Emigration to America During the Nineteenth Century," *Norwegian-American Studies and Records* 11 (1940): 78-80.

111. Blegen, *Norwegian Migration to America*, 2:3.

112. Peter Munch, "Social Adjustment Among Wisconsin Norwegians," *American Sociological Review* 14 (1949): 780-87.

113. Thomas, *Swedish Migration*, 169, 304-5; A. J. Youngson, "The Acceleration of Economic Progress in Sweden, 1850-1880," in *Possibilities of Economic Progress* (Cambridge, 1959), 176-77; Blegen, *Norwegian Migration to America*, 2:456.

114. Kirk, "Demographic Trends in Europe," 53-54; Willcox, ed., *International Migrations*, 2:244.

115. Kirk, "Demographic Trends in Europe," 83-88.

116. See Isaac, "International Migration and European Trends," 186-91; Kirk, *Europe's Population in the Interwar Years*, 148-49; Kirk, "Demogrpahic Trends in Europe," 53-54.

117. Thomas and Znaniecki, *The Polish Peasant in Europe and America*, 1:204-5, 2:1499; P. Hauser, "Present Status and Prospects of Research in Population," *American Sociological Review* 13 (August 1948): 380.

118. E. W. Hofstee in *Economics of International Migration*, ed. Thomas, 105-6.

119. G. H. L. Zeegers, "Some Sociographic Aspects of Emigration from the Netherlands," in *Proceedings, World Population Conference* (New York, 1954), 2:297-98.

120. Thomas, *Social and Economic Aspects of Swedish Migration 1750 to 1930*; *Emigrationsutredningen: Betänkande i Utvandringsfragen*, passim; Arne Skaug, "Memorandum on Fluctuations in Migration from Norway since 1900 Compared with Other Countries and Causes of These Fluctuations," Norwegian Memorandum 1, International Studies Conference, 10th Session, Paris, June 28-July 3, 1937; Blegen, *Norwegian Migration to America*; Ingrid Gaustad Semmingsen, "Norwegian Emigration in the Nineteenth Century," *Scandinavian Economic History Review* 8 (1960): 150-60.

121. Semmingsen, "Norwegian Emigration," 76.

122. Quoted in Blegen, *Norwegian Migration to America*, 2:468.

123. Semmingsen, "Norwegian Emigration," 76.

124. See Florence E. Janson, *The Background to Swedish Immigration, 1840-1930* (Chicago, 1931), 167-96; Franklin D. Scott, "The Causes and Consequences of Emigration in Sweden," *Chronicle of the American-Swedish Historical Foundation* (Spring 1955); Blegen, *Norwegian Migration to America*, 1:27-36, 159-60; Thistlethwaite, *The Anglo-American Connection in the Early Nineteenth Century*, chapters 1 and 3.

125. Blegen, *Norwegian Migration to America*, 1:56.

126. Halvdan Koht, *The American Spirit in Europe* (Philadelphia, 1949), passim; Thistlethwaite, *The Anglo-American Connection in the Early Nineteenth Century*, chapter 2; George D. Lillibridge, *Beacon of Freedom: The Impact of American Democracy upon Britain 1830-70* (Philadelphia, 1954), passim.

127. Blegen, *Norwegian Migration to America*, 1:162-63.

128. *Emigrationsutredningen*, 836.

129. Thomas and Znaniecki, *The Polish Peasant in Europe and America*, 1:passim.

130. That important bodies of emigrant letters may still be uncovered has been proved by the results of an advertising campaign in England, see Charlotte Erickson, ed., *Invisible Immigrants: The Adaptation of English and Scottish Immigrants in Nineteenth-Century America* (Ithaca, 1990).

Postscript

An addiction to history comes in various ways. For me, its wellspring was a sense of the past conjured by the historical imagination. I began not in the library but on the ground, with the study of medieval parish churches in and around York, as did A. J. P. Taylor, who went to the same boarding school before me and was taught by the same outstanding history master. Thereafter it became, for me, a quest for the historical past which existed before the blight of textile industrialization obliterated so much of my Lancashire home neighborhood, especially its scattering of sixteenth-century halls, farm houses, and hamlets. Later it was to be the Tudor and Stuart college buildings of Cambridge, a romantic evocation of the past no doubt, but a powerful stimulus to many a youth for historical exploration and research.

When I read for the history tripos at Cambridge in the mid-1930s, the only element of American history in the syllabus was Alexander Hamilton's *The Federalist* as a text for the history of political thought; and so, when I was elected to a Commonwealth Fund (later Harkness) Fellowship to study history in the United States and decided to learn about its past, I had to start at the beginning. With wisdom beyond my years, I accepted the Fund's proposal that I should go to the Midwest, to the University of Minnesota rather than to an Ivy League college, on the ground that I was more likely to get to the heart of the matter in what was then largely terra incognita for an English student rather than as just another British type at Yale. So it proved, and it was a decision for which I have ever been thankful. It resulted, after various vicissitudes, in making me not just an American historian, but one of migration. As far as orthodoxy was concerned, Minnesota was my undoing.

Once again I began on the ground, this time on the bluffs of the upper Mississippi, an islander somewhat at a loss in the heart of a continent, conscious of vast expanses of prairie, lakes, and forest and, as fall turned to winter, of a frozen north with more affinity to the great Canadian subcontinent than to any climate I had known. More significant, the Americans who welcomed me to Minneapolis were unlike any preconceived English stereotype: they seemed to me Americanized Swedes, Norwegians, Germans, Czechs, and Finns, in their physiognamies, their speech, their Lutheran or Catholic faith, their folk customs, and their European heritage. In short, the counters, the building blocks with which I began the humbling and sometimes painful job of constructing an America were what is now called "ethnic" and, moreover, a predominently Scandinavian mix. Above all, they were in a particular time-scale of migration and settlement: mostly second-generation immigrant. Such was my American mosaic. Only later did I discover that transplanted New England of old English origins which was the other Twin City, Saint Paul.

This was my first education in American history. Such staple subjects as constitutional and diplomatic history, although essential, seemed formalistic compared with the economic and the social. I was attracted especially by the teaching of George Stephenson, author of a pioneer book on the history of immigration published over a decade before. This modest, friendly, and important scholar, more than anyone else, set my compass for me. Stephenson had been a pupil of Frederick Jackson Turner, who exerted a powerful field of force. To one for whom the Upper Midwest seemed a physical—and certainly an intellectual—frontier, the Turnerian thesis was revolutionary, illuminating, and, like many great discoveries, obvious when you came to think about it. The formative influence of a moving frontier of settlement on European-derived institutions and on the social psychology of the Americans who experienced it explained to a European so much that seemed familiar yet strange about American institutions and values.

Although that famous hypothesis was to undergo the critical scrutiny of "revisionists" who emphasized the debilitating, rather than creative, effects of the edge of settlement or even challenged the whole concept, American history would never be the same again. To me as a European it seemed that the theory could be modified or refined to take into account the objections of the revisionists without diluting the value of the concept itself. From across the Atlantic what was significant was not the frontier of settlement per se, but the physical and psychological mobility of the society which a moving frontier of settlement induced in its wake. And so I evolved my own working model of America as the mobile society, a people on the move, in caravan. This proved a useful tool when after the war I was faced with the challenge of helping establish the teaching of American history at Cambridge. As part of this I was commissioned to write an introductory history of the United States for British students. The result, *The Great Experiment,* was more than an introduction; it was an attempt to explain America by reinterpreting her past in the neo-

Turnerian terms of the mobile society. As I wrote in the preface: "The writing of this book has strengthened the conviction that one set of influences has dominated American development: I mean those which relate to migration; and the underlying purpose of the book has been to show how as a result of the great process of migration from Europe across the new continent a new variant of western society has come into being."[1] As a hypothesis, for British students at any rate, it appears to have stood the test over thirty years' time. This, however, is to anticipate events so far as this historiographic pilgrim's progress is concerned.

That progress, as for most of my generation, was interrupted by World War II, but the experience of the war had its lessons to teach a young historian.

My sojourn in Minnesota covered the two years between the Munich Agreement of September 1938 and the German conquest of France in June 1940. This was the period of phony peace and war. For America it was the time of isolationism par excellence, and the Scandinavian communities of Minnesota responded with instinctive and deeply held convictions. Had not they, their parents, and even grandparents, however proud of and nostalgic for their homeland, turned their backs on Europe? Furthermore, coming from small, largely neutralist countries, they wished a plague on the houses of all Great Powers. Events, particularly the invasions of Finland and Norway, were to modify this, but my education in the deeper convictions of the Upper Midwest stood me in good stead when, at the conclusion of my fellowship, our ambassador asked me to stay awhile in New York before returning to England in order to help set up an information service to persuade the American press and radio that Britain was by no means defeated after the fall of France. A knowledge of the multifaceted attitudes of the immigrant communities was important for such work and was, indeed, similar to that whereby academics like Samuel Lubell were to transform the analysis of American political behavior. This was the first of my war lessons.

From the point of view of the Diplomatic Service, we of the British Press Service were an uncouth bunch of amateurs, chiefly journalistic and academic. But we had in common the fact that we shared American experiences of a variety and to a depth that our diplomats, with their limited time and experience in the United States, could not readily grasp. The tensions which developed between the embassy in Washington and we who were coping with what today is called the media in New York were persistent. I became aware that there existed across the Atlantic a disrupted network of Anglo-American relationships, professional, religious, and commercial for the most part, of which official channels knew little and which only needed technical skills and communications to become yet again a supportive network for the British war effort. Could it be, I asked myself, that this had been also true in the past, and that the history of Anglo-American relations could be found to be richer, more varied, and more substantial than the copybook analysis of diplomatic dispatches which was the stuff of the Bemis-inspired textbooks?

The third lesson was more general. I returned to the beleaguered citadel of the British Isles in 1941 convinced that only an Anglo-American war partnership more intimate than a conventional alliance could bring victory, that a postwar resurgence of American isolationism would be a disaster, and that something must be done about the ignorance, complacence, and conceit of most of my fellow countrymen concerning the United States. It was in such a spirit that I went back to Cambridge in 1945 to resume my education as an American historian and to do what I could to help establish the subject, not only at Cambridge but also at British universities in general. The phenomenal and lasting success of the American Studies movement of the 1950s goes far beyond the scope of autobiography but must be alluded to here as an important motivation for my professional progress.

More immediately pertinent to this narrative was the need to justify such an undertaking professionally, to make American history respectable to an academic establishment for whom the subject, if it existed at all, was a subordinate option in a Europe-centered world. Its credentials had to be proved as an independent discipline in its own right and as a valuable new dimension to historical studies. The intellectual argument was not enough that European scholars, by virtue of their different *points d'appui*, might contribute revealing interpretive insights for a subject that had developed introspectively. It was necessary to show that British scholars working on British sources could add to the sum of human knowledge about the history of the United States. For me, this meant taking a new look at the history of Anglo-American relations and more specifically to follow up my wartime hunch that there was considerably more to it than the old diplomatic bag. It also meant strengthening my Minnesota penchant for social and economic forces and for developing interdisciplinary skills. The history of the North American continent was too formidable an undertaking not to make use of the insights of all relevent disciplines, from physical geography through the social sciences to literary and intellectual history. And so I came to be thought not merely unorthodox but suspect, an interdisciplinary nutcase.

It also meant broadening one's angle of vision to take in the whole sweep of the North Atlantic basin as a geopolitical and geoeconomic entity, and preeminently to subsume Canada with the United States. I was by no means alone in this, and if I may claim discipleship at all, apart from to George Stephenson, it is to John B. Brebner, whose work, particularly *North Atlantic Triangle*,[2] was a seminal force and whose personality a tonic. Cambridge colleagues in the teaching of what we called "the expansion of Europe," and especially Gallagher and Robinson with their idea of "informal empire," helped me focus on the persistence into the early and mid-nineteenth-century of North America as England's colonial economy, of the metropolitan and the provincial; and Brinley Thomas sharpened up the macroeconomic and demographic theory of the movement of capital and labor westward across the Atlantic.[3]

Within the framework of this Atlantic economy I pursued my own lines of inquiry into what proved to be a whole network of relationships among elements in English society and North America in the early nineteenth century largely unknown to the government-to-government contacts which are the stuff of diplomatic history. For members of the early Victorian establishment, the young American republic was a fearful example of revolution, but for the new industrial and commercial classes of the north and midlands, America was the hope of the world. Radicals in politics from Chartists to Cobdenites, nonconformists in religion, evangelicals, and philanthropists, cultivated their own transatlantic connections with like-minded reformers in the northeastern United States. I developed a special interest in the Anglo-American antislavery movement and its connection with the emergence of feminism. Such networks had an important bearing on the forming of public opinion, especially in Britain, at the time of the American Civil War. The result of this work was a series of public lectures which I gave as visiting professor of American civilization at the University of Pennsylvania in 1958 and which became *The Anglo-American Connection in the Early Nineteenth Century*.[4]

An important element in this transatlantic traffic was the flow of passengers, at first seasonal but increasingly one-way, of those skilled emigrants from Britain who were to be so essential for the industrialization of the American economy and its ultimate emancipation from colonial status. In the mid-1950s the phrase "transfer of technology" had not yet, I think, been invented as a term of art; but the phenomenon—the migration from Britain's industrial metropolis of the technicians who formed the first skilled cadres for the new industries of America—invited investigation. It became my chief preoccupation and the means for my returning to that topic of migration which had first captured my imagination in Minnesota before the war.

I first turned my attention to the textile operatives. Textiles, and particularly cotton, was the architypal high-tech industry of the new order and the first to be established in the United States as a result of the inventive skills of English pioneers like Samuel Slater and the Scholfields. There was also a more personal reason for this choice. I happen to come from a family of Lancashire cotton manufacturers stretching back to a great, great, grandfather who started as a hand-loom weaver at the outset of that "industrial revolution"; another member of the family immigrated to the cotton mills of New England and died of a heart attack on the floor of the Massachusetts House of Representatives. I had something of a family "feel" for the technical processes of weaving cloth.

I then pursued this interest in the cases of other skilled occupations such as the Welsh ironworkers of Pennsylvania and the Welsh and Yorkshire coal, and Cornish tin, miners of Appalachia; and I made a special study of those migrant potters who brought their craft from Staffordshire to the claybanks of New Jersey and the Ohio Valley.[5] Gradually, patterns, now familiar to all students of migration, began to emerge: of "chains" of migration linking specific towns and neighborhoods, even families, on both sides of the Atlantic; of persistence in those skills like the Cornish miners, who would tunnel anything, from mines in upper Michigan to railways in the Rockies, rarely deserting their proud and esoteric calling; of key workers like the iron puddler or the mine captain, the elite of a new order, some of whom would emerge as trade union organizers and leaders, state mine and factory inspectors, and a minority as capitalist masters; and most preserving the folk customs, speech patterns, the foods and drinks, music, and sports of those Welsh valleys, Lancashire towns, and Cornish mining villages whence they had come, to a second and even third generation.

Plotting the trails of such specific groups of migrants reinforced my view that origins were as important as destinations in the history of migration, the particular circumstances leading to uprooting as significant as the experience of adjustment and assimilation. "Americanization" began not at Ellis Island but in innumerable but specific European neighborhoods: if there was an American frontier, it was the frontier of Europe. That vast efflux of European population across the Atlantic in the nineteenth and early twentieth centuries was a prime historical force which demanded to be studied for itself. The migration process transcended national barriers, and yet in terms of historiography it went unrecognized in a profession whose parameters were still so largely drawn by the nation-state. In countries of origin, those who left, the emigrants, were treated, if not as deserters, as a negative loss and written out of the story. George M. Trevelyan's *English Social History,*[6] still a ranking work of its kind after World War II, contains only one mention of emigration, and that a passing reference to the British colonies.

By contrast, in the United States the phenomenon could no more be ignored than the ocean tides. When Franklin Roosevelt teased the Daughters of the American Revolution by addressing them as "fellow immigrants" he was only underlining the obvious. Yet here, too, migration history was still regarded as a subdiscipline in a profession concerned with the evolution of the American nation. With a few towering exceptions, notably that of Marcus Lee Hansen, the writing of that period still used, almost exclusively, the word *immigration* and *immigrant* to describe the phenomenon. Ever since the wealth of documentation provided by the Immigration Commission, the underlying motive was to comprehend how Europeans became Americans. The prevailing ideas modulated from crude concepts of Americanization to progressively more sophisticated theories of assimilation, acculturation, pluralism, and images of melting pots and salad bowls. Scholarly standards had come a long way from the filiopietists—whether Bostonian genealogists or first-generation hyphenated Americans—and a new generation of classic writing was brilliantly illuminating the immigrant experience, from a literary genre like Alfred Kazin's *A Walker in the City*[7] to a whole corpus of historical writing. Prominent in this was, of course, the work of Oscar Handlin, an important and helpful influence for me. Yet, from across the Atlantic, even *The Uprooted*[8] sketched a Europe that was more like a stage back-cloth or, in English terms, the stylized landscape of Gainsborough before Wilson or Constable had learned to look upon its true nature. Europe was, simply, given.

Another aspect of this America-centerdness, this preoccupation with American exceptionalism, was a blind spot concerning any other emigrant destinations than the United States. Having learned to think of North America as a whole in terms of the flow of trade, people, and capital, it was an easy step for this European to ask, What of the other destinations for the great migration explosion? Ought one not to be setting the North American phenomenon in the even broader context of migration to South America and to explore these interrelationships and the dynamics of a movement which seemed ever more powerful and ramifying the more one attempted to chart its depths?

In short, by 1960 it had gradually dawned on me that the history of migration was an Andromeda, chained to the rock of national history and crying to be freed to become an independent force. Here was an opportunity for Europeans to take a lead. At this fortuitous moment I received an invitation to act as rapporteur for the migration session of the Eleventh International Conference of Historical Sciences, to be held in Stockholm in 1960. It was in response to this invitation that I wrote the paper airing these ideas that is reprinted herein. That it should have indirectly resulted in such a wonderful harvest of original scholarship, mostly by younger European colleagues, is a matter of great gratification to me. I feel honored that what was essentially a *pièce d'occasion* should have prompted such results.

NOTES

1. Frank Thistlethwaite, *The Great Experiment* (Cambridge, 1955), xi.

2. John B. Brebner, *North American Triangle: The Interplay of Canada, the United States and Great Britain* (New Haven, 1945).

3. Brinley Thomas, *Migration and Economic Growth: A Study of Great Britain and the Atlantic Economy* (Cambridge, 1954).

4. Frank Thistlethwaite, *The Anglo-American Connection in the Early Nineteenth Century* (Philadelphia, 1959).

5. Frank Thistlethwaite, "The Atlantic Migration of the Pottery Industry," *Economic History Review,* 2d series, 11 (1958): 264-78.

6. George M. Trevelyan, *English Social History* (London, 1942).

7. Alfred Kazin, *A Walker in the City* (New York, 1951).

8. Oscar Handlin, *The Uprooted: The Epic Study of the Great Migrations that Made the American People* (Boston, 1951).

2

Migration, Ethnicity, and the Rise of an Atlantic Economy: The Re-Peopling of British America, 1600–1790

RUSSELL R. MENARD

From an outsider's perspective, American immigration history is a strange field. Its oddity emerges clearly from the observation that the colonial era falls outside its terrain. Why that is so is a puzzle, although it clearly reflects the main "lines of force" in the two specialties, the way practitioners define the boundaries, the questions they pursue, and the themes that shape their inquiries. With a few notable exceptions, historians of the American immigrant experience have ignored the preindustrial age, confining their comments to obligatory and cursory introductions as they hurry to get to the truly important issues.[1] And despite some promising recent developments, immigration has failed to emerge as a central theme among colonialists, who have instead organized their field around other questions.[2]

This division is artificial and unfortunate, for immigration historians and colonialists ought to have much in common. Certainly the main themes of immigration history as they emerge from scholarship on the nineteenth and twentieth centuries are also key issues in the colonial period. Immigration and opportunity, assimilation and ethnicity, oppression and resistance, community-building and the construction of a national identity were as central to the colonial era as to the industrial age. Certainly, too, there is continuity in process as well as theme. The great transatlantic migrations of the industrial era — one of the major transforming events of world history — originated in the movements of the early modern age. Indeed, from some perspectives these are not two migrations but a single stream; at the very least the second will not be fully understood without knowledge of the first. Colonialists and immigration historians have much to learn from each other. And they have a grand opportunity. If they work together they can elaborate a consistent vision of the American

58

experience that spans more than four centuries and keeps the role of migrants in building a world economy at its center.

At one level this chapter is a plea for such a collaboration. It surveys the colonial period from an immigrationist perspective, asking what we know, what we need to find out, and how we can best get from here to there. Along the way, I will sketch out the shape of the field and point to some key continuities between the colonial period and the national history of the United States. It is surely an error in a discussion concerned to undermine boundaries of time and field to fail to question boundaries of nation and region. However, limits of space and my own competence combine to focus the essay on the colonies of British North America.

Native Americans

From the perspective of America's aboriginal inhabitants, the great transatlantic movement of the early modern age was not a migration but an invasion, and the process was not one of populating a wilderness but of re-peopling a once densely settled land. For Indians, the central consequences of that invasion were conquest and demographic disaster. Estimates of the native population of the Americas on the eve of the invasion show wild variation, from the just over eight million suggested by A. L. Kroeber in the 1930s to the more than a hundred million advanced by Woodrow Borah, Henry Dobyns, and others during the 1960s. Although it is unlikely that a universally accepted figure will ever be developed, William Deneven's estimate of fifty-seven million, cautiously offered with a range of 25 percent (forty-three to seventy-two million), reflects current opinion and probably captures the range of possibilities. That range is large, but it is nevertheless a robust result, sufficient to establish that the European invasion of America initiated a holocaust, one of the great demographic catastrophes of human history. By the middle of the seventeenth century there were fewer than ten million, and perhaps only five million, Indians left in the Americas. And, in contrast to the European and Asian experience with massive decline, where recovery was fairly quick, "the Indian population of America recovered only slowly, partially, and in highly modified form."[3]

Additional perspective is provided by the North American experience. The best estimates suggest a population of 4.5 million for North America in 1500, although some argue for a much higher total. In 1770, on the eve of Independence, some 1.8 million whites and fewer than a half million blacks lived in British North America. We do not know how many Indians remained at that date, but it is clear that their numbers had fallen considerably. In all probability there were fewer people in North America in 1770, more than century and a half after the settlement at Jamestown, than there had been at the beginning of the English invasion. That observation alone should be sufficient to destroy the myth of Europeans transforming an American wilderness into a garden.[4]

It ought to be but it is not, and the myth persists. Professional historians bear some responsibility for it staying power, for we have largely failed to assimilate the Native American experience into a comprehensive American history. That assimilation will be difficult, but one strategy emerges from the collaboration between immigration historians and colonialists advocated here. The unifying threads are the fabrication of ethnicity and the persistence of distinct cultures within a pluralistic society despite hostility and oppression. This is not to argue that American Indians can be understood as just another national group. The conditions they faced were extreme, while their aboriginal status, tribal structure, and segregation from white society set them apart from European immigrants. Still, one way of under- standing the Indian struggle with their English conquerors is to trace their transformation from independent tribal peoples into America's first ethnic groups.[5]

How Many Immigrants?

We can now turn to more familiar territory for historians of im- migration by asking how many people crossed the Atlantic to that part of North America that became the United States. This is a difficult question, for contemporaries kept track of new arrivals only sporad- ically and occasionally. No direct answer is available. It is possible to proceed indirectly, however. Given birth and death rates and the size of colonial populations, net migration can be calculated as a residual, as that portion of the change in population size not attributable to the difference between births and deaths. H. A. Gemery, David Gal- enson, and Robert Fogel and his collaborators have offered such estimates. Table 2.1 builds on their work to construct a series of net migration estimates for the years 1620 to 1780. These are net figures, it must be emphasized, for the method is unable to account for return migrants or for those who left for other regions in the Americas. As such, they should be read as absolute minimums: the true volume of transatlantic migration must have been a good deal higher.[6]

At least six hundred thousand people, these estimates indicate,

Table 2.1. Estimated Net Migration to British America, 1620-1780*

Date	New England			Middle Colonies			Upper South			Lower South			Total		
	E	A	T	E	A	T	E	A	T	E	A	T	E	A	T
1620-39	11	0	11	1	0	1	10	0	10	0	0	0	22	0	22
1640-59	8	0	8	1	0	1	25	1	26	0	0	0	34	1	35
1660-79	10	0	10	5	0	5	44	5	49	1	0	1	60	5	65
1680-99	-19	1	-18	20	1	21	32	11	43	3	3	6	36	16	52
1700-1719	15	1	16	8	4	12	7	22	29	3	11	14	33	38	71
1720-39	3	1	4	40	-1	39	19	49	68	8	29	37	70	78	148
1740-59	-25	-1	-26	48	1	49	-1	56	55	13	13	26	35	69	104
1760-79	-27	-5	-32	11	-5	6	39	32	71	45	18	63	68	40	108
Totals													358	247	605

* All numbers in thousands. E = Europeans; A = Africans; T = Total.
Sources: Estimates follow the procedures described in Henry A. Gemery, "Emigration from the British Isles to the New World, 1630-1700: Inferences from Colonial Populations," *Research in Economic History* 5 (1980): 179-231, and David Galenson, *White Servitude in Colonial America: An Economic Analysis* (Cambridge, 1981), 212-18. However, I used estimates of population (and occasionally of vital rates) based on material discussed in John J. McCusker and Russell R. Menard, *The Economy of British America, 1607-1789* (Chapel Hill, 1985). New England includes New Hampshire, Massachusetts, Connecticut, and Rhode Island. Middle colonies include New York, New Jersey, Pennsylvania, and Delaware. The Upper South includes Maryland, Virginia, and North Carolina. The Lower South includes South Carolina and Georgia.

crossed the Atlantic between 1620 and 1780 to the British colonies
that became the United States. By the standards of the industrial age,
that seems a minor movement, barely more than the average annual
migration of Europeans overseas in the century following 1820. That
is not the only yardstick, however. If we approach the numbers in
colonial terms and compare the migration to the base population, it
is more impressive. In 1730, for example, there were roughly 650,000
people in the colonies, exclusive of Native Americans: the nearly
150,000 immigrants who arrived between 1720 and 1740 were thus
more than 20 percent of the base population, clearly sufficient to
profoundly shape all aspects of life. In American history, the colonial
period, not the industrial era, was the age of the immigrants.

Those six hundred thousand immigrants were not evenly distributed by region, race, or time. One can divide the colonial period into
two broad eras, with a turning point or hinge in the late seventeenth
century. The first, from 1620 to 1680, witnessed a steady growth of
the migrant stream, although there were always sharp, short-term
fluctuations obscured by the high level of aggregation employed in
Table 2.1. The migrants were overwhelmingly white, indeed, almost
exclusively English, the great majority going to New England and the
Chesapeake colonies of Maryland and Virginia. The 1680s and 1690s
were marked by both a decline in volume and the beginnings of a
new pattern. Thereafter, New England ceased to be a major destination: more often than not it registered a net loss to migration in
the eighteenth century. Two more recently settled regions, the mid-
Atlantic colonies and the Lower South, emerged as major centers of
migration. And, perhaps most important, blacks came to dominate
the migrant stream, outnumbering whites in most years from 1700
to 1760. In the eighteenth century, America was as much an extension
of Africa as of Europe.

This last fact points directly to the profound Eurocentrism of immigration history as practiced in the United States. One of the grand
opportunities missed by historians of international migration who
ignore the colonial era is the chance to explore the African-American
experience in their terms. As with Indians, this is not to suggest that
blacks can be viewed as simply another ethnic group. Slavery and
racism clearly set them apart. But they did struggle against oppression
in a hostile environment to forge a new African-American identity
out of their common Old World heritage and their shared New World
experience. A comprehensive American history must include that
process.[7]

The Diversification of the Migrant Stream

The temporal pattern revealed in Table 2.1 suggests a considerable diversification of the migrant stream in the eighteenth century. Clearly, migrants became progressively darker. And a simple division by race obscures the full extent of that diversity. Fortunately, we have, in a surname analysis of the 1790 census originally conducted more than fifty years ago, a rough guide to just how diverse the migrant stream was in the late colonial period. Before turning to those data it is worth looking at their genesis, for they have often served as a starting point for the ethnic history of the United States, and they are a product of a rare collaboration between immigration historians and early Americanists.

The Immigration Act of 1924 established a quota system by apportioning the flow of migrants according to the "national origins" of the existing population. That seems a straightforward rule, but it required accurate—or, rather, generally accepted—estimates of the number of Americans descended from various ethnic groups. Since the Census Bureau had not asked where people were born until the 1850 enumeration, a scholarly disagreement with important policy implications developed centered on the composition of the U.S. population in 1790. By 1927, when the new rule went into effect, two sharply different sets of estimates contended for acceptance by immigration authorities. The first, advanced by W. S. Rossiter of the Census Bureau in 1909, concluded that 82 percent of the white population of the United States in 1790 was of English or Welsh descent. The second, offered somewhat later by J. Franklin Jameson, maintained that only 60 percent of the whites were English or Welsh and argued for a much larger proportion of Scots, Irish, Germans, and Dutch. Such substantial disagreements among distinguished scholars raised "grave doubts" about "the whole value of these computations" upon which the quota system rested.[8]

The American Council of Learned Societies waded into the fray in 1927, intending to use its prestige and wide scholarly contacts to settle the matter. The ACLS appointed a committee of distinguished academics, including historians Jameson and Max Farrand, the prominent statisticians Joseph A. Hill and Walter F. Wilcox, and Robert H. Fife, a linguist from Columbia University. The committee set the questions, supervised the research, took responsibility for the final report, and put its authority behind the results, but the work was done by Howard F. Barker, "an expert in the field of family names and indications of descent derived from them," and Marcus Lee Hansen, then the leading scholar of American immigration history.

The results were mixed. From one perspective, the ACLS report was a great success. The results were accepted by the Quota Board and helped shape the pattern of migration to the United States until 1965, when the system was finally changed. Its distribution of the white population into various national groups was widely accepted by scholars and entered the canon of American history, serving as an unquestioned baseline description on which analysis of ethnicity built for roughly a half century. From a different perspective the report was a disaster. With it the ACLS lent its authority to the racism that pervaded U.S. immigration policy and provided the Quota Board with an excuse to raise admissions from Great Britain and reduce those from Ireland and Southern and Eastern Europe. And it was a methodological mess. The report, as Donald Akenson has concluded, "is so full of errors, ranging from the minor to the fundamental, that it is beyond rehabilitation. It must be abandoned, erased from the historical literature, and forgotten." That gives me pause. Since the major intermingling of immigration and early American history produced such unfortunate results, perhaps we ought to leave the fences high and stick to our own gardens.[9]

Several historians have offered revisions of the ACLS estimates.[10] Table 2.2 amalgamates and summarizes their results. These scholars have demonstrated considerable energy and some ingenuity, and I wish I could report that they had overcome the deficiencies of the ACLS work to produce fully reliable results. Unfortunately, they have pursued refinements to the Barker-Hansen approach when a more radical shift is required. We need to abandon the effort to produce point estimates in favor of a method that will capture the range of possibilities, or at least generate some probability boundaries. Until that is done, these figures provide the best guesses we have of the ethnic makeup of the population before the 1850 census, and they offer valuable clues to the changing composition of the migrant group. At the least they are "ball-park" estimates consistent with "what immigration history tempered by common sense tells us."[11]

Perhaps the most striking aspect of these data is the diversity they reveal: from its beginning, the United States was an ethnic mosaic. People of English background were by far the largest group, but they constituted less than half the total and only 60 percent of the whites, a fact that raises questions about the persistent tendency of colonialists to portray early America as a simple extension of England. Blacks were the next largest group, nearly 20 percent of the whole, although that category conceals a variety of cultural backgrounds. The remainder of the population came from Britain's Celtic fringe and from

Table 2.2. Composition of the U.S. Population in 1790 (in Percent)

	European	African	English	Welsh	Scots-Irish	Scots	Irish	German	French
New England	98	2	82	3	6	3	3	—	1
Mid-Atlantic States	94	6	38	3	11	5	5	30	2
Upper South	64	36	36	4	8	4	5	5	2
Lower South	58	42	29	4	10	5	5	3	2
Kentucky and Tennessee	85	15	45	4	15	7	7	6	1
U.S.	81	19	48	4	9	3	5	10	2

Sources: American Council of Learned Societies, "Report of the Committee on Linguistic and National Stocks in the United States," American Historical Association, *Annual Report for the Year 1931* (Washington, D.C., 1932), 1:122; Forrest McDonald and Ellen Shapiro McDonald, "The Ethnic Origins of the American People, 1790," *William and Mary Quarterly*, 3d ser, 37 (1980): 198; Thomas L. Purvis, "The European Ancestry of the United States Population, 1790," *William and Mary Quarterly* 41 (1984): 98.

German includes some people of Dutch and Swedish background. New England includes Vermont, New Hampshire, Massachusetts, Connecticut, and Rhode Island. The Mid-Atlantic states include New York, Pennsylvania, New Jersey, and Delaware. The Upper South includes Maryland, Virginia, and North Carolina. The Lower South includes South Carolina and Georgia.

Western Europe, especially the Rhine Valley. It must be stressed that
Native Americans do not appear in these estimates: their presence
adds further variety to a highly diverse population.

The data also describe sharp regional variation. New England was
clearly the most homogenous area, its population overwhelmingly
white, its whites largely English. The mid-Atlantic states were also
largely white, but hardly homogenous, as large concentrations of
German, Dutch, and Scots-Irish settlers combined to outnumber the
English and produce a truly polygot population. The South too was
diverse, but in a different way. There the striking facts were the
substantial black population, nearly 40 percent of the total in 1790,
and the ethnic variety among whites due in large part to the heavy
Celtic presence. We need to be careful in generalizing about the South,
however, for the category obscures a major difference between plantation districts, where slaves were often a large majority and most
whites were English, and the mixed-farming regions of the back-
country, where blacks were few and whites more often of Celtic or
German background.

The Sources of Ethnic Diversity

Accounting for the ethnic and racial diversity of the American
population and for the particular regional pattern it describes is no
easy task. That variety reflected reproductive differences as well as
the interaction of numerous migrations, themselves the product of
countless individual choices made in three continents over two centuries. Research suggests that we can make some progress in sorting
out the complexity by distinguishing between types of migrants and
processes of recruitment. The bulk of people who moved to the
colonies came either as workers recruited through a transatlantic labor
market or as settlers recruited by land speculators.[12]

The largest group of migrants, perhaps three-quarters of the total,
came as workers, usually single, predominantly male, and generally
young, in their late teens and early twenties, recruited through a
transatlantic labor market developed during the first phase of England's invasion of North America. Initially, most of these migrants
were English—indeed, at first the majority came from London and
its immediate hinterland—who arrived as indentured servants in a
movement that extended and complemented patterns of labor mobility within England. Over time, however, the English-American migrant stream proved inadequate to the needs of colonial employers.
When it did so they turned to other areas to recruit workers, first

within Great Britain, later on the European continent and in Africa, in the process changing the composition of the migrant group.

We can get some sense of why the migrant stream became increasingly diverse and a better appreciation of the extent of the change by a close look at the Chesapeake colonies of Maryland and Virginia. Documentation for that region is relatively full, and it has been the subject of intense study by social historians. Further, sitting at the center of the demographic spectrum that was British America, the tobacco coast reveals the full range of possibilities in the composition of colonial populations.[13]

In the 1630s, when the English at last established permanent, secure colonies in North America, migrants to the Chesapeake were a homogenous lot. They were overwhelmingly young, single, English males in their late teens and early twenties, usually with some prior work experience and often sons of yeomen and artisans who arrived as indentured servants. By the end of the century the migrants were more diverse. The most obvious and striking change was the growth of slavery. By the 1690s, blacks were a majority among new arrivals. There were also significant shifts in the composition of white immigrants. The majority were still servants, but the migrant stream now included a greater proportion of women, of young boys in their early to middle teens, and of the children of the very poor. And they came from different parts of Great Britain. In the 1630s, the majority of servants to the Chesapeake were from London and the home counties. By the 1690s, the recruiting net was cast more widely and captured large numbers from the southwest and north of England as well as from the Celtic fringe, particularly from the Welsh counties near Bristol and Liverpool and from Ireland.

The greater diversity of the migrant stream was triggered by changes in the supply of indentured servants. The number of servants delivered to Maryland and Virginia rose steadily from the 1630s to the 1660s. The supply leveled out in the mid-1660s, or at least grew at a slower rate, before registering a sharp decline in the 1680s, a decline that persisted into the eighteenth century. Demand for workers continued to grow, however, producing a severe labor shortage for planters.

Why these changes in the rate of migration? Why, that is, did the number of English immigrants to the Chesapeake increase rapidly during the first half of the seventeenth century, level out or grow much more slowly in the 1660s and 1670s, and then decline after 1680? Two processes seem of central importance: changes in the size of the potential migrant group and changes in the relative attractiveness of the several destinations available to English men and women on the move. Although neither can be measured precisely, it is clear that during the seventeenth century both changed in ways that tended first to increase and then to reduce the number of servants willing to try their luck in tobacco.

The number of potential emigrants in seventeenth-century England was a function of total population, an assertion that must be qualified by a recognition that migration was highly age, sex, and probably class specific and that the propensity to migrate varied with time. Nevertheless, changes in the rate of population growth provide a rough index to changes in the size of the potential migrant group. Despite disagreements over the absolute size of total population and the rate and sources of change, it is clear that the pattern of growth within England changed sharply near the middle decades of the seventeenth century. The most reliable estimates describe an average annual growth rate of 0.4 to 0.5 percent for roughly two centuries, beginning from a base of 2.5 million in the mid-fifteenth century and reaching 5.5 million in 1650. England's population declined slowly over the next forty years to about five million, its level during the 1620s, and then began to grow again, slowly at first, more rapidly toward the middle decades of the eighteenth century.[14] If movement to the Chesapeake were a function of the size of the population alone, one would expect the rate of immigration to increase during the first half of the seventeenth century and then decline.

Other processes reinforced the impact of changes in the number of potential migrants, tending first to increase and later to reduce the attractiveness of the Chesapeake relative to other destinations. In part, this was a function of changing prospects at home. During the sixteenth and early seventeenth centuries, real wages in England fell as a growing number of workers competed for employment. Falling wages lowered the opportunity costs of migration and made movement to the colonies more attractive. Relieved of the pressure of a rapidly gowing population, wages rose across the last half of the seventeenth century.[15] Higher wages increased the opportunity cost to migration and worked both to reduce the size of the migrating population and, for those who still chose to move, to increase the attractiveness of destinations within England.[16]

The course of opportunity for ex-servants in Maryland and Virginia helped shape the pattern of migration. The likelihood that a young man who completed servitude along the Bay would achieve a comfortable position in society was high to about 1660 and then began to decline, a decline that became especially sharp after 1680 when former servants often left the region in search of better prospects elsewhere. The chances for success along the tobacco coast were initially a substantial encouragement to prospective migrants, but the size of that inducement fell as the seventeenth century progressed.[17]

Perhaps more important than the course of opportunity within the Chesapeake colonies was the changing attractiveness of the tobacco coast relative to other colonial regions. During the 1630s, poor English men and women who decided to cross the Atlantic could choose among three destinations, but in the 1640s sugar and disease gave the West Indies a bad reputation, while the failure of New England to find a profitable export prevented the growth of a lively demand for servants. These developments narrowed the options and focused the greatest part of the English transatlantic migratory stream on the tobacco coast. After 1680, the opening up of Pennsylvania and the Carolinas ended this near monopoly and diverted migrants away from the Chesapeake colonies. In short, changes in the size of the British-American migration stream and in the share of all migrants attracted to Virginia and Maryland worked first to increase and then to reduce the number of servants bound for the tobacco coast.

Planters and merchants were not passive in the face of these changes. Indeed, recruiting agents were a critical link in the process and could, by varying the intensity of their efforts, shape both the volume and direction of migration. During the seventeenth century their efforts were usually successful in the short run, and, as a consequence, the supply of new servants proved highly sensitive to short-term shifts in planter demand. Over the long haul, shifts in the composition of the servant group suggest some more permanent adjustment in recruiting practices as merchants cast their net more widely in the search for migrants.

In the middle decades of the seventeenth century, recruiters apparently focused on young men in their late teens and early twenties from the middling ranks of English families with some job skills and work experience. After 1660, however, as their numbers dwindled and their opportunities at home increased, few such men moved to Virginia and Maryland. Recruiters tried to meet the shortfall by drawing more heavily on other groups within Britain's population — Irish, women, convicts, homeless orphans, and the laboring poor. Despite these efforts it proved impossible to overcome the powerful secular processes — a stagnant English population and the increasing pull of other destinations — tending to diminish the ability of tobacco planters to attract willing workers. During the last decades of the seventeenth century merchants were unable to meet the growing demand for indentured labor without driving the cost of servants beyond what planters were willing to pay. The result was a major change in the composition of the Chesapeake work force as merchants tapped new sources of servants and planters turned increasingly to African slaves as their principle source of labor.

Work by H. A. Gemery and Jan Hogendorn suggests a way of generalizing this narrative of migration to the Chesapeake, of constructing a model that illuminates the movement of workers to the Americas as a whole.[18] Their key insight concerns the differences in supply between African slaves and all other sources of labor available to colonial employers. The developers of British America had several options in recruiting and organizing a work force. They could draw on free workers and servants from England, Ireland, Wales, and the European continent, on Native Americans from the vast North American interior, and on colonial-born youths not yet established in households of their own. All of those workers moved in small, localized markets characterized by sharp, unpredictable shifts in volume and price. However, as long as demand for labor in a particular region remained low, one of those sources was adequate to meet the need for workers. Thus New England, where the failure to develop a major staple export meant a sluggish economy and relatively low levels of labor productivity, found enough workers in its own sons and daughters, thereby retaining its ethnic homogeneity.[19]

Regions where demand for labor was higher, however, quickly ran into difficulty if they relied on a single source. The prices of workers in those small, localized markets rose sharply, pressed against profit margins, and set off a scramble by merchants who often exhibited considerable ingenuity in developing new sources of labor. Thus in the middle colonies, where a lively agricultural export sector and linked commercial development created a more expansive economy and higher levels of worker productivity, there emerged a complex and rapidly changing labor market that lay behind the ethnic diversity of that population. A different pattern emerged in the southern colonies. Those regions experimented with work forces drawn from a variety of sources early in the development of each area, but high productivity and increasing demand quickly exhausted those small and localized supplies and drove planters toward slaves, Africans trapped in a much wider net, commodities in a stable, large-scale, international labor market that made them the victims of choice in the rapidly expanding plantation colonies of European America.[20]

While an analysis of labor markets along the lines suggested by Gemery and Hogendorn explains much of the diversity of the American population, it cannot account for it all. A substantial portion of the white migration, particularly during the eighteenth century, was not caught up in the labor markets that brought servants and slaves to British America. These were free migrants who moved in family groups, often, as Bernard Bailyn has described them, "sizeable families of some small substance, hit by rent increases that threatened their future security, resentful of personal services they were still required to perform," and, I would add, occasionally pursuing a utopian vision of religious freedom and community. Most, Bailyn continues, were "eager for a fresh start as landowners or at least tenants of independent status capable of expressing their energies in expansive ways." Few were rich, but they were able to scrape together enough money to pay their passage, "buy or rent a stake in the land, equip themselves for the work that lay ahead, and tide themselves over the lean period before the first crops could be produced."[21]

Unfortunately, we cannot describe this migration with the precision possible in the case of workers caught up in the Atlantic labor market. It is clear, however, that land speculators, those much-maligned creatures of the American frontier, played a key role in the process. In efforts to develop their often vast holdings, speculators—perhaps it would be more accurate to call them estate developers—disseminated information, organized passage, provided creative financing, and offered a range of services, all at easy terms. Colonists from Britain and the European continent took up their offers, thus helping to create the ethnic complexity of early America.[22]

Accomodating Ethnic Diversity

It is possible to describe the diversity of the people of early America with precision and to provide a systematic account of the migrations that produced the complex ethnic mosaic of 1790. Moving beyond those issues to the other major themes of immigration history is more difficult. The problem is not an absence of work on such questions by colonialists. Indeed, on some of the major issues the literature is especially rich and detailed, exhibiting a lively creativity in teasing patterns out of seemingly intractable sources. We have, for example, useful studies of the opportunities confronting immigrants, not only in the Chesapeake colonies but also in the low country and in Pennsylvania.[23] There is also a literature on the transfer of culture, particularly among the English in New England, but also among Africans in the plantation colonies.[24] And there are imaginative studies of the role of ethnic differences in politics, of particular ethnic communities, and of relationships among various ethnic groups, especially in the area of attitudes.[25] The difficulty lies rather in the complexity of the subject and in the absence of compelling, comprehensive generalizations.

Without pretending that it captures the full complexity of the matter, I offer this as an integrating hypothesis: in certain critical respects, the people of British America exhibited more homogeneity—or, more precisely, less ethnic diversity—in 1776 than they had earlier in the colonial period. By exploring this proposition we can make some progress toward constructing a history of British America from an immigrationist perspective.

Timothy Breen suggests that the question of ethnic identity can be approached through a focus on the cultural interactions characteristic of early America. During the seventeenth century, he notes, those interactions fell into two broad categories, both of them fluid, diverse, and complex, marked by the "creative adaptation" of participants to new, unstable, rapidly changing circumstances. One type brought people of the same race or nation but from different localities together under conditions of relative equality in ways rare in the Old World outside of Europe's major metropolitan capitals. Thus, "East Anglians were forced to deal with West Country and Kentish migrants, Ibos with Akan. Strangers had to sort themselves out, making compromises about institutional structure and rituals connected with the life cycle." While the sorting process went on, Old World identities at first persisted in an almost bewildering diversity. Eventually, however, and by means that remain obscure, those migrants— and, more completely, their descendents—coalesced into creole cultures, what can be called "charter communities" that "set the rules for the incorporation of later arrivals."[26]

The second type of interaction involved people of different races: red, white, and black. Although it would be a gross exaggeration to claim that such encounters occurred among individuals or groups wielding equal power, those initial meetings were fluid, diverse, and flexible, and circumstances often made it "possible for individuals to negotiate social status on the basis of various attributes, only one of which was race."[27] Again, however, there was a coalesence—perhaps hardening is the better word—of racial ideologies, and racial identities as structured, hierarchical, castelike relationships based on color overwhelmed the more fluid interactions of the early settlements.

Despite the gradual development of creole societies and racial identities, British America exhibited a remarkable cultural diversity in the early decades of the eighteenth century. Much of that diversity rested in the local, parochial character of colonial settlements. The charter societies and the relationships among whites, blacks, and Native Americans were elaborated in different ways and with unique outcomes in each of the major regions—New England, the middle colonies, the Chesapeake, and the low country—regions relatively isolated from one another, each integrated into a larger Atlantic world more through contacts with England than by relations with other colonies. And even within those regions, pockets of ethnic diversity persisted for the still-developing creole cultures—the charter societies built by the early European and African settlers—had not yet overwhelmed or absorbed the customs, loyalties, and identities of more recent migrants.

Although the migrant stream became more varied as the Revolution approached, British North America exhibited progressively less cultural diversity. Two related processes account for the paradox. The first is what John Murrin has called the "Anglicization" of British America, a "general standardization of procedures, tastes, and assumptions" as white colonials in each of the major regions developed a heightened sense of cultural identity and a common set of values and institutions that linked them to settlers in the other areas while gradually eroding the parochial, localized cultures of the seventeenth century.[28] Anglicization had several roots: the creation of a centralized administrative bureaucracy, of standardized legal procedures, and of common institutional structures to govern the empire; the frequent imperial wars against Spain and France which helped forge a common consciousness; the religious revivals that crossed cultural boundaries; the growth of coast-wise trade which improved communications and linked colonial merchants and planters into a commercial network; an increase in migration between the major regions; the rapid economic growth and rising incomes which tied white Americans into a common consumer culture based on English manufactures; and, after 1763, the growing storm of protest against the encroachments of the British Empire which began the slow process of forging a national identity. These processes worked together rather than at cross-purposes to undermine local cultures and regional identities, leaving, as Jack Greene put it, "the separate colonies far more alike than they had ever been at any earlier time."[29]

The second process promoting homogeneity was the continued elaboration of creole cultures established earlier in the colonial period. Africans and Europeans who arrived in British America during the eighteenth century encountered an increasingly structured, articulated social system and powerful incentives and pressures to embrace the dominant culture, to become Anglo Americans or African Americans quickly and with little resistance. Those who moved to the

periphery of settlement sometimes maintained separate cultural identities, but most groups—the Scots of Vermont, the Pennsylvania Dutch
of Germantown, the Huguenots, the Africans in the Chesapeake—
quickly lost their distinctiveness, retaining only their names (and for
blacks not even those) as reminders that they had once been separate
peoples.[30]

It will not do to exaggerate. Pockets of ethnic identity persisted in
America through the late eighteenth and early nineteenth centuries.
And the young United States was a pluralistic society. It was, however,
a pluralism based on color, a multicultural society of reds, whites, and
blacks in which race rather than Old World origins proved the primary
determinant of ethnic identity.

NOTES

1. This seems a fair characterization, for example, of Thomas J. Archdeacon's treatment of the colonial period in *Becoming American: An Ethnic
History* (New York, 1983).

2. Bernard Bailyn's work makes immigration a central theme of early
American history. See *The Peopling of British North America: An Introduction*
(New York, 1986), and *Voyagers to the West: A Passage in the Peopling of America
on the Eve of the Revolution* (New York, 1986).

3. The introduction and epilogue to *The Native Population of the Americas
in 1492*, ed. William Denevan (Madison, 1976) provide a useful introduction
to the subject. The quotation is from page 7. Russell Thornton has argued
for substantially higher figures than those advanced by Denevan (more than
seventy-two million for the Western Hemisphere, more than seven million
north of the Rio Grande) while providing an excellent survey of the state
of the field in *American Indian Holocaust and Survival: A Population History
since 1492* (Norman, 1987).

4. Denevan, ed., *Native Population*, 291; John J. McCusker and Russell
R. Menard, *The Economy of British America, 1607-1789* (Chapel Hill, 1985),
54; Francis Jennings, *The Invasion of America: Indians, Colonialism, and the
Cant of Conquest* (Chapel Hill, 1975).

5. Anthony F. C. Wallace, *The Death and Rebirth of the Seneca* (New York,
1969), provides an especially compelling account of one such transformation.

6. Henry A. Gemery, "Emigration from the British Isles to the New
World, 1630-1700: Inferences from Colonial Populations," *Research in Eco-
nomic History* 5 (1980): 179-231; Gemery, "European Emigration to North
America, 1700-1820: Numbers and Quasi-Numbers," *Perspectives in American
History*, n.s., 1 (1984): 283-342; Robert W. Fogel et al., "The Economics of
Mortality in North America, 1650-1910: A Description of a Research Proj-
ect," *Historical Methods* 11 (1978): 75-108; David W. Galenson, *White Servitude
in Colonial America: An Economic Analysis* (Cambridge, 1981), 212-18. A note

of caution is in order regarding the figures in Table 2.1. These estimates rest on estimates. Although colonial demographic history has made great strides in recent years, our knowledge of vital rates and total population is still far from firm. Further, the residual approach used here channels all errors in rates and population sizes into the migration estimates. The figures are only rough approximations, perhaps too rough to support the analysis to which they are subjected. Recent work in early American population history is assessed in McCusker and Menard, *Economy of British America,* 211-35, and Jim Potter, "Demographic Development and Family Structure," in *Colonial British America: Essays in the New History of the Early Modern Era,* ed. Jack P. Greene and J. R. Pole (Baltimore, 1984), 123-56.

7. Ira Berlin, "Time, Space, and the Evolution of Afro-American Society on British Mainland North America," *American Historical Review* 85 (1980): 44-78, introduces the literature on these issues.

8. American Council of Learned Societies, "Report of the Committee on Linguistic and National Stocks in the United States," *Annual Report of the American Historical Association for the Year 1931* (Washington, D.C., 1932), 107-25.

9. Donald H. Akenson, "Why the Accepted Estimates of the Ethnicity of the American People, 1790, Are Unacceptable," *William and Mary Quarterly,* 3d ser., 41 (1984): 102-19. For recent, unquestioning uses of the ACLS report see, for example, Stephan Thernstrom, comp., *Harvard Encyclopedia of American Ethnic Groups* (Cambridge, 1980), 479, 503, and U.S. Bureau of the Census, *Historical Statistics of the United States: Colonial Times to 1970* (Washington, D.C. 1975), 2:1168.

10. Forrest McDonald and Ellen Shapiro McDonald, "The Ethnic Origins of the American People, 1790," *William and Mary Quarterly,* 3d ser., 37 (1980): 179-99; Thomas L. Purvis, "The European Ancestry of the United States Population, 1790," *William and Mary Quarterly,* 3d ser., 41 (1984): 85-101; Purvis, "The National Origins of New Yorkers in 1790," *New York History* 67 (1986): 133-53; David N. Doyle, *Ireland, Irishmen and Revolutionary America, 1760-1820* (Dublin, 1981), 75-76.

11. Forrest McDonald and Ellen Shapiro McDonald, "Commentary," *William and Mary Quarterly,* 3d ser., 41 (1984): 134.

12. This division is suggested by Bailyn, *Peopling of British North America,* 60.

13. This discussion of the Chesapeake region summarizes several of my essays. See especially "From Servants to Slaves: The Transformation of the Chesapeake Labor System," *Southern Studies* 16 (1977): 355-90, and "British Migration to the Chesapeake Colonies in the Seventeenth Century," in *Colonial Chesapeake Society,* ed. Lois Green Carr, Philip D. Morgan, and Jean B. Russo (Chapel Hill, 1988), 99-132.

14. E. A. Wrigley and R. S. Schofield, *The Population History of England, 1541-1871: A Reconstruction* (Cambridge, 1981), 528-29.

15. On real wages see Henry Phelps Brown and Sheila V. Hopkins, *A Perspective on Wages and Prices* (London, 1981).

16. This hypothesis finds support in work reporting a decline in both the intensity and scale of migration within England during the last half of the seventeenth century: after 1660, fewer English men and women moved than earlier, and those who did traveled shorter distances. Peter Clark, "Migration in England during the Late Seventeenth and Early Eighteenth Centuries," *Past and Present* 83 (May 1979): 57-90.

17. On the course of opportunity in the Chesapeake colonies see Russell R. Menard, "From Servant to Freeholder: Status Mobility and Property Accumulation in Seventeenth-Century Maryland," *William and Mary Quarterly*, 3d ser., 30 (1973): 37-64; Lois Green Carr and Russell R. Menard, "Immigration and Opportunity: The Freedman in Early Colonial Maryland," in *The Chesapeake in the Seventeenth Century: Essays on Anglo-American Society*, ed. Thad W. Tate and David L. Ammerman (Chapel Hill, 1979), 206-42; and Lorena S. Walsh, "Servitude and Opportunity in Charles County, Maryland, 1658-1705," in *Law, Society, and Politics in Early Maryland*, ed. Aubrey C. Laud, Lois Green Carr, and Edward C. Papenfuse (Baltimore, 1975), 111-33.

18. Henry A. Gemery and Jan Hogendorn, "The Atlantic Slave Trade: A Tentative Economic Model," *Journal of African History* 15 (1974): 223-46. David Galenson offers an insightful comment on their approach in *White Servitude in Colonial America*, 141-49.

19. On the New England economy see McCusker and Menard, *Economy of British America*, 91-116.

20. Richard S. Dunn surveys the labor systems of the several colonies and provides a guide to recent literature in "Servants and Slaves: The Recruitment and Employment of Labor," in *Colonial British America*, ed. Greene and Pole, 157-94. On the growth of slavery in the southern colonies see Menard, "From Servants to Slaves" and "British Migration to the Chesapeake Colonies," and Russell R. Menard, "The Africanization of the Lowcountry Labor Force, 1670-1730," in *Race and Family in the Colonial South*, ed. Winthrop D. Jordan and Sheila L. Skemp (Jackson, 1987), 81-108.

21. Bailyn, *Peopling of British North America*, 86.

22. A good description of the activities of land speculators in early America is provided by Thomas M. Doerflinger, *A Vigorous Spirit of Enterprise: Merchants and Economic Development in Revolutionary Pennsylvania* (Chapel Hill, 1986), 314-29.

23. Menard, "From Servant to Freeholder"; Carr and Menard, "Immigration and Opportunity"; Walsh, "Servitude and Opportunity"; Aaron M. Shatzman, "Servants into Planters: The Origins of an American Image: Land Acquisition and Status in Seventeenth Century South Carolina," Ph.D. dissertation, Stanford University, 1981; and Sharon V. Salinger, *"To Serve Well and Faithfully": Labor and Indentured Servants in Pennsylvania, 1682-1800* (New York, 1987).

24. See, for example, David Grayson Allen, *In English Ways: The Movement of Societies and the Transferal of English Local Law and Custom to Massachusetts*

Bay in the Seventeenth Century (Chapel Hill, 1981); Berlin, "Time, Space, and the Evolution of Afro-American Society."

25. See, for examples, Thomas J. Archdeacon, *New York City, 1664-1710: Conquest and Change* (Ithaca, 1976); Ned C. Landsman, *Scotland and Its First American Colony, 1683-1765* (Princeton, 1985); and Winthrop D. Jordan, *White over Black: American Attitudes toward the Negro, 1550-1812* (Chapel Hill, 1968).

26. Timothy Breen, "Creative Adaptations: Peoples and Cultures," in *Colonial British America,* ed. Greene and Pole, 216. Breen's essay provides an excellent summary of the literature on ethnic and cultural identities during the colonial period. Michael Zuckerman offers a somewhat different reading of the evidence in "Identity in British America: Unease in Eden," in *Colonial Identity in the Atlantic World, 1500-1800,* ed. Nicholas Canny and Anthony Pagden (Princeton, 1987), 115-57.

27. Breen, "Creative Adaptations," 218.

28. John M. Murrin, "Anglicizing an American Colony: The Transformation of Provincial Massachusetts," Ph.D. dissertation, Yale University, 1966; Breen, "Creative Adaptations," 221.

29. Jack P. Greene, "Search for Identity: An Interpretation of the Meaning of Selected Patterns of Social Response in Eighteenth-Century America," *Journal of Social History* 3 (1970): 216-17.

30. Breen, "Creative Adaptations," 223; Stephanie G. Wolf, *Urban Village: Population, Community, and Family Structure in Germantown, Pennsylvania* (Princeton, 1976); Jon Butler, *The Huguenots in America: A Refugee People in New World Society* (Cambridge, 1983); Allan Kulikoff, *Tobacco and Slaves: The Development of Southern Cultures in the Chesapeake, 1680-1800* (Chapel Hill, 1986).

3

International Labor Markets and Community Building by Migrant Workers in the Atlantic Economies

DIRK HOERDER

Were North American workers members of an international proletariat? Or were they ethnically fragmented? Was the recruitment of successive waves of peasant immigrants who supposedly had to be conditioned to industrial work specific to the North American labor force? By the 1870s, and in some cases earlier, economic structures, industrial development, and economic cycles were basically similar in the two North American economics (the United States and Canada) and in the Western European states. An "Atlantic economy" had come into existence. Within its confines, social mobility, both upward and downward, differed only by a few percentage points in areas of comparable industrial development and urbanization. Real wages, taking into account consumption patterns, were relatively similar for unskilled workers in Birmingham and Pittsburgh, while skilled workers earned considerably more in Pittsburgh. Inequality in wages in the United States had reached German and English levels by World War I.[1] Prospective labor migrants in England, Germany, and elsewhere could learn this information from union and social democratic periodicals.[2]

Research on the whole of the mass migrations in Europe and across the Atlantic has been somewhat spasmodic. From the 1860s to the 1920s, European observers — economists, socialists, and reformers — published "eyewitness accounts" often containing lucid analyses and also racial biases. Then came the monumental statistical study of Willcox and Ferenczi in the late 1920s. After a long period of neglect, studies of British migration were undertaken, and in 1960 Frank Thistlethwaite read his agenda-setting paper. His call was first taken up by the Swedish — later Nordic — Migration History Project at Uppsala, then by numerous East and Southeast European scholars, and finally by the Labor Migration Project at Bremen.[3] In addition, numerous detailed studies of specific migratory movements were published during the 1970s and 1980s.

Research on South America and on migratory flows — voluntary, military, and convict — in the British and French empires suggests that peripheral areas in the whole world reached by the Euro-American core have to be included in the model. A recently established new frame of reference, "migration in the Atlantic economics," combines the world-systems perspective with a view "from the bottom up" of millions of men and women making decisions according to economic constraints and opportunities, in response to family exigencies and personal experiences.[4] They moved in networks of information relays and migration traditions based on ties of community, friendship, kinship, and family that provided emotional and material support. "Chain migration" from a traditional community into an urban ethnic enclave served as the vehicle for ventures into a new culture and its labor markets.

This multitude of migration streams was initiated by entrepreneurs, steamship and railroad agents, and land office and labor recruiters, as well as by local artisans, fishermen, merchants, and sailors who had market connections and travel experience. Migration often was neither *e*migration nor *i*mmigration. Seasonal or temporary for a few years or for work life, it could become voluntarily permanent. Migration might take the form of one single long-distance move, or of a shuttling back and forth between area of departure and receiving society. Whatever the form, it was goal-directed and network-supported. Migrants might experience extreme changes and suffering, but few were "uprooted." They moved through processes of acculturation, with sometimes contradictory options and ambivalent experiences.

The new frame of reference for migration history discards the classic but misleading distinction between "old" and "new" immigration, terms originally loaded with racist overtones. No clear-cut break between old and new ever occurred, as a glance at the statistics proves: the migrants from Western and Northern Europe consisted only in part of settlers; they included skilled workers and artisans as well as unskilled workers, domestics, and rural laborers. Settlers included Eastern and Southern Europeans, while after the assumed break, migrants continued to come from Western and Northern Europe.[5] The distinction between a settlement migration (primarily family units) into agrarian areas and a labor migration (primarily single men and later single women) remains analytically useful. The former was directed to the Balkans, the Russian South and East, the North American West, Australia, and South America. The labor migration was directed to industrializing areas all over Europe and North America. The term *labor migration* is preferable to *proletarian migration* because the newcomers often had a rural or artisanal background and moved into wage labor only in the receiving society. Furthermore, many of these temporary proletarians intended to and often did return to their homeland with savings from their wages to secure improved social status, usually through land acquisition.

In this chapter the mobilization of labor in the Old Country will first be placed in a historical perspective. Next, the development of international labor markets, that is, the structures linking peasant cultures and societies within a worldwide capitalist market system, will receive attention. I will also argue that migration into new cultures did not produce uprooted individuals cast adrift; rather these persons were transplanted by economic forces yet decided to move of their own free will.[6] Cultural "baggage"[7] carried into the new society included a consciousness of social ranks and—for a portion of the migrants—a rudimentary class feeling. These views of social hierarchies had to be adapted to the new circumstances. In the concluding section of the chapter I will address the migrants' struggles for better working conditions, struggles fueled by resources provided by the ethnic communities. Kinship patterns and communication networks of immigrant women played a decisive role in the establishment of solidarities based on village ties.

Mobilization of Labor

Parallel to the east- and westward settlers' migrations, intra-European labor migration rose to high levels in the first half of the nineteenth century and increased further during the second half. Although it was considerably larger than the transatlantic flow, the intra-European migration has received less attention. Distances were shorter,[8] the voyages less spectacular, and the complex network of movements precluded easy generalizations. None of the receiving areas attained the renown of the "land of the free" with its "unlimited opportunities."

For most Europeans, "America" was not a country; it was a myth. During the Age of Revolution, the Declaration of Independence and the Constitution became standard reference points for European middle-class revolutionaries, many of whom assiduously contrasted its orderly character to the bloody "disorders" of the French Revolution.

That America's admirers knew little about the social and economic realities of the United States was demonstrated by the disenchantment of many "Fortyeighters," whether Czech, Hungarian, or German. The ideological construct "America" had an impact on the working classes of Europe as well. After the Civil War, in addition to a more desirable state of political affairs, it implied more desirable material conditions and greater opportunities. For example, the newly opened territories of Siberia were called "another America"; large factories or mines produced "on an American scale," while cities were being planned "in the American way."[9] Letters of immigrants before the Civil War were more realistic: the two big advantages they reported were that one could make an independent living through hard work and that one did not have to doff one's cap when asking for a job. While the myth persisted, after the Civil War information about the economic and social conditions in the United States contained in the European labor press left little room for illusions.[10]

Yet "America" was not the only myth that attracted surplus labor from the rural areas of Europe. Industrializing capital cities like Vienna or Paris had similar reputations, offering visions of rich and lively cities full of architectural masterpieces and a confusing multitude of people and languages. "In Bohemia, Vienna was looked upon as a kind of Eldorado and people sent their children there to make their fortune."[11]

Mobilization of labor for the industrializing economies proceeded in several stages, drawing on older traditions which included the rural-urban migrations; the migrations of skilled journeymen artisans; and the circulation of upper-middle-class groups among cities. Shifting borders between the European empires (including the Ottoman) had involved involuntary migrations and labor force changes. Mercantilist states had attracted skilled labor (often expelled from areas of origin for religious reasons). Entrepreneurs or state and municipal agencies also recruited needed workers for planned towns, new mines, or factories. Seasonal agrarian migrations from naturally less productive to more productive regions and journeymen artisans' migrations throughout the whole of Europe were long established. From the 1840s, male migration took place in connection with railroad and canal construction, initially involving local surplus labor but eventually attracting more and more laborers from far-off regions. Meanwhile, women migrated to domestic service in the cities. The system of protoindustrialization, patterns of putting-out work or establishment of manufactories on agrarian estates, while retarding migration, changed living habits and brought the economic behavior of peasants closer to marketplace relationships. Mechanization and concentration of production in factories could lead to sudden declines in living standards and rapidly increasing out-migration. With the establishment of large factories, skilled workers were recruited to train the local labor force, while skilled women migrated as cooks and needleworkers.[12]

After the 1860s—earlier in Great Britain—these localized movements merged into the proletarian mass migrations in the Atlantic economies. Much of this movement was directed toward rising centers of industry, but a hobolike "Wanderarbeiter" emerged, driven by necessity or by an acquired habit of migrating, losing family ties and living in camps or "Herbergen." Eventually, millions of migrants moved in part because of demographic pressures (out-migration was often due to a relative population surplus), or because of differences in stages of economic development even when labor supply and demand were in equilibrium. In the latter case, better working conditions, higher wages, or perceived opportunities elsewhere might attract workers. Such out-migration was usually accompanied by in-migration from even less-developed areas. Rigid social structures, determined by inheritance patterns and old patterns of family life, sometimes added to the pressures to leave. These push factors, varying from region to region, form the societal background of migration. Economic changes which affected the work and earning capacity of men and women, such as an abrupt end to homework patterns or expanding markets for mass-produced goods, led to a high propensity to migrate.

Within the reservoir of potential migrants, who actually left was often determined by personal circumstances: unsuccessful courtships, unacceptable pregnancies, death or remarriage in the family, and avoidance of compulsory military service (especially of ethnic minorities in imperial armies). Such considerations introduced an individual factor into migration decisions.[13]

To recruit skilled urban or unskilled peasant-workers from labor pools, whether national or foreign, information networks had to be established. "Pioneer" migrants, sometimes artisans with market connections, induced others to follow. They became "migration entrepreneurs" providing help at the point of arrival and often also profiting from the newcomers. Recruiting agents for shipping and railroad companies either came from among a firm's work force or were government officials or independent entrepreneurs. Once initiated, a migratory movement became self-sustaining through an information network of letters, travel accounts, and return migration. Such communications served to screen potential migrants: "let him not risk coming, for he is too young"; "too weak for America"; "America for the oxen, Europe for the men."[14] Protoindustrialization, seasonal factory work during slack times in agriculture, and temporary factory work over years with other family members tending the land prepared rural migrants for industrial work.[15]

In the second half of the nineteenth century, the demand for labor in the industrializing areas of the Atlantic economies increased rapidly. Berlin, for example, grew from almost a million inhabitants in 1871 to two and a half million in 1900; in Upper Silesia, miners and industrial workers increased from 18,700 in 1852 to 193,500 in 1913; in the Ruhr district, they increased from 14,300 to 383,000 in the same period. Of the work force in Upper Silesia, about 10 percent were foreigners, most of them Poles from Russian Poland and Ruthenians. However, about 50 percent of the workers in the metal industries and most of the miners were local Poles. Many of the latter were subsequently recruited for work in the Ruhr district, where they concentrated in the "Polish mines." After World War I, between 50,000 and 150,000 of them moved on to French and Belgian mines.[16] An average of 54 percent of the urban population in Germany and in Vienna at the turn of the century were in-migrants from the relative surplus population in the agrarian sector and from unevenly developing industrializing areas.[17]

Labor was mobilized by the variations in economic development among the various regions. To take the example of colonial Ireland, out-migration came from the eastern modernizing areas where commercialization of agriculture was accompanied by growing unemployment. Collapse of the domestic textile industry, which had provided supplementary income, and the introduction of agricultural "machinery" as simple as the plow forced parts of the population below subsistence levels. The penetration of the cash economy into subsistence farming areas and tax collection in cash also forced people into wage labor.[18] More traditional areas of noncommercial farming resisted the pull of British or American jobs in the first decades of the nineteenth century. Later, these areas of family farming with only a limited surplus of labor provided seasonal laborers for Britain, while the more developed areas provided permanent immigrants to Britain and North America. The selection of destination was partly determined by finances; the fare to Britain was cheaper. But it was also regulated by tradition: once a seasonal job had been taken in Britain, there was a strong likelihood of return during the following harvest seasons. By 1851, about half a million Irish had settled in Britain, and a decade later more than 180,000 first- and second-generation

Irish lived in London alone. Although there was no language barrier—except for the Irish who spoke only their native tongue, Gaelic—
they suffered as much from labeling by the dominant "race" as in
the United States. Irish middle-class migrants acculturated quickly,
while an Irish working-class subculture became a distinct part of British
society.[19]

In nineteenth-century Europe as in North America, one-half or
more of the emerging urban industrial proletariats were first-generation in-migrants. From this finding some historians have deduced a
linguistic fragmentation of the newly formed working class. While
this argument can be sustained in general, it has to be qualified for
all areas of ethnically mixed settlements in Europe where multilingualism was a common phenomenon. Germans and Poles, Slovaks
and Magyars, Czechs and Austrians frequently spoke both languages.
The newspaper of the Hungarian Social Democratic party, *Népszava,*
published a German supplement, *Volksstimme.* Strike calls or announcements of mass meetings in Budapest were often published in
four languages. German unions published special newspapers for Italian and Polish labor migrants.[20] To what extent such multilingualism
facilitated communication and thus class solidarity among immigrant
workers in the Americas remains to be determined.

The Development of International Labor Markets

After the middle of the nineteenth century, the Atlantic economies
became divided into an industrialized Western European and eastern
North American core and a predominantly rural Eastern and Southern European and western North American periphery. To be more
exact, the industrializing areas consisted of rural districts with market-
oriented cottage production and of urban industrial islands which
drew a considerable proportion of their new labor force from the
surrounding countryside. Central Europe had such labor-importing
industrial centers as Berlin, Vienna, Prague, Budapest, and St. Petersburg. England, Germany, France, and Switzerland were the primary labor-importing countries, as England and Germany were exporting labor to North America. England drew workers primarily
from its Irish colony, Switzerland from Italy and Germany, Germany
from Poland and Italy, France from its neighboring countries, and—
after 1900—from Poland. Belgium and the industrializing sections
of Austria, particularly Vienna, attracted streams of migrants but
contemporaneously experienced heavy out-migration. The Scandinavian and southeastern European countries exported labor to other

European countries and North America but attracted skilled workers in certain occupations. North America, for its part, imported labor from many European countries. Two types of migrants came: rural people from areas not directly within the pull of any one of the European centers and industrial workers, artisans, and shopkeepers, who first moved to European cities and then in a second stage migrated across the Atlantic.[21]

While the character of emigration was primarily determined by economic and demographic factors, with governmental policies like tax collection in cash, encouragement of commercial farming, and subsidies for large estates playing at best a secondary role, the character of immigration was defined by both economic factors and governmental policies.[22] The French and German governments adopted opposing policies concerning labor migrants. France, where internal migration was a way of life for up to one-fifth of the population, became the main European country of immigration. The number of foreigners in a population that ranged between 35 and 40 million increased from 381,000 in 1851 to 1,160,000 in 1911 (400,000 Italians, 287,000 Belgians, 117,000 Germans and Austro-Hungarians, and 110,000 Spanish and Portuguese, as well as Swiss, Russian [Jewish], Dutch, and others). Emigration from France's North African colonies was negligible. In 1911, 12 percent of these foreign workers were in agriculture, 3.1 percent in mining, 40.7 percent in industry, 15.6 percent in transportation, 14 percent in commerce, 9.7 percent in domestic service, and 4.8 percent in education, administration, and liberal professions. Some of the immigrants rose to the level of skilled workers, and a few into the lower middle class as shopkeepers, tavern owners, and the like, catering primarily to their immigrant countrymen. Acculturation was expected of the migrants but not forced upon them.[23]

Germany, for nationalist and racist reasons, chose a different path. From the late 1870s onward the demand for workers increased beyond the supply available at the prevailing wages, conditions, and low social status. For Saxon and East Elbian agriculture the natural recruiting areas were the densely populated Polish territories under Russian and Austrian control. In 1885, a nativist movement that included a heavy dose of anti-Catholicism led to the expulsion of Polish migrants working in Silesian mines and in eastern agriculture. But efforts to redirect migrating Italian or "racially desirable" Flemish workers failed because the cultural and economic attraction of their customary labor markets proved stronger, and their migratory traditions could not easily be overcome.[24] A coalition of East Elbian Junkers and Westphalian "industrial barons" brought about a reversal of the policy in 1890. In-migration of Poles was permitted under tight governmental control and on condition of their return to Poland in the winter. Thus the estate owners saved on wages, and the government prevented acculturation. Jobs were to rotate to a different set of temporary migrants each year. Mining and industrial interests forced a suspension of this rule because their work was less seasonal and involved the cost of training newcomers. These sectors also recruited Ruthenian and Russian workers, while the building industry hired Italian workers in large numbers. The latter's migration was naturally seasonal because construction work ceased in winter. In addition, Swedes and ethnically heterogeneous workers from the Austro-Hungarian empire came to Germany.[25]

With the declaration of war in 1914, voluntary migration came to an abrupt end. Demand for workers, however, expanded, and German authorities tried to prevent foreign workers from leaving the country. Like France, Germany recruited workers in neutral countries. German military authorities forced workers from the occupied Eastern territories at gunpoint to sign contracts for work in the German war economy. One of the secret but explicit war aims in 1914 had been to control the East European labor supply upon conditions dictated by the Germans. Documents from the government and from economic interest groups prove this continuity between voluntary and forced migrations.[26]

In the decades before World War I, migration of workers cannot in all cases simply be subsumed under the heading "proletarian mass migration." Highly skilled workers and technicians from industrializing countries moved to Great Britain, Germany, and the United States to improve their skills and advance in their own country upon return. This entailed a transfer of technology without proletarianization and growing class consciousness. In-migration of skilled workers and technicians to train a local labor force and to support the initial phase of industrialization characterized Budapest and other less industrialized areas. Other examples of migration of skilled workers are skilled cigar makers of Spanish, Cuban, and German origin to Cuba, Tampa, and New York City, and of Welsh miners to U.S. pits.[27] Skilled Italian tile-layers were likewise in demand all over Europe. German skilled workers in southeastern Europe improved their personal position, rising to supervisory positions over the inexperienced local labor forces. In addition to transferring technological knowledge, such skilled workers also transported experience in labor organization. Many were active in the first labor unions in southeastern Europe.

The transfer of class-conscious ideologies through migration has not been studied adequately in relation to the growth of the labor movement throughout Europe. Meanwhile, migrant workers, particularly from Czech and Polish areas, came under the influence of social democratic movements in Western Europe and upon returning home introduced increased political awareness into their societies.[28]

The heightened political consciousness of migrant workers since the Russian Revolution of 1905, as well as their alleged racial characteristics, led to immigration restrictions in the United States. During and after World War I, the internal migration of blacks from the South to the North increasingly substituted for immigrant laborers. During the 1920s, transatlantic migrations were directed primarily toward Canada, while internal labor migrations within Europe were resumed at a slower pace than before the war. Polish workers went to Denmark and France; many who had migrated to the Ruhr district before 1914 moved to Belgium and France, where anti-Polish feeling was less virulent. Italians went to France and overseas. World War II brought about yet another change, with forced labor being imported to Germany by the army and the Gestapo. After the war, voluntary migration resumed within Europe, but alien workers were called "guest workers."[29]

Thus the great numbers of internal migrants in the Atlantic economies were supplemented by foreign workers. The latter, however, rarely reached North American proportions in Europe. In the United States, 12.9 percent of the population was foreign born in 1920, whereas in France, this figure, 2.8 percent in 1911, climbed only to a high of 7 percent in 1930. Germany and Belgium fluctuated between 2 and 4 percent foreign born. Swiss statistics (referring to the percentage of the industrial labor force) reported 12.7 percent foreigners in 1895 and 22.3 percent in 1911. Although the proletariats in the Atlantic economies can hardly be described as international, they included internationally mobile segments.

Migration has been considered in terms of flows between nations because of specific national policies toward recruiting and because statistics were compiled only when workers crossed borders. A result is that internal migrations have received less attention, another is that nationality has been confused with ethnicity. Rather than using nation-states, that is, political entities, as areas of reference, regions of common culture and integrated labor markets need to be the focus of migration studies. Migration from the Walloon parts of Belgium into France, for example, involved little change: language, culture, and occupation (agriculture) remained the same. Internal migration from

Flanders to Wallonia, on the other hand, signified a change of language
and culture and usually a change from agrarian to industrial work.[30]

The development of international and multiethnic labor markets
may be illustrated by two examples. When mining expanded in the
Ruhr district, Polish, Silesian-German, and Italian workers responded.[31] When industrialization in the urban centers of Denmark
and Norway expanded to the southern areas of Sweden and Finland,
the labor supply was recruited from the entire southern part of Scandinavia and Finland. The Russian center, St. Petersburg, also exerted
a pull on those areas. Thus a four-state area and the Russian territories
along the Baltic Sea were incorporated into one labor market dominated by an industrial core, which drew upon a common periphery
for labor regardless of national boundaries.[32]

Patterns of migration could be highly complex, as a look at the
western part of the Austro-Hungarian Empire toward the end of the
nineteenth century reveals. Upper and lower Austria as well as the
Czech and some Slovak areas had a relatively mobile labor force;
Tyrol, the Slovenian section of the South Slav territories, Galicia, and
Bukowina were only marginally integrated into the imperial labor
market. Prague attracted workers from neighboring areas over distances of up to 150 kilometers, as well as from abroad; but Vienna
exerted a dominant pull throughout the empire and into adjacent
countries as well. An analysis of migration to Vienna in the 1850s
and 1890s reveals that the newcomers consisted of short-, middle-,
and long-distance migrants, and that these three groups also differed
according to occupational and social status. Among short-distance
migrants, unskilled laborers and domestic servants (mainly women)
were heavily overrepresented. Middle-distance migrants (especially
from Bohemia and Moravia) sought employment primarily in small-
scale industry and in the crafts. Long-distance migrants included some
craft workers (probably showing a continuity of artisan-journeymen
migrations) and a disproportionate number of highly educated persons
and property owners. In the 1880s, domestic service ceased to be
attractive, and short-distance migrants began to move into small-scale
industry or unskilled labor. The three groups also differed concerning
patterns of family migration and living arrangements. By the 1880s,
the in-migrants increasingly lived in their own quarters. They were
thus less subject to control by their masters and could strengthen class
ties. But because ethnic segregation in residential areas increased from
the 1880s to World War I, new bases for organization along ethnocultural lines developed at the same time.[33]

Because many migrants, whether in Vienna, Scandinavia, or the

Ruhr, could not be permanently absorbed by the respective labor markets, they moved on to other cities or to mining districts in Europe or North America. Others, coming from areas distant from industrializing centers in Europe, often moved directly overseas. A dual labor market emerged in the Atlantic economies. The native working class of each country received the more stable and more skilled jobs, while foreign workers entered the labor market on the internationalized lower-skill levels of employment such as heavy manual labor and piecework, in both industry and agriculture. Here the reserve army of aliens operated as a buffer against structural changes and market fluctuations.[34] The buffer function was explicit in Germany with its government-controlled yearly work-permit system and implicit in the United States with its flow of information through migrants' letters, which reduced immigration with only a short time-lag after each economic downswing at the same time that return migration increased.[35] This buffer function is an indicator of the exploitation of periphery by core countries. The social cost[36] of raising children to working age, of education, of support during return because of unemployment or physical disability was absorbed by the sending country.[37] In certain skilled occupations the internationalization of labor markets also occurred in periods of high demand. In this case, too, the cost-benefit analysis shows advantages for the receiving countries only.

Herbert Gutman and others have argued that migrant workers had to adjust to industrial time and work routines. From migrants' letters and their references to the inexorable clock we know that many had to become used to rigorous time-keeping.[38] But as concerns daily, weekly, and monthly work patterns, peasants did not necessarily arrive with unsteady work habits. The seasonal character of agricultural work was regularized by home work for manufacturers or by additional tasks. Breaks in fieldwork, be it for a day of rain or for a season, were filled with repair of implements, inside chores, and home production. Men, women, and children had regular work habits, whether enforced by internalization, custom, family, or overseers. Only those harvest workers for whom no other jobs were available worked irregularly. As labor migrants, the former would have been likely applicants for the primary sector with steady employment and hours, the latter for the secondary sector with irregular employment and varying hours. But since industrializing economies in general and leading industries, steel in particular, in the initial phase of growth could or would not offer regular employment to these peasant workers, the adjustment to industrial time and routine was not necessarily one to regular work habits. For the former seasonal workers, the experience of waiting for a job at factory gates each morning may have involved little change, although in the economic system of origin they had usually been hired for a whole season. For former peasants, industrial time with all its irregularities often involved a socialization to unsteady work patterns.[39] One large difference, of course, was that there was no remedy against rain and seasons. Against employers, although not against economic cycles, there was the possibility of direct action and organization. Employer-imposed routines or irregularities may also have been experienced as more arbitrary than harvest and other traditional cycles.

Thus the internationally mobile section of the proletariats in the Atlantic economies had a highly structured but also highly flexible system to guide them into jobs. Contemporary union activists as well as labor historians have assumed that this flexibility meant job competition, strikebreaking, and wage undercutting through the Atlantic economies. Were the Atlantic working classes fragmented, or did they achieve organization beyond the confines of national labor movements? Was their class consciousness of a national or international nature? What effects did the bigotry of workers, themselves often earlier migrants, toward more recently arrived migrants, based on race, nationality, religion, and skill, have upon their capacity to organize?

Migration, Labor Markets, and Class Consciousness

Labor migrants, particularly from countries judged to be less developed with regard to standard of living and culture, have been depicted as strikebreakers, unorganizable, and content with low wages. They have also been viewed as lost in the bewildering array of city life and frightened by the roaring machinery in the factories. I will argue that the transition from old to new society could largely be without trauma. It was less a move into an alien culture than a voyage from a village (or a region) to a specific job and into a specific ethnic enclave.

Labor-market theory may help us understand the transition in the sphere of work, as community studies and women's history do, the transition in the reproductive sphere. Both approaches show that class solidarity and mutual aid crossed ethnic boundaries. Throughout the following discussion it must be kept in mind that working-class militancy often was a grass-roots phenomenon, not to be measured by membership in labor organizations; community solidarity cannot only be measured by political success, but by cooperation on the street. Even in an ethnic group as militant as the Finnish migrants, those active in the labor movement amounted to only one-third of the group.[40] The case of the U.S. working class has been assumed to be exceptional because of the high percentage of migrants and resulting high turnover in union membership. We have established that migration frequency was as high in Europe, and labor historians have found comparably high rates of membership turnover in Europe.[41]

European union periodicals regularly published information about ongoing strikes, warning potential migrants not to believe advertisements about job opportunities. This implies that labor organizations viewed any migrating workers, whether native born or foreign, as a potential danger to jobs, wage levels, and bargaining power.[42] In 1907, the International Socialist Congress at Stuttgart endorsed a resolution that encouraged unions to organize migrant workers from wherever they came. The resolution had been preceded by heated debates about the effects of migration, and trade unions continued to discriminate against foreign workers.[43]

The debate continues in scholarly literature. John S. MacDonald has argued for southern Italy that labor militancy and migration were different and mutually exclusive responses to unacceptable conditions. Donna Gabaccia, however, has shown that in Sicily labor militants migrated and returned and remained militant in both cultures.[44] The debate may be reduced to two opposing ideal positions. One assumes that labor migrants moved with the sole intent of improving their personal circumstances, the other maintains that migrations were a form of class-based collective protest. According to the first, labor migrants left their homes intent to improve their personal or family fortunes. At first glance this set them off from more passive members of the society, who never moved and who never organized. But it also set them off from those who remained, struggled, and sacrificed for the sake of the class or at least of the co-workers in the local community or factory. First, migrants expected to makes sacrifices for the sake of their families (even if these stayed behind) or for their children. If they did not receive wages because they were striking, they would have to change the expectations of their families. Second, social involvement of migrants in the area of arrival depended on the intended duration of stay.[45] Propensity to organize and fight grew as the length of stay increased. Seasonal migrants showed little propensity to organize according to the rules of the receiving society, even when a long stay resulted because of few or no opportunities to return. Third, if a propensity to organize was present, a period of acculturation preceded effective involvement in the labor movement because a minimum knowledge was necessary about structures and processes in the new social environment. Finally, community-building efforts in the new culture may have absorbed organizational energies that could otherwise be used for class organization.[46]

From the opposite perspective, labor migration may be considered a working-class strategy of resistance to exploitation. "In Scandinavia it can be observed that emigration led to a scarcity in labor supply in the labor exporting countries which favored a redistribution of incomes. . . ." The wage differential between Sweden and other European countries as well as the United States informed individual decisions to migrate.[47] In England, Scotland, and Wales some trade unions, in fact, advocated emigration as a means to reduce the surplus of workers in their respective trades.[48] This withdrawal of labor through migration was met by industry and agriculture through increased wages and rationalization as well as the importation of foreign labor.

Both of these hypotheses, personal improvement or collective resistance, find only limited support in the sources. Migration to settle in farming areas was in pursuit of personal improvement, and the letters of migrants were explicit about this aim. Artisans and skilled workers also sought personal improvement, or, in some cases, at least a delay in adjustment to new mechanized and more divided tasks. Few, except political refugees, openly talked about "resistance." But to leave low-wage industries, abusive bosses, or below-subsistence agrarian conditions was itself an expression of discontent. Blacklisted workers, militant tenants, and landless laborers moved to work and to struggle where societal conditions seemed more favorable. Their aims were "living wages" and "independence."

After reaching their destination — whether in the United States, Germany, or France made little difference — the migrants immediately entered the labor market but did not necessarily compete with other more highly paid workers. Labor markets are not filled by homogenous labor forces as postulated by classical theory. Rather, according to recent theory, they are divided into a primary sector with relatively stable employment, an unstable secondary sector, and a marginal but highly flexible tertiary sector. The homogenization of labor markets, which according to D. M. Gordon, Richard Edwards, and Michael Reich took place at the turn of the century, increased the number of unskilled jobs but did not reduce the multiplicity of labor markets. Edna Bonacich and J. B. Christiansen advanced "the split labor market" approach to explain ethnic antagonism over jobs.[49] A more differentiated model may also explain noncompetitive labor-market behavior.

Newly arriving migrants in cities or mining camps did not expect all jobs to be open to them; only specific labor market segments suited their qualifications, physical conditions, and language skills. In segregated labor markets, some jobs were never given to foreign, female, or black migrants; in stratified labor markets, other jobs could never be reached because of lack of qualifications.[50] Stratification and segregation often coincided when groups defined by ethnicity, color, or sex were refused admission to education and vocational training or were labeled as "ignorant" by those who had jobs to distribute — capitalists, or to defend — unions.[51] Because migrants would consider or be considered for entry only into some segments of the labor market, there was no direct competition with workers in other segments.

Competition, on the other hand, did occur in "split labor markets" where at least two groups competed for the same jobs — each equally qualified and desirable from the employers' point of view — but differing in the price of their labor. Thus segmented or stratified labor markets may have decreased job competition and fragmentation, whereas split labor markets increased competition. The conflict diffusing effect of segmentation operated only as long as its existing border lines were accepted by all. When employers changed the composition of the labor force in a segment, when a group rejected its subordinate position, when the jobs in one segment were insufficient to accommodate the applicants, conflict occurred. In fast-growing economies, displaced native-born, or "senior" migrant workers often either found equal-paying positions elsewhere or moved up into better jobs. In other cases, new low-paying jobs became available, and in a process of substratification new groups entered a labor market at the bottom level. This theoretical framework provides a setting for a new interpretation of class consciousness, ethnic antagonism, and fragmentation.

Likewise, the wage issue should not be simplified to a merely bipolar model of "cheap" workers undercutting organized and miltantly class-conscious ones. Victor Greene's classic study portrayed the aspirations and struggles of Poles and Lithuanians in Pennsylvania coalfields, while Michael Barendse argues that the assumption by native-born and earlier migrant workers, as well as of historians, that East European workers would be content with comparatively lower wages contains an ethnic bias.[52] In fact, ethnic or labor historians have never addressed the question of why migrants should consider their work inferior, worthy only of lower wages. The assumption was that migrants were used to lower standards of living in their cultures of origin. However, research indicates that the point of reference, at least among unionized workers, was quickly transferred from the general standard of living in the old to that of the new society.[53] The oral autobiographies of some Italians suggest that immediately after arrival immigrants took any job they could get; then, after gaining even a precarious foothold, they looked for better-paying positions.[54]

Differences between migrants from rural backgrounds and workers conditioned through industrial work or craft traditions may be detected in patterns of living and class feelings rather than in aspirations. Peasant workers, used to doing all the chores on the farm, substituted one kind of labor for another: the quintessential boardinghouse culture in which they raised pigs (goats in the case of in-migrating miners in the Ruhr district), tended vegetable gardens, built fences or sheds, or went hunting after work hours. Wages were supplemented by such after-hours work for sustenance. Skilled workers, on the other hand, achieved higher and regular wages through collective bargaining, but thereby lost work flexibility and were dependent on skilled butchers and grocers. To reduce complex forms of consciousness and action to a simple dualism: given their respective positions in the labor market, peasant workers could not afford craft consciousness, whereas skilled workers could not do without. Both could strike, one group relying on union benefits, the other on their strike "fund," the garden and the pig.[55]

Analysis of labor-market behavior as well as of aspirations for job security and living wages may also help one understand migrant workers' reactions to employers and unions. Orthodox labor-market theory assumed that workers, male or female, were hired according to supply, demand, and productivity. Empirical studies show that subjective factors such as customs and favoritism were as important as formal procedures regulated by management in open shops, by collective bargaining procedures in unionized shops, and by informal procedures determined by foremen.[56] Migrant workers did not necesssarily benefit from unions which were often not even open to them. A foreman of one's own ethnic group could provide better job or promotion access than a hostile union of native-born, English-speaking workers. Migrants secured a niche in labor markets through ethnic clustering which enabled them to negotiate with existing labor organizations or to establish their own. Organizations might be on an ethnic basis, for example, the Polish political and mutual benefit associations in the Ruhr district, Czech ones in Vienna, regional French ones in Paris, and diverse ones in the United States and in Canada; in trade unions, as indicated by the foreign-language labor periodicals published by the German, French, and North American trade unions; or along political as well as welfare-oriented lines, as with the socialist emigrant aid "Società Umanitaria" in Milan or the Hungarian Social Democratic party.[57] Whether parallel organizaitons along ethnic and native-born lines led to antagonism or mutual support depended on cultural, political and economic circumstances and varied over time in each particular setting.[58]

Multiethnic organization of migrant workers, or so it has commonly been assumed, was difficult if not impossible because of language barriers. But migrants coming from the Polish territories or the Austro-Hungarian monarchy often had rudimentary knowledge of languages other than their own. In most of eastern and southeastern Europe, the resident ethnic population was faced with the administrative language of the dominant power, German, Russian, or Turkish, or with church languages. Merchants spoke German in the north, Italian or Greek in the south. Artisans and skilled workers used German as a lingua franca. With the penetration of West European capital into southwestern Europe, French and English were occasionally used. Most travel accounts from the dual monarchy express fascination about the mixture of languages to be heard in the streets; urban and rural populations were usually of ethnically mixed origins. Marketplace, military service, and contacts with authorities all demanded knowledge of more than the ethnic language.[59] In 1873, a Chicago court reporter noted that Poles sentenced for some misdemeanor left the court swearing in three languages: probably Polish, some English, and Russian or German.[60] For southeastern Europe, where literacy was low, scholars speak of the "multi-lingualism of the illiterates." Class-based organization, communication at the work place as well as in the community, was possible at least for a segment of the immigrant population. Sufficiently large to provide interpreters for the others, this segment was not necessarily free of ethnic biases or sufficiently large to overcome all ethnic antagonisms.[61] More and more, studies pay attention to this multiethnic cooperation of immigrant workers, although ethnic antagonisms often transplanted from the societies of origin remained of great importance.[62]

The question remains whether labor migrants could communicate with native workers on a common basis of perceptions of the social, economic, and political sphere. Were not U.S. labor republicanism and European traditions much too different?[63] Workers used to call U.S. police units, whether the notorious coal and steel police or the state militia, "Cossacks." A Homestead worker, probably of Slovak origin, paraded in a Hungarian uniform of 1848 during the Fourth of July celebration of 1876. Alberta miners either enlisted to fight the "Kaisers" of Europe or went on strike to fight the "Kaisers" of the mines during World War I.[64] During the American Revolution, women attacked British soldiers and the "swarms" of fee-gobbling officials because they were strangers who came "to take the bread out of the mouth of the people." A century later, Pinkertons and strikebreakers were harassed with the same words by women who had been born a continent away. On that continent, a Lithuanian shoemaker explained to a peasant family that "America" would be the hope for their son, where strong men could make it and which meant escape from Russian military service. However, not all was well in "America": there was no support in case of illness, and "man-wolves" were around, John D. Rockefeller in particular.[65]

Peasant workers from Eastern Europe like other immigrants of the turn of the century no longer shared the myth of "America." They felt that they were treated in the mills like beasts of burden at home: "Put horse in wagon, work all day. Take horse out of wagon—put in stable. Take horse out of stable, put in wagon. Same way like mills." The Pole who said this bought Liberty bonds during the war to make the world safe for democracy: "For why we buy Liberty Bonds? For the mills? No, for freedom and America—everybody. No more horse and wagon. For eight-hour day." This worker struggled in the United States for freedom, equality, and the eight-hour day, for a better society not dominated by the owners of steel mills. The myth of "America" had been replaced by political and social programs. Shared concepts of economic democracy and political equality beyond that at the polls seem promising approaches to understanding the manifold affinities that working men and women shared across cultures.[66]

Community, Kinship, Landslayt, and Gender Roles

The ability to communicate across language barriers on the basis of shared social and political tenets which make workplace cooperation possible also had an important function in the neighborhood. Ethnic neighborhoods were often less segregated than designations such as "Little Italy" or "Little Germany" suggest. One or two houses, occasionally a whole block or even street, were occupied by the one ethnic group. Other groups filled the next blocks. For the outside observer the most visible group—shop signs, saloon windows, and street living patterns—may have dominated a whole quarter. The research of turn-of-the-century social workers and the manuscript censuses provide a more differentiated picture.[67]

Many migrants were guided into their ethnic communities in Vienna, Budapest, New York, or Chicago by letters or by returned kinspeople and fellow villagers. Prepaid tickets often provided a direct link. By the turn of the century, more than 70 percent of the newcomers at Ellis Island intended to go to relatives of friends.[68] The large number of labor migrants who crossed the Atlantic more than once could act as guides to the "greenhorns." For example, a Lithuanian boy traveled thousands of miles from his parents' plot and ended up in a Chicago boardinghouse where friends of his father's sister expected him. Sardinians, who migrated to dig the Panama Canal and then moved on to the United States, conveyed the impression that wherever they were, other Sardinians were already present. Although geographical distance may have been great, social distance was minimal. Hungarian villagers traveled to specific locations, if male to the Pennsylvania coalfields, if female to the New Brunswick factories.[69] Much has been said about migrant bewilderment at the strange new world through which they traveled, never understanding the language, but the planned, guided, and goal-directed movement was the larger reality.

Labor migrants, steeped in the oral culture, knew where fellow villagers and kin resided. Letters show that they kept track of a large number of acquaintances with whom they never communicated in written form. It seems that updating the information about this network of social relations was primarily a task for women, although single men and "pioneer" male migrants did function in similar ways. Oral histories suggest that women reported about their past in terms of relations to others: kinsfolk, children, and acquaintances; men discussed what they did or "achieved" in the first-person singular. Letters from German immigrants suggest that men might mention a presidential election, while women wrote about family affairs in a way that only the dateline indicated they were living in a foreign country.[70] This seems to be a clue to understanding chain migration and the reconstitution of families across continents and over long timespans. If chain migration was to function without severe strains on family, kinship, and village-community ties, a considerable amount of shared information was necessary for the migrants and their hosts.[71] In periods of thoroughgoing economic and social changes, the family seemed to increase in importance as haven, as has been argued for Italians and German socialists in New York City.[72]

The strong emphasis on living with people from the same area (not just the same country) indicates a similar tendency to retain old culture relations and customs, to transplant into the new society the non-material conditions of living while improving the material conditions of living. Jewish attempts to settle among *landslayt*, the German clustering of people from the same region, and Italian *campanilismo* have been interpreted by native-born contemporaries, whether working class or middle class, as backward-looking attempts to avoid acculturation into a new dynamic society. They can better be understood as an attempt to retain the structures of life and relations to others in ways learned during the first socialization in childhood and not easily abandoned. Cultural self-confidence was the springboard to venture into the new society.

The community-building process in the culture of arrival involved on the first level a reconstitution of personal relations, often primarily a woman's job. The next level, establishment of ethnic institutions like churches, mutual benefit associations, a press, and singing and gymnastic societies, was predominantly assumed by male migrants. With the establishment of male institutions, women were excluded and informal networks became invisible because ethnic men were not interested, and they were difficult for historians to trace. As a result, women were considered unorganizable by male ethnics, just as male ethnics were considered unorganizable by native-born workers who did not understand their cultural ways. When women created organizations, at least to some degree on their own terms, or when direct action against strikebreakers was necessary, women were as active as men. If working for wages, many women fought for improvements in sweatshops and factories. When working without wages at home, they fought for improvements in childcare and sanitary conditions. Considerable attention has been given to changes in work patterns in factories and artisanal workshops. To understand patterns of acculturation and class consciousness of migrants in gender-specific ways, workplaces in homes and the whole reproductive sphere need the same attention.

For women, the connections among the spheres were obvious. An Orthodox Jewish woman, active in a boycott of expensive kosher meat, remarked: "Our husbands work hard. . . . They try their best to bring a few cents into the house. We must manage to spend as little as possible. We will not give away our last few cents to the butcher and let our children go barefoot." A daughter of Mexican immigrants, who had seen many children, including one of her own, die, rejected the common belief that the fault was the mothers': "I know it wasn't that that killed them, it was hunger, malnutrition, no money to pay the doctors. When the union came, this was one of the things we fought against."[73]

The common struggle, common suffering, and common longing for labor organization described by these women have been the main theme of this chapter. Mass migration throughout the Atlantic economies, interrelated labor markets, and networks of kinship and community linked the men and women. Gender, ethnicity, and job competition could divide them. Divisions could be and were overcome in labor struggles, only to reemerge in political matters. While labor historians on the whole have not paid sufficient attention to ethnicity,[74] ethnic historians still do not sufficiently take into account class solidarity. A look at U.S. sources demonstrates that Supreme Court decisions were based on notions of "class war" and that the National Guard was formed as a middle-class institution against the "dangerous classes."[75] A look at ethnic labor newspapers indicates the class feeling from below. I have argued elsewhere, taking foreign workers and German unions as an example, that rhetoric about class solidarity often masked discriminatory practices by the hegemonic unions. But ethnic groups acted in solidarity in most strikes. From autobiographies and newspapers I detect a common class consciousness that did not devote much thought to complex analyses of relations of production, but rather demanded living wages (and roses, too). It divided society in a simple "we–them" dichotomy. This consciousness seems to have been an almost universally shared one. Whether class inequities were accepted as natural, considered unjust but passively accepted, or the target of militant struggles, depended on personal, societal, ethnic, and gender-specific patterns.

While migration and ethnicity could be disruptive elements, the diverse cultural backgrounds at times resulted in a creative fusion of many traditions of struggle. Through the columns of the immigrants' press and letters rather than the AFL *Federationist*, we see striking foreigners transpose the American motto *e pluribus unum* into a class basis rather than fitting themselves into "business unionism." A migrant culture existed that connected communities and workplaces in the Atlantic economies. The experience of exploitation was similar. Hunger remained the same, whether felt by a Sicilian, an East Elbian, a Californian rural worker, or a Slovak or Romanian in Budapest, Vienna, or Pittsburgh. Other experiences varied. Old World ethnic antagonisms continued in the new; hierarchies of skill prevented common actions. Peasants becoming mineworkers felt the terror of darkness and experienced sharp disruptions in their life-styles. Women moving from one home to another over large distances experienced similar disruptions in their lives. For most migrants, kin and *landslayt* eased the transition into new communities,[76] the establishment of which was to a large degree women's work, and into work places. Migration and acculturation have to be understood as self-determined processes within a framework of social and economic constraints. The establishment of institutions and informal networks on an ethnic basis meant, to continue Bodnar's metaphor, the intentional if gradual sinking of new roots, while almost imperceptibly the old roots began to wither away. Cooperation within and among the groups eased migrant workers' lives; conflict persisted, all common experiences and common world views notwithstanding.[77]

NOTES

1. Hartmut Kaelble, *Historical Research on Social Mobility: Western Europe and the USA in the Nineteenth and Twentieth Centuries* (Darmstadt, 1978; New York, 1981); Peter R. Shergold, *Working-Class Life: The "American Standard" in Comparative Perspective 1899-1913* (Pittsburgh, 1982); Jeffrey Williamson and Peter Lindert, *American Inequality: A Macroeconomic History* (New York, 1980).

2. Dirk Hoerder, "German Immigrant Workers' Views of 'America' in the 1880s," in *In the Shadow of the Statue of Liberty: Immigrants, Workers and Citizens in the American Republic 1880-1920*, ed. Marianne Debouzy (Saint-Denis, 1988), 17-33; on the same theme, see the other essays in this volume.

3. Walter F. Willcox and Imre Ferenczi, *International Migrations*, 2 vols. (New York 1929, 1931); *Les migrations internationales de la fin du XVIIIe siècle à nos jours* (Paris, 1980); Frank Thistlethwaite, "Migration from Europe Overseas in the Nineteenth and Twentieth Centuries," XI. Congrès International des Sciences Historiques, *Rapports* (Uppsaia, 1960), 5:32-60.

4. Dirk Hoerder, ed., *Labor Migration in the Atlantic Economies: The European and North American Working Classes During the Period of Industrialization* (Westport, 1985).

5. U.S. Bureau of the Census, *Historical Statistics of the United States: Colonial Times to 1970* (Washington, D.C., 1970), "Series C 89-199," 120-37. By the 1840s settlers accounted only for one-third of the in-migration.

6. Oscar Handlin, *The Uprooted: The Epic Study of the Great Migrations that Made the American People* (Boston, 1951); Rudolph J. Vecoli, "The Contadini in Chicago: A Critique of the Uprooted," *Journal of American History* 51 (1964-65): 404-17; John Bodnar, *The Transplanted: A History of Immigrants in Urban America* (Bloomington, 1985).

7. The cultural "baggage" was in fact the whole process of primary socialization in the culture of origin whereby it was internalized.

8. For the migrants, short distances were not necessarily easier to cover. Italian agricultural workers who migrated to Argentina each year for the

grain harvest refused offers to come to the eastern section of Germany; travel was more difficult and more expensive, and the wages were lower, A. Sartorius Freiherr von Waltershausen, *Die italienischen Wanderarbeiter* (Leipzig, 1903), 13, 20, 22, 27.

9. Otto Heller, *Sibirien, ein anderes Amerika* (Berlin, 1930).

10. Hoerder, "German Immigrant Workers' Views," 18-20. A variety of contemporary accounts, diplomatic dispatches, and industrial commission and trade union publications gave a relatively realistic account of living and working conditions in the United States. See the essays on Scottish miners' views (Claudius H. Riegler), Swedish labor migrants' views, and Swiss technicians' views (Hannes Siegrist) in *The Press of Labor Migrants in Europe and North America, 1880s to 1930s*, ed. Christiane Harzig and Dirk Hoerder (Bremen, 1985), 521-80; Dirk Hoerder, ed., *"Plutocrats and Socialists": Reports by German Diplomats and Agents on the American Labor Movement 1878-1917* (Munich, 1981); and Debouzy, *In the Shadow of the Statue of Liberty*.

11. Heinz Fassmann, "A Survey of Patterns and Structures of Migration in Austria 1850-1900," in *Labor Migration in the Atlantic Economies*, ed. Hoerder, 79.

12. Detailed information on streams of migration has to be culled from local and regional histories. See Introduction and Bibiology, ibid., 3-31, 449-65. See also Peter Kriedte, *Peasants, Landlords and Merchant Capitalists: Europe and the World Economy, 1500-1800* (Cambridge, 1983); Peter Kriedte, Hans Medick, and Jürgen Schlumbohm, *Industrialization Before Industrialization: Rural Industry in the Genesis of Capitalism* (Cambridge, 1981); Jan Lucassen, *Migrant Labour in Europe 1600-1900: The Drift to the North Sea* (Beckenham, 1986).

13. The research of Julianna Puskás in Hungarian villages and of Donna Gabaccia in Sicilian towns as well as studies of putting-out work suggest this pattern.

14. Quotes taken from Herbert Gutman, "Work, Culture and Society in Industrializing America, 1815-1919," in *Work, Culture and Society* (New York, 1976), 30; Ewa Morawska, " 'For Bread with Butter': Life Worlds of Peasant Immigrants from East-Central Europe, 1880-1914," *Journal of Social History* 17 (1984): 392; compare David Brody, *Steelworkers in America, the Nonunion Era* (New York, 1960, repr. 1969), 99.

15. This phenomenon has been studied for the period of early industrialization in Russia. For Hungary, see Julianna Puskás, *From Hungary to the United States, 1880-1914* (Budapest, 1982), 45-56.

16. Lawrence Schofer, *The Formation of a Modern Labor Force: Upper Silesia, 1865-1914* (Berkeley, 1975); Wilhelm Brepohl, *Der Aufbau des Ruhrvolkes im Zuge der Ost-West-Wanderung* (Recklinghausen, 1948); Krystyna Murzynowska, *Polskie wychodztwo zarobkowe w Zaglebiu Ruhry w latach 1880-1914* (Wroclaw, 1972; Dortmund, 1979).

17. Wolfgang Köllman, *Bevölkerung in der industriellen Revolution* (Göttingen, 1974), 117; Reinhard E. Petermann, *Wien im Zeitalter Franz Joseph I.* (Vienna, 1908), 143-44.

18. Donna Gabaccia, investigating Sicily, described the economic changes there as resulting in a "cash crisis," *Miltants and Migrants: Rural Sicilians Become American Workers* (New Brunswick, 1988).

19. Lynn Hollen Lees, *Exiles of Erin: Irish Migrants in Victorian London* (Ithaca, 1979); John Archer Jackson, *The Irish in Britain* (London, 1963); Hasia R. Diner, *Erin's Daughters in America: Irish Immigrant Women in the Nineteenth Century* (Baltimore, 1983); Kerby A. Miller, *Emigrants and Exiles: Ireland and the Irish Exodus to North America* (New York, 1985).

20. Armin Hetzer and Dirk Hoerder, "Research Note: Linguistic Fragmentation or Multilingualism among Labor Migrants in North America: The Socio-Historical Background," in *The Immigrant Labor Press in North America, 1840s-1970s*, 3 vols., ed. Dirk Hoerder and Christiane Harzig (Westport, 1987), vol 2; *Volksstimme*, Budapest, 1894-1924, Archive of the Museum of Hungarian Labor Movement, Budapest.

21. This discussion is based on Hoerder, "An Introduction to Labor Migration in the Atlantic Economies, 1815-1914," in *Labor Migration in the Atlantic Economies*, ed. Hoerder, chapter 1.

22. Before World War I, attempts were made on an international level to regulate the supply of labor. A conference to organize the continental European labor markets was held at Budapest in 1910. *Verhandlungen der Budapester Konferenz betr. Organisation des Arbeitmarktes. 7./8. Oktober 1910* (Leipzig, 1911). Of special importance for these questions is the research of Lothar Elsner and others at the Institute for Labor Migration under Imperialism of the University of Rostock. A survey is Ulrich Herbert, *Geschichte der Ausländerbeschäftigung in Deutschland 1880-1980* (Bonn, 1986).

23. Nancy Green, " 'Filling the Void': Immigration to France before World War One," in *Labor Migration in the Atlantic Economies*, ed. Hoerder, 143-62; Willcox and Ferenczi, *International Migrations*, 2: 201-36.

24. Italian workers, although Catholics, did not threaten German cultural dominance in the areas settled partly or largely by Poles (Silesia and partitioned Polish areas).

25. Klaus J. Bade, "German Emigration to the United States and Continental Immigration to Germany in the Late Nineteenth and Early Twentieth Centuries," *Central European History* (December 1980): 348-77, repr. in *Labor Migration in the Atlantic Economies*, ed. Hoerder, chapter 5.

26. Gary S. Cross, "Toward Social Peace and Prosperity: The Politics of Immigration in France during the Era of World War One," *French Historical Studies* 11 (1979-80): 610-32; Lothar Elsner, "Foreign Workers and Forced Labor in Germany during the First World War," in *Labor Migration in the Atlantic Economies*, ed. Hoerder, 189-232; compare also the series edited by Elsner and his institute at Rostock University, *Fremdarbeiterpolitik des Imperialismus* (1975 onward). Research in progress by Peter Shergold and others demonstrates that forced migration has been relied upon to supplement voluntary migration whenever demand exceeded labor supply in imperial or hegemonic countries.

27. Research by Hannes Siegrist (West Berlin) on Swiss technicians' migration; Claudius H. Riegler, *Emigration und Arbeitswanderung aus Schweden nach Norddeutschland, 1868-1914* (Neumünster, 1985).

28. A number of specialized studies analyze this transfer of class-consciousness for specific trades, cities, or ethnic groups. The emphasis on theory, Lassalle versus Marx, in labor historiography has prevented an assessment of the impact of migrations. The 'Labor Migration Project' of the University of Bremen is taking up this subject; Peter Sipos, "Die Rolle der Migration im Entwicklungsprozess der Arbeiterklasse [. . .] Das Beispiel Ungarn," in *Internationale Tagung der Historiker der Arbeiterbewegung, 1986* (Vienna, 1987), 15-28.

29. Herbert, *Ausländerbeschäftigung*, 120-236; Georges Mauco, *Les étrangers en France* (Paris, 1932).

30. Jean Stengers, "Les mouvements migratoires en Belgique au XIXe et XXe siècles," in *Les migrations internationales*, 292.

31. Christoph Klessmann, *Polnische Bergarbeiter in Ruhrgebiet 1870-1945* (Göttingen, 1978); Schofer, *The Formation of a Modern Labor Force*; Brepohl, *Der Aufbau*; Murzynowska, *Polskie wychodzstwo*.

32. Hans Norman and Harald Runblom, "Migration Patterns in the Nordic Countries," in *Labor Migration in the Atlantic Economies*, ed. Hoerder, 35-68.

33. Fassman, "Migration in Austria 1850-1900," ibid., 69-93.

34. Bade, "German Emigration," ibid., 374.

35. According to the evidence available internal migrants hardly corresponded by letter with their areas of origin. Lack of statistics makes research on internal return migration during economic downswings almost impossible.

36. In 1892 the U.S. Commissioner of Immigration estimated the value of each immigrant (not counting cash and material goods carried) at $1,500, *Annual Report*, 1892. The Polish-American newspaper *Glos Polek* asserted that migration had drained Poland of "strength, health, youth," that is, the "capital of our land" to build "the well-being and wealth of this nation," quoted in Maxine Schwartz Seller, ed., *Immigrant Women* (Philadelphia, 1981), 178-79.

37. Studies on behalf of the European Organization for Economic Cooperation and Development on present-day labor migration support this view. "None [of the researchers] was able to quote any really conclusive instance in which the returning labour was used in a manner at all conducive to development. In no way do the returning emigrants help to further their country's economic growth, whether by the use of the savings they have accumulated abroad or the experience they have acquired," *OECD-Observer* 47 (1970): 11, quoted by K. P. Dietzel in *Argument* 68 (1971): 772. Savings sent back by migrants are of no help to the country of origin's development without a government directed and enforced investment strategy. The surplus value created by migrant workers in the core countries may in fact

increase the relative disparity to the periphery (society of origin), wage remittances notwithstanding. Even the migrants' families in the old societies generally used the remittances for consumption or ostentatious proof of a better condition rather than for investment to secure their position.

38. Gutman, "Work, Culture and Society," 5-8, 23-24, passim; compare also Tamara K. Hareven, *Family Time and Industrial Time: The Relationship Between the Family and Work in a New England Industrial Community* (Cambridge, 1982).

39. F. C. Valkenburg and A. M. C. Vissers, "Segmentation of the Labour Market," *Netherlands Journal of Sociology* 16 (1930): 155-70, discuss a "spoiled identity" (152).

40. Auvo Kostiainen, "The Finnish-American Labor Press" (unpublished manuscript).

41. For example, for Germany, see Klaus Schönhoven, *Expansion and Konzentration: Studien zur Entwicklung der Freien Gewerkschaften im Wilhelminischen Deutschland, 1890-1914* (Stuttgart, 1980).

42. See the organ of the German federation of trade unions, *Correspondenzblatt*; Martin Forberg, "Freie Gewerkschaften und ausländische Industriearbeiter, 1890-1918," M.A. thesis, University of Münster, 1985; Hans-Peter Winter, "Analyse der Ausländerpolitik der deutschen Gewerkschaften," diploma thesis, University of Erlangen-Nürnberg, 1980; for Hungary, see *Népzava* and *Volksstimme*.

43. Winter, "Analyse," 73-83; Dirk Hoerder, "The Attitudes of German Trade Unions to Migrant Workers, 1880s-1914," *Migracijske Teme* 3 (1988): 21-37.

44. J. S. MacDonald, "Agricultural Organization, Migration and Labour Militancy in Rural Italy," *Journal of Economic History*, 2d ser., 16 (1963-64): 61-75; Gabaccia, *Militants and Migrants*, passim.

45. The two positions refer to the past, but the debate is still being conducted concerning contemporary labor migrants.

46. Dirk Hoerder, "Migration in the European and American Economies: Comparative Perspectives on Its Impact on Working-Class Consciousness," in *Emigration from Northern, Central and Southern Europe: Theoretical and Methodological Principles of Research* (Kraków, 1983), 314-15. Community and class, juxtaposed here for the sake of argument, may be complementary as much recent work shows, but may also be conflicting.

47. Claudius H. Riegler, "Emigrationsphasen, Akkumulation und Widerstandsstrategien: Zu einigen Beziehungen der Arbeitsemigration von und nach Schweden, 1850-1930," in *Migration und Wirtschaftsentwicklung*, ed. Hartmut Elsenhans (Frankfurt/M., 1978), 31-69, quote, 32.

48. Charlotte Erickson, "The Encouragement of Emigration by British Trade Unions, 1850-1900," *Population Studies* 3 (1949): 248-73. Horst Rössler is carrying out a research project on this topic at the University of Bremen, Labor Migration Project.

49. David M. Gordon, Richard Edwards, and Michael Reich, *Segmented*

Work, Divided Workers: The Historical Transformation of Labor in the United States (Cambridge, 1982); Edna Bonacich, "A Theory of Ethnic Antagonism: The Split Labor Market," *American Sociological Review* 37 (1972): 547-59; John B. Christiansen, "The Split Labor Market Theory and Filipino Exclusion, 1927-1934," *Phylon* 40 (1979): 66-74.

50. Clark Kerr, *Labor Markets and Wage Determination: The Balkanization of Labor Markets and Other Essays* (Berkeley, 1977); Peter Doeringer and Michael Piore, *Internal Labor Markets and Manpower Analysis* (Lexington, Mass., 1971); Randy Hodson and Robert L. Kaufman, "Economic Dualism: A Critical Review," *American Social Review* 47 (1982): 727-39; Walter Licht, "Labor Economics and the Labor Historian," *International Labor and Working-Class History* 21 (1982): 52-62; Sar Levitan, Garth Magnum, and Ray Marshall, *Human Resources and Labor Markets: Labor and Manpower in the American Economy* (New York, 1976); B. Harrison, "Human Capital, Black Poverty and Radical Economics," *Industrial Relations* 70 (1971): 285.

51. Particularly AFL unions and in Germany the miners and the building trades' unions showed massive prejudices against in-migrating workers.

52. Victor R. Greene, *The Slavic Community on Strike: Immigrant Labor in Pennsylvania Anthracite* (Notre Dame, 1968); Michael A. Barendse, *Social Expectations and Perception: The Case of the Slavic Anthracite Workers* (University Park, 1981).

53. Dorothee Schneider, "'For Whom Are All the Good Things in Life?' German-American Homewives Discuss Their Budgets," in *German Workers in Industrial Chicago, 1850-1910: A Comparative Perspective*, ed. Hartmut Keil and John B. Jentz (DeKalb, 1983), 145-60.

54. Salvatore J. LaGumina, ed., *The Immigrants Speak: Italian Americans Tell Their Story* (New York, 1979), 20, passim.

55. In German, the term *Sparschwein* [piggy bank] may originate in the custom of raising pigs to save money; the term could not be traced in dictionaries of historical meaning.

56. Valkenburg and Vissers, "Segmentation," 161, passim.

57. Klessmann, *Polnische Bergarbeiter,* English summary "Polish Miners in the Ruhr District: Their Social Situation and Trade Union Activity," in *Labor Migration in the Atlantic Economies,* ed. Hoerder, 253-75; *La Società Umanitaria: Fondazione P.M. Loria, Milano, 1893/1963* (Milan, 1964); Monika Glettler, *Die Wiener Tschechen um 1900: Stukturanalyse einer nationalen Minderheit in der Grossstadt* (Munich, 1972); Isabelle Bertaux-Wiame, "The Life History Approach to the Study of Internal Migration: How Women and Men Came to Paris Between the Wars," in *Our Common History: The Transformation of Europe,* ed. Paul Thompson and Natasha Burchardt (London, 1982), 186-200.

58. Numerous studies analyze migrant and immigrant workers' organizations in individual cities, but no general theory of "class and ethnicity" has yet been developed, even comparative studies are lacking.

59. Hetzer and Hoerder, "Linguisitic Fragmentation or Multilingualism among Labor Migrants."

60. *Illinois Staats-Zeitung,* November 19, 1873.

61. Ethnic newspapers were usually edited by journalists who had acquired some knowledge of English and sometimes other languages; union organizers spoke several languages; public meetings of several ethnic groups usually included speakers from different language groups who could, however, understand each other.

62. A summary of recent research is in *"Struggle a Hard Battle": Essays on Working-Class Immigrants,* ed. Dirk Hoerder (DeKalb, 1986).

63. John B. Jentz and Richard Schneirov, "Social Republicanism and Socialiasm: A Multi-Ethnic History of Labor Reform in Chicago, 1848-1877" (unpublished manuscript, 1985); Paul Krause, "Labor Republicanism and 'Za Chlebom': Anglo-Americans and Slavic Solidarity in Homestead," in *"Struggle a Hard Battle,"* ed. Hoerder, 143-69. The metamorphosis of this social republicansim to class consciousness, as well as Old World-oriented nationalism from 1919 to 1921, to the drive for industrial unions in the 1930s, has not yet received adequate attention.

64. Krause, "Labor Republicanism," 154; reference to "Kaisers" in unpublished paper of Allen Seager.

65. Ibid., 158; Antanas Kaztauskis, "From Lithuania to the Chicago Stockyards: An Autobiography," in *Plain Folk: The Life Stories of Undistinguished Americans,* ed. David M. Katzman and William M. Tuttle, Jr. (Urbana, 1982), 103.

66. Quote in David Montgomery, "Nationalism, American Patriotism, and Class Consciousness among Immigrant Workers in the United States in the Epoch of World War I," in *"Struggle a Hard Battle,"* ed. Hoerder, 346.

67. *Hull-House Maps and Papers: A Presentation of Nationalities and Wages in a Congested District of Chicago* (New York, 1895, repr. 1970); Heinz Fassmann found similar living patterns for Vienna.

68. At the turn of the century about one-third of the labor migrants returned, compare Stephan Thernstrom, comp., *Harvard Encyclopedia of American Ethnic Groups* (Cambridge, 1980), 1036-937; essays in Part 3, *Labor Migration in the Atlantic Economies,* ed. Hoerder; Commissioner General of Immigration, *Annual Reports* (1890s-1915) (Washington, D.C., 1891-1915).

69. Julianna Puskás "Hungarian Migration Patterns 1880-1930: From Macro-Analysis to Micro-Analysis" (unpublished paper); Kaztauskis, "From Lithuania."

70. Bertaux-Wiame, "The Life History Approach to the Study of Internal Migration," 186-200; Wolfgang Helbich and Ulrike Sommer, "Immigrant Letters as Sources," in *The Press of Labor Migrants,* ed. Harzig and Hoerder, 39-58; Micaela di Leonardo, "The Female World of Cards and Holidays: Women, Families, and the Work of Kinship," *Signs* 12 (1987): 440-53.

71. This type of information, usually contained in letters, has until now been considered irrelevant by historians. It has to be viewed in a different perspective from a family or women's history approach. The same holds

true for news about weather conditions: unimportant for historians but highly important as a reflection of the minds of peasant workers and peasants back home, for whom the weather decided the size of the crop and, in extreme cases, whether there would be anything to eat during the next winter. In 1900 more than six million letters crossed the territory of the German Reich from West to East (plus four times that amount in closed packages), most of them probably letters of immigrants.

72. Christiane Harzig, "The Role of German Women in the German-American Working-Class Movement in New York, 1878-1885," *Journal of American Ethnic History* 8 (1989): 87-107; also Jutta Schwarzkopf, "Chartist Women" (unpublished paper, Bremen, 1986); Donna R. Gabaccia, *From Sicily to Elizabeth Street: Housing and Social Change Among Italian Immigrants, 1880-1930* (New York, 1984), 80-83, 100-102.

73. Both quotes *Immigrant Women*, ed. Seller, 242.

74. For example, see the research conference, "The Future of American Labor History: Toward a Synthesis," Northern Illinois University, DeKalb, October 1984.

75. Income Tax Cases, 1894; Sidney L. Harring, *Policing a Class Society: The Experience of American Cities, 1865-1915* (New Brunswick, 1983); Jerry M. Cooper, *The Army and Civil Disorder: Federal Military Intervention in Labor Disputes, 1877-1900* (Westport, 1980).

76. Just as the concepts of *class, community,* and *ethnicity* shape historians' interpretations, *kin* has led to an exmphasis on old-new culture continuity and family cooperation. Just as the other concepts refer only to aspects of the migrants' experience, kin may have been idealized. Family structures often include massive friction and conflict.

77. The aspect of conflict among ethnic groups will receive specific attention in a project I plan with East European colleagues on comparative acculturation patterns of ethnic groups in Cleveland and Budapest.

PART TWO

Microanalyses:
Migration Traditions
and Chain Migrations

4

Migration Traditions from Finland to North America

REINO KERO

Migration studies often use the concept of *chain migration*, usually meaning that those immigrants who were the first to arrive in a particular locality drew after them relatives, friends, and acquaintances, who, in turn, attracted their own relatives, friends, and acquaintances. The term indicates the continuity of the migration process.

Chain migration is not quite the same thing as a *migration tradition*. The latter term has been seldom used[1] and has not perhaps been precisely defined. In what sense is the term *migration tradition* used in this chapter? It denotes the existence of migration between two specific areas, of greater or lesser size, extending over a prolonged period (including at least two economic cycles). An example of a migration tradition might be the continuity of migration from a particular Finnish village to Hibbing, Minnesota, extending over a period of at least a decade. A strong migration tradition usually involved a countercurrent, in that some of the immigrants returned to their point of departure. The phenomenon of the migration tradition is, of course, not only related to migration between countries; such a tradition may exist in the case of internal migration as well.

Basic Features of Finnish-American Migration

Emigration from Finland to America began at the end of the 1840s, when the news of California gold reached Finland. The first Finnish emigrants, seamen sailing the oceans, felt the attraction of America far more strongly than it was felt inside the boundaries of Finland.[2] Finnish vessels sailing in U.S. waters were in serious difficulty around 1850; sailors had a tendency to desert their ships in order to seek a share of the gold.[3]

For the following twenty years connections between Finland and

111

America continued to be weak; there were small settlements of Finnish sailors in North American seaports, but they rarely if ever sent messages to the home country. By the 1860s, however, the Finns' connections with America no longer depended only upon sailors. The contacts that the inhabitants of northern Finland, and particular Vaasa Province (Figure 4.1) maintained with Norway and Sweden now played a central role, and the urge to emigrate to America apparently spread from there to the Tornio River Valley. Swedish-speaking inhabitants of Vaasa Province also had connections with Sweden. As a result of these contacts, emigration began as early as the middle of the 1860s among the Swedish-speaking population of the province. At the beginning of the 1880s emigration spread beyond Oulu and Vaasa provinces to other parts of Finland, and by the beginning of the 1890s people were emigrating from all of Finland.[4]

Although Finnish emigration had a late start compared to other Nordic countries, at the beginning of the twentieth century, emigration from Finland to North America was stronger than at any time before or since. During the first decade of the twentieth century the number of Finnish overseas emigrants was about 150,000. By the 1920s the number of Finnish emigrants had declined to about 60,000, and emigration was very small in the 1930s. The total number of Finns who migrated overseas was about 350,000; in other words, some 1 percent of all immigrants arriving in North America were of Finnish origin.[5] Although Nordic emigrants in America were included in the group of so-called "old immigrants," those from Finland were termed "new immigrants."[6]

Almost 90 percent of the Finns emigrated from rural districts; more than half of the early group were farmers and their children.[7] Later, the proportion of not only farmers but also of their children declined, while that of farm hands and workers increased. This was due in part to the fact that when Finnish emigration began, only farmers had enough money to purchase tickets for the trip. The change in the occupational structure of the emigrant group probably also resulted from the fact that as emigration spread from Oulu and Vaasa provinces to the rest of Finland, the population base for emigration changed. It is also of some importance to note that in the late nineteenth century the economy of Finland as a whole changed from a purely agricultural system to one that included some industry.[8]

Finnish emigration was male-dominated compared to that of other Nordic countries: almost 65 percent of Finnish emigrants were men. They, like emigrants in general, consisted of relatively young age groups, about half were between sixteen and twenty-five. In Finland,

Figure 4.1. Provinces of Finland and Principal Localities

immigration to America was particularly an Ostrobothnian phenomenon; most of the emigrants came from this area in western Finland.[9]

The areas of destination for Finnish emigrants were quite similar
to those of emigrants from other Nordic countries: Michigan, Minnesota, Wisconsin, Ohio, New York, Massachusetts, Montana, Washington, Oregon, and California. Ontario and British Columbia were
the most important destinations in Canada.[10]

Some Examples of Finnish Migration Traditions

The immigration goals of Finns provide numerous examples of the
way in which immigrants who had known each other in the home
country tended to cluster in America in particular cities or rural areas.
In the case of Finnish migrants it is perhaps easier than for many
other nationalities to study the extent to which immigrants from the
same area of origin traveled to the same target region in North
America, the size of the groups that left the same locality and clustered
in the same destination in the new country, and the duration of these
migration traditions. Source material is available in Finland in the
form of passport registers kept at the time, passenger lists of the
shipping companies that carried emigrants from Finland and Sweden
to England, and the membership registers of the Finnish-American
churches.

Emigrants leaving Finland had to have a passport, and authorities
kept lists of those who were issued passports, including not only the
name of the recipient but also his or her home village or town. The
destination, on the other hand, was entered more or less vaguely, for
example, "America" or "abroad." The passport registers thus do not
provide direct information on specific destinations.

The shipping companies selling tickets to emigrants compiled passenger lists, which for the most part have survived. The lists were
necessary because the companies at the same time often sold tickets
that covered the whole voyage, from the port of departure to England,
from England to America, and from the American port by rail to,
for instance, Hibbing, Minnesota. Thus it is possible to determine
from passenger lists the final destination of the immigrants. To know
the original home localities of Finns who bought tickets to Minnesota,
we have to combine information from passport registers and passenger
lists. The names and home towns of intending emigrants appear upon
the passport registers; these names then have to be searched in the
passenger lists. By these means the number of immigrants traveling,
for instance, from northern Finland to Minnesota in 1905 can be

determined, and we can pinpoint the origins of immigrants to a high degree of precision—at the level of the parish.

Because as many as twenty thousand emigrants left Finland in some years, the compilation of data from passport registers and passenger lists is a laborious task. This information, however, has been compiled for the years 1873, 1882, 1890, and 1905.[11] The names found in both lists for these years number 528, 1,697, 3,111, and 15,751, respectively. Examples of findings based upon these data follow.

In 1882, forty-eight emigrants departed for transatlantic countries from the neighboring parishes of Ylistaro and Isokyrö. Of these, twenty-four (50 percent) had purchased tickets to Ohio. Eighty-one emigrants departed from these same parishes in 1890, ten (12.3 percent) of whom went to Ohio; and in 1905, 365 emigrants left, eighty-eight (24.1 percent) of whom were destined for Ohio. Only 6.3 percent, 2.5 percent, and 3.4 percent, respectively, of the total Finnish emigration during these years was directed to Ohio.

Emigration from Finland to Utah came from a comparatively small region in the vicinity of Vaasa: in 1882, there were sixteen; in 1890, twenty; and in 1905, eighty. Of the area's total emigration, the portion going to Utah during these years was 4.7 percent, 3 percent, and 6.8 percent respectively; whereas only 1 percent, 1.2 percent, and 0.7 percent of Finland's total emigration was destined for Utah. Mormon missionaries had been active in the area around 1880, however, there is no conclusive evidence that the emigrants whose destination was Utah were either Mormons or under the influence of Mormon ideas. It is as likely that the Utah immigrants intended to work in the mines, like the Finns who immigrated to Wyoming.

Emigration from southwest Finland was distinctly directed to New York.[12] In 1890, of the 108 emigrants who left this area, 46 (42.8 percent) had purchased tickets to New York, as did 424 (44.5 percent) of the 953 who left in 1905. Of the total Finnish emigration, 27.2 percent and 14.6 percent were directed to New York in 1890 and 1905.

Finnish emigration to Canada originated especially from the southern parts, in particular from a few parishes from the southeastern part of Vaasa province. Emigration to Canada may have begun from the area earlier than from anywhere else in Finland. In 1890, from the seven parishes in the core area of emigration to Canada, ten (6.1 percent) emigrants of a total of 164 purchased tickets to Ontario. Only 1 percent of the country's total emigration during this year was directed to Ontario. In 1905, of the area's 1,079 emigrants, 191 (17.7

percent) went to Ontario; while of Finland's total emigration, 5.1 percent (947) was directed to Ontario.[13]

Of fourteen emigrants in 1882 from Rantsila in Oulu Province, nine (64.3 percent) purchased tickets to Michigan. In 1890, nine (42.9 percent) of twenty-one emigrants and in 1905, twenty-three (52.3 percent) of forty-four immigrated to Michigan. Meanwhile, 39.4 percent, 30.2 percent, and 19.4 percent, respectively, of the total Finnish emigration during these years was directed to Michigan.

On the basis of these examples, it is clear that in many cases the main emigration flows from certain areas had the same destination in North America from decade to decade. The destination of the emigrants from a particular Finnish parish, however, was often much more specific; for example, Crystal Falls, Michigan, was the destination of a majority of the approximately two thousand emigrants from the parish of Merikarvia in Finland before World War I.

The Birth of Emigration Traditions

There were two basic conditions for the birth of migration tradition. On the one hand, there had to be some kind of continual migration pressure in the areas of departure, for example, poor employment opportunities. The second condition was the availability of nearly free, good agricultural farming land at the areas of destination in North America during the early stages of emigration, and perhaps even into the 1880s. In later stages, the most important factor was the demand at the destination for labor and the comparatively higher level of wages available there than in Europe. However, it was not enough that the first emigrants from specific districts knew that farming land could be obtained almost for nothing in North America or that higher wages were paid in America than in Europe. They also had to know exactly where they were going and how to get there. It is therefore important to know how the first emigrants obtained such information.

In the early days of emigration, a few emigrant recruiters traveled around northern Finland. These people were earlier immigrants who had come back to recruit labor for the mines of northern Michigan, which to some extent they succeeded in doing. The importance of Michigan as the destination area of Finnish emigration was probably due to such recruitment.

Another case in which recruitment probably created a strong migration tradition that lasted for several decades was in the Kristiin-ankaupunki area, where leaflets containing information on Canada were distributed in the early 1880s. It was this area that emigration from Finland to Canada began, and for at least thirty years the Kristiinankaupunki-Isojoki-Karijoki-Karvia region was the core area of Finnish immigration to Canada.[14] Recruitment activity, of course, did not necessarily create a tradition. It might have been totally without results, as was the case with Hans Mattson's effort in 1874 to recruit Finns to Manitoba. Mattson is known to have printed leaflets intended for Finland.[15]

In some cases the steps of recruited emigrants were not followed by others. A Finn named Charles Linn, who had migrated to the United States in the 1830s, took more than fifty emigrants from the Helsinki area to Alabama in 1869, however further emigration from this area to Alabama seems to have been nonexistent. Emigration from Uusimaa province to North America, excluding perhaps Helsinki, does not appear to have occurred until the 1890s.[16]

Examples of migration traditions created by recruiters are also known outside of Finland, even though migration traditions have seldom been researched. For example, migration traditions from the iron industry areas of Sweden to Worcester, Massachusetts, originated when an industrialist from Worcester came to recruit Swedish craftsmen for his enterprise.[17]

Emigrant recruiters were thus one source of migration traditions, as were sailors. Because the emigration from the Åland Islands and the coast of southwest Finland was directed expressly to New York, it seems undeniable that in this case sailors had a particular influence. A large part of the area's population was concerned with shipping, and the number of sailors was considerable; some from southwest Finland are known to have lived in New York by the mid-nineteenth century. When emigration became a mass phenomenon in the 1880s in the Åland Islands and a little later in coastal parishes, it was thus natural to expect it to be directed to New York.[18] Emigration from many localities began when persons departed from one locality under the influence of emigrants from neighboring villages and parishes. In this way, emigration traditions spread from village to village and parish to parish.[19]

Conditions for the birth of a migration tradition were exceptionally good if the first emigrants from a certain locality happened to arrive at a place in North America with acceptable long-term employment. For the Finns, the first such area was the Upper Penninsula of Michigan. Migrants from northern Finland had first sought work in Norway, where they had labored for some time as fishermen or in the copper mines. Along with Norwegians and Swedes, they were recruited for the copper mines of Michigan, where jobs suitable for immigrants were available from the 1860s on.

Even though a few Finns settled in Minnesota fairly early, the state possessed no special magnetism before the 1880s or 1890s, when the mines of the Vermillion and Mesabi ranges were opened. The earliest Finnish immigration to Minnesota had been directed either to Minneapolis or certain small farming areas, areas that continued to attract emigrants but in comparatively low numbers. In the eastern parts of the United States, New York City and certain industrial towns in Massachusetts, particularly Fitchburg and Worcester, provided economic opportunities that made for lasting and strong migration traditions. Industrial locations in Pennsylvania, Ohio, and Illinois, such as Monessen, Ashtabula Harbor, and Waukegan, attracted a considerable portion of the emigrants from some Finnish localities. However, this was not a significant portion of Finland's total emigration. Comparatively weaker migration traditions restricted to smaller areas focused upon centers of Canadian mining and forest industries, mining in the Rocky Mountain states, and fishing on the Pacific coast.

To what extent did the occupational structure of the departure area affect the choice of area of settlement in the destination area? In Sweden it has been observed that emigrants from agricultural areas generally settled in the farming region of the Midwest, whereas those from the iron industry districts congregated in the manufacturing cities of Massachusetts. Can comparable observations be made for Finland? A comparison of the destinations of the urban and rural emigrants of 1905 reveals more urban Finnish arrivals in New York City and Illinois.[20] Of the Finns who came to New York, 435 (10 percent) originated from urban centers, accounting for 19.9 percent of the Finns who arrived in New York. Meanwhile, Illinois received 47 urban emigrants, or 15.3 percent of the total number of arrivals in Illinois. By way of contrast, only 8.9 percent (129) of Finns who went to Minnesota originated from cities; 5.2 percent (160) of those who went to Michigan were of similar origin. When compared to those from rural areas, emigrants from urban areas had the advantage of higher levels of occupational skill and even specific crafts. The urban areas of New York City and Chicago would be their "natural" choice, evidence that the occupational structure of the departure area determined to some extent the settlement areas of the emigrants.[21]

The Overlapping of Migration Traditions

The emigration stream consistently flowed to Michigan from quite a large part of Oulu Province and certain parts of central Finland.

An example from the other extreme is offered by the rather small Peräseinäjoki parish, whose emigrants, unlike those from neighboring parishes, settled exclusively in New York City. Thus, territories dominated by migration traditions seem to have been in some cases very large and in some cases very small.

Soon after emigration had begun, many Finnish localities evidently possessed several migration traditions concurrently. The emigration flow was divided among different destinations in transatlantic countries. Thus, for example, emigrants from Kälviä in 1873 went to either Pennsylvania or Ohio and in 1882, to Minnesota, Michigan, Ohio, New York, or Oregon. In 1890, their goals were Michigan, Ohio, New York, and Oregon, and in 1905, Minnesota, Michigan, Massachusetts, Wisconsin, Ohio, New York, Oregon, Montana, Colorado, Vermont, Maine, and Quebec. Emigration from Alahärmä was directed to three states in 1882, to eight in 1890, and to nineteen in 1905. Even though the emigration flow became more and more dispersed, Ashtabula Harbor in Ohio and Astoria in Oregon continued to remain very important destinations for emigrants from Kälviä. Those from Alahärmä seem to have had Ishpeming, Michigan, and New York City as constant destinations. A departure area the size of a Finnish parish often possessed one or two strong and long-established migration traditions, but over time, new traditions were continually born. In general, late migration traditions never became very strong; typically, each year the migration pattern tended to be fragmented among more and more different destinations.

How broad then were the areas of origin of Finnish immigrants to such typical communities as Harlem, New York; Worcester, Massachusetts; DeKalb, Illinois; Negaunee, Michigan; Virginia, Minnesota; Copper Cliff, Ontario; and Astoria, Oregon? Many Finnish churches in North America kept careful membership registers, similar to those of parishes in Finland. The registers included not only the member's name but also the locality in Finland where he or she had been born. Although not all Finns arriving in America joined a church, the registers offer a good picture of the origins of Finns who lived in a given locality.[22] This picture can be given further precision by comparing the information thus obtained to that provided by passenger lists and passport registers.

In this way, the parishes of origin of Finnish immigrants living in a number of different localities in various parts of North America have been studied. It appears that Harlem, New York, received immigrants from 119; Worcester, Massachusetts, from 107; DeKalb, Illinois, from 63; Negaunee, Michigan, from 154; Virginia, Minnesota, from 121; Copper Cliff, Ontario, from 55; and Astoria, Oregon, from 137 Finnish parishes (Figures 4.2-4.8). However, about 63 percent of the immigrants who arrived in DeKalb, 45 percent in Worcester and Copper Cliff, 34 percent in Astoria, 29 percent in Negaunee, 25 percent in Harlem, and 24 percent in Virginia originated from the five parishes that had the strongest migration traditions with those American places.

The Duration of Migration Traditions

How long did the emigrants from certain small or large areas of departure remain settled in the same area in North America? How long did the migration tradition last between two localities situated on opposite sides of the Atlantic? Even though emigration from Finland began late in comparison with that from other Nordic countries, traditions lasting for thirty to forty years can also be found in Finland. For example, the traditions to migrate from Isokyrö, Ylistaro, and Kälviä to Ohio, and from Kälviä to Oregon, seem to have lasted at least that long.

What were the connections between the communities of the old and the new world? Of what, concretely, did the migration tradition consist? The most important means of contact were returning emigrants and correspondence between relatives and friends. The proportion of emigrants from Finland to North America who returned permanently to the home country has been estimated at 20 percent. In other words, some seventy thousand emigrants remigrated and naturally offered information to their relatives and friends, on the basis of their own experience, about what localities were good places for immigration.

Among those emigrants who returned to Finland intending to remain were also some who later changed their minds and reemigrated. In exceptional cases the same person might emigrate up to seven or eight times. Such persons, traveling back and forth between the old and the new country, were important sources of information. Back home in Finland they played the part of the great expert, and their information might serve as the basis for the emigration plans of many others. It was also common that when such persons left once more for America they were accompanied by other, first-time emigrants. The new emigrants sometimes traveled under their guidance to relatives who already lived in America. In other cases, the more experienced immigrants helped the newcomers to find work, and in fact determined the destination of the new immigrants.

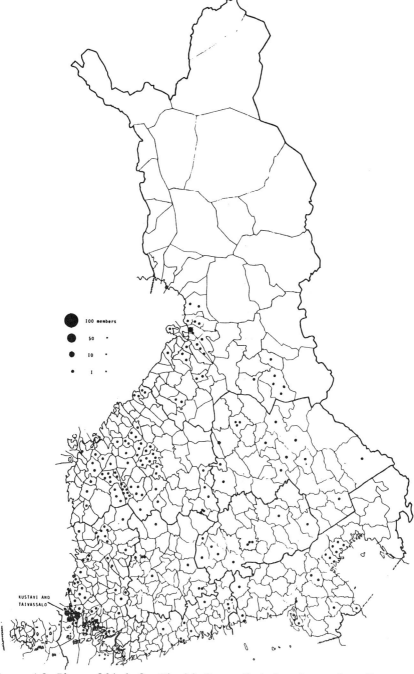

Figure 4.2. Place of birth for Finnish Evangelical church members from Harlem, N.Y.

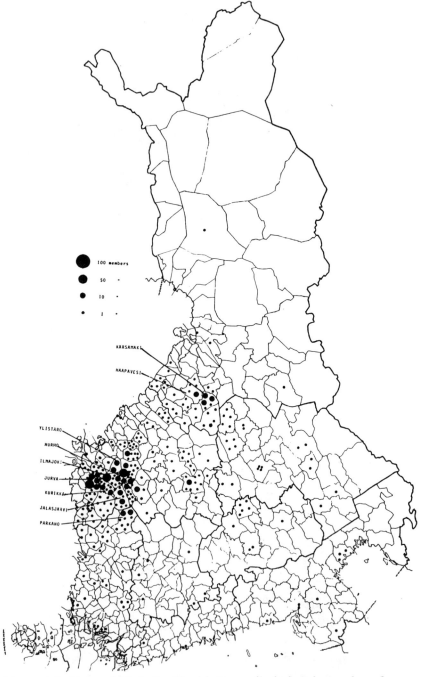

Figure 4.3. Place of birth for Finnish Evangelical church members from Worcester, Mass.

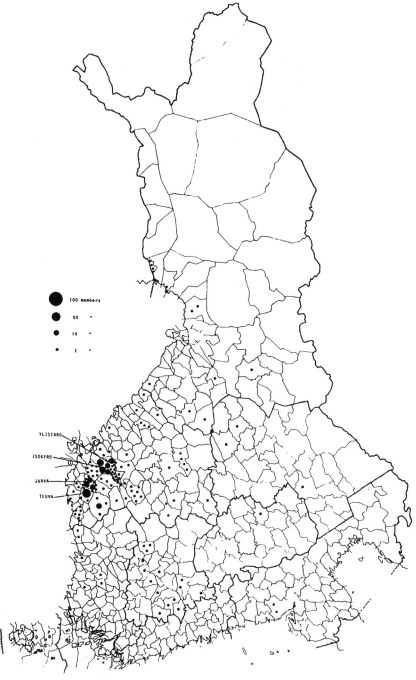

Figure 4.4. Place of birth for Finnish Evangelical church members from DeKalb, Ill.

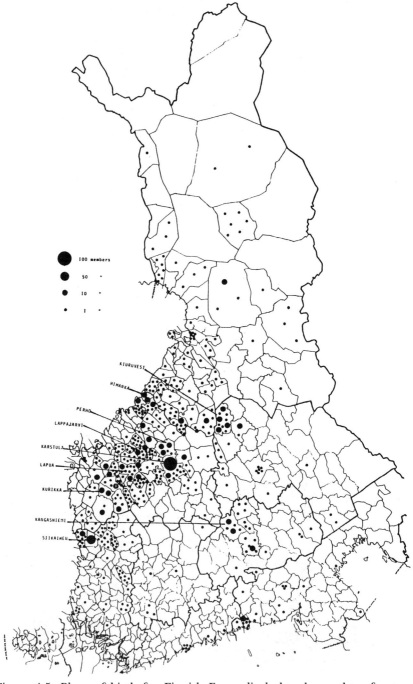

Figure 4.5. Place of birth for Finnish Evangelical church members from Negaunee, Mich.

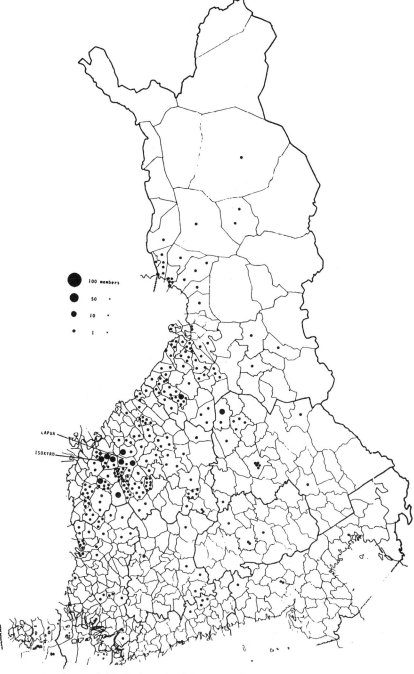

Figure 4.6. Place of birth for Finnish Evangelical church members from Virginia, Minn.

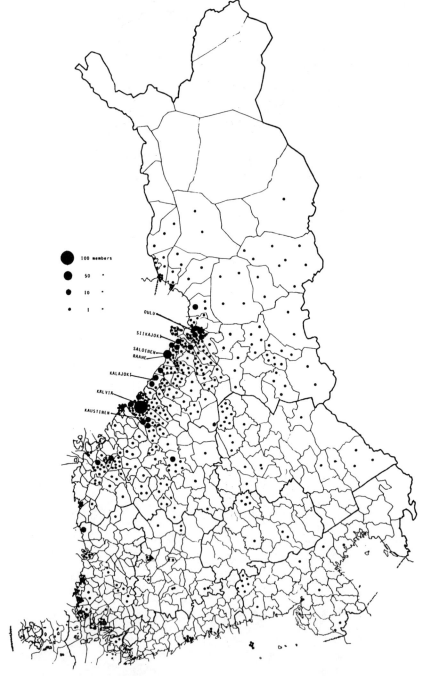

Figure 4.7. Place of birth for Finnish Evangelical church members from Astoria, Ore.

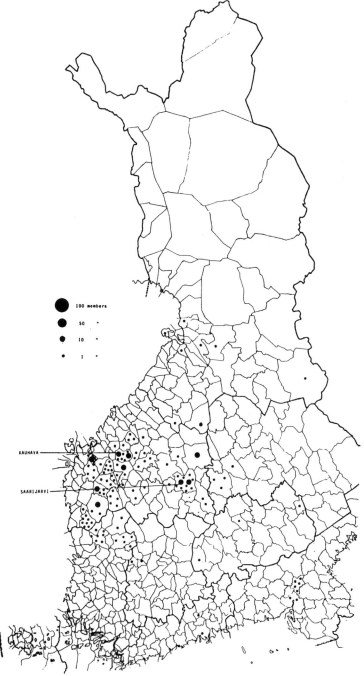

Figure 4.8. Place of birth for Finnish Evangelical church members from Copper Cliff, Ont.

Letters also provided a great deal of information from Finnish immigrants in America to their relatives in the home country, and, of course, vice versa. Almost all Finnish emigrants were literate, but writing was not as common a skill among Finnish emigrants as reading. The life of the immigrant, the need to maintain contact with relatives back home, nevertheless forced many individuals to write who would not ordinarily have done so. Altogether, some thirty thousand Finnish immigrant letters have been collected. The letters allow us to form a picture of the typical letter sent home by an immigrant in North America, provide the image of America that such a letter offered, and indicate the way in which the information letters transmitted guided the decisions of potential emigrants.

What was the typical immigrant letter like? It might contain information about America in general; it might praise American food, high wages, and "American freedom"; or it might complain about unemployment, the poor conditions in the lumberjacks' camps, and so on. More typically, however, such letters told about the writers' own lives, their health, and their high wages, describing how easy the work was or the availability of land in the neighborhood. We can perhaps even describe the America of the typical immigrant letter as identical with a particular mining town, lumber camp, or farm region. And it was this information that served as the basis for decisions made in Finland: when to emigrate and where to go. The following examples demonstrate the kind of information on the basis of which emigration decisions were made. When the first Finnish immigrants came to Minnesota, one of them, a farmer, wrote to his home locality: "Dear Brother: Now let me invite you to come here, to live and to die. Dear brother, leave the country of our fathers and come here. . . . I promise to help you set up your farm as my neighbor . . . buy a ticket by railroad to the town called Minneapoli [sic] . . . I will come to meet you."[23]

In the 1890s, when Finnish immigration to the United States was already a large-scale phenomenon, a Finnish immigrant in Ohio wrote, "If you come, send me a letter. And when you get to Nyyork [sic], telegraph me from there, so I will come and meet you at the depot, so that you do not get lost."[24]

In 1908, a year of severe depression in America, the immigrants looked forward to better times: "You wrote that Kalle intends to come here. If he really means to come, it seems to me that it would be best to come in the spring, since work will begin to improve in the spring, and times will probably otherwise improve for a couple of years."[25] Another letter, written about the same time, offers a similarly optimistic forecast: "How old is your oldest boy, Eino? Has he already gone to confirmation school? I would like send a ticket to him in the spring so that he could come here this spring, since there were presidential elections here, and the better party won. Thus it looks like next spring and summer work will be going at full swing."[26] The information that traveled back and forth between relatives and friends tended to reinforce the migration tradition: an immigrant living in Hibbing, Minnesota, would never suggest that his relative should go to, say, San Francisco, but encouraged him to come to Hibbing.

In addition to these two sources of influence, returning emigrants and messages contained in letters, a third important factor played a part in determining the forms, destinations, and timing of migration: the prepaid ticket and travel funds that immigrants sent from America. We know that some of the emigrants leaving Finland bought their passage with money that had been sent from America for this specific purpose. Of even greater importance were the prepaid tickets that were purchased in America from the agents of shipping companies and sent to relatives and friends in Europe. The prepaid ticket often covered the whole voyage, from the port of departure to a remote destination deep in the heart of the North American continent, entitling the immigrant to travel both by a particular steamship line and by train in America. In the case of Finland, we know that during the years 1891-1914 some 30 percent of emigrants traveled on prepaid tickets. The system was also used by emigrants from the other Scandinavian countries; some 50 percent of Swedish emigrants in the 1880s, for example, actually made use of prepaid tickets.[27]

How did the system of the prepaid ticket stimulate emigration? The initial impetus for migration might come from the emigrant, but it might also arise in America. The immigrant was often an enthusiastic "recruiter" who tried to alleviate homesickness by sending prepaid tickets to those back home: life in America would be better with relatives and old friends nearby. In many cases, the motives for sending prepaid tickets undoubtedly also involved the desire to help kin who were in difficulties in the Old Country, even if they had not asked for help.

Whether the initiative came from Europe or America, the sending of a prepaid ticket in any case speaks of close relationships, and of confidence that the recipient would repay the debt. By the early 1900s the journey was much less expensive than during the early stages of Finnish emigration, but even then the sum of money involved required a considerable outlay on the part of the immigrant in America. Even in the best-paid job, it required saving for a period of at least months, but more often more than a year. The cost of a steamship ticket from Finland to New York in 1905, for instance, was about $40, and the train ticket from New York to Duluth cost $25; from New York to San Francisco, as much as $45.[28]

The person who had provided the prepaid ticket needed some sort of assurance that the recipient would repay the debt. In general, kinship or close friendship was sufficient guarantee. Usually, such an agreement between relatives or friends was not put in writing; this was not considered important because the assumption was that the newcomer would not disappear into America. The recipient was coming to the same region, often to the same working place, as the person who had sent the ticket. And the same "terms" were naturally advantageous for the newcomer as well, who arrived among familiar faces and was assured of help in finding work or in dealing with other problems relating to the new life in America. This form of financing migration thus tended to reinforce the migration tradition.

The Importance of Migration Traditions

Because Finnish immigration to the United States ended almost completely during World War I and was quite small during the 1920s, migration traditions developed during the end of the nineteenth century and the beginning of the twentieth century were broken. The longest had lasted three or four decades. Some migration traditions had probably been broken off even before World War I interrupted the emigration flow. For example, many hundreds of Finns traveled to Orange, Texas, to work in the forests at the end of the 1880s and in the 1890s; but by the early twentieth century the city was an unknown migration objective. When the numbers of Finns in some Rocky Mountain states began to decline at the beginning of the twentieth century, it would appear that the particularly strong traditions born in the 1880s and 1890s of mirgration to this area from parishes in northern parts of Vaasa Province were also dying.

What did a long-lasting migration tradition between a locality in the departure area and one in the area that received emigrants signify? It is impossible to give a definite answer to this question. But if emigrants who departed from a certain locality arrived in an area where there was abundant, long-term work available, their experience helped create the conditions for the further expansion of the emigration from the departure area. As time passed, the destination area became well known to the population of the departure area and the adventure-seeking character of emigration disappeared. Then again, the breaking off of a migration tradition may have "disturbed" the emigration of the departure area. The emigrants then could not expect to move to the "other home village" in America but rather to a locality about which comparatively little was known and where there were perhaps only a few relatives and friends. This could at least temporarily cause emigration to decline until a new migration tradition was born.

NOTES

1. The term may have been used previously in only three publications: Reino Kero, *Migration from Finland to North America in the Years between the United States Civil War and the First World War* (Vammala, 1974), 60-61; Kero, "The Character and Significance of Migration Traditions from Finland to North America," *American Studies in Scandinavia* 9 (1977): 95-104; Kero, *The Finns in North America: Destinations and Composition of Immigrant Societies in North America before World War I* (Turku, 1980), 35-36.

2. Kero, *Migration from Finland*, 17.

3. An example of the situation that arose in connection with the California gold rush is reflected in a letter mailed from San Francisco in 1851 by the captain of a Finnish vessel and published some months later in a Finnish newspaper. According to this letter, nine crew members had jumped ship. The crew's wages were doubled, but in spite of this, the vessel had to leave San Francisco undermanned, *Åbo Underrättelser*, June 20, 1851.

4. Kero, *Migration from Finland*, 17-21.

5. Ibid., 24-47; Reino Kero, "Migration from Finland in 1866-1970," *Les migrations internationales de la fin du XVIIIe siècle à nos jours* (San Francisco, 1975), 392-93.

6. Kero, *Migration from Finland*, 22-23; Sten Carlsson, "Chronology and Composition of Swedish Emigration to America," in *From Sweden to America*, ed. Harald Runblom and Hans Norman (Uppsala, 1976), 114-26; Ingrid Semmingsen, *Veien mot Vest: Utvandringen fra Norge til Amerika, 1825-1865* (Oslo, 1941), 20-25.

7. The term *farmer* here means those Finnish cultivators who owned the land they cultivated. In addition, there were also "tenant farmers" (*torppari*, Sw. *torpare*); the land they cultivated might sometimes be quite extensive by Finnish standards, but they did not own it. In 1873, 53.6 percent of immigrants came from the former group and 11.2 percent from the latter. By 1902, the former had fallen to 28.4 percent and the latter increased to 13.6 percent. I have derived the first figures from passport and passenger lists; those for 1902 are from the official Finnish migration statistics.

8. Kero, *Migration from Finland*, 81-90.

9. Ibid., 48-55, 90-119.

10. Kero, *The Finns in North America*, 16-27.

11. Data were collected in the early 1970s at the University of Turku

from both passport and passenger registers concerning emigrants who left Finland in the years 1873, 1882, 1890, and 1905. For details see Kero, *Migration from Finland*, 9-13, and *The Finns in North America*, 11-13.

12. The area includes the area around the city of Rauma, Laitila, Karjala, Kuusjoki, Pöytyä, Koski Tl., Kiikala, Nummi, Pusula, Pyhäjärvi Ul., Vihti, Kirkniemi, and the parishes to the southwest in southwest Finland and the Åland Islands.

13. For an account of the earliest Finnish immigration to Canada see Reino Kero, "Emigration from Finland to Canada before the First World War," *Lakehead University Review* 1 (1976): 7-16.

14. Kero, *Migration from Finland*, 160-67, and "Emigration from Finland to Canada," 8-13.

15. In 1874 *Uusi Suometar* and *Sanomia Turusta* published selections from a Finnish-language book by "Colonel H. Mattson" in which Canada was highly praised, *Uusi Suometar*, July 20, 1874; *Sanomia Turusta*, July 17, 1874. Mattson's reminiscences show that he had attempted to recruit immigrants to Manitoba, Hans Mattson *Minnen af öfverste H. Mattson* (Lund, 1890), 162. However, no names of Finns going to Canada can be found in the passenger lists for 1874, so it appears that this recruiting attempt was wholly without results.

16. Kero, "The Character and Significance," 97.

17. Hans Norman, "Swedes in North America," in *From Sweden to America*, ed. Runblom and Norman, 255.

18. Salomon Ilmonen, *Amerikan Suomalaisten Historiaa* 1 (Hancock, 1919), 127-48; Kero, *The Finns in North America*, 34.

19. This conclusion can be drawn from a study of the emigrant groups and their places of origin, based on the passenger lists for the early phases of migration; a common destination is a reliable indicator of the existence of a group. If, for example, we look at the beginnings of emigration from the parish of Parkano, we find that the first Parkano emigrants left together with emigrants from the neighboring parish of Jalasjärvi, where emigration had begun a few years earlier. In Parkano itself we see how emigration began in the northern part of the parish and gradually spread southward.

20. Finnish immigrants in Illinois settled chiefly in Chicago, DeKalb, and Waukegan; it was rare for a Finnish immigrant to Illinois to settle in a rural area.

21. Norman, "Swedes in North America," 249-52; Kero, *The Finns in North America*, 37-39.

22. The congregations belonging to the Suomi-Synod and the National Church kept careful membership registers. Missing from the registers are chiefly those immigrants who moved frequently from one place to another. In the first decade of the 1900s there were conflicts between the Finnish churches and the Finnish labor movement, and members of the latter generally did not belong to a congregation. Because a relatively large proportion of the supporters of the labor movement were from southern Finland (south

of the primary focus of emigration in Finland), church membership lists include relatively few emigrants from this part of Finland. Likewise, church registers do not provide reliable information concerning the origins of immigrants in those areas where the immigrants, usually from northern Finland, established Laestadian (pietistic) congregations. The clergy in charge of Laestadian congregations generally had relatively little professional training, and the keeping of membership registers did not receive much attention.

23. Adam Onkamo (in Minnesota), March 2, 1868, to Hannu Salla; letter published in *Oulun Wiikko-Sanomia*, May 30, 1868.

24. Henrik Mikkola, April 8, 1893, to his friend G. Rosliin, Institute of General History, University of Turku, TYYH:S:m:Satakunta:MER:XX:1.

25. Viktor Myllymäki, November 25, 1908, to his relatives, TYYH: S:m:Satakunta:SIIK:LXVIII:8.

26. K. A. Hemia, December 23, 1908, to Johan Riihimäki, TYYH: S:m:Satakunta:KAN:XII:3.

27. Kero, *Migration from Finland*, 177; Kristian Hvidt, *Flugten til Amerika eller drivkraefter i masseudvandringen fra Danmark 1868-1914* (Odense, 1971), 133, 348.

28. The passenger lists for 1905 of Suomen Höyrylaiva Osakeyhtiö, White Star, TYYH.

5

Local Patterns of Dutch Migration to the United States in the Mid-Nineteenth Century

ROBERT P. SWIERENGA

Frank Thistlethwaite in 1960 first encouraged scholars to explore the "true anatomy of migration" by placing the mass data under a microscope and identifying the "honeycomb of innumerable particular cells."[1] This chapter explores individual cells in one such anatomy of migration, that of sixty-two thousand Dutch emigrants in the years 1835-80. A comprehensive migration profile has been created for this population, which identifies each family and local subgroup in their Old Country communities of origin and traces to their final destination the 90 percent who went to the United States.[2] The relatively small overseas emigration from the Netherlands in these years and the high quality of the government records makes such an approach feasible, given modern technology.

Among European nations, the Dutch ranked only tenth (above France, Belgium, and Luxemburg) in the proportion of their population that emigrated overseas in the nineteenth century. In the United States they ranked a lowly seventeenth among foreign-born groups. The proverbial Dutch attachment to family, faith, and fatherland seemingly vaccinated the populace against the disease known as "American fever," except in a relatively few villages. The Dutch who did leave acted not out of desperation or a failed political revolution but in the hope of economic betterment for themselves and their children. Religious and cultural motives were secondary except among several thousand Seceders from the Netherlands Reformed church (*Hervormde Kerk*) who spearheaded the Dutch emigration in the 1840s.

Characteristics of the Immigrants

What kinds of people emigrated from the Netherlands?[3] The behavioral characteristics of the sixty-two thousand documented emigrants (out of an estimated eighty-six thousand emigrants)[4] in the forty-five years (1835-80) can be described quite precisely. Generally they were energetic rural folk of the lower rungs of society who had the most to gain by leaving. Four out of five were from the countryside and rural villages, and only one out of five lived in a Dutch city. Two-thirds were classified in the Netherlands documents as middling in economic status, and a fifth were needy (i.e., on the public dole). Only one in eight was wealthy. It is notable that 96 percent of those in middling circumstances and 85 percent of the needy emigrants went to the United States, compared to only 60 percent of the well-to-do. Of the wealthy, 40 percent opted for the Dutch colonies.

Demographic data likewise indicate the exodus of young peasant families seeking upward mobility and trying to avoid a seemingly inevitable decline in status.[5] The average age of all Dutch arrivals in the United States was 23.1 years, adult males outnumbered females by a ratio of six to four, and more than three-fourths of all immigrants left with family members. This high degree of family involvement exceeds by fifteen to thirty points the German and Scandinavian migration and reveals the Dutch as a "folk" migration rather than a "labor" migration of solitary adult males, as with the British and Irish. Of the emigrating families, two-thirds were couples with children, and the remaining one-third were single-parent families and childless couples. The average age of husbands was 36 years, wives, 33.5 years, and children of all ages, 8.3 years. These were young, still growing families. The average family size at the time of immigration was only 4.3 persons.

The religious makeup of the immigrants was, in part, a reflection of the historic religious geography of the Netherlands in which the majority Protestants dominated the nine northern provinces and minority Catholics inhabited the two southern provinces below the Waal River.[6] The Catholics were generally second-class citizens, shut out of political power. Most of the Protestants were members of the privileged Reformed church (the church of the monarchy), but in the 1830s a secession by more orthodox conservatives led to the founding of a small ultra-Calvinist church, the Christian Seceders (*Christelijk Afgeschiedenen*). Bitter government suppression of the Seceders, including heavy fines, imprisonment, disruption by soldiers of worship services, and social and economic discrimination, prompted many to immigrate to the United States for religious freedom in the mid-1840s.

Although the Seceders comprised only 1.3 percent of the Dutch population in 1849, they totaled nearly one-half (48.7 percent) of all emigrants in the initial phase of emigration, 1845-49, and 18.4 percent in the whole period through 1880. More than six times as many Seceders departed the fatherland as their share of the total population. A major reason that the Seceders were so heavily overrepresented among the emigrants was that their dominies (ministers) took the lead in stimulating, promoting, and organizing the emigration. Frequently, the dominies would themselves emigrate, along with the majority of their congregations. Over 99 percent of the Seceder emigrants settled in the United States.

Catholics, by contrast, were greatly underrepresented among emigrants. As the most traditional cultural group in the Netherlands, they listened when their priests strongly discouraged emigration so as not to disrupt their communities and risk losing control over their flocks in Protestant America. The southern Netherlands also was developing an industrial base that opened new jobs. As a result, Catholics comprised 38 percent of the Dutch population in 1849 but made up only 17 percent of the total emigration through 1880. Twice as many Catholics should have emigrated to match their share of the population. In sum, the religious configuration of the Dutch emigrants was as follows (in percent): Seceder 18, Catholic, 17, Reformed 62, other Protestants 2, and Jewish 1.

Occupationally, farmers and farm laborers comprised 26 percent of household heads, which was 10 points above the national average in 1859, day laborers—many of whom also worked in agriculture—made up another 39 percent (20 points above the national average), 21 percent were village craftsmen, and 4 percent worked in the industrial sector, mainly in textiles and small instruments (Table 5.1). Only 10 percent of household heads held white-collar positions as professionals, administrators, merchants, and clerks. This was 30 points below the national average. Blue-collar workers thus made up less than half of the Dutch labor force in 1859, but they comprised two-thirds of the emigrant labor force.

As one would expect in a preindustrial migration, there was a noticeable lack of occupational diversity among Dutch immigrant household heads, and *none* of the new industrial jobs is found among the top twenty occupations (Table 5.2). The three most common occupations—unskilled day laborers, farmers, and farm hands—included nearly 60 percent of the emigrant heads. Almost nine out of ten (86 percent) worked in fewer than twenty occupations. Apart from the top three, only carpenters and merchants accounted for more than 3 percent of the total. Merchants, clergymen, government officials, and teachers were the only non-blue-collar occupations among the top twenty. Nor does the pattern change substantially over time, at least before 1880.

Geographically, Dutch emigration varied greatly between the major soil regions of the Netherlands: the dairy areas of the west central area, the inland sandy-soil regions, and the sea-clay-soil areas along the North Sea (Figure 5.1). More than half (57 percent) of all emigrants originated in the rich clay-soil areas; a third (32 percent) hailed from the thin, sandy soil areas, and only 11 percent came from dairy regions (Table 5.3).[7] The dairy farms were small, single-family operations. Dairy farmers enjoyed stable prices, and technology had little impact, so the propensity to emigrate was almost nil. Agriculturalists in the inland sandy regions also had less pressure to emigrate, because land reclamation in the nineteenth century and improved soil productivity (due to the introduction of artificial fertilizers) allowed several generations of farmers to subdivide their farms to keep their married sons at home.

By contrast, the prosperous clay-soil regions along the North Sea coast of the provinces of Zeeland, Groningen, and Friesland led in the development of commercial farming, cattle breeding, and participation in international markets. Agriculture was highly specialized and the farm owners were more entrepreneurial-minded in the coastal areas than elsewhere. The clay-soil farms were especially large and prosperous by Dutch standards. They employed numerous farm workers who comprised a landless proletariat. Formerly the laborers were part of a patriarchal and mutually dependent communal society. But with the introduction of capitalist economics in the eighteenth century, farmers sought higher profits by changing from stock raising to grain farming, by introducing scientific agricultural practices, by consolidating ancient holdings, and by cutting the work force and reducing farm workers to the status of independent day laborers. The laborers, who had formerly been members of the farmer's family group, became strangers to be hired as needed during peak seasons of planting and harvesting. The workers thus became especially vulnerable to periodic food crises. This occurred in the mid-1800s when rising potato and grain prices brought hunger to the farmers.

These distressed workers, forever immortalized in Vincent Van Gogh's painting "The Potato Eaters," were thus the prime candidates for overseas migration. More than 80 percent of all emigrant farm laborers originated in the clay-soil regions, compared to only 24 percent of the farmer emigrants (Table 5.3). In sharp contrast, 65 percent of the emigrant farmers tilled sandy soil, compared to only 16 percent of the farm laborers. More than three-quarters of all emigrant un-

Table 5.1. Occupations by Industrial Sector, Dutch Emigrants, 1835-80

Sector	1835-57		1858-68		1869-80		Total	
	Row N	Row Percent	Row N	Row Percent	Row N	Row Percent	Row N	Col. Percent
Primary								
Farmers	1,245	44	779	28	813	29	2,837	16
Farm laborers	540	31	465	27	738	42	1,743	10
								26
Secondary								
Preindustrial crafts:								
Building trades	653	43	371	25	484	32	1,508	8
Food processors	261	33	295	37	235	30	791	4
Metal workers	162	49	76	23	93	28	331	2
Wood workers	487	49	234	23	273	23	994	5
Clothing trades	148	40	113	30	112	30	373	2
								21

Industrial:							
Textiles	160	60	56	21	49	18	265	2
Iron and steel	6	35	5	29	6	35	17	0
Engineers	14	37	12	32	12	32	38	0
Watch/instrument	134	38	96	27	122	35	352	2
Printers	4	16	11	44	11	40	26	0
Misc.	14	25	17	30	26	46	57	0
								4
Laborers (unspecified)	2,176	31	2,256	32	2,673	38	7,105	39
Tertiary								
Clerical	24	19	41	32	64	50	129	1
Commercial	310	37	218	26	300	36	828	4
Officials, government	31	15	98	46	82	39	211	1
Professional	148	26	212	38	199	36	559	3
Gentlemen/students	44	44	25	25	31	31	100	1
Service	29	52	10	18	17	30	56	0
								10

Source: Robert P. Swierenga, Dutch Emigrants data file.

The 2,043 individuals with no occupation, trade, or unemployed are excluded. The categories are those employed by Charlotte Erickson, "Emigration from the British Isles to the U.S.A. in 1831," *Population Studies* 35 (July 1981): 175-97, Tables 11, 13, 14, 15.

Table 5.2 Twenty Most Frequently Listed Occupations, Dutch Emigrant
Males, 20 Years and Older, 1835-80

Rank	Occupations	N	Cumulative Percentage	Rank 1835-57	Rank* 1858-68	Rank† 1869-80
1	Laborer	5,712	36	1	1	1
2	Farmer	2,668	53	2	2	2
3	Carpenter	880	58	3	4	3
4	Farmhand	851	63	4	3	4
5	Merchant	580	67	5	5	5
6	Tailor	356	69	6	9.5	7
7	Shoemaker	343	71	7	11	8
8	Sailor	287	73	11	8	6
9	Baker	275	75	9	12	9
10	Blacksmith	257	77	10	14	10
11	Weaver	234	78	8	13	18
12	Soldier	200	79	11	5	17
13.5	Clergyman	198	80	14	9.5	13.5
13.5	Painter	198	81	12	16	11
15	Mason	175	82	13	18	13.5
16	Govt. official	166	83	21	7	12
17	Teacher	154	84	15	15	15
18	Miller	115	85	16	21.5	19
19	Clerk	101	86	23	17	16
20	Wagonmaker	88	86	18	19	20

Source: R. P. Swierenga, Netherlands Emigration data file.
* Period 1-Period 2 R_s = .61   p < .01.
† Period 1-Period 2 R_s = .74   p < .001.

skilled laborers also left from sea-clay areas. Many of these likely
worked in agriculture or related industries.

This displaced agricultural work force had two options—migrate
to Dutch cities and seek factory jobs or go to another country needing
farm hands and offering the prospect of land ownership. The generous
American land policy in the mid-nineteenth century made the second
option more attractive than the first, especially for peasants who preferred a rural way of life. Moreover, factory jobs were scarce because
the industrial revolution in the Netherlands was delayed until after
1900. Thus, emigration was the only viable choice for the surplus
rural laborers.

Nor were many disappointed in the United States. A comparison
of the last occupation in the Netherlands with the occupations recorded in the U.S. population censuses within ten, twenty, and thirty
years after immigration shows that most of the farm laborers, day

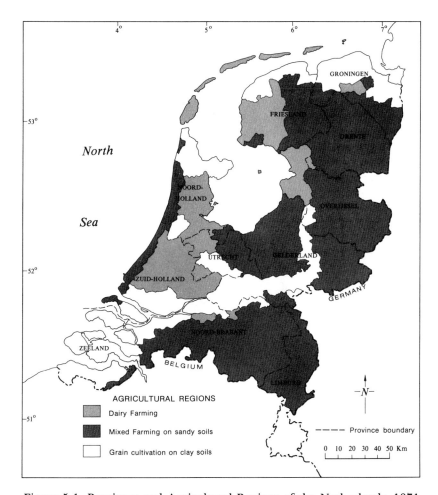

Figure 5.1. Provinces and Agricultural Regions of the Netherlands, 1871

laborers, and the jobless became farmers.[8] In the first immigrant cohort, 1841-50, 48 percent of the farm laborers became farm operators by 1850 (i.e., within ten years), and by 1860, 90 percent were farmers (Table 5.4). Of the unskilled nonfarm laborers in this first cohort, 36 percent were farming by 1850, 60 percent by 1860, and 76 percent by 1870 (i.e., within thirty years). Of the jobless male household heads or adult singles in this cohort, 59 percent were farmers in 1850, 72 percent in 1860, and 78 percent in 1870.

For the second immigrant cohort, 1851-60, farm-making opportunities lessened slightly; only 35 percent of the farm laborers became

Table 5.3. Occupational Class by Economic Region, Dutch Emigrant
Household Heads and Solitaries, 1835-1880

Occupational Class*	Economic Region							
	Dairy Area		Sandy Soils		Clay Soils		Row Totals	
	N	%	N	%	N	%	N	%
High white collar[†]	176	24	251	34	312	42	739	4
Low white collar[‡]	370	31	286	24	524	44	1,180	6
Farmer	278	10	1,828	66	679	24	2,785	15
Farm laborer	27	2	223	16	1,117	82	1,367	7
Skilled/semi-skilled	775	17	1,711	38	1,989	44	4,475	24
Unskilled	337	4	1,513	20	5,893	76	7,743	42
Column totals	1,963	11	5,812	32	10,514	57	18,289	98

$X^2 < .001$ C = .43

Source: R. P. Swierenga, Netherlands Emigration data file.
* The occupational social class categories follow the codebook of Lynn Hollen Lees, "Patterns of Lower-Class Life and Irish Slum Communities in Nineteenth-Century London," in Stephen Thernstrom and Richard Sennett, eds., *Nineteenth-Century Cities: Essays in the New Urban History* (New Haven, 1969), 359-85.
[†] Includes professionals, subprofessionals, owner-entrepreneurs, submanagerials, gentlemen and students.
[‡] Includes clericals, civil service employees, merchants, shopkeepers, and peddlers.

farmers by 1860 and 71 percent by 1870 (compared to 48 percent and 90 percent, respectively, for the initial cohort). Among the unskilled day laborers, the percentage entering farming remained the same within ten and twenty years as among the first cohort: 37 percent in 1860 and 84 percent in 1870. The jobless emigrants fared less well—only 41 percent and 44 percent, respectively, were farming within ten and twenty years (compared with 59 percent and 72 percent of the first cohort).

The third cohort, 1861-70, had the least success: only 22 percent of the laborers and 14 percent of the jobless emigrants were farming within ten years. Clearly, farmland in Dutch-American colonies was becoming too scarce and expensive by the middle 1860s to permit ready access by the later emigrants. Neverthless, these findings show a marked improvement in occupational status among the immigrants from the lowest levels of the Dutch work force. Many gained the coveted status of farmer. The dream of land ownership, which these people could hardly imagine in the Old Country, had become a happy reality. Only longitudinal studies, however, will reveal whether the Dutch farmers held onto their land during the financial crisis in

Table 5.4. Occupational Mobility from Premigration Occupation
to U.S. Farmer or Farm Operator, 1841-70: Dutch Immigrant
Household Heads and Single Adults

Premigration Occupation	U.S. Farmers and Farm Operators			
		1850	1860	1870
	N	Percent	Percent	Percent
1841-50 emigrant cohort:				
High white collar	18	33	33	31
Low white collar	55	51	44	56
Farmer	195	76	78	87
Skilled	181	34	51	54
Unskilled	183	36	60	76
Farm laborer	31	48	90	87
Jobless	37	59	72	78
	700			
1851-60 emigrant cohort:				
High white collar	14		21	36
Low white collar	51		31	40
Farmer	249		77	80
Skilled	290		28	35
Unskilled	489		37	54
Farm laborer	68		35	71
Jobless	27		41	44
	1,195			
1861-70 emigrant cohort:				
High white collar	17			18
Low white collar	55			22
Farmer	272			64
Skilled	262			21
Unskilled	728			22
Farm laborer	99			22
Jobless	14			14
	1,447			

Source: Compiled from Tables 5.4, 5.5, 5.6, and 5.8 in R. P. Swierenga, "Dutch International Migration and Occupational Change: A Structural Analysis of Multinational Linked Files," in *Migrations Across Time and Nations: Population Mobility in Historical Contexts*, ed. Ira A. Glazier and Luigi De Rosa (New York, 1986), 107, 109-10, 112.

American agriculture in the 1870s. In the Pella, Iowa, colony, which was a quintessential farming community, the farmers weathered the depression with little difficulty.[9]

Geography of Migration

Although the total Dutch immigration was relatively small, its impact on the United States was significant for several reasons. First, the Dutch who did depart had a strong "America-centeredness." Ninety percent of all Dutch overseas emigrants before the mid-1890s settled in the United States; the remaining 10 percent went to Netherlands colonies in the East Indies and South America, or they went to South Africa.[10] Only Norwegians surpassed the Dutch in the desire for "destination—America." This funneling pattern, like a megaphone, amplified the Dutch visibility in America.

Netherlanders also had a greater presence in the United States than their numbers warranted because of their clustered settlements. By the time of the 1870 census, twenty-five years after immigration began in earnest, 59 percent of all the Dutch born resided in only twenty-two counties in seven midwestern and two mid-Atlantic seaboard states (38 percent lived in only forty-six rural townships or city wards).[11] The primary settlement field was within a fifty-mile radius of the southern Lake Michigan shoreline from Muskegon, Grand Rapids, Holland, and Kalamazoo on the east to Chicago, Milwaukee, Sheboygan, and Green Bay on the west side (Figure 5.2). Secondary settlement areas were in central Iowa, southeastern Minnesota, and the New York City region including northern New Jersey (Figure 5.3). Subsequently, of course, the Dutch dispersed themselves over a wider area of the Great Plains and Far West in search of cheap farm land. But few immigrant groups, if any, have clustered more than the Dutch. Thus, in spite of a relatively weak volume of overseas migration, the Dutch single-mindedness for the United States and their clannish settlement behavior created a choice environment in which to nurture and sustain a strong sense of "Dutchness" for many generations.

Settlement Behavior

Dutch immigrants carried a traditional familism and localism to America as part of their cultural baggage. Like other European peasants from areas generally isolated from the forces of the industrial revolution, Dutch immigrants valued an ordered, traditional society based on kinship, village, and church. When these people emigrated, and this is especially true of the Calvinists, they sought to transplant their village cultures, churches, and kin networks. Most were not innovators seeking to break free of their identity group, but conservatives intending to maintain their culture in a new environment.

Group identity and the desire for religious and cultural maintenance dictated settlement in segregated communities on the frontier or in urban neighborhoods.[12]

Because Dutch immigrants from the same Old Country villages preferred to settle together in order to lessen the emotional shock of leaving the homeland and to facilitate the adjustment to a new environment, provincial or local loyalties remained strong in most settlements in the United States, at least until the first generation passed from the scene. In the classic example of this phenomenon, nearly every village and town in half a dozen townships surrounding the largest Dutch colony of Holland in Ottawa County, Michigan, boasted a Dutch place-name derived from the province or town where most of the first settlers originated. The central city of Holland, founded in 1847 under the leadership of Dominie Albertus C. Van Raalte, consisted largely of people from Gelderland and Overijssel provinces. New arrivals soon founded villages within a ten-mile radius bearing provincial and municipal names of their places of origin where they spoke the local dialect and perpetuated dress and food customs. The entire settlement was know as *de Kolonie,* but it required the passing of the first generation before the colony became a community.

Holland's sister colony of Pella, Iowa, also founded in 1847 by Dominie Henry P. Scholte, similarly had its cultural divisions. Settlers from the large cities of Utrecht and Amsterdam lived in or near the village center, while on the periphery was the "Frisian Neighborhood" northwest of town, the hamlet of Kockengen to the north for people from that village in Utrecht Province, and the Herwijnen neighborhood of those from the village of that name in Gelderland Province. The entire colony consisted initially of religious Seceders from the Netherlands Reformed church, yet their provincial differences caused friction for many years, despite a shared religious bond.[13]

In frontier settlements in the 1880s and 1890s, new Dutch immigrants continued to perpetuate such provincial distinctions. In Charles Mix County, South Dakota, for example, a group of Calvinist immigrants from the provinces of Friesland and Overijssel in 1883 established separate communities five miles apart, bearing the names of their respective provinces. Each insisted on their own church congregation and edifice, although they belonged to the same denomination and shared a minister between them.[14]

In American cities and villages that predated Dutch occupancy, the new immigrants likewise clustered in neighborhoods with kin and friends. In Grand Rapids, the quintessential Dutch-American large city where 40 percent of the population was of Dutch birth or ancestry

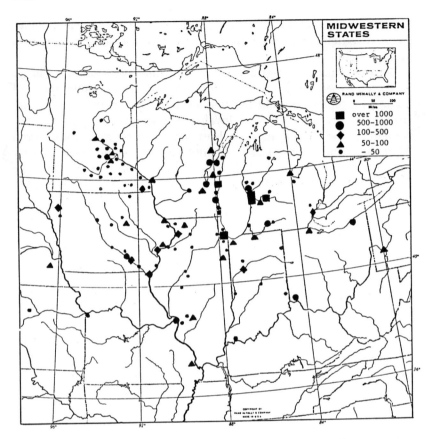

Figure 5.2. Dutch-born in Midwestern States, 1870

in 1900 (the largest population of Dutch in any American city over twenty-five thousand), the Dutch isolated themselves not only from the west-side Poles but also from other Dutch. David Vanderstel, in his doctoral dissertation on the Dutch in Grand Rapids from 1850 to 1900, identified twelve distinct neighborhoods, each composed mainly of immigrants from certain communities and regions in the Netherlands. As Vanderstel stated: "Even though each neighborhood could easily be characterized as a 'little Holland,' it would be more accurate to identify each residential cluster as a 'little Zeeland,' 'little Groningen,' or 'little Friesland,' thereby affirming the provinciality of the particular settlements."[15] Not only did immigrants from the same province settle together, they often hailed from the same villages. Even later moves within the city were often dictated by these con-

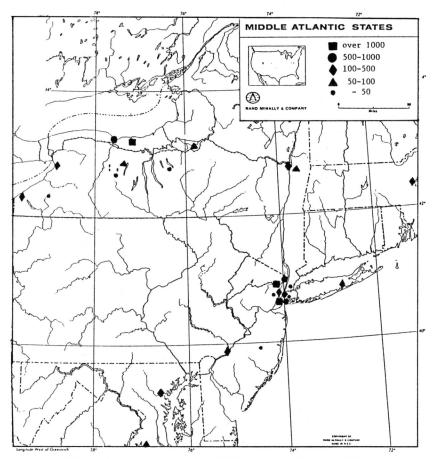

Figure 5.3. Dutch-born in Middle Atlantic States, 1870

nections; only one-fourth of the families that moved within the city left their own neighborhoods. The magnet at the center of each locality was the church where the people could worship in the old way in the Dutch language, and even be served in many instances by pastors called from their home villages in the Old Country.

Migration Streams

The linked Netherlands emigration and U.S. census file allows for the analyses of both sending and receiving communities. Emigrants from each Dutch locale were traced to their destinations in order to find the geographic migration streams throughout the Netherlands.

Figure 5.4 provides a map of the Netherlands showing the historic cultural-geographical regions.

Zeeland Province in the southwest had the greatest overseas emigration, both in raw numbers (14,296) and per capita (87.8 per 1,000 average population). Geographically, Zeeland consisted of three distinct regions; Zeeuws Vlaanderen on the Belgian border to the south with 5,300 emigrants, and two island clusters: Walcheren-Beveland (Zuid and Noord) lying between the Eastern and Western Schelde rivers with five thousand emigrants, and Schouwen-Duiveland-Tholen lying north of the Eastern Schelde with three thousand emigrants.

The Western Schelde served as a clear demarcation line—emigrants to the south went primarily to New York and Wisconsin and those to the north went to Michigan. Two-thirds of the emigrants from Zeeuws Vlaanderen settled in Rochester, Clymer, and Buffalo, New York, and one-third settled in southeastern Wisconsin (mainly Oostburg, Sheboygan, Alto, and Milwaukee). Two-thirds of all Zeelanders in New York originated in Zeeuws Vlaanderen; one-third hailed from only three municipalities (similar to U.S. townships)— Groede, Zuidzande, and Cadzand. In Wisconsin, 15 percent of the Zeelanders came from one municipality, West Kapelle (Walcheren). Zeelanders from north of the Western Schelde went almost exclusively to Zeeland, Michigan, but no one place of origin dominated. Indeed, sixty-six municipalities contributed at least one emigrant to the Michigan frontier, led by Zierikzee and Goes. Despite the many villages represented, the emigrants shared a common religious bond—most were persecuted Seceders.

The province of Zuid Holland, to the north of Zeeland, is one of three urban provinces (with Noord Holland and Utrecht). It includes Rotterdam, the government center of The Hague, and such historic cities as Dordrecht, Delft, and Gouda. Emigration from Zuid Holland was minimal (7,500 persons) and centered in two rural localities where Seceders were concentrated: (1) the island of Goeree-Overflakke south of the Haringvliet on the North Sea, which was tied economically and culturally to the Zeeland islands; and (2) the regions of the Hoeksche Waard and Ablasserwaard, which were wheat-growing areas "between the rivers," the Lek, Waal, and Maas.

The island of Goeree-Overflakke, centered at Middelharnis, had 4,200 emigrants, fully 56 percent of all emigrants from the entire province. This poor, isolated, and thinly soiled island had the highest per-capita emigration in the Netherlands; indeed, it was three times higher than anywhere else. The village of Ouddorp in the Goeree region had 1,840 emigrants between 1835 and 1880 for a rate of

1. Lauwers Zee
2. Achterhoek
3. Zeeland
4. Uden
5. Boekel
6. Roermond
7. Zeeuws Vlaanderen
8. Western Schelde
9. Eastern Schelde
10. Goeree-Overflakke
11. Utrecht
12. Amsterdam
13. Geestmer Ambacht
14. Den Helder
15. Harlingen
16. Barradeel
17. Ferwerderadeel
18. West Dongeradeel
19. Oost Dongeradeel

Figure 5.4
Historical-Geographical Landscape
of the Netherlands

Source: H. J. Keuning, *De Historisch-Geografische Landschappen van Nederland* (Gorin-
chem, 1946), 72-73.

716 per 1,000 average population from 1849 to 1878. From the
village of Goedereede, less than two miles to the east, another 942
persons emigrated, for a rate of 846 per 1,000. These two rates were
more than one hundred times the national average of 7.2 per 1,000.
Both villages and indeed the entire island suffered an absolute population decline in the second half of the nienteenth century.

The reason for the mass exodus from Goeree-Overflakke was a

combination of religious unrest and an agricultural crisis in the 1840s. The main cash crop, *meekrap*, a root processed in local factories to produce red dye for cloth, became outmoded. The loss of this mainstay forced the marginal farmers to leave. More than three-fourths of the Flakkeers settled in northern New Jersey (Paterson and Passaic), where they made up 92 percent of the Zuid Hollanders in the Garden State. This was by far the most focused emigration from any of the islands of the southwestern Netherlands. In total, 37 percent of Zuid Hollanders went to New Jersey, 24 percent (mainly from the wheat-growing Hoeksche Waard between the rivers) went to the main Iowa colony of Pella, 21 percent chose the Holland, Michigan, colony (especially the village of Noordeloos), and 9 percent settled in South Holland, Illinois (these were also from the area between the rivers). Thus, more than 90 percent of Zuid Hollanders settled in four colonies—Paterson, Noordeloos, Pella, and South Holland.

Noord Holland, the most populous province, contained very few emigrant "hot spots." Only 5,406 persons left for overseas destinations in the period, and fully one-third went elsewhere than the United States. Many of these were white-collar workers and skilled craftsmen from Amsterdam and the nearby cities of Haarlem and Zaandam. At least nine cultural regions were in the province, but three areas contributed the most emigrants: Amsterdam (42 percent), the rural North Sea islands of Texel and Terschelling, and the northern regions of Geestmer Ambacht and Den Helder. One-quarter of Amsterdam emigrants were Jews bound primarily for New York City and Newark, with secondary destinations in Philadelphia, Boston, Baltimore, Cincinnati, Detroit, Chicago, St. Louis, Indianapolis, and San Francisco. Many Protestant Amsterdam emigrants were Seceders who followed Dominie Scholte to Pella.

The small northern islands of Texel and Terschelling sent out seven hundred emigrants and in the decade from 1865 to 1875, these two islands had the highest emigration in the province. Texel's rate was 46 per 1,000 in the 1860s and Terschelling's was 66 per 1,000. This compares with a rate of less than 3 per 1,000 for Amsterdam and fewer than 6 for Haarlem. Texel emigrants showed a proclivity for northern New Jersey, where one-third settled. Another fifth went to the village of Noord Holland in the Michigan colony. Terschelling emigrants favored the Iowa prairies. Some thirteen families (forty-five persons) settled in German Township in Grundy County in 1865 and seven families (thirty-four persons) went to Washington Township in Butler County between 1865 and 1869.

The rural Geestmerambacht region (some thirty to forty miles north of Amsterdam) and especially the villages of Schoorl and Zijpe sent emigrants mainly to the suburban Chicago village of Roseland, a market gardening region that became a Seceder colony in the 1840s and 1850s. Pieter de Jong, the schoolmaster in Schoorl, led a group of fourteen families to Roseland in 1849. Only four of the fourteen families were not interrelated.

The distribution of Noord Hollanders in the United States was 33 percent in Michigan, 19 percent in Illinois, 14 percent in New York, and 11 percent in New Jersey. Half of the Noord Hollanders in Michigan originated in three municipalities (Texel, Den Helder, and Amsterdam), and half of those in Illinois came from the villages of Schoorl and Zijpe.

Utrecht, the third of the urban provinces, was the least important emigration area. Only 1,171 persons emigrated by 1880. The one focused migration was a band of Scholte's followers from the city of Utrecht who left in the first decade for Pella. After 1860, however, 80 percent of the emigrants from the province went to non-U.S. destinations, mainly the Netherlands East Indies. That the three urban provinces thus experienced only minimal emigration confirms a common theme in emigration research.

The northern province of Friesland also had a low emigration rate before 1880, but it became a major emigration region during the agricultural depression of the 1880s. Friesland had three agricultural regions: the North Sea clay-soil area from Harlingen to the Lauwers Zee, the western dairy region, and the eastern sandy-soil area of three-field agriculture. Half the Frisian emigrants came from the sea-clay area, where cash-grain farming without rotation was the norm. The dairy area had one-third of the emigrants and the sandy area one-sixth. The municipalities of Het Bildt and Ferwerderadeel in the center of the clay-soil region led all localities each with an emigration rate of 53 per 1,000, compared to the provincial average of 14 per 1,000.

The preferred destination of northern Frisians was western Michigan, especially Grand Rapids and the village of Vriesland in the Holland colony. One-half of the northern Frisians settled in Michigan, including 80 percent of the emigrants from Ferwerderadeel, 70 percent from Barradeel, and 60 percent from Kollumerland. The "Frisian Hoek" in Pella primarily attracted people from Het Bildt and Westdongeradeel. The remaining northern Frisian emigrants went to Frisian colonies in La Crosse (led by Opke Bonnema) and Friesland, Wisconsin, and Lancaster, New York.

Emigrants from the eastern sandy-soil area of Friesland preferred

Pella, where half settled. The remainder went to Friesland, Wisconsin; Chicago; and Lancaster. From the dairy area one-third of the emigrants were Mennonites from Gasterland, who went to Goshen, Indiana. Another one-third were Reformed, who settled in western Michigan, and 12 percent went to Pella. Frisians, always more independent-minded, dispersed themselves in America more than other Netherlanders.

The province of Groningen ranked second in the Netherlands (behind Zeeland) in its emigration rate of 41 per 1,000 average population. The three cash-grain regions of northern Groningen led in the emigration. The Hunsingo area was dominant with 5,900 emigrants (68 percent), the Fivelingo area had 1,000 (12 percent), and the Westerkwartier on the Frisian border had only 800 emigrants (9 percent). The early emigration was a movement of ultra-Calvinist Seceders, who comprised 70 percent of all Groningen emigration in the 1840s. After 1845, when the pace of emigration quickened, two-thirds of the emigrants were members of the Reformed church.

The preferred destination for two-thirds of the Groningen emigrants was western Michigan, notably Grand Rapids and Muskegon and the village of New Groningen in the Holland colony. The "Groninger Hoek" or quarter on Chicago's near west side attracted one-quarter, and the remainder went to Lafayette, Indiana, a farm settlement, and to Wisconsin. The Fivelingo municipalities of 't Zandt and Stedum were particularly oriented toward Chicago; one-third of their emigrants settled in the Groninger Hoek. By contrast, emigrants from the Westerkwartier municipalities of Grijpskerk and Zuidhorn went almost exclusively to western Michigan, but most nearby Aduard emigrants chose Chicago. The causes of these differing patterns is unclear, but it probably stemmed from the influence of early immigrants who enticed family and friends to follow.

The three eastern provinces, all sandy soiled, are Drenthe, Overijssel, and Gelderland. Drenthe was the most isolated and least densely populated province.[16] Nevertheless, the province ranked fourth, with an emigration rate of 15 per 1,000, double the national rate. The clannish Drenthers did not choose to leave; they felt forced to go because of religious persecution. Almost half of all Drenthe's emigrants were Seceders who came from fewer than a dozen villages that had become Seceder strongholds. In the village of Erm, 10 percent of the inhabitants emigrated, from Sleen 5 percent departed. Emmen, Bielen, and Assen, the provincial capital, were other centers. The mass exodus depressed farm prices in the entire Zuiderwolde region.

More than 90 percent of all Drenthe emigrants settled in the western Michigan colony, primarily in the village of Drenthe.

Overijssel Province, like Drenthe, had small family farms, but it also boasted a major textile industry in the Twente district on the German border, centered in the cities of Enschede, Hengelo, and Almelo. The emigration rate from the province was 12.5 per 1,000. Geographically, Overijssel had three distinct regions: a large central area of general three-field farming (Salland) from which two-thirds of the emigrants originated, the Twente textile district to the east from which a quarter of the emigrants came, and a small meadow area of dairying along the Zuider Zee (Land van Vollenhave and Kamperland) from which one-sixth of the emigrants came.

As was the case elsewhere, the American migration first began in earnest in the 1840s among Seceders, particularly in the puritanical and austere village of Staphorst. The Staphorsters followed Dominie Van Raalte to the Holland (Michigan) colony, and settled in the village of Overisel, very near the village of Drenthe. Staphorsters numbered 30 percent of the Overijsselers in Michigan, where they lent a particular flavor to the settlement. Roman Catholic emigrants from the Twente district comprised a second, lesser emigration, numbering about 250 persons, many singles, most of whom settled in Cleveland and Bay City, Michigan. These were industrial emigrants, skilled craftsmen, and white-collar workers, who went from Dutch to American cities.

The large province of Gelderland ranked second behind Zeeland in total emigrants (12,400) and third in the rate of emigration: 32 per 1,000. Gelderland consisted of three distinct regions: The Achterhoek (or de Graafschap) on the German border, the Veluwe to the southeast side of the Zuider Zee, and the Betuwe astride the Rhine River in the south. The Achterhoek was always the focal point of Gelderland emigration and even of Dutch emigration nationally.[17] People departed earlier and in greater numbers from the Achterhoek than from anywhere else. More than 6,300 persons, which was more than half of all Gelderland emigrants, came from the Achterhoek, and particularly from one community, Winterswijk, the seat of municipal government. The mass emigration of Germans to America in the 1830s and early 1840s directly instigated the Winterswijk emigration from the generally poor-soil area of small farms and cottage textile industries. Again, Seceders were the first to depart in groups from Winterswijk led by a minister, Lammert Rademaker, and a weaver, Dirk Meengs. Rotterdam emigration agents were active in the district, selling transatlantic tickets in 1846 and 1847 for $12 to $15. In two villages, Neede and Wisch, up to two-thirds of the Seceder congregations departed. These Achterhoekers settled primarily in Dutch colonies in western New York in Monroe County (Ontario, East Williamson, and Palmyra) and in Sheboygan and Alto, Wisconsin.

The other half of Gelderland emigrants came equally from the Betuwe and Veluwe. The Betuwe region, centered in Nijmegen, had the largest Catholic population outside of Limburg and Noord Brabant. Hence, nearly half (45 percent) of Betuwe emigrants were Catholic. A quarter came from Nijmegen and other lesser cities. These Catholics, 60 percent of whom were singles, scattered widely in America, but Calvinists from the Betuwe villages of Vuren, Kerkwijk, and Herwijnen went primarily to Scholte's Pella Colony in Iowa, and those from Haaften preferred Van Raalte's Holland Colony. Emigration from the Veluwe began later, after 1865. Those from the northern sector, called Overveluwe, went to Holland and Grand Rapids; those from the southern sector chose Iowa.

The two Catholic provinces round out this brief survey. Noord Brabant is a large and diverse province, but only the northern region centered in the municipalities of Uden, Boekel, and Zeeland had significant overseas emigration.[18] This area experienced the demise of the cottage textile industry in the 1840s and 1850s just at the time when the potato and rye crops failed. The result was a large group migration led by Father Theodore Van den Broek to Little Chute, Wisconsin, in the Fox River Valley south of Green Bay (in Brown and Outagamie counties). More than three-fourths of all Brabant emigrants settled here, and two-thirds of the Wisconsin Brabanters originated in only ten municipalities led by Uden, Boekel, and Zeeland, with 14.5, 9.5, and 8.6 percent respectively. The eastern part of Brabant had several Protestant regions; emigrants from this area, while few in number, settled in western Michigan (Ottawa and Allegan counties).

Limburg was an agrarian province characterized by small, inefficient farms of ten acres or less in which a cottage textile industry augmented family incomes. Struggling Limburgers historically worked as seasonal laborers in Belgium and Germany. Others moved to the rising industrial city of Maastricht in the extreme south. Only a few decided to emigrate to the United States.[19] Although Limburg emigration was low (1,849 persons emigrated, a rate of 8.7 per 1,000) and began in earnest only after 1860 yet it is also the most clearly focused. One can draw a line bisecting the province near the center immediately south of Roermond. Emigrants north of the line settled in Wisconsin on the fringe of the Fox River settlement of fellow

Catholics from Noord Brabant. Emigrants south of line, from the region of middle Limburg, went exclusively to Carver County, Minnesota, beginning during the Civil War years. The emigration from middle Limburg was so concentrated in time and place that in one municipality, Montfort, 13 percent of the populace emigrated in one year. An Antwerp emigration agent, Adolph Strauss, worked the middle Limburg villages, especially promoting the raw Minnesota land offered in large quantities by an Amsterdam land company. Nowhere else in the Netherlands is the local character of emigration so clearly demonstrated as in the demarkation line in Limburg between Wisconsin and Minnesota destinations. Never did the twain mix.

This discussion suggests that Dutch immigration, as European immigration generally, was both region-specific in origin and focused in destination. Each region had its own pattern of response, or lack of it, to the forces of change that stimulated emigration. In the Dutch case three main factors instigated an emigration tradition in the several regions: the religious schism in the Reformed church, the modernization of agriculture in the sea-clay grain regions, and the decline of the cottage textile industry in the sandy-soil regions. Where a migration tradition began early, it continued long and strong. And since moving to America was a risky and permanent venture, the migrants used the information chain of family, friends, and neighbors already there. As a result, strong links were formed between specific Dutch and American localities.

NOTES

1. Frank Thistlethwaite, "Migration from Europe Overseas in the Nineteenth and Twentieth Centuries," XIe Congrès International des Sciences Historiques, *Rapports* (Uppsala, 1960), 32-60.

2. The source files are Robert P. Swierenga, comp., *Dutch Emigrants to the United States, South Africa, South America, and Southeast Asia, 1835-1880: An Alphabetical Listing by Household Heads and Independent Persons,* (Wilmington, 1983); Swierenga, *Dutch Immigrants and U.S. Ship Passenger Manifests, 1820-1880: An Alphabetical Listing by Household and Independent Persons,* 2 vols. (Wilmington, 1983); Swierenga, *Dutch Households in U.S. Population Censuses, 1850, 1860, 1870: An Alphabetical List by Heads of Family,* 3 vols. (Wilmington, 1987).

3. The standard histories are Henry S. Lucas, *Netherlanders in America: Dutch Immigration to the United States and Canada, 1789-1950* (Ann Arbor, 1955), 44-58; Jacob van Hinte, *Netherlanders in America: A Study of Emigration and Settlement in the Nineteenth and Twentieth Centuries in the United States of*

America, ed. Robert P. Swierenga, trans. Adriaan de Wit (Grand Rapids, 1985); and Gerald F. DeJong, *The Dutch in America, 1609-1974* (Boston, 1975).

4. For a critique of the completeness, reliability, and biases in the Dutch immigration records, see Robert P. Swierenga, "Dutch International Migration Statistics 1820-1880: An Analyses of Linked Multinational Nominal Files," *International Migration Review* 15 (Fall 1981): 445-70, esp. Table 4, p. 461.

5. Swierenga, *Dutch Immigrants in U.S. Ship Passenger Manifests.* See also Robert P. Swierenga, "Dutch Immigrant Demography, 1820-1880," *Journal of Family History* 5 (Winter 1980): 390-415.

6. The information in this and following paragraphs is from Robert P. Swierenga, "Religion and Immigration Patterns: A Comparative Analysis of Dutch Protestants and Catholics, 1835-1880," *Journal of American Ethnic History* 5 (Spring 1986): 23-45.

7. The economic context is more thoroughly described in Robert P. Swierenga, "Dutch International Labour Migration to North America in the Nineteenth Century," in *Dutch Immigration to North America*, ed. Herman Ganzevoort and Mark Boekelman (Toronto, 1983), 1-34.

8. The information in this and the next two paragraphs is summarized from Robert P. Swierenga, "Dutch International Migration and Occupational Change: A Structural Analysis of Multinational Linked Files," in *Migration Across Time and Nations: Population Mobility in Historical Contexts*, ed. Ira A. Glazier and Luigi de Rosa (New York, 1986), 95-124.

9. Richard L. Doyle, "The Socio-Economic Mobility of the Dutch Immigrants to Pella, Iowa, 1847-1925," Ph.D. diss., Kent State University, 1982.

10. The information in this paragraph and the next is derived from the data files cited in note 2.

11. Based on my compilation of Dutch-born persons in the U.S. manuscript population censuses cited in note 2.

12. Findings indicate that transplanted homogeneous communities were the norm rather than the exception among all European immigrant groups. See John Gjerde, *From Peasants to Farmers: The Migration from Balestrand, Norway, to the Upper Middle West* (New York, 1985); Robert Ostergren, *A Community Transplanted: The Transatlantic Experience of a Swedish Immigrant Settlement in the Upper Middle West, 1835-1915* (Madison, 1988); and Walter Kamphoefner, *The Westphalians: From Germany to Missouri* (Princeton, 1987).

13. See, for example, the pamphlet published in the Netherlands written by the Pella pioneer Sjoerd Aukes Sipma. An English translation is Robert P. Swierenga, ed., "A Dutch Immigrant's View of Frontier Iowa," *Annals of Iowa* 38 (Fall 1965): 81-118. Cf. Van Hinte, *Netherlanders in America*, 150.

14. *75th Anniversary Booklet 1883-1953*, Platte Christian Reformed Church, Platte, S.D., 7-9.

15. David G. Vanderstel, "Dutch Immigrant Neighborhood Development in Grand Rapids, 1850-1900," in *Dutch in America*, ed. Swierenga, 125-55, quote on p. 131. This article is based on Vanderstel's primary work,

"The Dutch in Grand Rapids, Michigan, 1848-1900: Immigrant Neighborhood and Community Development in a Nineteenth Century City," Ph.D. diss., Kent State University, 1983, esp. chapters 4 and 5.

16. H. J. Prakke, *Drenthe in Michigan* (Grand Rapids, 1983), contains the story of the 1847 Seceder emigration.

17. G. H. Ligterink, *Emigratie naar Noord-Amerika in het Gelders-Westfaalse grensgebeid tussen de jaren 1830-1850* (Zutphen, 1981); Verena M. de Bont, "Ik druk voor het laatst uw hand in het oude vaderland: Emigratie uit de Gelderse Achterhoek naar Noord-Amerika in de periode 1848-1877," doctoral thesis, University of Tilburg, 1983.

18. The Noord Brabant Catholic emigration is analyzed carefully in Yda Saueressig-Schreuder, "Emigration, Settlement, and Assimilation of Dutch Catholic Immigrants in Wisconsin, 1850-1905," Ph.D. diss., University of Wisconsin, 1982.

19. Anja F. M. Koeweiden-Wijdeven, "Vergeten Emigraten: Landverhuizing van noord- en midden-Limburg naar Noord-Amerika in de jaren 1847-1877" (typescript, Venlo, May 1982). See also G. C. P. Linssen, "Limburgers naar Noord-Amerika," *De Maasgouw* 93 (1974): 39-54; and H. C. W. Roemen, "Vertrek uit de provincie Limburg naar overzeesche gewesten in de jaren 1851 tot en met 1877," *Tijdschrift voor economische geografie* 12 (1946): 372-76.

6

Chain Migrations from the West Coast of Norway

JON GJERDE

While traveling through the Midwest on a tour of the United States in the 1880s, Kristofer Janson was impressed by many aspects of American society. In particular, Janson was struck by how his countrymen in America had created ethnic clusters "isolating and clumping themselves together in colonies and maintaining their Norwegian memories and customs. I often had to rub my eyes," he continued, "and ask if I really was in America. . . . Farmers' wives plodded down the road speaking dialect. They had a church [which was] like the churches at home with a pulpit . . . and with a pastor in gown and collar. They sang Norwegian psalms and listened to Norwegian sermons. Was this America?"[1]

Janson's question was rhetorical, a variation on a century-old theme of Crevecoeur. As such, it was neither unique nor original. Even so, his observations underscore a lasting impression of contemporaries and historians alike: Norwegian settlements—like those of other ethnocultural groups in the rural Upper Midwest—were often tightly knit communities which practiced many customs from the Old Country. The transplantation of custom, moreover, was enhanced, especially in those many settlements composed of people who came largely from one particular locale in Europe.[2]

Such settlements, made up of those with common European pasts, were the results of migration patterns that sent people from particular communities to specific destinations. Scholars of the European immigration have repeatedly stressed the importance of information provided by family, friends, and former neighbors who had already moved in precipitating the decision to migrate. By providing not only information, but also encouragement and promises of emotional and material support, early migrants played an essential role in influencing the timing and destinations of subsequent migration. Particularly in movements covering great distance, such as transatlantic migrations, reliance on kith and kin was of extreme importance to the migrant. Since reliable information often originated from friends or family, the migration from Europe was directed toward them.[3] This behavior, labeled "chain migration" by scholars, influenced the volume of migration as well. Researchers, using national or regional aggregates of migration flows, repeatedly have discovered the significance of family and friends in influencing migration intensity.[4] Flows of information eastward across the Atlantic Ocean, in short, were followed by flows of migrants westward.

Yet throughout the European continent and over a century of immigration, the character, timing, and volume of migration varied enormously. In some areas, migrations occurred early and were undertaken by large numbers of families who considered their moves as permanent ventures. In other regions, migrations characteristically began late in the nineteenth century and were limited to relatively small numbers of unmarried men, many of whom returned home.[5] Given these variations, we might expect corresponding differences in the degree of influence exercised by family and friends regarding choice of destination. Unmarried men seeking to accrue capital, for example, might have found the support of family and community in America less important, because they tended to return home to Europe after a time. Even if a portion of these men did move to family and friends, one might anticipate that they would be prone to migrate again to locations where opportunities for economic success appeared even more plentiful. Finally, the timing of migration meant that destinations would differ in terms of geographical location and size. Those who moved later in the nineteenth century, to a more industrial United States, would be more inclined to move to America's cities.

This chapter uses individual-level data from two diverse regions on the west coast of Norway to explore differential migration behavior with particular reference to the chain migration phenomenon.[6] In the inland area of Luster, emigration began earlier and occurred in family units, whereas emigration from the coastal region of Ørsta consisted primarily of single men and women who did not move in significant numbers until the 1880s. The migration patterns of the two regions also differed in terms of the number of moves each migrant typically made and his or her ultimate destination. Those from the earlier migration were more likely to remain in their original settlement than were later migrants who experienced a high degree of secondary migration. And when the members of the first group chose to relocate, they continued to opt for the open land on the frontier or small market towns in the Upper Midwest, while the coastal immigrants generally located in major cities.

In spite of these differences, a significant segment of migrants from both areas created and maintained a tradition of chain migration. And most surprisingly, both migrant streams initially gravitated toward rural places in the Upper Midwest, establishing and continuing a Norwegian tendency to direct transatlantic migration to the countryside. Only after a period of acclimatization did the coastal migrants continue on to the cities. Understanding these similarities is essential, for chain migration had a profound effect on community development and interaction, influencing the character of relationships within the self-contained Norwegian settlements and also those between Norwegians and other nationality groups.

Migration Patterns from the Western Coast of Norway

The western coast of Norway, which extends from Bergen north to Ålesund (Figure 6.1), is one of rugged beauty. Islands of varying size dot the shore providing coves and inlets for fishermen as they prepare to harvest the wealth from the sea. Major fjords—the Sognefjord, the Sunnfjord, and the Nordfjord—originate at the sea and then cut into the rocky terrain. As one moves inland, the fjords offer stark contrast to the mountains above. The wide expanses of the coast disappear, and immense mountains seem to shoot out of the sea. Waterfalls plunge hundreds of feet down the hillsides as they continue their slow, inexorable erosion of the mountains of rock.

This juxtaposition of rock and water created two separate worlds for the inhabitants of the region. Near the coast, the sea's fish provided a means for a livelihood. As population increased in the nineteenth century, greater emphasis was placed on netting larger catches to supply a growing market; this expansion increased economic prospects for coastal residents, and it attracted many others to the fishing villages in hopes of enjoying the opportunities along the coast. In contrast, the mountain pastures in the inland fjord regions encouraged animal husbandry. Over time, although grain harvests and dairy production kept pace with the growing inland population, land ownership became rarer and rarer. Inevitably, more and more young people in this area were forced to work as cotters (husmenn) and nonlanded laborers in a society that ascribed status to land holding.

These two worlds differed culturally as well. Residents on the coast were more cosmopolitan than their inland neighbors. Fishing and commerce provided opportunities for increased mobility and exposure

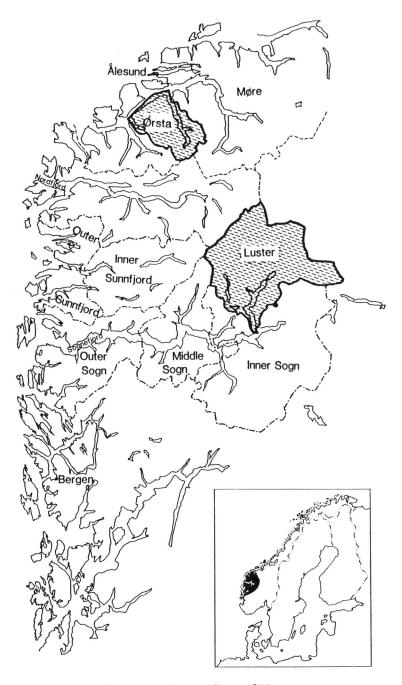

Figure 6.1. Western Coast of Norway

to the outside world. People on the coast were more likely to visit distant cities like Bergen and were therefore more comfortable in such urban surroundings. Within the fishing villages, too, residents were more worldly because decades of incoming migrants assured the infusion of new attitudes and ideas. The inland inhabitants, on the other hand, found fewer occasions to venture out of their communities, making only infrequent and reluctant visits to the city. As a result, they were more isolated culturally.[7]

Within this framework, the migration patterns of Norway's west coast during the nineteenth century are explicable (Table 6.1). Stated simply, economic conditions meant that people on the coast had less reason to move away in search of greater opportunities; if they did move, cultural dispositions and information networks led them to migrate elsewhere on the coast or to other major coastal areas in Norway rather than America. Nearly one-third of the migrants from Outer Sogn and more than two-fifths of those from Outer Sunnfjord, for example, moved to Bergen, the major city on the west coast between 1835 and 1855 (Table 6.1). Those coastal dwellers in Møre nearer to the growing city of Ålesund directed their migration there, swelling the population of a once quiet fishing village.[8] In contrast, dwindling opportunities to become landed led to massive early migrations to the north of Norway or to the United States. Nearly two-thirds of the migrants from Middle Sogn and more than half from Inner Sogn between 1835 and 1855 made the United States their new home, and nearly one-tenth of the migrants from each region moved to the "internal Americas" of north Norway's frontiers. Ratios of migration patterns underscore the varying destinations (Table 6.2). Although more than eleven immigrants from Middle Sogn departed for the United States for every migrant to Bergen between 1839 and 1855, the ratio was ten to one in the other direction for migrants from Outer Sunnfjord.

While coastal dwellers were generally attracted to Norway's cities and inlanders to other agricultural areas, some exceptions to this pattern did occur. One of the major sending areas to Bergen in the nineteenth century was the inland area of Fjalar and Gaular. These communes had developed close ties to the city due to a tradition dating from the eighteenth century of sending its young women to Bergen as nursemaids. Unlike those of other inland regions, residents of Inner Sunnfjord had fewer premarital births and generally lower levels of fertility, perhaps a reflection of new patterns of behavior learned in the city. The combination of knowledge of urban oppor-

Table 6.1. Principal Destinations of Migrants
(Regions of Western Norway)

	Bergen		Ålesund		North Norway		America		
	N	Percent	N	Percent	N	Percent	N	Percent	Total
1835-65*									
Outer Sogn	285	31.6	—	—	17	1.9	51	5.6	903
Middle Sogn	123	5.7	—	—	193	9.0	1,394	65.1	2,141
Inner Sogn	342	9.1	—	—	272	7.2	1,895	50.4	3,757
Inner Sunnfjord	684	42.9	—	—	—	—	121	7.6	1,594
Outer Sunnfjord	256	43.3	—	—	—	—	21	3.5	591
Møre†	14	3.3	200	46.8	3	.7	8	1.9	427
1866-85‡									
Inner Sunnfjord	921	39.2	—	—	—	—	851	36.3	2,347
Outer Sunnfjord	268	24.6	—	—	—	—	423	38.9	1,088
Møre	18	1.8	170	17.3	4	.4	574	58.6	980

Sources: Leiv H. Dvergsdal, "Emigration from Sunnfjord to America prior to 1885," *Norwegian-American Studies* 29 (1983): 127-58; Ragnar Standal, *Mot Nye Heimland: Utvandringa frå Hjørundfjord, Vartdal og Ørsta* (Volda, 1985); and Aage Engesaeter, *"Rift om Brøtet"? Befolkning, Ressursar og Økonomi i Sogn 1801-1855* (Sogndal, 1985).
* Sogn: 1839-55.
† Hjørundfjord, Vartdal, and Ørsta
‡ Møre: 1866-1900.

tunities and slower rates of natural growth resulted in lower rates of emigration to the United States.[9]

Although the coast responded to economic rhythms different from those in the inland regions, it too was eventually touched by "America fever." When the amount of fish netted mysteriously diminished later in the nineteenth century, emigration to the United States increased, approaching the level experienced inland. The demographic patterns of emigrants from the coast, however, did not parallel those from the inner regions, which were disproportionately family-based. Rather, the coastal emigrant patterns were similar to those already extant in the urban migration within Norway. Those who emigrated in the late nineteenth century were overwhelmingly single people, predominantly men who were much more likely to remigrate. The coast, in short, did not experience a family migration.[10]

Paradoxically, although the inland areas were more conservative and traditional than the coastal regions, it was in the interior that emigration first occurred. As information about America filtered through the valleys into Sogn, a tradition of emigration developed

Table 6.2. Patterns of Migration
(Regions of Western Norway)

	Ratios*		Rates:[†]
	America: Bergen	America: Norway	Migrants per 1,000
1839-55			
Outer Sogn	18	6	9.8
Middle Sogn	1,133	187	28.7
Inner Sogn	554	99	19.2
South Outer Sunnfjord	9	4	8.1
South Inner Sunnfjord	0	0	9.9
North Inner Sunnfjord	3	1	5.4
North Outer Sunnfjord	13	4	1.7
1856-75			
South Outer Sunnfjord	190	127	5.9
South Inner Sunnfjord	17	10	13.4
North Inner Sunnfjord	182	106	12.1
North Outer Sunnfjord	62	22	3.9

Sources: Leiv H. Dvergsdal, "Emigration from Sunnfjord to America prior to 1885," *Norwegian-American Studies* 29 (1983): 127-58; Ragnar Standal, *Mot Nye Heimland: Utvandringa frå Hjørundfjord, Vartdal, and Ørsta* (Volda, 1985); and Aage Engesaeter, *"Rift om Brøtet?" Befolkning, Ressursar og Økonomi i Sogn 1801-1855* (Sogndal, 1985).
* Number of immigrants to America per hundred migrants to Bergen and within Norway, respectively.
[†] Number of migrants annually per thousand of median population.

rapidly. Heavy migration from Sogn continued after the massive flows between 1839 and 1855. In the ten years after 1855, the region of Sogn as a whole experienced the highest rate of emigration in Norway, a fact made all the more noteworthy in light of limited emigration from Outer Sogn. Indeed, the rate for Sogn between 1855 and 1865 averaged more than seventeen per thousand per year throughout the decade.[11]

The inland regions, in fact, were areas of migration even before their inhabitants discovered America. As early as the mid-eighteenth century, people began moving to the less-hospitable yet unoccupied land in such northern regions as Trøndelag, Nordland, and Finnmark. And the migration continued well into the nineteenth century. One-eleventh (9.1 percent) of the registered emigrants from Inner Sogn between 1839 and 1855 during the incipient phases of emigration to the United States still moved north. In certain communes, moreover, the proportions were significantly higher. Nearly one-sixth (16.2 percent) of Luster's emigrants and more than one-seventh of Hafslo's emigrants traveled in that migrant stream followed by Knut Hamsun's ancestors.[12]

Chain Migrations from the West Coast

Regions within western Norway, therefore, evinced varying communitywide migration patterns. Whereas people from some regions tended to migrate to cities, those from other areas were bound primarily for America. Yet within each community, potential migrants were aware of numerous options. Given the multiplicity and complexity of migration opportunities and decisions, aggregate statistics of large regions in which the migration originated do not provide the specificity necessary to unravel migrant behavior. Rather, we must concentrate on the multitude of individual decisions to migrate. Because the direction and intensity of migration from western Norway was bifurcated into two basic patterns, moreover, each should be analyzed within a comparative framework. That opportunity is provided by community histories of two areas: Luster in Inner Sogn and Ørsta, situated on the coast. Each compilation includes detailed information on each individual who migrated, the social background at home, demographic characteristics, timing of migration, and places of residence following migration. The individual migration histories of 2,145 people and 842 migrant parties who moved from the parish of Fortun within Luster and 597 emigrants from Hjørundfjord parish in Ørsta provide an adequate population on which to base the analysis.[13]

Luster, situated on the Sognefjord, was the place of origin for one of the most intense immigrations to the United States. Like other inland regions, Luster's economy revolved around a transhumance farming system; like other inlanders, most of Luster's residents were landless poor. Although these conditions made Luster fairly typical of other interior areas, and although migration from Fortun parish in Luster generally conformed to patterns found throughout Inner Sogn, Luster did depart from the norm in some aspects. As noted, internal migration to the north, rather than outright emigration, was more significant in Luster than elsewhere, particularly in the early nineteenth century. Throughout the century, Luster's poor were more likely than its landed citizens to take this route of migration. Whereas just over one-fifth of all internal migrants were of the landed class, well over one-fourth (27.4 percent) of the landless migrants moved within Norway. Another departure from the migration patterns of

Inner Sogn in Luster was the relatively significant migration to Bergen. Fully three-tenths of internal migrant parties (30.1 percent) moved to the city or its suburbs in the century of migration.

In 1845, meanwhile, the first emigrants from Luster seized the opportunities promised by a new frontier in America. Thereafter, the United States dominated the volume and direction of migration. From earliest emigration until 1890, 3,031 people registered as emigrants from Luster; unregistered emigration probably puts this number closer to 3,300.[14] In large part as a result of this movement, the population of the region decreased from 4,428 to 3,276 people between 1845 and 1891.[15] The migration was particularly intense in the middle decades of the nineteenth century. More than two-fifths (40.5 percent) of those who would emigrate from Fortun parish moved between 1850 and 1865. The annual rate during that period, moreover, was 19.2 per thousand, fully two per thousand higher than the average rate for Sogn.[16]

In comparison, the commune of Ørsta, situated to the north of Luster, typified the coastal ecological zone with its very different patterns of emigration. Emigration occurred later in Ørsta than in Luster, and with less intensity because fishing opportunities offered relative prosperity and the nearby urban center of Ålesund tended to attract those who might otherwise move to America. Although an isolated group of emigrants did depart in 1852, it was not until fifty-one people left the region in 1882 that migration across the sea became numerically significant. Emigration peaked in 1887 when an additional seventy-two departed. Despite a belated bout of America fever, then, Ørsta never experienced emigration like that in Luster. Only in one five-year period in one parish did the proportion of emigrants top ten per thousand.[17]

Like most of the coastal region, the initial phase of emigration from Ørsta, unlike Luster, was carried out by individuals rather than in family units.[18] For every hundred people who migrated in family units, 414.4 left as individuals. The Ørsta migrants, moreover, were overwhelmingly young, mostly male adults, many of whom later returned to Norway. Whereas the sex ratio of emigrants from Luster was 116.3, for example, that of Ørsta was 212.2, indicating that twice as many men as women moved across the sea. Likewise, while boys under ten comprised 4 percent of the male emigrant population between 1866 and 1915, young men fifteen to twenty-nine constituted 86.8 percent in Hjørundfjord. Finally, of those who emigrated from Ørsta, nearly one-sixth (16.4 percent) returned home, 6.6 times greater than the rate of 2.5 percent from Luster.

Although the characteristics of the transatlantic migrant streams of Fortun and Hjørundfjord differed, migrants from both areas had a pronounced tendency to move to destinations where family and friends already lived. Many incentives enticed people to move to kinship colonies throughout the Upper Midwest; the most obvious was simply the information that earlier emigrants provided to those considering emigration. Letters that recounted the opportunities in a new land attracted many who had been left behind. On occasion, "Americans" who returned home illustrated even more dramatically the purported riches of America and thereby heightened America fever. A resident of Ørsta, for example, remembered that the visits of emigrants "so elegantly outfitted with topcoats and fine suits, golden watch chains, and other grand things" provided a strong incentive to emigrate.[19] The most graphic representation of this was the return in 1876 of Paul Pederson Sæbø, the first emigrant from Hjørundfjord in 1852. His visit home so impressed some of Hjørundfjord's residents that forty-four people followed him back to his home near Echo, Minnesota in 1877.[20]

Migration to clustered settlements also ensured the presence of material and emotional support to ease the burden of emigration. When immigrants arrived in a settlement, temporary housing was often provided for those who needed it. The communities settled by kin also offered opportunities to work and accumulate capital at wages that were usually higher than those in Europe. Indeed, emigration was often funded by advance wages in the form of prepaid tickets. Unmarried men looking for work were often found in settlements peopled by former residents of their home community. A group of landless immigrants in 1883 used community ties to search for work, moving from one settlement to another; eventually, they settled permanently in an immigrant Ørsta community. Economic aid continued. One immigrant remembered that when he arrived in the Echo community in 1892, "we could get all we desired . . . on credit only by showing that we were from Hjørundfjord."[21]

Because the immigrants from Luster and Ørsta moved at different stages in the colonization of the Upper Midwest, the location of their primary settlements differed and followed the frontiers of agricultural settlement. The early immigrants from Luster initially settled near earlier migrants from Sogn who had established settlements in Dane County, Wisconsin (Table 6.3). As land became less available in these early settlements, immigrants from Luster quickly seized the open land to the west in the coulees of western Wisconsin. In less than five years, a region along the border between Crawford and Vernon coun-

Table 6.3. First Place of Residence, Immigrants from Fortun
(by Date of Emigration)*

	Quartiles				
	1 (Before 1861)	2 (1861-69)	3 (1870-85)	4 (After 1886)	Total
Crawford/Vernon County, Wis.	52.3	52.4	51.6	25.3	45.7
Buffalo County, Wis.	2.5	18.3	3.3	22.6	11.3
Dane County, Wis.	25.4	5.0	6.9	1.2	19.6

* Figures in percent.

ties rapidly became the focus of migration.[22] After the first emigrant from Fortun parish arrived in Christiania township in Vernon County in 1853, emigrants from Fortun rushed to the region. Two years later, emigrants entered the townships of Freeman and Clayton in Crawford County and Franklin in Vernon County, which eventually became the center of the Luster settlement. By 1861, after one-fourth of the emigrants had departed from their Norwegian home, 52.3 percent of them had settled in the two-county area. A similar proportion of the emigrants from Fortun moved initially to the colony in Crawford and Vernon counties in the 1860s. As immigrants from Luster either moved directly from Norway or via other Norwegian settlements in Wisconsin, the population of the settlement swelled. An estimated four thousand immigrants from Luster and Årdal, a commune to the east of Luster, eventually peopled the region and formed thirteen Norwegian church congregations there. "Nowhere in America," wrote an early observer, "can one hear the resounding Sogning dialect so pure and genuine as here."[23] In the later periods, other land to the west beckoned to the emigrants. Nevertheless, one-fourth of the immigrants from Fortun after 1886 made the settlement in Crawford and in Vernon counties their first home in America.

Despite the importance of the settlement, emigrants from Fortun parish established other smaller colonies. The most notable was a settlement based in three townships in Buffalo County, Wisconsin, to the north. The colonization of the Buffalo County settlement commenced in 1854, one year after the first immigrants reached the Crawford-Vernon County site. Although emigrants in Crawford, Vernon, and Buffalo counties had moved from a common parish in Luster at about the same time, and although they settled only ninety miles apart from each other, it appears that the two migrations were separate. First, the farms of origin in Fortun for the two areas differed

(Table 6.4).[24] Whereas just under one-tenth (9.2 percent) and just under one-sixth (15.6 percent) of the immigrants who settled in Vernon and Crawford counties were from the Svensøy farm, for example, no one from that place moved to Buffalo County. Conversely, nearly two-fifths of the people from Fortun who settled in the Buffalo County settlement originated from the Hauge farm, which sent few migrants to either Vernon or Crawford counties. Second, the primary initial place of residence in Dane County differed. Those initial immigrants who colonized Crawford and Vernon counties had previously lived in eastern Dane County in the Koshkonong settlement, while the Buffalo County settlers migrated first to the Springdale area in western Dane County.[25] Finally, the social classes of the settlers differed. The majority of those who first moved to Crawford and Vernon counties were of the landed-farmer class, a percentage somewhat higher than the norm for emigrants from the entire parish. In the Buffalo County settlement, on the other hand, the vast majority of settlers were *husmenn* (Table 6.5). In this case, the axes of communication and migration were oriented not only spatially, but in terms of class as well.

Regardless of whether they moved to Buffalo, Vernon, or Crawford counties, the early emigrants from Fortun parish migrated within the confines and under the "auspices" of people from their home community. Between 1848 and 1860 more than four-fifths moved to one of the four major Wisconsin counties (Table 6.3). The intensity of the movement clearly lessened over time, but even after 1886, nearly half of the emigrants from Fortun parish first settled in Vernon, Crawford, or Buffalo counties.

The immigrants from Hjørundfjord of Ørsta also focused on specific regions of settlement. Because they moved later than their Luster counterparts, their destinations were to the west and north of the early Norwegian farming settlements of the Luster emigrants. The first of two settlements in west central Minnesota was situated around the small Minnesota River valley town of Echo, where many took up farming. In the Echo neighborhood, 40.4 percent of the Hjørundfjord emigrants initially settled in this area after Sæbø arrived in 1876 (Table 6.6). Another settlement area, centered on the town of Benson, attracted a smaller contingent. The industrial wood pulp mills around Marinette, Wisconsin, were a primary focus for the emigration from Ørsta parish, but they attracted a small contingent from Hjørundfjord as well. Like the early settlement areas of Luster immigrants, those of Ørsta became less attractive over time. Whereas nearly two-thirds of the emigrants up to 1893 migrated first to the three settlement areas, just over one-quarter moved there after 1908.

Table 6.4. Proportion of Emigrants Moving to American Settlement Areas by Farm of Origin, Fortun Parish

Percent	Total	Crawford County	Vernon County	Buffalo County
Ormelid	2.4	3.3	1.3	4.2
Øyene	1.1	2.2	1.3	—
Bjørk	5.5	5.6	2.6	2.1
Svensøy	5.5	15.6	9.2	—
Holmestad	2.5	8.9	1.3	—
Steig	.6	—	2.0	—
Eidsøy	—	—	—	—
Yttri	6.8	3.3	12.5	12.5
Skagen	2.7	6.7	3.9	—
Søvde	2.0	7.8	—	—
Optun	1.6	—	3.3	—
Berge	3.5	8.9	1.3	2.1
Fortun	11.5	13.3	10.5	8.3
Drægni	3.8	2.2	2.6	—
Fuglesteg	3.1	—	7.9	—
Furåsen	.6	—	2.0	—
Eide	8.7	2.2	7.2	8.3
Gjerseggi	1.9	—	.7	—
Skjolden	.6	1.1	—	—
Bolstad	18.3	11.1	18.4	18.8
Heltne and Rebni	2.2	—	.7	2.1
Skåri	.9	—	—	—
Moen	6.0	5.6	7.9	—
Mørkrid	7.6	2.2	3.3	39.6
Hauge	.6	—	—	2.1
Total	100.0	100.0	99.9	100.1

Note: Table organized to give a rough approximation of the spatial location of the farms. Those farms positioned near one another on the table are geographically propinquitous as well.

Despite the strong chain migrations from both the inland region of Fortun and the coastal area of Hjøringfjord, those from the coast were more likely to move again (Table 6.7). One-third of the immigrants who first settled in the Echo neighborhood, for example, later departed. In contrast, only 15.7 percent of those inland immigrants who moved into the eleven-township complex of the settlement in Vernon and Crawford counties left it.[26]

Table 6.5. County of First Residence by Economic Background,
Fortun Emigrant Parties

	Farmers (Landed)		Husmenn (Landless)	
	N	Percent	N	Percent
Crawford County, Wis.	49	51.0	47	49.0
Vernon County, Wis.	92	52.3	84	47.7
Buffalo County, Wis.	8	14.8	46	85.2
Total	277	43.6	358	56.4

If both the coastal and inland immigrants settled initially on the countryside, the former commenced a distinctive pattern of urban destinations in its secondary migrations. Nearly one-fourth (24.4 percent or twenty-two out of ninety) of those Ørsta immigrants who first moved to rural settlements in Minnesota before remigrating often chose major American cities from San Francisco to New York as their second destination. Seattle was an especially popular choice; as a growing number of Ørsta immigrants moved directly from Norway to the Pacific Northwest, one-sixth (17.8 percent) of those secondary migrants from the Echo settlement remigrated to Seattle. The development of an ethnic community then continued in a new locale. A church north of Seattle in Silvana was formed in 1894 as the area became a center for immigrants from the region of which Ørsta was a part.[27]

Those immigrants from Fortun who relocated from the primary western Wisconsin settlements, on the other hand, tended to move to other rural places in the Dakotas and Canada. The only noticeable rural-to-urban movement was reflected in the tendency of farmers to migrate to small market towns upon retirement. The clearest examples of westward secondary group migrations from rural regions to the moving frontier occurred from small peripheral settlements rather than from the large colonies in Crawford, Vernon, or Buffalo counties. Eastern Winneshiek County, Iowa, for example, was the first American home of seventy-eight immigrants from Fortun. One group of fifty-four who moved from the Fuglesteg farm in 1858 migrated as a group fifteen years later to Summer Hill township in northeastern Nebraska. An additional twenty immigrants from Bjørk farm joined the first group in the Iowa settlement in 1868, but they too moved in 1873, probably to join friends and relatives in Crawford County. These and

Table 6.6. First Place of Residence of Immigrants from Hjøringfjord
(by Date of Immigration)*

	Quartiles				
	1 (Before 1887)	2 (1887- 93)	3 (1894- 1907)	4 (After 1907)	Total
Echo community, Minn.	49.1	47.3	41.3	25.5	40.4
Benson community, Minn.	10.1	7.2	4.8	.0	5.4
Marinette community, Wis.	6.2	12.0	.7	.0	4.9
Seattle community, Wash.	1.6	1.8	8.8	12.8	7.5

* All figures in percent.

similar secondary migrations on the Middle Border underscore the
significance of family and friends in influencing patterns of movement
within the region.

We must avoid reification of the chain migration. It was neither a
thing nor a simple mechanistic response, but rather the result of untold
numbers of decisions by historical actors. And embedded within the
decision to move were the hopes and fears of migration and strategies
to maximize its benefits and ease its burdens. Unfortunately, we cannot
identify those strategies as well as we can recreate migration behavior.
Yet when comparing the immigration patterns of coastal and inland
residents, we observe the greater tendency of the former to drift to
major American cities through secondary migration. The more rural
immigrants from Fortun were less likely to relocate, and when they
did migrate again, they eschewed urban settings. That experience was
deferred to their children. Whatever the ultimate place of residence,
however, both migrant streams initially focused on rural communities.
The preference for the countryside not only influenced the migration
patterns of the immigrants, but it also deeply affected the development
of settlements and communities in rural Middle America.

Chain Migration in the Rural Community Context

Chain migration can be viewed from a number of angles. For those
who emigrated, the opportunity to move to a place already settled
by friends or family could not only precipitate the act of migration
but also ease the adjustment to the new locale. An alternative focus
is the effect of chain migration on residence patterns, community
development, and cultural adjustment in new settlements.[28] With this
approach, we concentrate less on the chain migrations linking migrants

Table 6.7. Percent Remaining in First American Residence

Crawford County, Wis.	85.7
Vernon County, Wis.	83.3
Buffalo County, Wis.	67.4
Echo neighborhood, Minn.	66.5

across space as on the impact of chain migration on the settled communities which the migrants form. Nearly half (45.7 percent) of the emigrants from Luster, for example, settled in the Vernon-Crawford settlement, but they did not comprise the entire Norwegian contingent there. Indeed, one of the central factors in the development of ethnic communities was the interaction *between* and *within* the different subgroups of the same nationality.[29]

The nature of this interaction is of profound importance in understanding development in the rural Midwest. Scholars have repeatedly stressed the significance of what Helge Nelson terms "kinship colonies" in influencing settlement patterns and community creation.[30] After their arrival in America, many rural immigrants remained in their original settlement and participated in community affairs. Social institutions, the most prominent being the church, were formed around Old World ties of nationality, region, and kinship. The community provided a market for trade of labor and land, facilitating the economic adjustment to circumstances in the new land. Thus, from the immigrant settlements—not only Norwegian, but also German, Swedish, Irish, and Luxemberger—that spread out on the prairies or took root in the coulees, emerged ethnic communities, the major focuses for economic and social interaction among their members.

That settlement patterns resembled an "ethnocultural patchwork quilt," therefore, is more than a colorful metaphor; a structurally segmented society was forged in the rural Midwest. Probably the most noticeable aspect of ethnocultural division was the strained interaction among nationality groups. Stories of conflict between Yankees and Germans or Norwegians and Irish are legion. Another component of community interaction is more difficult to detect but no less significant: the extent of conflict and cooperation within the settlements peopled by those of a single nationality.

A multifarious combination of migration and situational factors resulted in great variability of community development among immigrants in the rural Midwest. For example, three distinct patterns of interaction occurred among immigrants in communities of the Upper Midwest. First, those emigrants who were a part of a chain migration community accrued advantages—pecuniary and other-wise—not enjoyed by nonmembers of the community. In settlements such as the Vernon-Crawford County Luster community with its embedded networks of kinship, the process of cultural change was slowed, while the opportunities for economic and social interchange increased. Conversely, those individual households without close ties faced relative deprivation. Their members might marry into the community to enjoy its benefits. If they did not, these immigrants were more likely to move again than their neighbors who had close ties of kinship originating in Norway. Finally, settlements oftentime consisted of multiple chain migrations originating from various places in Norway. While each segment within the settlement enjoyed the community benefits within its confines, it also interacted with the other groups within the settlement. This interchange was both informal in everyday socializing or courtship, or formal in the formation of communitywide institutions such as the church. Although the community operated as an integrated unit, an underlying tension among the subcommunities often erupted in conflict.

Dwelling within a settlement largely peopled by those from the same community in Europe deeply colored patterns of interaction. Socializing in the form of visiting was often based not only on nationality, but also on regional background. Peter A. Munch, who conducted fieldwork in the Vernon County settlements in this century, still perceived distinct "gossip circles" based on Old World ties.[31] More formal social relationships, such as those formed through marriage, were also circumscribed by region background. More than half of the people from Luster who lived within the Vernon-Crawford County settlement married others from their home community, a proportion much higher than that of Luster immigrants as a whole (Table 6.8). As endogamous conjugal ties were formed in American settings, they enlarged complex kinship networks carried from Norway.[32]

Economic interrelationships were fostered by common European background as well. Opportunities for credit were often centered on one's background in Europe. Scholars have stressed the importance of these same ties, moreover, in facilitating land sales and opportunities for labor.[33] Information about economic opportunity, channelled through social exchanges, carried no financial costs. Although it was "free," the information nevertheless brought a high rate of return to those within the community who possessed that information.[34] Economic mobility thus was often achieved through the trust created by membership in such an ethnic community. Martin Bekkedahl, for example, was a Norwegian-born tobacco merchant in Crawford County.

Table 6.8. Place of Birth of Marriage Partners of Fortun Emigrants
Married in the United States by Place of Residence, 1845-1920

	Total		Within Craw-ford/Vernon Settlement		Outside Craw-ford/Vernon Settlement	
	N	Percent	N	Percent	N	Percent
Luster	117	34.8	71	51.4	46	23.2
Neighboring communities*	62	18.5	30	21.7	32	16.2
Elsewhere in Sogn	11	3.3	3	2.2	8	4.0
Elsewhere in Norway	74	22.0	15	10.9	59	29.8
Elsewhere in Europe	16	4.8	3	2.2	13	6.6
American†	23	6.8	7	5.1	16	8.1
Norwegian American	33	9.8	9	6.5	24	12.1
Total	336	100.0	138	100.0	198	100.0

* Including Hafslo, Sogndal, Lærdal, Árdal, Vang, Lom, Skjøk, Stryn, Jolster, and Balestrand.
† Includes Canadian-born.

By positioning himself "between the community and the outside," he was able to garner the trust of the Norwegian tobacco growers while becoming adept at marketing the product.[35]

Despite the advantages of community membership, a number of migrants did not move into settlements peopled by former neighbors or friends. Certainly some were connected by marriage or kinship to migrant groups of other communities. Yet some chose to travel without the succor of family and friends. We can only speculate on the motives for their behavior, but given their behavior in kin communities to which they were attached, these immigrants fit the mold of the atomized individual so popular in mobility studies of a decade ago. Not surprisingly, these immigrants from Fortun were less likely to marry those from their old home (Table 6.8). And because they did not enjoy the benefits of community membership, their migration behavior could differ from those who were a part of the community. In an area of central Minnesota peopled principally by Irish, Swedish, and Norwegians, for example, it was precisely those people who were not integrated into church communities formed around Old World membership who, independent of wealth or nativity, were most likely to move again.[36]

The most fascinating community interaction was that which developed between Norwegian subcommunities of different cultural backgrounds that came together to form a Norwegian settlement. On the one hand, those from varying regions formed a community based on common nationality and religion centered on the central cultural institution—the church. On the other hand, however, those from particular regions were members of a subcommunity which shared similar customs and dialects that often differed dramatically from those of the other subcommunities around them. Such situations could result in cultural conflict based on different attitudes. One settlement in Wisconsin was inhabited by a group of people from the region of Hardanger and others from districts to the south of Hardanger who were recognized in the settlement for their piety. After a house had been built by a Southerner, four Hardanger-born brothers who were skilled fiddlers asked permission to hold a house-warming dance. "But the Southerner didn't like this," one man remembered, "He looked at [the fiddlers] awhile and then he answered, 'No,' he said, 'we're not like the Hardanger people with dancing every evening.' "[37]

In spite of the inherent tension within such settlements, outright conflict was relatively rare. Few expressions were discovered within the Fortun and Ørsta settlements. But conflict did occur elsewhere. One particularly dramatic instance took place when cleavages based on regional background were expressed in the form of theological differences over the nature of predestination.[38] A segment of the Crow River Lutheran Church, located in rural central Minnesota, had emigrated from Gausdal, a commune in central Norway. In the early 1890s, members of the church were torn between differing interpretations of grace and the nature of predestination offered by leaders within the synod to which the church belonged. The majority of the community backed the orthodox interpretation which the minority claimed smacked of "Calvinistic predestination." The conflict grew so rancorous that the minority withdrew to form their own congregation based on what it considered a correct theological base.

Although the discord was centered on church-related issues, it was also emblematic of other underlying tensions. The people from Gausdal formed a clear cultural minority within the church community. Cultural practices such as courtship among the Gausdal immigrants were at odds not only with late nineteenth-century American patterns but also with those of the other subcommunities within the settlement, largely from coastal regions of Norway. Moreover, since the Gausdal immigrants arrived later, they held less wealth than other subgroups within the community. When a question over the interpretation of the nature of predestination and grace arose, then, it was the Gausdal people who made it an issue and ultimately withdrew from the church. They rapidly formed their own church which joined a competing synod and was named, appropriately enough, the Gausdal Lutheran Church.

Kristofer Janson observed one moment in a process of migration, settlement, and acculturation when he made his visit to a rural Norwegian community a century ago. He provided a small window through which to view an immigrant settlement. Clearly, his observation that farmers' wives spoke dialect indicates that they, like many immigrants from Luster and Ørsta, had created a community on the basis of a common past which had been preserved through intricately organized migration. Because Janson was writing about only one settlement, however, he failed to provide a comparative perspective of migrations and settlements from different areas in Norway. By analyzing two migrations with very different demographic and temporal characteristics, this chapter has attempted to discover variations within migration and settlement processes. However, there are many similarities. Both migrations were characterized by strong chain migrations to the rural Midwest. The later immigrants from Ørsta were only slightly less likely to migrate to their principal settlements than the earlier, more family-oriented migration among those from Fortun. They were more likely to move again, however, often to a major American urban center.

If chain migration affected the immigrants, it profoundly influenced their settlements as well. Conflict and cooperation, which characterized the immigrant colonies, was in large part the result of the patterns of in-migration and community development. Since the rural Midwest was composed of a complex array of ethnic settlements based not only on nationality but also on more specific Old World ties, moreover, those settlement patterns which arose out of chain migrations merit even greater emphasis.

Janson provided only one snapshot of the process, and this discussion enlarges the view somewhat; many scenes are still missing, and others are not fully in focus. Other comparative studies of migration patterns and migrant behavior would be valuable, and analysis would be improved if we could find more explicit expressions of immigrant motivations. Moreover, the process of migration and community formation continued. Whereas the Luster immigrants remained nestled in their rural communities, many of their children left for the big city. If impressionistic evidence is accurate, many also moved in a chain migration fashion. Yet even those who remained in the rural community faced a changing world. Ethnic identifications continued to change as increased intermarriage, attendance at the common school, and acculturation worked to alter interaction.

NOTES

I have benefitted immeasurably by the helpful comments and criticisms provided me by James Gregory, James Kettner, and Anita Tien. I would also like to thank Robert Angres for his help in data input.

1. Kristofer Janson, *Hvad jeg har oplevet* (Kristiania, 1913), 180.

2. Robert C. Ostergren, "A Community Transplanted: The Formative Experience of a Swedish Immigrant Community in the Upper Middle West," *Journal of Historical Geography* 5 (1979): 189-212; John G. Rice, *Patterns of Ethnicity in a Minnesota County* (Umeå, 1973); Jon Gjerde, *From Peasants to Farmers: The Migration from Balestrand, Norway to the Upper Middle West* (New York, 1985).

3. See Charles Tilly and C. Harold Brown, "On Uprooting, Kinship, and the Auspices of Migration," *International Journal of Comparative Sociology* 8 (1967): 139-64; Harvey M. Choldin, "Kinship Networks in the Migration Process," *International Migration Review* 7 (1973): 163-75; John S. MacDonald and Leatrice D. McDonald, "Chain Migration, Ethnic Neighborhood Formation and Social Networks," *Milbank Memorial Fund Quarterly* 42 (1964): 82-97; Rudolph J. Vecoli, "The Formation of Chicago's 'Little Italies,' " *Journal of American Ethnic History* 2 (1983): 5-20; Robert C. Ostergren, "Cultural Homogeneity and Population Stability among Swedish Immigrants in Chisago County," *Minnesota History* 37 (1973): 255-69; Hans Norman, "Swedes in North America," in *From Sweden to America: A History of the Migration*, ed. Harald Runblom and Hans Norman (Minneapolis, 1976), 256-61.

4. James A. Dunlevy and Henry A. Gemery, "Some Additional Evidence on Settlement Patterns of Scandinavian Migrants to the United States: Dynamics and the Role of Family and Friends," *Scandinavian Economic History Review* 24 (1976): 143-52; Michael Greenwood, "The Influence of Family and Friends on Geographic Labor Mobility in a Less-Developed Country: The Case of India," *Review of Regional Studies* 3 (1972-73): 27-36; Allen R. Newman, "The Influence of Family and Friends on German Internal Migration, 1880-85," *Journal of Social History* 13 (1979): 277-88; Mildred B. Levy and Walter J. Wadycki, "The Influence of Family and Friends on Geographic Labor Mobility: An International Comparison," *Review of Economics and Statistics* 55 (1973): 198-203; B. Lindsay Lowell, *Scandinavian Exodus: An Analysis of Nineteenth Century Communities* (Boulder, 1987).

5. The earlier family-oriented migration, often known as "folk" migration, and the later individually based migration, often called "labor" mi-

gration, have been observed in many regions of Europe. See, for example, William Petersen, "A General Typology of Migration," *American Sociological Review* 23 (1958): 256-66; Robert P. Swierenga, "Dutch Immigrant Demography, 1820-1880," *Journal of Family History* 5 (1980): 390-405; and Sten Carlsson, "Chronology and Composition of Swedish Emigration to America," in *From Sweden to America*, ed. Runblom and Norman, 131-32.

6. Ragnar Standal, *Mot Nye Heimland: Utvandringa Frå Hjøringfjord, Vartdal, and Ørsta* (Volda, 1985), and Lars E. Øyane, *Gards-og Ættesoge for Luster Kommune* (Oslo, 1984).

7. See, for example, Gjerde, *From Peasants to Farmers*, 133-35.

8. Standal, *Mot Nye Heimland*, 92-94.

9. Leiv H. Dvergsdal, "Emigration from Sunnfjord to America prior to 1885," *Norwegian-American Studies* 29 (1983): 127-58; Eilert Sundt, *Om Sædelighheds-Tilstanden i Norge: Tredie Beretning* (Kristiania, 1866; repr. Oslo, 1976), 447-88.

10. Standal, *Mot Nye Heimland*; Dvergsdal, "Emigration from Sunnfjord."

11. Andres A. Svalestuen, "Om Den Regionale Spreiinga av Norsk Utvandring før 1865," in *Utvandringa: Det Store Oppbrotet*, ed. Arnfinn Engen (Oslo, 1978), 76-77.

12. Aage Engesæter, *"Rift om Brødet"? Befolkning, Ressursar og økonomi i Sogn 1801-1855* (Sogndal, 1985), 122; see also Arnfinn Engen, "Nordland: Småkårsfolks Amerika? Trekk ved Befolkningsutvikling og Migrasjon i Nordlandsamt, 1801-1865," in *Vandringer: Festskrift til Ingrid Semmingsen på 70-årsdagen 29 Mars 1980*, ed. Sivert Langholm and Francis Sejerstad (Oslo, 1980), 53-72. Hamsun, a Nobel Prize winner in literature, wrote among other works *The Growth of the Soil*, a novel about farming in northern Norway.

13. Standal, *Mot Nye Heimland*; Øyane, *Gards-og Ættesoge*. Norwegian communities have a vital interest in local history. Most have commissioned histories which vary in focus and rigor. These two volumes serve our purpose despite their different focuses. Standal's work is a rich study of emigration; Øyane's is strictly genealogical, but he has included emigrants into the second generation. Because of their interests, however, some problems of comparison do exist. Øyane, for example, includes individual migration information on those who moved within Norway, which permits analysis and comparison of patterns of internal migration and emigration. Both studies include material on secondary migrations, so we have a relatively complete picture of the patterns of migration not only to the initial destination, but also beyond it. Because the collection of individual migration behavior was so immense, we would expect some error in charting the multiple migrations of thousands of people within two continents. Residences of people for short periods was probably lost to the researcher, so the dataset is most likely biased toward homes where the stays were lengthy. Since the data include information on death, however, I am confident that the place of final residence is accurate.

14. Most surviving data on migration behavior are derived from emigrant protocols or emigration notations taken by the parish minister. On occasion,

those in charge of monitoring migration from a region failed to do so, which resulted in undercounting. This problem was particularly acute in short-distance migration. Both Standal and Øyane take pains in using multiple sources to derive as full a picture of the migration as possible.

15. Øyane, *Gards-og Ættesoge*, viii.

16. Calculated from the population at 1855 as a linear rate of the total migration between 1850 and 1865.

17. Standal, *Mot Nye Heimland*, 641.

18. Ragnal Standal, "Emigration from a Fjord District on Norway's West Coast, 1852-1915," *Norwegian-American Studies* 29 (1983): 189.

19. Standal, "Emigration," 202.

20. Standal, *Mot Nye Heimland*, 262-63.

21. Ibid., 268.

22. Hjalmar R. Holand, *De Norske Settlementers Historie: En Oversigt over den Norske Indvandring til og Bebyggelse af Amerikas Nordvesten fra Amerikas Opdagelse til Indianerkrigen i Nordvesten* (Ephraim, 1908), 268.

23. Holand, *De Norske Settlementers*, 268.

24. Norwegian farms were nucleated settlements which could contain many households of varying wealth and status. Their population size varied, but they usually were much more complex socially and demographically than the standard American family farm.

25. Holand, *De Norske Settlementers*, 299.

26. We are examining the immigrant generation in both of these populations. If the proportion of people who left their first American home was small in the first generation, their children behaved differently as they participated in large migration to the cities.

27. Standal, *Mot Nye Heimland*, 348, 372.

28. See Tilly and Brown, "On Uprooting Kinship," 146, which hypothesizes that "migration under the auspices of kinship" tends to slow down "assimilation."

29. See, for example, Vecoli, "Formation of Chicago's 'Little Italies' ''; Donna Gabbaccia, "Kinship, Culture, and Migration: A Sicilian Example," *Journal of American Ethnic History* 3 (1984): 43-47; and Walter D. Kamphoefner, *Transplanted Westfalians: Chain Migration from Germany to a Rural Midwestern Community* (Princeton, 1987).

30. See Robert C. Ostergren, *A Community Transplanted: The Trans-Atlantic Experience of a Swedish Immigrant Settlement in the Upper Middle West, 1835-1915* (Madison, 1988); Rice, *Patterns of Ethnicity*; Arnfinn Engen, "Emigration from Dovre, 1865-1914," *Norwegian-American Studies* 29 (1983): 241; Kjell Erik Skaaren, "Emigration from Brønnøy and Vik in Helgeland," *Norwegian-American Studies* 29 (1983): 310; Sverre Ordahl, "Emigration from Agder to America, 1890-1915," *Norwegian-American Studies* 29 (1983): 332; Helge Nelson, *The Swedes and the Swedish Settlements in North America* (Lund, 1943), 64. The saga of Norwegians in the United States was set primarily in a rural locale. Indeed, few nationality groups were as likely as Norwegians

to direct their migration to the countryside. That both the inland and coastal communities were initially directed toward rural places underscores the Norwegian tendency to move to the country. See Robert P. Swierenga, "Ethnicity and American Agriculture," *Ohio History* 89 (1980): 325.

31. Peter A. Munch, "Segregation and Assimilation of Norwegian Settlements in Wisconsin," *Norwegian-American Studies and Records* 18 (1954): 128-35.

32. Robert C. Ostergren discovered a similar pattern among Swedish immigrants. See "Kinship Networks and Migration: A Nineteenth-Century Swedish Example," *Social Science History* 6 (1982): 293-320.

33. Jon Gjerde, "The Effect of Community on Migration: Three Minnesota Townships 1885-1905," *Journal of Historical Geography* 5 (1979): 403-22; and Ingolf Vogeler, "Ethnicity, Religion, and Farm Land Transfers in Western Wisconsin," *Ecumene* 7 (1975): 6-13.

34. Robert T. Aubey, John Kyle, and Arnold Strickon, "Investment Behavior and Elite Social Structure in Latin America," *Journal of Interamerican Studies and World Affairs* 16 (1974): 71-95.

35. Arnold Strickon, "Ethnicity and Investment Behavior in a Wisconsin Rural Community," in *Entrepreneurship in Cultural Context*, ed. S. M. Greenfield, A. Strickon, and R. Aubey (Albuquerque, 1979), 173-77.

36. Gjerde, "The Effect of Community," 414-21.

37. Einar Haugen, *The Norwegian Language in America: A Study in Bilingual Behavior* (Philadelphia, 1953), 2:358.

38. Jon Gjerde, "Conflict and Community: A Case Study of the Immigrant Church in the United States," *Journal of Social History* 19 (1986): 683.

7

A Pioneer Chicago Colony from Voss, Norway: Its Impact on Overseas Migration, 1836–60

ODD S. LOVOLL

A tradition of overseas migration to the United States was established early in many rural communities on Norway's west coast. The characteristics of this rural exodus varied, depending on local circumstances, as well as on settlement patterns in America. Voss, one such community, is a distinctive highland district, actually a large valley with several branches, located about fifty miles east of the Norwegian west coast city of Bergen between the Sogn region to the north and Hardanger to the south. Its expansive mixture of valleys, rivers, lakes, woods, and enormous mountain areas covers about seven hundred square miles within present administrative boundaries. The local humorous saying is that "The world is wide, but Voss is wider."[1]

In 1836, the year marking the beginning of overseas migration from this district, Voss had a population of about 9,400. No roads connected it to neighboring districts until in the late 1860s, when roads were built to both the Hardangerfjord and the Sognefjord. Transportation of goods in and out of Voss was in summer by pack horse and in winter by sled; people also carried heavy loads across the mountains themselves. It was an agricultural community, relying on the cultivation of barley, oats, and potatoes, and on cattle raising. Butter, cheese, and livestock could be marketed in the city of Bergen. Even the tiny village of Vangen, located in the center of the district, was dependent on farming as a main source of income; its most prominent resident, the Lutheran dean of the area, operated the largest farm in Voss. Others who lived at Vangen were a curate, a precentor who was in charge of the congregational singing and taught the children, an innkeeper, and one shopkeeper; a few artisans practiced their crafts in the village and there were many paupers.[2]

During the period under consideration, from the 1830s until the beginning of the American Civil War, a barter economy prevailed in the district, and people lived in self-sufficient households, satisfying as much as possible the material needs on each farm. The situation did not prevent activities related to capitalistic enterprise. Within the local agricultural system peasant shoemakers, tailors, and weavers, as well as blacksmiths, tinsmiths, and even silversmiths, provided specialized services.

Rapid population growth, especially after 1815, exceeded the community's resources, and farm production could not keep pace with the increase. Historians have determined that the community would have to have cleared from thirty-five to fifty acres annually to feed the growing population. Given the primitive farming methods as well as the limitations on arable land, it was far beyond the group's ability to do so. There were clear repercussions on the social structure. Within peasant society the main social distinction was between the independent farmers and the cotters, that is, the landless peasants. Population pressures were producing a downward mobility, so that farmers and sons of farmers sank down into the lowly cotter rank.[3]

Certain local characteristics and patterns of adjustment emerge which are important in a discussion of the American experience of emigrants from Voss. Historians, taking the practice of bartering for goods and services into account, have nevertheless identified considerable commercial activity and capitalistic enterprise in Voss, more so than in its neighboring communities. Within the economic life of the peasant community, with its self-sufficient ways, there were clear indicators of an emerging money economy. Business dealings and trade represented a response to inadequate resources. Vossings were thought to possess a special talent for commercial venture. The dialectologist Ivar Aasen, who spent five weeks in Voss in 1844, recorded that the Vossings "distinguish themselves for their high level of industry and ingenuity, and in many ways stand significantly above all other inhabitants of the county." Financial straits, frequently a result of increases in poor relief and other taxes and general hard times, were, however, the cause of many land transactions between 1800 and 1860. The frequency of sales was particularly high in Voss, some farms being sold as many as nine times. The owner might buy a poorer farm or might leave the community and move to the far north, to the counties of Nordland or Troms, where there was plenty of good land to be had. Between 1820 and 1865, 250 people from Voss moved to these parts. A tradition of migration which can be traced back to about 1750 to other regions in western Norway was reinforced by the later migration to the distant north.[4]

Seasonal work in the herring fisheries moved many men from Voss to the coastal districts and involved them in a large commercial venture. In this manner they established personal contacts over a wide area and received important information about events and developments elsewhere; it is conceivable that news of the first Norwegian emigrants who departed from the coastal town of Stavanger in 1825 was spread along the coast and brought inland to Voss by the men who engaged in fishing. Other local enterprise prepared people to survive in a money economy. Horsebreeding and the sale of horses was a significant part of the district's economic life, and horses were driven to distant markets. "Horsetrading has been a major business since time immemorial," the district physician reported in 1891, claiming that to a Vossing his horse was more important than his wife.[5]

A cottage industry provided the basis for an extensive trade. "Craftsmen prepared," wrote Knut Rene, a student of the Vossings in Norway and in America, "saws, scythes, knives, carding combs, loom reeds, bells, and finery of different kinds," and sold them to young men in the community who during the winter months became peddlers and carried these modest articles all over the country along appointed routes. As many as a hundred men from Voss might be thus occupied. On their return they became the center of attention as people flocked around them to hear about people and places they had seen; returned Norwegian Americans were later to become the objects of a similar interest about the United States.[6]

One might conclude that a sense of adventure, a receptiveness to new opportunities, and entrepreneurial attitudes and skills were encouraged by these activities. Meanwhile political reforms and popular movements gave the peasants increased influence and brought them into a direct political confrontation with the ruling official class of civil servants, the most visible local representative of which was the Lutheran parish priest. Local self-government was granted in 1837, a democratic reform that created local councils, albeit the franchise was limited to the propertied classes. Voss was one of a few of the 322 country municipalities to elect a farmer as council chairman (mayor); the others generally elected a member of the official class. Greater class consciousness in the peasantry in Voss is evident by the fact that in 1844 no member of the old elite was elected to the council. A religious schism between a pietistic laity and the ordained clergy of the official church encouraged peasant solidarity. Several memorable confrontations with the authoritarian district dean M. W. Münster occurred in the 1830s and were later reflected in the actions of emigrated Vossings; his attempt to collect the equivalent in money or kind of one day's work from all cotters at Voss during the harvest season produced a bitter conflict and much hostility.[7]

Münster held to a philosophy of rationalism and enlightenment which made him promote the education of the peasants and neglect their need for a more devout religious life. In a sense he thereby undermined his own position. Aasen, in 1844, commented on the many knowledgeable peasants he had encountered in Voss and their capacity for independent thought. Improved schooling gave the peasants not only knowledge but also self-assurance. Lack of religious fervor opened the way for pietistic lay preachers to gather converts, further alientating the population from the Lutheran clergy. The pietists were orthodox Lutherans and remained as members of the state church, but their religious assemblies were illegal without the presence of an ordained minister until 1842. A heightened class solidarity and assertiveness were also evident in conflicts with such temporal authorities as the sheriff and district judge. The pioneer emigrants from Voss carried with them a deep resentment of the social and religious situation they had experienced. According to their own testimony, stated in letters sent back to Voss, their dissatisfaction had influenced their decision to emigrate.[8]

The Norwegian-American Community

The early expansion of Chicago, platted in 1830, owed much to the projected Illinois and Michigan Canal. A great westward movement of people of European origin began upon the removal of the last Indian threat in 1832. In the account book of John Calhoun, who in late 1833 launched Chicago's first newspaper, the *Chicago Democrat,* the name "David Johnson" is entered on August 22, 1834. Johnson, a young Norwegian sailor who found employment as a pressman on Calhoun's newspaper, is credited with being the first Scandinavian resident of Chicago.[9]

An urban colony of Norwegians had its genesis in 1836, when a few families decided to remain in Chicago rather than continue on to the Fox River, Illinois, settlement, a three-day trek by wagons pulled by oxen. The early Norwegian-American scholar Rasmus B. Anderson called the Chicago colony the third permanent Norwegian settlement in America, with that at Kendall, New York, in 1825 as first, and that at Fox River in 1834, as second. One of the families to settle in Chicago in 1836 was Nils Knutson Røthe, his wife Torbjørg, and their three children. They were the first emigrants to leave Voss for America.[10]

Chicago was the gateway to the Northwest—a prairie seaport—and the port of entry for most immigrants. The metropolis became for most who landed there merely a dispersion point or at best a temporary home. But the city did offer immediate income to impecunious newcomers, many of whom stayed only long enough to save up money to go farther west to purchase or claim the farm of which they had dreamed. Although Norwegian emigration, like the European movement as a whole, may be viewed in the context of a general process of urbanization—a move from the country to town that was occurring on both sides of the Atlantic—Norwegian immigrants demonstrated a much greater rural orientation than the other ethnic groups arriving in American in the pre–Civil War period. While the Irish, for instance, rarely settled on the land, Norwegian peasants overwhelmingly moved to America to continue a rural way of life. A sufficient number did, however, become permanent residents in Chicago to secure the growth of a Norwegian enclave. Attractive employment possibilities, special skills best used in the city, or at times confining poverty kept people in the city once they had arrived. Later, when a community of fellow Norwegians stood ready to assist, many Norwegians headed directly for Chicago to take up permanent residence.[11]

Exactly why Røthe and his family decided to remain in Chicago, a place probably unknown to them before their departure from Voss, is unclear, but the fact that Røthe found employment on the Illinois and Michigan Canal was a likely reason. Many others worked on the canal as an immediate means of supporting themselves. Even though work conditions were unhealthy and strenuous, wages were attractive. Røthe was joined by many Vossings; from 1836 to 1840 about 120 came to America. By then it was said that there were more Vossings in Chicago than all other Norwegians taken together. They were referred to by other Norwegians as the "Voss Circle." In July 1858, the Norwegian-language newspaper *Wossingen* listed the names of all two hundred Vossings in Chicago, about 20 percent of the Norwegian colony.[12] Many were likely only temporary residents; a detailed examination might provide the names of those who remained in Chicago and those who eventually left the city.

Emigration was a structured and selective process; it was engaged in by individuals who made considered and realistic decisions about their own and their children's lives. Confining conditions caused by population pressures might make parents act to find opportunities for the next generation. Anticipated difficulties and a fear of a decline in social status could lead to migration, but no immediate hardship appears to have pushed the pioneer emigrants from Voss out of the community. Poverty was not a direct cause of early exodus; Norwegian scholarship has instead focused on the relative wealth of those who sought America in the period before 1850. Once America became a realistic alternative to traditional strategies engaged in by Vossings, they considered emigration as a means to advancing their material and social well-being. In Voss, the many sales of farms during these years financed the move to America; others, like Røthe who belonged to the cotter class, had saved money from various business and employment ventures. A Norwegian historian has claimed, based on quantitative as well as qualitative evidence, that to a certain extent the pioneer emigration can be viewed as a phenomenon caused by a modicum of material surplus. The immigrants were people who reached out for what in their judgment would be a better future. A broadening of the social base of emigration occurred only in the 1850s, when tickets and money sent back from America gave poor people of Voss the means to cross the Atlantic.[13]

The early emigration from Voss was not only selective in terms of economic ability, but also in regard to personal relationships. The emigrants were people who were tied together by kinship or neighborhood; it was a dispersal and a reunion in America. There is little doubt that many of these early emigrants from Voss arrived in America with an entrepreneurial attitude, which may be related to their capitalistic and commercial experiences in Voss, and which were best used in an urban economy. Some were peasant craftsmen with skills comparable to those of urban artisans. In a study of skilled peasant boys who moved to Oslo in the nineteenth century, the Norwegian historian Sivert Langholm has shown that in crafts with traditions in peasant society, such as carpentry, shoemaking, leather tanning, tailoring, and even fashioning silver jewelry, the boys did as well as craftsmen who had learned their trade in the city. A comparable development might be seen among the Vossings in Chicago. By 1850 the majority of Norwegian men were listed in the census as skilled workmen, especially in the building sector, as carpenters and painters. Language barriers and ignorance of the American market place prevented some immigrants from immediately practicing their trade. One of the early Vossing leaders, Iver Lawson (Boe), abandoned his trade as a tailor for this reason. By the 1850s, Chicago's Norwegian colony, which in 1850 numbered 1,313 Norwegian-born individuals, could itself employ people in specialized occupations. A case in point was the clothing store which Lewis A. Brown (Lars Anfinson Bryn), like Lawson a

peasant tailor, operated on North Clark Street. It was a popular meeting place for Norwegian immigrants.[14]

Most early settlers accepted whatever employment was available
and worked as day laborers. Of the fifty or so Vossings who emigrated
in 1839, "a number of them took work on the Canal, thirty miles
from town." An emigrant of 1836 was in charge of hiring newly
arrived Norwegians, indicating how immigrants were recruited and
obtained employment. It was necessary to live close to where work
could be found; early Norwegians squatted near the lake on government Canal land in a swampy and unhealthy area north of the Chicago
River known as "the Sands." The devastating cholera epidemic of
1849 hit the locality hard, and as many as a hundred of them may
have succumbed. The growth of the colony slowed as people left or
new immigrants bypassed the city. But Norwegians gradually moved
from this immigrant slum to more favorable areas to the north and
west. An immigrant from Voss, Kjel Vikingson Gjøsten (Kiel Williams),
who together with his wife Sigrid Johnsdatter and their children
Viking, Lars, and Ingeborg came to Chicago in 1839, exemplified
this movement. As Rene relates: "Like several of the other Vossings
he got himself a small house on Canal land, and in 1840 even had
saved a little money. Later he built a house near the cemetery, or
where Lincoln Park now is, and had a valuable piece of property."
Gjøsten subsequently sold his property. Many took advantage of their
property's appreciation and sold their lots to purchase cheaper land
farther from the center of town, where they might even engage in
light farming.[15]

Many Norwegians with experience as saltwater seamen became
sailors and captains on lake vessels; women who worked outside the
home became domestic servants. By 1850 about one-fifth of all Norwegian women in Chicago, most of whom were single, were thus
employed. Although this figure included some married women, most
in that group were listed in the census simply as housewives, which
concealed their work outside the home, at the time mainly as domestic
servants or laundresses. Synneve B. Fletre wrote back to Voss in 1843
to relate that she had found work as a servant for 50 to 75 cents a
week, but "when I become more used to the work and understand
the language better, then I think I will get $1.00."[16]

The most successful immigrants realized their wealth through property speculation; business dealings in Norway had prepared them to
take part in the purchase and sale of real estate. Realizing the future
value of Chicago they invested in land while they retained their jobs
as common laborers. "[They] came into wealth effortlessly under this

wonder city's fantastic growth," as Knud Langeland, an early immigrant, expressed it. Andrew Nelson (Brekke), for instance, who emigrated from Voss in 1839, invested money from meager savings, earned at first from working on the canal, in central Chicago. As in the peasant community in Voss, the family functioned as an economic unit, sons, daughters, and wives contributing to its income. Nelson's wife Inger baked flatbread to sell and used her home as a small restaurant; the single men in the colony were her best customers. The Nelsons eventually amassed a large fortune, as did Iver Lawson, who emigrated from Voss in 1844. After giving up his trade as a peasant tailor, he found employment wherever he could and early entered into speculation in real estate. A number of Vossings did remarkably well using the formula for success of hard work and the investment of frugal savings in property. Examples are Andrew Larson (Flage) an emigrant of 1839 and Baard Johnson (Rogne) who had arrived in 1837. Both Larson and Johnson had owned farms in Voss, which they sold to finance their move to America. Entrepreneurial skills could also be profitably employed in Chicago's large lumber business, where Johnson's son Andrew B. Johnson became wealthy. These men had an exceptional ability to take advantage of existing opportunities in a rapidly growing urban economy.[17]

The Norwegian colony in Chicago in the pre–Civil War period tended to be a homogeneous community; most of those who did not come from Voss were from the same general area in western Norway. A tight-knit group of people, their existence was based on kinship and contacts with people with whom they felt a kindred spirit. This in spite of the religious dissent and tensions which developed between the pioneer immigrants and later arrivals. Like the population of Chicago in general the Norwegian colony was composed of young people, but had a more pronounced family character than the overall population. Very few married outside the Norwegian group; many of course emigrated as married couples. In 1850, 94 percent of all married couples were endogamous, nearly two-thirds having been married in Norway. During the 1850s, a frontier colony of Norwegian immigrants slowly emerged as an important Norwegian-American center, prosperous enough to support religious and cultural institutions.[18]

The Vossings and Emigration Promotion

What was, then, the impact of the Chicago colony on Norwegian emigration, in particular on the one from the Voss area? Why, for instance, did so many from Voss settle in Chicago? Quite obviously we may speak of a chain migration. Once a nucleus of immigrants from Voss had been created, it would naturally attract others from the same community. Andrew Larson (Flage) and his family, as an example, stayed with Baard Johnson and other Norwegians in Chicago until they could move into their own home. It was a frequently re- peated pattern in all regions of Norwegian settlement, encouraging the formation of settlements of people from one specific locality in Norway. The Vossing group in Chicago was thus not much different, save for the fact that the colony emerged in an urban setting. But given the commercial activities in Voss and the entrepreneurial atti- tude they seemed to foster, it might be argued that many Vossings arrived in America with skills particularly suitable to an expanding urban economy, and that they remained in Chicago precisely because of the opportunities they discovered there. This hypothesis finds sup- port in the success of the Voss Circle leaders, whose financial activities reveal a quick grasp of the basics of American capitalism.[19]

The arrival of news about America was in the initial phase of overseas migration a prime factor in determining its timing from specific districts. Knowledge of opportunities in America might be the final incentive to leave. How information was transmitted, its intent and quality, thus become important to understanding migratory pro- cesses. Holger Wester in his doctoral thesis in 1977 examined inno- vations in population mobility patterns in a small Swedish-speaking parish in Finnish Ostrobothnia; he looked at information channels and the diffusion of "innovation," which he defined as changes in the propensity of inhabitants to migrate. The destination of those who left was usually America, but sometimes Sweden. The community maintained a long-standing relationship with Sweden, the source of most information about America. Wester's assessment that the inde- pendent farmers were most receptive to the news of America also seems applicable to the situation at Voss. People from the farm-owning class predominated in the initial emigration. Information then spread to the lower classses, primarily at events such as church services, where public announcements were read.[20]

Nils Røthe, the pioneer emigrant from Voss in 1836, had been convinced to emigrate after reading a copy of a letter by a well-known writer of so-called "America letters," Gjert Gregoriussen Hovland. A lay preacher, Elling Eielsen from the farm Sundve at Voss, who himself emigrated in 1839, received the copy on one of his travels and in- troduced it to the peasants in Voss. Hovland had emigrated to the Kendall settlement in western New York in 1831; his letter about pleasant and fertile land was brought back to Norway in 1835 by another emigrant of 1831, Knud Andersen Slogvig. Copies of it circulated widely. One might suspect that both the letter and Slogvig's visit represented an example of emigrant recruitment by Norwegians in America.[21]

There is no record of letters back to Voss from Røthe once he had settled in Chicago, although a report about his safe arrival in New York had come back. From the half hundred who emigrated in 1837, however, and from later emigrants, there were many letters that provided reliable information about the new land and how to reach it. The Vossings took one step further; they engaged in direct promotion of emigration.[22]

From the late 1830s Norwegian authorities became alarmed at the growing movement overseas. An agitation against leaving the homeland ensued: "Stay in the land and support yourself honestly," Bishop Jacob Neumann in Bergen admonished. In their propaganda against emigration the authorities used America letters and other writings sent home by discontented emigrants. An example is a letter written by one Sjur Jørgensen Lokrheim (also known as Sjur Jørgensen Haaeim) and published in *Bergens Stiftstidende* (Bergen Diocese Times) in 1839. Published with the aid of Bishop Neumann, it is a mournful account of conditions among Norwegians in America and an earnest expression of a desire to return to Norway. Lokrheim accomplished this in 1841, and the following year, likely again with Neumann's help, published a ten-page pamphlet titled "Oplysninger om Forholdene i Nordamerika" (Information on Conditions in North America), which also discouraged emigration. In this pamphlet he told that he had emigrated from Hardanger in 1836 and together with others in his party was destined for the Fox River settlement, but when they arrived in Chicago after a long journey some of the emigrants had no money left and were thus forced to remain. This might explain why some immigrants from Hardanger settled in Chicago that year.[23]

The Lokrheim letter of 1839 came to the attention of the Vossings in Chicago through Lars Nesheim, a bachelor farmer in Voss given to literary pursuits, who acted as their correspondent. Group solidarity in an immigrant population from a common locality, a need to justify their own emigration and to defend the new society, roused the Vossings to action. In an early and notable act of immigrant self-assertion, the Vossings mailed a joint letter back to Voss, penned by Andrew Larson. It denounced as false the statements and allegations by Lokrheim. "It is not true," the letter declared, "that it is so bad in America as that Sjur Valdres has written. . . . We have enough food and clothes."[24]

Lokrheim hailed from the district of Valdres, and one senses a local bias in how he was identified as an East Norwegian. But he had emigrated from the parish of Ulvik in the district of Hardanger just to the south of Voss. The impact of positive or negative information on the volume of emigration as well as on the choice of specific destination in America cannot be precisely determined. It is nevertheless obvious that at a time when letters were the main, if not the only, source of information on which to make far-reaching personal decisions, they had some impact. They were written by people from the peasant community itself, and whether they gave good news or bad, their authors were trusted friends and neighbors. Norwegian peasants, at a time of increasing class consciousness, relied upon their own authorities on America.[25]

Knut Rene, attempting to assess the influence of Lokrheim's letter, quoted from a letter by Arne Andersen Vinje, one of the twenty Vossings to emigrate in 1840. Vinje, who settled in Chicago, wrote that that year many Vossings had abandoned plans of going to America after having read the Lokrheim letter. But Rene insisted that the letter's effect was temporary because of the countermeasures taken by Vossings in Chicago. From immigrants in America from Hardanger, however, no letters arrived to either contradict the negative reports or to encourage emigration, and parish priests read Lokrheim's letter from the pulpit to convince people to remain in Hardanger. Other woeful reports also arrived. On June 11, 1841, *Bergens Stiftstidende* printed a letter from three dissatisfied emigrants who in 1839 had left Ulvik, the same parish from which Lokrheim emigrated. Twenty people from the community were in their party; they came to Chicago on August 25 after a journey of about three months. Several found jobs on the canal, some on a schooner on the river, and others as woodcutters in the forests about Chicago. The letter told of trials and hardships and many deaths; it advised people not to come to America. The historian George Flom concluded that this discouraging news without any rebuttal from other Hardanger emigrants in America caused a break in the emigration from individual parishes until 1846 and explained why so few of the later emigrants from Hardanger located in Chicago, even though the first, like those from Voss, had arrived in 1836.[26]

The Vossings were again moved to take action in 1848 to challenge another document. This time it was an official report by the Swedish-Norwegian consul general in New York, Adam Løvenskjold, following his visit to "Norwegian settlements in the western districts of the United States" in the summer of 1847. His report was published in Bergen the following year. Løvenskjold's official description of immigrant life was not intentionally distorted or wicked, but it painted a negative picture: the immigrants lived in wretched houses; there was poverty and illness; Norwegians enjoyed little respect; they were slovenly and ignorant. The report was seen by the immigrants as an anti-emigration document and it created great bitterness.[27]

That same fall the Vossing Correspondence Society was organized to give "systematic enlightenment to the Norwegian people concerning the status of their emigrated compatriots and to refute false assertions regarding America and the Norwegian immigrants." Andrew Nelson became president and Iver Lawson vice president. The Vossings had in their midst a number of capable and talented letter writers. They banded together to meet the mailing costs and possibly pay for the postage of correspondence from Norway. The society may very well have been the very first secular organization among Norwegians in America; it is significant that it emerged in a city where residential concentration encouraged active social life. Immigrants in an urban center like Chicago consequently could play an important central role within the entire Norwegian community.[28]

That the eight letters the society sent back to Norway from September 30, 1848, to May 1, 1849, drew the comparison between the confining circumstances in Norway and the freedom and opportunity in America was perhaps not unusual. One is nevertheless impressed by an extreme spirit of optimism expressed in the midst of struggle and illness. Directly or indirectly the letters also constituted a biting criticism of social conditions in Norway, venting considerable bitterness against public officials, social injustice, and class differences. A careful analysis of the letters would reveal much about attitudes and conditions in the small immigrant community in Chicago. The correspondents took pains to show that when given opportunity members of the lower classes in Norway had the ability to succeed, and they gave personal information about thirty-two Vossings, probably the members of the society, and emphasized their material advances. Freedom, equality, and opportunity for everyone—the common citizen just as much as the educated person—were for the letter writers the basic elements of the American social order. They concluded that "it is high time the civil, as well as the religious organizations make justice, freedom, and equality a common measure also in Norway."[29]

In one respect the letters were unique among those arriving in Norway in the 1840s; they tended to promote a rural to urban migration not, as in the great number of America letters, a rural to rural. The Vossing correspondents described life in a city and success in urban occupations and professions. One reads, for example, about Claus Knutsen Saude, whose work was to build houses as a carpenter, to lay sidewalks, and to load and unload vessels, for which he earned about 75 cents to $1.00 daily. His wife did laundry, making from $1.00 to $1.50 weekly. These were clearly Norwegian peasants entering urban occupational patterns and adjusting to an urban setting.[30]

It is clear from later actions that the broader purpose of the society's work was not merely to justify the immigrants' existence in America but just as much to encourage further emigration. Knut Rene thinks that Løvenskjold's negative report merely provided the immediate incentive to organize, as the Vossings were already concerned about a decline in emigration from Voss and the small numbers that were coming to Chicago. The letters made a compelling case for moving to America. The letter writers' motives might simply have been a strong wish to be joined by kinfolk and neighbors from home; thereby a familiar environment could be partly recreated, and religious and secular institutions would find support. The expanding Norwegian farming communities in Illinois and Wisconsin required a steady infusion of new immigrants. As the spread of settlement westward reduced their populations, Norwegian-American farmers sought reliable and reasonable labor from home, as did immigrant entrepreneurs in Chicago.[31]

The ultimate purpose of the society became obvious in the fall of 1849 when three of its members went to Voss with the clear errand of encouraging Vossings to go to America. The fact that no replies had been received to their correspondence was given as a partial reason for their visit. Perhaps one concern was to allay fears about the cholera epidemic that year. Cause and effect can by no means be established, but one may fairly conclude that their efforts deserve some credit for the sudden jump in emigration from Voss in 1850, when an estimated 300 to 350 Vossings went to America. Most of them only passed through Chicago or avoided the city altogether, because of the dreaded disease. They sought instead rural settlements in Illinois and Wisconsin, where they entered farming and either invested in land or became farm laborers. Vossings, in the manner of other Norwegian emigrants, preferred a rural life and sought to become farmers; it was always a minority that remained in the city.[32]

After 1849 the Correspondence Society continued as a discussion group with regular meetings which attracted new members. In February 1848, a Lutheran congregation had been established in the

Norwegian colony, and the society held its meetings in a small room above the entrance of its church on Superior Street. Social and religious concerns merged, as the leaders in these various undertakings were the same. In the spring of 1856 Iver Lawson and Andrew Nelson, two of the society's most prominent members, made a trip to Voss. They discovered that many people in their old home community wished to emigrate but could not finance the move. An American tourist, Charles L. Brace, who visited Voss that same summer stayed at the village inn at Vangen where the two men also found lodging. Brace later recorded his impressions and his understanding of their mission. "The two Norwegians," Brace wrote, "had spent fifteen to sixteen years in our western states and there had acquired a fortune. They had now returned partly to visit friends and relatives, and perhaps partly for the purpose of speculation—in order to bring suited emigrants to their own claims or to the expanding cities. . . . The contrast between the American Norwegians and their countrymen was striking. . . . They [Larson and Brekke] thought Norway to be intolerably backward."[33]

On returning to Chicago in the fall, Lawson and Brekke were instrumental in organizing the Vossing Emigration Society on October 23, 1856. The Correspondence Society must have merged with the new organization, whose object was "to collect funds through free subscription to be used simply and only to help needy and deserving families to America." Aid was to be given in the form of a loan and repaid to the original fund, which in this manner would perpetuate itself, although direct gifts were made from it in special cases. Iver Lawson was president of the society, Andrew Larson, treasurer, and Andrew Johnson joined as vice president. Endre Tesdahl was secretary, as he had been in the Correspondence Society; his special qualification was a better formal education in Norway than the others. An outgrowth of the new organization's activities was the appearance in December 1857, of the small monthly newspaper *Wossingen* published at Leland, Illinois. Copies were sent to Voss, perhaps as an effort to continue the work of the Correspondence Society, and it printed letters from both sides of the Atlantic. The issue of May 1858 told of the arrival in Voss of Iver Lawson, who had returned to aid in the emigration of Vossings. Lawson remained in Norway for an entire year, actively recruiting emigrants and supervising the disposition of funds.[34]

It is difficult to estimate how many of the about 630 Vossings who emigrated between 1856 and 1860 were aided by the Emigration Society. The fact that the Chicago group organized chapters in Norwegian rural settlements suggests its perceived broader goal. A chapter founded at Jefferson Prairie in Wisconsin sent in 1859 the considerable amount of $106 to aid impoverished potential emigrants in Voss. These people would in turn supply needed farm labor for established Norwegian settlers. It became a common practice for Norwegian newcomers to work off their debts to the farmers who had advanced tickets to America. It has not, however, been possible to find solid evidence of this kind of indenture in connection with the society's activities, although it is likely that it existed. The society's aid was in the form of a loan, and repayment through labor would be an obvious arrangement for people arriving in America penniless. The society functioned until the Civil War, and Rene thought that its activities had a significant impact by assisting disadvantaged people who wished to emigrate. It became one of the factors that helped to broaden the social base of the overseas exodus.[35]

The societies formed in 1848 and 1856 were a part of the social life of the Vossings in Chicago, and had direct links to the immigrant religious institutions. The goals of the two societies placed them as well within the larger context of promoting emigration; during the founding phase of Norwegian overseas migration they were undoubtedly the most spectacular expressions of immigrant self-assertion. Efforts to induce emigration might have had a strong element of economic self-interest combined with what must be understood as a genuine will to help people of a common origin improve their lot. The stream of immigrants provided ready and trusting customers for a multitude of business ventures, from selling tickets to America and operating boardinghouses and employment agencies, to land sales and colonization promotion. Several of the society's members were engaged in such pursuits; Iver Lawson himself operated a steamship agency and transferred money to the Scandinavian countries. Life in America would also be more pleasant if it could be shared by people from the Norwegian home community: a common dialect, social customs, traditions, and landscape bound them together. A pronounced regional impulse and a sense of kinship with other Vossings are clearly evident in the writings and activities of the two organizations. Their sympathy was on the side of the ordinary person, and they embraced the American ideals of equality and liberty.[36]

The early appearance of the two societies can be explained by the urban environment, with its residential concentration that encouraged social life. Their central role in the Norwegian-American community was a consequence of their location in the main port of entry for most Norwegian emigrants. A cohesive and substantial regional immigrant contingent established itself, and resourceful and prosperous leaders emerged in its midst. Their success and progress were demonstrably linked to general economic and social circumstances in Voss, which had prepared them to compete in a rapidly evolving urban economy. Official Norwegian attitudes toward the overseas movement prompted decisive action. Although other Norwegian immigrants during the 1840s and 1850s encouraged their compatriots to join them in America, only the Vossings organized societies for this purpose. The coming of the Civil War might conveniently mark the end of the founding phase of Norwegian emigration and the end of the Vossing Emigration Society's activities. The issues of the Civil War absorbed the attention and energy of all Americans. Besides, the broadening stream of Norwegian emigration in the 1850s had established points of contact over a wide area and provided new sources of information and financial support. The Vossing colony in Chicago became less unique as the Norwegian-American community matured and acquired greater resources. But it had played a crucial role in the pioneer phase, receiving and aiding newly arrived emigrants, giving systematic information and in many cases financial assistance to potential emigrants, and enlightening Norwegian society in general about life in America.

NOTES

1. William Brøgger et al., eds., *Norges geografiske leksikon*, vol 3 (Oslo, 1963), 196-211.

2. Lars Kindem, *Vossaboki* (Voss, 1981), 23-39, 86-91; Thrond S. Haukenæs, *Gammelt og nyt fra Voss og Vossestranden* (Bergen, 1896), 51-53.

3. Johannes Gjerdåker, "Life and Development in Voss, 1836-1986," in *Gamalt frå Voss*, ed. Eirik Røthe et al. (Voss, 1985), 61-77.

4. Gjerdåker, "Life and Development in Voss," 61-62, 64-66, 74; Ivar Aasen, *Reise-erindringer og reise-indberetninger 1842-1847*, comp. Halvdan Koht (Trondheim, 1917), 34-42, quote on 40.

5. Gjerdåker, "Life and Development in Voss," 63-64; Medisinalberetning (medical report) for Søndre Bergenhus Amt for 1891 in *Norway's Official Statistics* (Oslo, 1891), 146.

6. K. A. Rene, *Historie om udvandringen fra Voss og vossingerne i Amerika* (Madison, 1930), 101-3; Gjerdåker, "Life and Development in Voss," 63.

7. Gjerdåker, "Life and Development in Voss," 68; Rene, *Historie om udvandringen*, 102-3.

8. Aasen, *Reise-erindringer*, 40-41; Gjerdåker, "Life and Development in Voss," 71-75.

9. John Calhoun papers, Manuscripts Library, Chicago Historical Society; A. T. Andreas, *History of Chicago: From the Earliest Period to the Present Time*

198   ODD S. LOVOLL

(Chicago, 1884), 1:360; Homer Hoyt, *One Hundred Years of Land Values in Chicago: The Relationship of the Growth of Chicago to the Rise in Its Land Values, 1830-1933* (Chicago, 1933), 14, 24-35; George T. Flom, *A History of Norwegian Immigration to the United States: From the Earliest Beginning Down to the Year 1848* (Iowa City, 1909), 232.

10. Rasmus B. Anderson, *The First Chapter of Norwegian Emigration (1821-1848): Its Causes and Results* (Madison, 1906), 194-95; Rene, *Historie om udvandringen*, 103-4; Flom, *Norwegian Immigration*, 95-96.

11. Ingrid Semmingsen, "Origin of Nordic Emigration," *American Studies in Scandinavia* 9 (1977): 14; Carlton C. Qualey and Jon A. Gjerde, "The Norwegians," in *They Chose Minnesota: A Survey of the State's Ethnic Groups*, ed. June Drenning Holmquist (St. Paul, 1981), 220-33; Maldwyn Allen Jones, *American Immigration* (Chicago, 1960), 121; Flom, *Norwegian Immigration*, 230-40.

12. *Wossingen* (Leland, Ill.) July 1858; Rasmus B. Anderson, *Bygdejævning: Artikler af repræsentanter fra de forskjellige bygder i Norge om, hvad deres sambygdinger har udrettet i Vesterheimen* (Madison, 1903), 43; Rene, *Historie om udvandringen*, 110-12.

13. Nils Kolle, "Den tidlegaste utvandringa frå Hordaland," in *Eit blidare tilvere?*, ed. Ståle Dyrvik and Nils Kolle (Voss, 1986), 15-28; Ståle Dyrvik, "Pionérane i utvandringa frå Indre Sunnhordland," in *Eit blidare tilvere?*, ed. Dyrvik and Kolle, 43-61.

14. Sivert Langholm, " 'Noget at fare med.'—Angående handverksmestere i Christiania," in *Vandringer: Festskrift til Ingrid Semmingsen på 70-årsdagen 29. mars 1980*, ed. Sivert Langholm and Francis Sejersted (Oslo, 1980), 141-62; Justin B. Galford, "The Foreign Born and Urban Growth in Chicago, 1850-1950," manuscript in the Chicago Historical Society, 96, 98; Rene, *Historie om udvandringen*, 262, 327, 369. The immigrants frequently chose their patronymic in America, regularly giving it an American form, but among fellow Norwegians continued to be known by their farm name, given here in parenthesis.

15. *Vossingen*, no. 3 (1922): 4-11; *Chicago Daily Democrat*, May 14, 16, 30, June 21, July 30, 1849; Mari Lund Wright, "The Pioneer Norwegian Community in Chicago before the Great Fire, 1836-1871," M.A. thesis, University of Wisconsin, 1958, 49-50; Bessie Louise Pierce, *A History of Chicago*, vol. 1: *The Beginnings of a City, 1673-1848* (Chicago, 1937), 79; Rene, *Historie om udvandringen*, 140.

16. Knut Gjerset, *Norwegian Sailors on the Great Lakes: A Study in the History of American Inland Transportation* (Northfield, 1928): 75-77; Lund Wright, "Pioneer Norwegian Community," 49-51; *Vossingen*, no. 3 (1922): 10-11; no. 1 (1923): 11-12; quote from *Vossingen*, no. 1-2 (1925): 12.

17. Knud Langeland, *Nordmændene i Amerika: Nogle erindringer om de norskes udvandring til Amerika* (Chicago, 1889), 41; Rene, *Historie om udvandringen*, 112-14, 136-39, 260-63.

18. Wright, "Pioneer Norwegian Community," 48-51, 94-96.

19. Rene, *Historie om udvandringen*, 137.

20. Holger Wester, *Innovationer i befolkningsrörligheten: En studie av sprid-ningsförlopp i befolkningsrörligheten utgående från Petalax socken i Österbotten* 93 (Uppsala, 1977), see 9-10 for a discussion of the investigation.

21. Flom, *Norwegian Immigration*, 62; Odd S. Lovoll, *The Promise of America: A History of the Norwegian-American People* (Minneapolis, 1984), 11-12, 33-34, 54-56.

22. Rene, *Historie om udvandringen*, 103-12.

23. Lovoll, *Promise of America*, 14; Gunnar J. Malmin, tr. and ed., "The Disillusionment of an Immigrant: Sjur Jørgensen Haaeim's Information on Conditions in North America," *Norwegian-American Studies and Records* 3 (1928): 1-12.

24. Rene, *Historie om udvandringen*, 172-73; *Vossingen*, no. 4 (1924): 6-9.

25. Malmin, "Disillusionment of an Immigrant," 1-2.

26. Rene, *Historie om udvandringen*, 171-72, 173; Flom, *Norwegian Immigration*, 234-35.

27. Lars Fletre, "The Vossing Correspondence Society of 1848 and the Report of Adam Løvenskjold," *Norwegian-American Studies* 28 (1979): 245-73; Knut Gjerset, tr., "An Account of the Norwegian Settlers in America," *Wisconsin Magazine of History* (September 1924): 77-78.

28. Albert O. Barton, "Norwegian-American Emigration Societies of the Forties and Fifties," *Norwegian-American Studies and Records* 3 (1928): 26-27.

29. Rene, *Historie om udvandringen*, 260-62, 380; Fletre, "Vossing Correspondence Society," 259-72. Quote in Barton, "Emigration Societies," 33.

30. Rene, *Historie om udvandringen*, 371.

31. Rene, *Historie om udvandringen*, 362-64; Lovoll, *Promise of America*, 33-51.

32. Barton, "Emigration Societies," 34; Rene, *Historie om udvandringen*, 437-38.

33. Barton, "Emigration Societies," 35-39; Haukenæs, *Natur, folkeliv og folketro paa Voss og Vossestranden* (Voss, 1887), 66-72, quote from 71-72.

34. The activities of the Emigration Society are reported in *Wossingen*, which came out from December 1857, until February 1860; a complete file is preserved at the Wisconsin Historical Society in Madison.

35. Rene, *Historie om udvandringen*, 499; Andres A. Svalestuen, "Om den regionale spreiinga av norsk utvandring før 1865," in *Utvandringa: Det store oppbrotet*, ed. Arnfinn Engen (Oslo, 1978), 75.

36. *Skandinaven*, May 30, 1867.

8

Moving into and out of Pittsburgh: Ongoing Chain Migration

JUNE GRANATIR ALEXANDER

In 1913, John Ciganik left his native village in northern Hungary for the United States. He knew exactly where he was going. He proceeded to the Detroit area where his father and other Slovaks from his village were working. The thought of traveling to America was not original with John Ciganik; he was following a pattern set by his father and other relatives who had migrated several times to the United States to work. Although he was from an agricultural background, John was certain his father or a fellow countryman could help him find work in a factory. His optimism was well-based. He did find employment and, moreover, so many immigrants from his own as well as adjacent villages lived in the area that it seemed "just like home." When his father heard through a friend that good jobs existed in Pittsburgh, he left Detroit for the "Steel City." John Ciganik stayed behind but subsequently decided to join his father. He later explained that his father wanted the family to be together. He found that not only did his father and persons from his village area reside in Pittsburgh's North Side, but his godfather did also. For the remainder of his life, John Ciganik stayed in the North Side.[1]

John Ciganik, his father, and godfather were part of the massive migration that provided the labor supply that fueled the industrialization of the United States. John Ciganik's emigration clearly represented what contemporary observers as well as students of immigration have termed "chain migration." Personal ties with a preceding migrant directed him from his village to the Detroit area. The successive moves that the Ciganiks made to Pittsburgh were also part of the internal migrations that occurred among America's working classes in the late nineteenth and early twentieth centuries.[2] John's second move, however, suggests a different view of internal migration than that conjured up by some studies of this movement. Once his father established that going to Pittsburgh would be wise, John Ciganik followed; he and his father were mobile, but neither could be described as a transient "buffeted about by the vicissitudes of the casual labor market."[3] Nor did they wander randomly in search of employment. Their decisions to leave Detroit were complex and based in part on the fact that they knew persons in Pittsburgh.

An examination of some Slovaks who left Pittsburgh, where Ciganik decided to remain, offers further insight into the nature of the internal migration that took place among America's immigrants. Indeed, evidence from Pittsburgh's early-twentieth-century Slovak population suggests that chain migration, typically associated with international migratory movements, was an ongoing process that affected internal migration in the United States. In short, some of the same factors that first encouraged chain migrations to the United States influenced successive moves of the foreign born after they arrived in America.

The following analysis of the migration patterns of Pittsburgh Slovaks places them within the context of ongoing chain migration. The available sources, however, do not permit an exhaustive examination. This chapter will consider the migration patterns of members of the Pittsburgh lodge, Branch 50 of the First Catholic Slovak Union from approximately 1902 to 1910. Before turning to Branch 50's members, some attention must first be given to chain migration as a process and to the characteristics of the Slovak migration to the United States in general and to western Pennsylvania in particular.

In seeking to describe chain migration and its impact on the United States, observers have stressed different components of the process. Critics of immigration maligned what they saw as a never-ending process. Complaining in 1907 that immigration to the United States was characterized by "endless chains," the commissioner general of immigration pointed to letters as the crucial links in these chains. In his view, personal communications that promised jobs to friends and relatives or carried news of favorable employment situations were encouraging persons to emigrate.[4] Investigations of the international mail service at the turn of the century supported the commissioner's claim. When investigators counted the number of letters and estimated the amount of money sent to Europe for travel tickets, they found a constant transoceanic flow of materials. The link was clearly there. However, correspondence was only one of several factors encouraging emigration. For instance, contemporaries found that "birds of passage," those workers who crossed the ocean several times, further stimulated immigration.[5]

While contemporaries often used the term *chain migration* to help explain why so many persons were coming to the United States, scholars have employed the concept to refine our understanding of the immigration process. Chain migration has been used, for example, to uncover the weaknesses of the "American fever" or the "push-pull" theories of emigration. The concept also supports the argument, so cogently presented by Frank Thistlethwaite, that demographic and economic pressures are not the only mechanisms stimulating emigration. Indeed, the chain-migration metaphor takes emigration beyond demographic and economic determinants and explains how these movements could become self-generating.[6]

As students of the subject have long recognized, the chain migration concept can be used to explain how socioeconomic conditions intertwined with traditions and influenced the decision to emigrate as well as the choice of specific destination. Whether explaining why persons chose to emigrate or where they went, scholars and contemporary observers have stressed one vital point: chain migration relied on personal relationships. Sometimes personal relations simply involved a letter carrying the news of potential jobs; at other times, the letters contained steamship fare or even a ticket itself. Talking with a returned "bird of passage" convinced others to leave their homeland. Thus personal relations, sometimes through oral contact and sometimes via the written word, influenced where many immigrants, both the transient and the permanent, initially went in the United States.[7]

Slovaks were part of the migratory work force that entered the United States at the turn of the century. While observers disagree about how Slovaks first learned of opportunities in America, there is general agreement on the characteristics of this migration that was underway by the early 1880s.[8] During the period up to 1914 when the war temporarily halted emigration, the majority of Slovak immigrants were young males. Between 1899 and 1910, slightly over 70 percent of the 377,527 Slovaks who entered the United States were males.[9] The age and sexual composition of this immigration reflected the sojourners' objectives. Unskilled, and primarily from agricultural regions, these residents of northern Hungary sought jobs in America's burgeoning industries. A significant portion, perhaps one-third, of the Slovaks were not immigrants but instead "migrants" seeking temporary employment and planning to return to their homeland.[10] Transients formed an especially large contingent of the early stages of the Slovak emigration, but migrants remained a common feature of the movement throughout the pre–World War I era. Between 1908 and 1910, for instance, immigration officials recorded 80,797 Slovaks as entering the United States while 41,726 left. According to statistics compiled in 1910, at least 19 percent of the Slovaks who entered an American port from 1899 to 1910 had been in the United States at least once before. Slovak immigrants themselves, between 1908 and 1910, stated that they were chain migrating: approximately 98.4 percent said they were coming to join relatives or friends.[11]

Migrating back and forth between the United States and their homeland was a lengthy trip for Slovaks, but traveling in search of seasonal employment was a tradition among this ethnic group. During the eighteenth and nineteenth centuries, a subsistence peasant economy helped create a migrant mentality among Slovaks. Some Slovaks engaged in "wandering trades" and traveled throughout northern Hungary to sell wares or repair household and farm implements. Others migrated to lower Hungary or neighboring countries in search of seasonal employment.[12] By the mid-nineteenth century, the backward economy of northern Hungary as well as its increasing population reinforced the practice of temporary migration. The journey that some began making in the 1870s to the United States was longer but, by this time, migration was a tradition among Slovaks.

There is little information on how the first Slovaks in America, many of whom were probably migrant workers, found employment. Some were met in New York by recruiters who directed unskilled laborers to America's inland factories, mills, and mines. Representatives of the Frick Company, based in Pennsylvania, were among the earliest of these recruiters. Consequently, by 1873 Slovaks were reportedly working in the coke plants and coal mines around Connellsville in southwestern Pennsylvania.[13] As the prewar migration movement gained momentum, this region remained a popular destination for Slovak immigrants.

The expanding economy of western Pennsylvania suited the objectives of a migrant work force. Dominated by Pittsburgh, this section of the state experienced rapid industrial growth at the turn of the century. The steel and iron industries of Pittsburgh gave rise to sundry allied industries in the city and its immediate environs. Pittsburgh's growth was accompanied by the emergence of mill towns that both supported and were dependent upon the growing economy of the "Pittsburgh District."[14] South of Pittsburgh lay the coke-producing region and coal mines that supplied Pittsburgh and small industrial towns with fuel. For unskilled migrants, Pittsburgh and southwestern Pennsylvania clearly offered a variety of job choices.

By the mid-1880s, more Slovaks were taking advantage of the economic opportunities available in western Pennsylvania. Although the coke and coal region south of Pittsburgh was the most popular destination of the earliest migrants, during the 1880s and 1890s Slovaks migrated in increasingly large numbers into Pittsburgh and the mill towns of western Pennsylvania. These immigrants formed mutual aid societies and built churches to serve their religious needs. Consequently, by the early 1900s, Slovak churches existed throughout the region and, during the pre–World War I era, their number continually increased.[15] These churches indicated that not all of the Slovaks who came to southwestern Pennsylvania were migrants; some persons planned to settle in the area. Nevertheless, these permanent institutions also served the transients who continued to be a significant segment of the Slovak migration.

When Slovak newcomers arrived in western Pennsylvania during the first decade of the twentieth century, then, it was not difficult to find a "Slovak" settlement, complete with a church. But the evidence suggests that Slovaks who went to the region were not looking simply for Slovaks. They were looking instead for persons specifically from their home regions. Such persons could perhaps help them find jobs. The tendency to migrate to areas where immigrants from one's village or region were living was evident both among recent arrivals from Europe and among those Slovaks coming to western Pennsylvania from other locales in the United States.

An extensive examination of the Slovak movement into Pittsburgh at the turn of the century demonstrates that these immigrants chain migrated to specific city neighborhoods.[16] Although some sections of the "Steel City" claimed Slovaks from a variety of counties and villages, a breakdown of individual origins reveals clear-cut chain-migration patterns. Some chains were based on individual villages, some on districts, whereby residents from clusters of neighboring villages or towns migrated to the same Pittsburgh neighborhood. For example, Slovaks from southern Zemplín County settled in Frankstown, the southeastern part of Pittsburgh. Natives from the central sections of Zemplín, however, moved to Woods Run, a neighborhood located in the northwestern part of the city. Natives of the western counties of Nitra and Bratislava uniformly chose Frankstown over other neighborhoods. Slovaks from northern Spiš County went almost exclusively to the South Side while those from central Spiš, just north of the Hornád River, settled in Pittsburgh's North Side.

The power of chain migration by village clusters was evident even among those who professed different religions. Slovak Catholics and Lutherans from Liptov County settled together in Pittsburgh's Sixth Ward. Regional migration by village clusters was such a strong characteristic of the movement of former inhabitants of northern Hungary into Pittsburgh that it also crossed ethnic boundaries. For example, Slovaks and Hungarians from the same sections of Zemplín County lived in the same sections of the "Steel City."[17]

The chain migration strikingly evident in the distribution of Slovaks in Pittsburgh was also occurring in the mill and mining towns outside Pittsburgh. Table 8.1 lists the county origins of Slovaks living in various locales in western Pennsylvania, from 1908 to 1912.[18] As the table indicates, natives of the eastern agricultural county of Zemplín apparently preferred the industrial mill towns over the mining regions. Persons from Trenčin, a western county with a tradition of wandering tradesmen, showed a similar preference for factory work. At the same time, Slovaks from the mining regions of central Spiš County could be found in Pennsylvania's southwestern mining regions (Figure 8.1).

Despite some correlation, the economy of homeland regions cannot fully explain the destinations of Slovaks in western Pennsylvania. Some Slovaks may have had an occupational preference based on their premigration work experience, but the evidence strongly suggests that over time this did not remain a significant factor influencing choice of occupation or destination. Instead, it appears that Slovaks established networks that helped direct subsequent migrants into unskilled jobs. For example, persons from the northern, extremely poor, agricultural regions of Orava County could be found in the mining regions south of Pittsburgh as well as in the industries of McKees Rocks. The same was true of immigrants from Spiš and Šariš counties. Natives of Šariš migrated to the highly industrial Braddock and Duquesne as well as to the mining town of Leisenring. Persons from the mining region of central Spiš County did move to the coke region of southwestern Pennsylvania, but they could be found in mill towns as well. Indeed, Pittsburgh's South Side boasted a significant number of immigrants from the Spiš mining area. And persons from the northern agricultural sections of Spiš moved both to Pennsylvania's mining and mill towns as well as to Pittsburgh[19] Hence, an examination of county origins shows that there was, at times, a correlation between the economy of the homeland regions and migration destinations; however, this correlation was decidedly not a constant nor characteristic feature of Slovak settlement patterns.

Previous work experiences also cannot explain the variety of village and county origins evident among Slovaks living in different towns in western Pennsylvania. Yet, origins of persons in these various towns do reveal a striking pattern of chain migration by individual villages or by districts comprised of village clusters. For example, the Trenčin natives who went to Ford City and worked in its glass factory came

Table 8.1. Places or Origin and Destinations of Slovaks in Select Towns of Western Pennsylvania

Town*	Abov	Bratislava	Gemer	Liptov	Nitra	Orava	Spiš	Šariš	Trenčín	Užhorod	Zemplín	Zvolen
Industrial												
Braddock	11	0	4	0	4	0	1	43	4	1	19	0
Charleroi	1	15	1	0	2	0	0	0	1	0	0	0
Donora	2	1	0	1	1	1	8	11	0	10	3	6
Duquesne	2	0	2	0	0	1	3	16	23	7	79	0
Ford City	0	9	0	0	0	1	0	0	23	0	0	0
McKees Rocks	1	0	0	0	0	6	0	10	0	0	3	0
Monessen	2	0	4	0	0	0	6	15	0	8	6	2
Mining												
Brownsville	6	0	0	0	1	3	0	2	4	0	0	0
Canonsburg	0	0	0	0	0	3	1	8	5	0	0	0
Connellsville	3	0	0	0	0	0	4	5	0	0	0	0
Imperial	0	0	0	0	0	0	4	0	0	2	0	0
Leisenring	1	0	0	0	2	1	12	13	0	0	0	0
Moon Run	1	0	0	0	0	1	6	0	0	0	0	0
Smock	3	1	1	0	0	11	6	2	0	0	0	0

Sources: Membership and insurance applications, 1908-12, branches, 35, 38, 95, 108, 155, 197, 200, 210, 219, 246, 247, 252, 311, 323, 369, 380, 434, 487, 564, 565, Immigration History Research Center, University of Minnesota, St. Paul; First Catholic Slovak Union Papers.

* Towns are grouped according to the dominant characteristic of the economy of the town or region in which it is located.

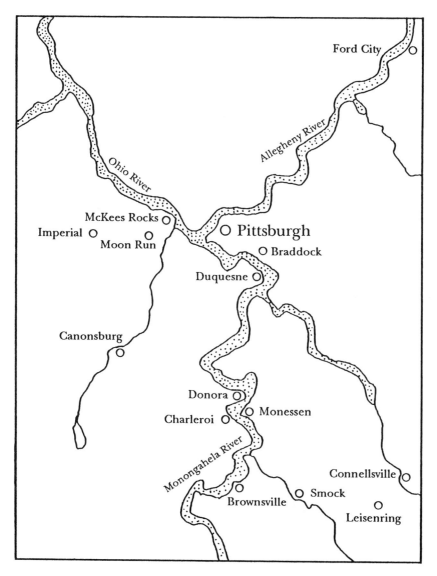

Figure 8.1. Slovak Settlements in Pittsburgh and Vicinity

primarily from a series of neighboring villages in the county's northern region.[20] Those who migrated from Trenčin to Duquesne showed a remarkable consistency of origins that differed from the Slovaks in Ford City. The twenty-three immigrants from Trenčin County who joined one of Duquesne's two Catholic male lodges hailed from just six villages: four were located close together in north central Trenčin; the other two were adjacent villages located in the extreme northeastern part of the county. Significantly, none of the village origins of the persons in Duquesne lodges were the same as for those in Ford City.

The same patterns occurred among persons from Orava County who lived in Smock and worked in mines, or who resided in McKees Rocks and labored in its factories. The Orava movement to these two areas was a chain migration, but persons who went to Smock originated from different villages than those who went to McKees Rocks. In sum, Slovaks who migrated from northern Orava came from the same agriculturally based economy, but they worked in clearly different types of industries. The similarity among the persons who chose one of these towns rested on their village origins. The same chain migration patterns were evident among Slovaks from other counties who moved into the various communities in western Pennsylvania.

A close examination of village origins thus reveals no clear-cut relationship between homeland local economies and choice of destination in western Pennsylvania. During the early stages of the Slovak migration into Pennsylvania such a correlation *may* have been evident. By 1908, however, the relationship had been replaced by migration networks. That is really not surprising, for the characteristics of the Slovak emigration, combined with its pace and degree, could not have sustained a persistent correlation between the job experience Slovaks had in Europe and their choice of destination in western Pennsylvania. This was the case because, although there was some industry in sections of northern Hungary and mining in central Spiš County, most Slovaks were typically unskilled and from agricultural districts.[21]

The movement of unskilled Slovak workers into the industrial regions that surrounded Pittsburgh as well as into the city itself was, then, marked by numerous migration chains. Besides influencing perhaps the place of first destination, regional ties influenced successive moves. This was dramatically illustrated in 1901 at Pittsburgh's Jones and Laughlin Steel Plant. An explosion at the company's Soho division killed eight Slovaks and injured three others. The Slovaks involved were from five neighboring villages in northern Hungary. Pittsburgh had not been the first destination for several of the men. Three of the victims, all from the same village, had come to Pittsburgh after having lived elsewhere in Pennsylvania. Yet, they worked in the same department as persons from their own or nearby villages who had come to the city before them.[22] It is certainly reasonable to conclude that these men did not randomly wander into Pittsburgh. Instead, family or friendship ties continued to give direction to their successive movements.

The Slovaks involved in the accident at Jones and Laughlin did not belong to the South Side's Branch 50, but their mobility was indicative of what was happening among members of that local lodge of the First Catholic Slovak Union. Pittsburgh's highly industrialized South Side, situated along the southern banks of the Monongahela River, attracted Slovaks from different sections of northern Hungary. At first glance, the diverse origins evident among the membership of Branch 50 in the period from 1902 to 1910 belie the idea of chain migrations into the South Side. But a closer look shows the variety of chains that characterized the movement into that neighborhood. A comparison of lodge membership with that of other lodges in the city, when combined with analyses of church records, documents a striking pattern of chain migrations to this industrial region.[23]

When the secretary of Branch 50 completely updated the membership roster in January 1902, forty-four (52 percent) of the lodge's eighty-five members lived outside Pittsburgh.[24] It cannot be determined how many of these out-of-town members had previously resided in Pittsburgh. Still, it is safe to assume that many of them had migrated in and out of the "Steel City." Between January 1902 and January 1910, another 148 persons joined Branch 50. Eighteen of these men definitely left Pittsburgh by January 1910 and another twenty dwelled outside of the city when they joined the lodge. In addition, eight men, for whom no addresses were given when they became Branch 50 members, resided outside Pittsburgh within two years of affiliating with the lodge. The following discussion is based upon an analysis of the fifty-six men for whom Branch 50 records contain reliable information on their out-of-town residences.[25]

In January 1902, twenty-seven of Branch 50's out-of-town members lived in eleven communities in western Pennsylvania. Between 1902 and 1910, twenty-four other persons left Pittsburgh's South Side for seven of these same destinations.[26] A breakdown of this post-1902 exodus of Branch 50 members does not show a consistent correlation between possible premigration work experiences and secondary movements.[27] However, there is evidence of ongoing chain migration. Half of the twenty-four later migrants went to towns where Branch 50 members from the same villages had gone before them. In another 25 percent of the cases, the later migrants went to towns where Branch 50 members from a village in their district had gone before them.[28] Significantly, by 1908, other Slovaks from the same villages or village districts as the Branch 50 migrants were also going to these towns.

The force of ongoing chain migration is particularly well demonstrated by the movement of Slovaks into Moon Run, Imperial, and McKees Rocks. Located on the outskirts of Pittsburgh, these three towns were easily accessible to Branch 50 members who decided to leave the South Side. And in 1902, fifteen of the lodge's out-of-town residents did live in one of these three towns. When Branch 50 members left the South Side for these regions, the evidence indicates this was not a random movement: those who left shared a common origin. In 1902, the seven members who lived in Moon Run came from just four villages in two counties; four came from the single village of Švedlár; two came from nearby villages; and one came from Zemplín County. Subsequent Branch 50 members from these villages also went to Moon Run. The same pattern was clearly evident in Imperial. In 1902, all three Branch 50 members who resided there came from Spiš County. All members from Branch 50 who later migrated to Imperial came from the same Spiš villages as did the 1902 residents.

The movement of Branch 50 members into McKees Rocks reveals the broader impact of ongoing internal migration on the general migration process. In 1902, five lodge members resided in that small industrial town. Four of the five came from three villages in northern Orava County; the other hailed from Šariš County. All the Orava people worked at the same company manufacturing steel cars.[29] One can speculate—but only speculate—that a steel strike in 1901 in Pittsburgh caused these men who had traveled together to Pittsburgh to make a subsequent move to McKees Rocks.

The decisions of two men, Albert and Wendelin Karkoška, illustrate the ongoing migration patterns of persons from Orava County. In 1902, these two Branch 50 members resided in McKees Rocks. They had joined Branch 50 in 1900 and 1901 respectively and presumably lived in the South Side. Even after they left Pittsburgh, both men remained members of the lodge until they were expelled from the lodge in 1904. Sometime between that date and 1909, they returned home. When they came back to the United States, they went to McKees Rocks and in 1909, decided to become members of that town's Branch 95 of the First Catholic Slovak Union. By 1909 other persons from the Karkoškas' village district were also migrating to McKees Rocks.[30]

Albert and Wendelin Karkoška were clearly part of a continual chain migration of Orava Slovaks into and out of Pittsburgh. The evidence is that, over the decade, the South Side was but one stop in this ongoing process. Between 1902 and 1910, eighteen persons from Orava County had joined Branch 50. In 1902, seven of the lodge's nine Orava members did not live in the South Side. During the next eight years, five of the nine new Orava members also left the South Side.[31] These men had all come from a well-defined area in Orava: fourteen of the eighteen hailed either from the villages of Liesek and Babín or from communities located between them.[32]

When Orava Slovaks left Pittsburgh, they continued to move in a uniform pattern. In 1902, Branch 50 members from the village of Babín resided in McKees Rocks while natives of Liesek lived in Smock and Canonsburg. When other persons from Babín subsequently left the South Side, they went to McKees Rocks. Two Liesek natives also left the South Side: in 1903 one did go to McKees Rocks, the other went to Canonsburg in 1904. Records of Slovak lodges show that persons from Babín continued to settle in McKees Rocks while those from Liesek moved to Smock.[33]

Orava Slovaks were not exceptions, but rather were representative of other members of Branch 50. While this South Side lodge claimed persons from a variety of villages and village clusters in northern Hungary, the migration of lodge members was typically by persons from the same villages. For example, during the period from 1902 to 1910, every member of Branch 50 from the village of Švedlár left the South Side and, with one exception, so too did natives of Malý Hnilčik, located in the same region and west of Švedlár.[34]

The migration of Slovaks to western Pennsylvania clearly represented a varied crisscross of chains. Some of these chains linked European villages and American destinations; others directed internal migration in the United States. In the absence of personal letters written by immigrants who moved from place to place, it is difficult to generalize about what motivated them. Unfortunately, compiled statistics are what often remains of the experience of these immigrants, and it is hard to endow statistics with human feelings. Nevertheless, the kinds of economic dislocations that affected the working classes in general surely caused Slovaks to migrate in and out of Pittsburgh. In 1901 a steel strike in Pittsburgh forced Slovaks to leave the city. The reverse was true when, in 1902, a strike in eastern Pennsylvania's anthracite coal regions caused Slovaks to move to the "Steel City."[35]

In 1905, when Pittsburgh's steel manufacturers broke a promise to increase wages after they had been lowered, a Slovak newspaper reported that "as a result . . . many Slovaks are looking elsewhere for work."[36] In bold type, another newspaper warned: "Nechod'te do Pittsburgu za robotou!" [Do not go to Pittsburgh for work!].[37]

The foregoing discussion considers only a small segment of the persons who migrated to the United States and, consequently, the following generalizations about the broader significance of their experience are tentative and, to some extent, speculative. Branch 50's records do provide clues that point to a process of ongoing chain migration that influenced migration not only to the United States but within it as well. Because the migration patterns of the Slovaks analyzed for this study were so consistent, their experience might well provide a deeper understanding of the internal migration that occurred among immigrants in general.

The migration patterns of Slovaks serve as reminders that chain migration was not an inexorable process that inevitably led immigrants from one village to a particular destination. Slovaks from the same village went to different areas of the United States. This trend has been discovered among Italian immigrants, and it is certainly true for other immigrants as well.[38] These exceptions, however, do not challenge the existence of chain migrations. Rather, deviations indicate the elasticity of familial and kinship ties in the migration process as some later immigrants followed the path of a relative who, for whatever reason, had settled in an area where fellow villagers were not living. Deviations thus show that chain migration was not a whirlpool process that controlled the destinies of those who decided to emigrate. Some immigrants, especially during the early stages of a movement, did strike out on their own. After all, the chain had to begin with someone.

In addition, despite the emphasis of this discussion, it is vital to remember that there was stability amid the migration that was taking place among the foreign born. Between 1902 and 1910, more of Branch 50's members remained in the South Side than left. Church records also demonstrate that immigrants remained in the same place long enough to be married and have several children. These permanent immigrants provided a stable base of support for ethnic institutions. The communities they established attracted chain migration not only from Europe to America but also from other locations within the United States.

Nevertheless, the Slovak experience also confirms the conclusions of studies that emphasize the mobility of immigrants as they confronted the realities of America's industrializing economy. Indeed, an examination of South Side Slovaks offers support for scholars who have cited the intensity of this movement to challenge the traditional image of immigrants as trapped in ghettos.[39] The fact that 52 percent of Branch 50's membership did not live in Pittsburgh as of 1902 attests to the mobility that did take place among America's working classes.

Furthermore, Slovak immigrants, as others, were victims of the vicissitudes of a capitalist economy and of its ethos that stressed making profits and cutting costs.[40] As with other immigrant groups, Slovaks faced crises when a Carnegie or a Frick instituted labor-saving measures that meant thinner pay envelopes or, even worse, no job. The practice of advertising jobs in such a way as to create a labor surplus that drove down publicized wages was another reality unskilled workers had to face. In 1908, a Slovak wrote that he had come to Pittsburgh because he heard there were jobs but when he arrived he found there were none.[41]

Placed within the context of recessions and also dislocations caused by the push for profits, the movement of Slovaks in western Pennsylvania does offer statistical support for those who stress economic factors as generating internal migrations among America's working classes. However, examined from a different perspective—even with the same economic emphasis—the Slovak example provides added dimensions to this view. Instead of transforming "birds of passage" into members of America's "floating proletariat," this perspective views mobile Slovaks and other immigrants as the migrant workers they were.[42]

Immigrants themselves realized that many of their compatriots responded to bad economic times by moving. One Slovak, who was particularly aware of the propensity of Slovaks to migrate back and forth between the United States and northern Hungary, was disturbed by this tendency. As a permanent immigrant he was afraid that Slovak churches and fraternal societies would die for lack of support.[43] In 1909, he pleaded with his fellow Slovaks in the United States to pray for better economic times because with them, he contended, would come the return of Slovaks. Based on census records or, perhaps city directories, many of these "birds of passage" have been classified as part of America's floating proletariat wandering in search of jobs. However, those who went back and forth between the United States and Hungary were adjusting to the realities of the economic system that, at least temporarily, did not fulfill their objectives. These return immigrants were maintaining control of their lives as were, it appears, those Slovaks who, for one reason or another, moved several times within the United States.

The "migration mentality" that has been advanced by some scholars as influencing transoceanic and other international population movement influenced internal migration as well.[44] Having made several trips to the United States, John Ciganik's father was not adverse to moving again when someone he knew informed him there were good jobs in Pittsburgh. His objective in coming to the United States was, after all, to make money for his family that remained in Europe. His son's subsequent decision to go to Pittsburgh demonstrated the intertwining of economic considerations with personal motivations. John Ciganik assuredly would not have left Detroit for Pittsburgh if his father had not informed him there would be a job. But, equally significant, he would not have left without his father's request that he do so. John's reasons for migrating from Detroit to Pittsburgh were voluntary and personal. Certainly other immigrants who traveled to new locations had similar motives.

Once in the United States, economic conditions and forces beyond their control could indeed compel Slovaks to leave a city or town and go elsewhere. However, migrant laborers had options that allowed them to avoid becoming part of a working class wandering in and out of towns and cities in search of employment or a better job. As migrant workers, they could do what many had always planned to do—go home. Certainly they may not have been happy with this alternative because they might not have attained their financial objectives; nevertheless, they had the choice of going home.

Those who, for whatever reason, could not return or simply chose not to go home if they suddenly found themselves unemployed or faced with unacceptably low wages, had options. They could remain where they were, or they could go to another locale.[45] The decision about where to go was based on a complex set of factors—ones quite similar to those that had first brought them to a particular city or town. For those who left, it appears, this often meant going to where persons from their homeland districts lived. In these instances, internal migration was part of the larger chain migration process that directed immigrants to specific destinations.

NOTES

I am grateful to John K. Alexander for preparing Figure 8.1.

1. Interview with John Ciganik, May 17, 1977, Pittsburgh.
2. For example, see Stephan Thernstrom and Peter R. Knights, "Men

in Motion: Some Data and Speculations About Urban Population Mobility in Nineteenth-Century America," in *Anonymous Americans: Explorations in Nineteenth-Century Social History,* ed. Tamara Hareven (Englewood Cliffs, 1971), 17-47; Stephan Thernstrom, *Poverty and Progress: Social Mobility in a Nineteenth Century City* (Cambridge, 1964), and *The Other Bostonians: Poverty and Progress in the American Metropolis, 1880-1970* (Cambridge, 1973); Howard P. Chudacoff, *Mobile Americans: Residential and Social Mobility in Omaha, 1880-1920* (New York, 1972); Gordon W. Kirk, Jr., and Carolyn Tyirin Kirk, "Migration, Mobility and the Transformation of the Occupational Structure in an Immigrant Community: Holland, Michigan, 1850-80," *Journal of Social History* 7 (1974): 142-64. See also, Rowland Berthoff, "The American Social Order: A Conservative Hypothesis," *American Historical Review* 15 (1960): 495-514.

3. Thernstrom and Knights, "Men in Motion," 39.

4. U.S. Department of Commerce and Labor, "Report of the Commissioner-General of Immigration, 1907," in *Reports of the Department of Commerce and Labor, 1907* (Washington, 1907), 136-37.

5. Frank J. Sheridan, "Italian, Slavic, and Hungarian Unskilled Immigrant Laborers in the United States," *Bulletin of the Bureau of Labor* 15 (1907): 407-8, 479-80; U.S. Immigration Commission, *Reports* (Washington, 1911), 1: 187-90; Emily Greene Balch, *Our Slavic Fellow Citizens* (New York, 1910), 119, 152-55, 181-82, 186, 471-73. This statement is not meant to imply that the investigations were made simply as a result of the commissioner's statements.

6. For example, see John S. MacDonald and Leatrice D. MacDonald, "Chain Migration Ethnic Neighborhood Formation and Social Networks," *Millbank Memorial Fund Quarterly* 42 (1964): 82-97; Julianna Puskás, *Emigration from Hungary to the United States Before 1914* (Budapest, 1975), 14-19; Jozsef Gellen, "Emigration in a Systems Framework: The Case of Hungary, 1899-1913," *Hungarian Studies in English* 17 (1984): 85-112; Frank Thistlethwaite, "Migration from Europe Overseas in the Nineteenth and Twentieth Centuries" in *Population Movements in Modern European History,* ed. Herbert Moller (New York, 1964), 73-92.

7. In addition to sources cited in note 6, see Virginia Yans-McLaughlin, *Family and Community: Italian Immigrants in Buffalo, 1880-1930* (Ithaca, 1977), 59-64; John W. Briggs, *An Italian Passage: Immigrants to Three American Cities, 1890-1930* (New Haven, 1978), 69-72; Judith E. Smith, *Family Connections: A History of Italian and Jewish Immigrant Lives in Providence Rhode Island, 1900-1940* (Albany, 1985); Donna Gabaccia, "Kinship, Culture, and Migration: A Sicilian Example," *Journal of American Ethnic History* 3 (1984): 43-47; Rudolph J. Vecoli, "The Formation of Chicago's 'Little Italies,'" *Journal of American Ethnic History* 2 (1983): 5-20.

8. Emily Balch suggested that Slovaks discovered America through Jews who had emigrated earlier. Some contemporaries blamed the Slovak emigration on steamship and company agents who enticed laborers with promises of high wages. Konštantín Čulen, a historian of the movement, also stressed

the catalytic affect of agents. Balch, *Our Slavic Fellow Citizens*, 100-101, 239; Konštantín Čulen, *Dejiny Slovákov v Amerike* [A history of Slovaks in America], 2 vols. (Bratislava, 1942), 1: 38; Minister of the Interior to the Peoples of Spiš County, 24 April 1884, in *Slovenské vyst'ahovalectvo: Dokumenty I do roku 1918* [Slovak emigration: documents I to the year 1918], ed. František Bielik and Eli Rakoš (Bratislava, 1969), document 26.

9. The number of males may have been inflated because of the tendency of individual Slovaks to make several trips to the United States. U.S. Immigration Commission, *Reports*, 3: 47, 89-94.

10. The term *migrant* is used here and throughout this discussion to refer to persons who remained temporarily in the United States and also to those persons who remained only temporarily in one of the local towns analyzed later in this study.

11. U.S. Immigration Commission, *Reports*, 3: 46, 348, 365, 372. Because it was common for Slovak males to leave their families in Europe and send for them later, a significant number of these persons were surely women and children going to join their spouses and fathers.

12. Balch, *Our Slavic Fellow Citizens*, 97-98; Čulen, *Dejiny Slovákov*, 1: 53-55; Emil Lengyel, *Americans From Hungary* (Philadelphia, 1948), 100; Ján Hanzlík, "Začiatky vyst'ahovalectva zo Slovenska do USA a jeho priebeh až do roku 1918, jeho príčiny a následky" [The beginnings and course of emigration from Slovakia to the United States in 1918, its course and results], in *Začiatky českej a slovenskej emigrácie do USA* [The beginnings of Czech and Slovak emigration to the United States], ed. Josef Polišenský (Bratislava, 1970), 50-55; Puskás, *Emigration from Hungary to the United States*, 13-14.

13. Sheridan, "Italian, Slavic and Hungarian Unskilled Immigrant Laborers in the United States," 407; Jozef Kushner, *Slováci Katolíci Pittsburghského Biskupstva* [Slovak Catholics of the Pittsburgh Diocese] (Passaic, 1946), 15-16.

14. U.S. Department of Commerce and Labor, Bureau of the Census, *Industrial Districts: 1905*, bulletin 101 (Washington, 1911), 9-45. The "Pittsburgh District" included the area surrounding Pittsburgh and also Allegheny City. In 1907 Pittsburgh annexed Allegheny City, which became known as the North Side.

15. Kushner, *Slováci Katolíci*, 17-132.

16. For a detailed discussion of Slovak chain migration into Pittsburgh, see June Granatir Alexander, "Staying Together: Chain Migration and Patterns of Slovak Settlement in Pittsburgh Prior to World War I," *Journal of American Ethnic History* 1 (1981): 56-83.

17. Based on data derived from First Hungarian Reformed Church (Pittsburgh), baptismal records (1891-1903) and marriage records (1891-1903), Historical Society of Western Pennsylvania, Pittsburgh (microfilm); Presbyterian Beneficial Union, Kniha Zomrelých do roku 1913 [register of deaths to 1913]; Presbyterian Beneficial Union, Kniha Zomrelých udov prestúpivsich a zmenie smrtnej podpory od jula 1913 do juna 1916 [register of

members dying, joining, and changing death benefits from July 1913 to June 1916]; Presbyterian Beneficial Union, Kniha Zomrelých, 1914-53 [death register, 1913-53]; all of these registers are deposited at the Presbyterian Beneficial Union Headquarters (formerly the Slovak Calvinistic Presbyterian Union), Philadelphia. St. Joachim Slovak Roman Catholic Church, baptismal records (1909-13) and marriage records (1909-13) maintained at St. Joachim Church, Pittsburgh. I compiled data from these records that show interethnic regional migrations; see "The Ties That Bind: Regionalism, Religion and the Slovak Immigration into the Pittsburgh Region, 1885-1918," paper presented at the Annual Meeting of the Organization of American Historians, Minneapolis, April 1985.

18. The towns included in Table 8.1 and on Figure 8.1 are limited to those towns where Branch 50 members migrated after leaving Pittsburgh. Church records are more comprehensive sources for determining the origins of the general Slovak population in any given locale. These records were used extensively in my analyses of Pittsburgh's Slovak population. Using these records, however, requires the permission and assistance of each individual pastor. It was not feasible to consult the records of Slovak churches for all of the towns considered in this present study. Instead, this analysis relies on local male lodges of the First Catholic Slovak Union. My research in and comparison of the records of Pittsburgh's Slovak churches and local lodges demonstrates that the lodge records did reflect the same origins for individuals as did church records, although church records are definitely far better for revealing the extent of the regional migration by Slovaks. In addition, fraternal records provide no information on nonfraternalists and only rudimentary information on the migration patterns of women. Lodge applications did list the marital status of applicants and whether wives were living with their husbands, elsewhere in America, or in Europe. Fraternal records, when combined with local church records, can be useful in determining migration patterns of some married women. However, conclusions about the internal migration of Slovak men cannot simply be applied to single Slovak women. These women typically followed the same chain migration patterns characteristic of Slovak immigration to the United States. But whether these women, and particularly those who were part of the work force, made successive moves and followed patterns of internal migration similar to Slovak men awaits further analysis beyond the scope of this study.

Unless otherwise indicated, all information on the origins and destination of Slovaks in western Pennsylvania were derived from membership and insurance applications for the period 1908-12. The specific lodges analyzed are branches 26, 35, 38, 95, 108, 155, 197, 200, 210, 219, 246, 247, 252, 303, 311, 315, 323, 369, 380, 434, 487, 564, 565, and 618. Membership and insurance applications, 1908-12, Immigration History Research Center, University of Minnesota, St. Paul; First Catholic Slovak Union Papers (hereafter, FCSU).

19. In addition to lodge records cited in note 18, data were derived from

St. Matthew Slovak Roman Catholic Church, baptismal records (1903-10) and marriage records (1904-10), St. Matthew Church, Pittsburgh; St. Elizabeth Slovak Roman Catholic Church, baptismal records (1895-1910) and marriage records (1895-1910), St. Wenceslaus Church, Pittsburgh.

20. Data on occupations were derived from membership applications, FCSU, branches 38, 200, 350. The jobs of applicants but not their specific employers are listed on the application forms. All data presented in this study on occupations were derived from membership applications for the FCSU lodges in the relevant town.

21. This is not an attempt to challenge the conclusions of numerous studies of specific immigrant groups that have discovered there was indeed a correlation between the homeland economy and choice of occupation in the United States. Scholars have found that this correlation was especially evident among skilled tradesmen from specific countries. Nor is this an attempt to deny the occupational differences that existed among America's different immigrant groups at the end of the nineteenth century. Among the points being argued here (and which are in agreement with conclusions made by John Bodnar) is that unskilled immigrants entering an industrial economy—going essentially from rural to urban, industrial areas—had few occupational choices that would correspond with their previous work experience. John Bodnar, *The Transplanted: A History of Immigrants in Urban America* (Bloomington, 1985).

22. *Amerikánsko-Slovenské Noviny,* December 26, 1901.

23. Alexander, "Staying Together," 66-69; St. Matthew Church, baptismal records (1903-10) and marriage records (1904-10).

24. Učtovníca Sp. sv. Antona z Padua. Č 50, I.K.S.J., 1902-12 [account book of the Society of St. Anthony of Padua, Branch 50 of the First Catholic Slovak Union] (hereafter, Branch 50, Učtovníca), Slovak Museum and Archives, Middletown, Pa., Branch 50 Collection. There are no extant membership records for the lodge before 1902. In January 1902 the secretary compiled a roster that listed the name, birthplace, date of lodge affiliation, and current address of each member. During the next five years, the secretary noted the same information for all new members. He also recorded address changes. In 1907, a new secretary again updated the list, and he completely redid the list each year from 1907 to 1910. Unless otherwise noted, all subsequent data presented on Branch 50 members were derived from the Učtovníca.

25. Branch 50 members excluded from this analysis include: (1) persons from Galicia, (2) members whose destinations are imprecisely listed in the records, and (3) those for whom there is no information on the origins of Slovaks in the towns where Branch 50 members subsequently moved.

26. Branch 50, Učtovníca does not list when members initially arrived in Pittsburgh nor when they left.

27. For example, two of the lodge's members from Trenčin County decided to go respectively to McKees Rocks, a factory town near Pittsburgh, and Brownsville, in the mining region south of the city.

28. The other 25 percent of the members who left went to towns where the records used for this work do not reveal that persons from their village regions were residing. However, as stated in note 18, the fraternal records do not include every person who lived in a town. Some persons either did not join fraternal societies or did not join them during the period for which there are extant records. The fact that 75 percent *did* go to where persons from their village or village districts had gone is, by itself, compelling evidence of internal chain migration.

29. Branch 50, Účtovníca.

30. If the men had been living in McKees Rocks in 1900 and 1901, it is reasonable to assume that they would have joined the existing lodge there or even one of the three First Catholic Slovak Union lodges located in western Allegheny City and thus located much closer to McKees Rocks than Pittsburgh's South Side. The two men applied for membership in Branch 95 in April and December 1909 respectively. Both stated on their subsequent applications to Branch 95 that they had temporarily returned to Europe. In 1910, one of their relatives also joined Branch 95; ibid.; membership applications, FCSU, Branch 95.

31. One of the Orava members who did live in the South Side in 1902 left the city by 1904. Four of the nine men who joined the lodge after 1902 were expelled, and there is no information on whether or not they remained in Pittsburgh.

32. In fact, individuals from the villages of Liesek and Babín dominated the general migration from Orava County into the South Side. Between 1905 and 1910, the Slovak church in the South Side, St. Matthew's, listed twenty families with both parents from Liesek; eleven other families had either one parent from Liesek or both parents came from villages in its immediate area; St. Matthew Church, baptismal records (1903-10) and marriage records (1904-10).

33. Smock was the only town (1909-12) where the Slovak lodges recorded members from Liesek. The Orava Slovaks who joined lodges located in other towns considered in this study came from different villages than those recorded in the Smock, Canonsburg, and McKees Rocks lodges.

34. While studies of chain migration have demonstrated that kinship ties were influential in the process, I was unable to establish such a correlation in the out-migration by Branch 50 members. With few exceptions, there was no clear kinship relation among these migrants. However, it must be noted that the records used may simply not reveal such relationships. Besides not including all of the Slovaks in a given locale, the records do not provide information on male migrants who may have been related through their wives or who were cousins and, hence, had different surnames.

35. *Slovák v Amerike*, July 2 and September 24, 1901, March 28, 1905; Alois B. Koukol, "A Slav's a Man for a' That," in *Wage-Earning Pittsburgh*, ed. Paul Underwood Kellogg (New York, 1914), 64; *Jednota*, January 18, 1905.

36. *Jednota,* January 18, 1905.

37. *Slovák v Amerike,* March 28, 1905.

38. For example, see Briggs, *An Italian Passage,* 69-119; and, cf., Vecoli, "Formation of Chicago's 'Little Italies' "; Yans-McLaughlin, *Family and Community,* 55-63.

39. For example, see Thernstrom and Knights, "Men in Motion"; Thomas Kessner, *The Golden Door: Italian and Jewish Immigrant Mobility in New York City, 1880-1915* (New York, 1977); Humbert S. Nelli, *The Italians in Chicago, 1880-1930* (New York, 1970); Howard P. Chudacoff, "A New Look at Ethnic Neighborhoods: Residential Dispersion and the Concept of Visibility in a Medium-Sized City," *Journal of American History* 60 (1973): 76-93. For criticism of studies of population turnover, see Donald H. Parkerson, "How Mobile Were Nineteenth-Century Americans?," *Historical Methods* 15 (1982): 99-109.

40. For a discussion of how immigrants adjusted to this capitalist economy and a synthesis of the literature dealing with this subject, see Bodnar, *The Transplanted.*

41. *Jednota,* January 29, 1908.

42. See, for example, John Bodnar, Michael Weber, and Roger Simon, "Migration, Kinship, and Urban Adjustment: Blacks and Poles in Pittsburgh, 1900-1930," *Journal of American History* 66 (1979): 548-65; John Bodnar, Roger Simon, and Michael P. Weber, *Lives of Their Own: Blacks, Italians, and Poles in Pittsburgh, 1900-1960* (Urbana, 1982), 29-54.

43. *Jednota,* January 20, 1909. *Národné Noviny* also reported that the bad economic conditions in 1907 had caused "thousands" of Slovaks to return to their homeland. According to the paper, they were returning to the United States in 1910, *Národné Noviny,* January 13, 1910.

44. Thistlethwaite, "Migration from Europe Overseas in the Nineteenth and Twentieth Centuries," 79-80; Puskás, *Emigration from Hungary to the United States,* 14-18.

45. The intention here is *not* to deny or even downplay the misery that many immigrants faced because of strikes, loss of jobs, low pay, or unsafe working conditions. The purpose here is to point to the alternatives that some migrants did, in fact, have and resorted to when faced with such situations.

9

Hungarian Overseas Migration: A Microanalysis

JULIANNA PUSKÁS

Research into the history of international migration in Hungary could be characterized as a struggle between demands and possibilities. The challenge put forth by Frank Thistlethwaite[1] and the studies which have resulted (for example, those in Scandinavia) have awakened the need for new approaches in us as well. We have begun to look at the emigration of Hungarians with even greater interest in relation to migration in Europe as a whole and as a comparison to bring to light its general and specific features. This has entailed the reexamination of our earlier evaluations, the freeing of earlier conclusions from the direct influence of politics so closely associated with research work on emigration in this part of Europe in particular. A greater emphasis has been placed upon comparative studies of the history of international migration and in the application of research methods and theories of the various branches of sociology. Study has been widened beyond the sending country to include the receiving country as well, and attention has been directed toward the study of the life histories of individuals.

From the results of these studies, it has been possible to begin to piece together the characteristics of the basic pattern of Hungarian migration.[2] Compared to Western and Northern Europe, emigration from Hungary began only in the 1880s, with the main wave in the first fourteen years of the twentieth century. Analysis of quantitative data for the period from 1899 to 1913 reveals several characteristics. A pronounced two-way movement is evident: aside from those emigrating, a large number were remigrating.[3] Among the male emigrants were a relatively high number of married men; among the women were a high number of single individuals.[4] The number of female migrants gradually increased, but it was only immediately before World War I that their number equaled that of the men.[5] The overwhelming majority of migrants were peasants or farm laborers, social strata

221

which do not comprise as large a proportion of the migrants from either Western or Northern Europe, or even from Czarist Russia.[6]

But the desire for a more exact specification of the typical characteristics of Hungarian migration required a systematic study of individual migrants. In this, however, we were not able to employ the methods of Swedish and Danish research (i.e., taking a given amount of individual-level information from the available records and using computers to create a typical profile), as our own sources and research conditions would not allow it.[7] However, a "more precise and detailed analysis of fewer cases" has appeared promising. Just as the water of an entire ocean is contained in a single drop of seawater, international migration is embodied in all its complexity in a small group (for example, in the biographies of the emigrants of a particular village and of their children and grandchildren). For these family studies I have selected a village from the northeastern part of Hungary, an area which emerged as an important region of emigration and from which transatlantic migration was most frequent.[8]

The choice of my native village of Szamosszeg promised to be especially advantageous because I already had knowledge of the community. In the course of my research trips to the United States, I visited New Brunswick, New Jersey, where a good number of immigrants from Szamosszeg and their descendants live. I was connected to several not only by personal contact and acquaintance but also by family ties, and it appeared that these connections would simplify the process of systematically collecting information outside the sending village — in the settlement areas.

I collected information from a wide range of historical sources: aside from oral interviews I consulted written documents and even referred to photographs and other memorabilia.[9] In the course of my questioning, however, I soon came to realize that such sources of written information as personal correspondence and such documents as passports have only survived in rare instances. For the most part, it never occurred to the Szamosszegeans on either side of the ocean to keep such documents, nor did the political developments of the postwar period do much to encourage preservation. As a result, I began to place more and more emphasis in my research upon the collection and analysis of oral sources. In gathering information on individual migrants from Szamosszeg I interviewed those older villagers who were considered by the community to have the most knowledge about past events in the village. For each individual emigrant I prepared a separate card on which I recorded all available information. This in turn gave me further leads to other village elders, to family members of the emigrants, and even to living emigrants themselves. In order to check their demographic and economic situations, I cross-checked the oral interviews against available written documents such as church registers in the village and in New Brunswick. Out of the mosaic of the various written and oral sources, I was able to reconstruct some of the more important episodes in the life histories of a number of individuals.

Collective memory proved useful as it widened and increased the number of sources of information and offered the opportunity to counterbalance various subjective evaluations. In the course of interviewing it was my experience that in the memory of the old people, facts considered important on the basis of an earlier, older value system were fixed in their minds with great exactness. Without the least bit of doubt, those interviewed on both sides of the ocean were able to relate accurately such facts as who had owned how much land in the village and how they had gotten it. With similar certainty, they were able to tie together the emigrants, family lineages, and extended relations. In their oral information on almost three hundred individual emigrants, only occasionally did their accounts differ from what was written in the church records. In fact, their information on property ownership was more accurate from time to time than the property records. In written records, the recording of change of ownership rarely followed the actual turn of events: often land had long been divided among the children while the deed continued to list the parent as the owner.

Past experiences were viewed from the standpoint of the present and interpreted accordingly. When I asked a fellow migrant seemingly straightforward questions such as "Why did such and such a person go to America?" or "Why did he come back?" I would invariably get more information than when I directly asked the migrants, their families, or the village elders. People tended to leave out those details of their past experiences which dealt with ideological or political developments to which, from their present-day viewpoints, they were not so partial. In this way, evidence of documented radical behavior in esteemed friends or family members during the 1930s had fallen from memory. In this area, the village "outsiders"—those not involved in the events—were much more communicative.

In my originally planned program of research, I had intended to conduct an interview with at least one individual from each emigrating or remigrating family. The "Who can I meet and where?" questions gradually revealed enough information to render my original goal unrealistic. In spite of being able to make numerous personal contacts and to hold interviews outside of New Brunswick,[10] the emigrant generation, and particularly their children, are dispersed over such a wide geographic area that I was not able to visit all of their locations. Fortunately, however, someone was always able to more or less fill in the missing information on those families and on their offspring with whom I was unable to visit personally. In this way, the gathering of information—apart from a few exceptions—covers the entire emigrant group from Szamosszeg. Research across three generations does not go as deeply into each of the generations, and the emphasis of the questions was primarily on uncovering, in as much detail as possible, the fates of the first generation. I would ask the second generation, above all, about the lives of their parents. Instead of asking about their own lives or about their children's lives I concentrated on collecting information on their geographic and social mobility, language usage, and connection to their ethnic community. The latter mainly focussed on the question "Did people marry those within or outside of the Hungarian community?" On the basis of this information, I attempted to explore the path from one identity to another, for example, the changing manifestations of ethnicity and assimilation. In my investigation, I sought to discover more, through microanalysis, about the mechanism of migration and about the "transplanted community."

I do not claim that the example of Szamosszegeans is a valid one for the peasant migration of every new immigrant group. Neither do I claim that there were no other patterns within the Hungarian overseas migration at the same time. The history of the Szamosszegeans does, however, reveal an important pattern. It corresponds to other family histories already recorded in other Hungarian villages and confirms those trends already uncovered by macroanalysis.

The Mechanism of Migration

The development of overseas migration across Hungary over time forms an S-shaped curve on a graph. Migration from Szamosszeg developed in a similar way, although slightly later. At the beginning of the century, a few sporadic departures occurred, and from year to year the number increased at such a rate that by the 1910s, as the channels of information took shape, it took the form of "migration fever."

The village pioneers of migration to America were not typical peasants. They were craftsmen—half peasant, half tradesmen—those individuals whose jobs had already given them a certain degree of mobility before their move to America. Thus, they were more receptive to the new opportunities presented by such work. News of their experience motivated their relatives, immediate neighbors, and closest friends to make the move as well. In this way, chain migration was created. In almost every case a blood relationship existed between those who left first and those who followed. The few exceptions had individual reasons for going. The nearly three hundred individuals who left the village for the United States or Canada since the early 1900s can be linked by family connections into a chain of migration that began with the first pioneers and that still continues.

Young men—married and single—were the first to migrate. In almost every case, only one family member at a time would leave. An exception to this were a few older heads of households, thirty-five to forty, who took a teenage son along. None of the emigrant families set off together as a complete unit (i.e., both parents together with all the children); rather, part of the family left and part remained in the village.

The value system of the village was much slower to accept the migration of the single young women. The first to leave did not go to join a father or a brother. Rather, their motivation was a personal crisis of some sort—an unsuccessful love affair, an illegitimate child, family discord, or the arrival of a stepfather or stepmother. The villagers' negative opinion of a few of the girls who went to America even found its way into satirical verses. Although it never disappeared completely, the critical attitude tended to fade over the course of time. At the peak of the migration fever—1912 to 1913—as in other parts of the country, more women than men set off for America; the majority, 76 of 103, were single. The fact that they were not going to a husband chosen for them in the village is shown by how many of them married men outside the extended village community.

At the peak of the "fever," the typical migrant was quite young, often sixteen or seventeen. Many migrants who returned to visit the village went back to America with a group of teenagers under their "guardianship." Naturally, when interviewed by immigration authorities, the youngsters would add a few years to their age.[11] Large families, those with six to eight children, were thinned out by the departure of three or four children, one after the other. Some couples who emigrated together left their children in the village under the care of the grandparents. In three families only the wife emigrated, and the children and the household were left in the care of the husband.

The goal in every case was to work for the good of the family, yet the family did not always decide who would emigrate. An example of a sibling or relative who emigrated, or stories told by those who had returned from America building up and exaggerating its possibilities and prospects, sometimes carried away young people who never asked their family for permission to go.

In the village the most effective and alluring enticements to emigrate came from those who had already emigrated, sometimes as a result of their recruiting new emigrants. A few of them even invited others for material gain. For example, wives with boarding houses in America would send messages back to the village promising work and housing to those willing to emigrate. One sister of an immigrant woman made money from those leaving without passports, advising them which way to go and which ship to take. She became the "transporter" (*liferans*, a German word with a Hungarian ending)—the nickname by which old people in the village still refer to her.[12]

Migration to America was noticeably individualized in its development over time, with one family member at a time leaving. The decisions connected with these departures, though, were usually part of an overall family strategy. There were those families whose members had no opportunity to work in their own farm or household. They had to make their living on the outskirts of the village, or in a neighboring village, by hiring themselves out as seasonal workers or sharecroppers. "We sweated on somebody else's land," they recalled. "Opportunities became fewer and fewer."[13] "There were more and more people, and the bigger farms were always needing fewer and fewer workers." The combination of demographic pressure and the modernization of farming methods made it all the more difficult to get by in Hungary at the turn of the century. "The people lived in great poverty."[14] Under these conditions, the temporary emigration of part of the familial work force overseas became a more and more attractive alternative, particularly when families saw concrete proof of the opportunities to make money in America.

At the turn of the century a strategy of remaining permanently apart from the community, which could advance the lot of an individual, was still a strange idea in the world view of the peasants. At that time industrialization in Hungary had still not given the peasant mobility in every rural area. Where such mobility did exist—around Budapest—emigration to America did not catch on.[15] It was an integral part of the peasants' view of the world that the reason to go to America was to make money in order to improve and continue their lives in their original communities. A number of practical and concrete goals were listed: pay off taxes, redeem the inheritance (i.e., the house), and earn money for farm equipment and land. There were young people who dreamt of even more than these things and saw leaving as a way to become independent of parental authority. Still, their dreams always revolved around the acquisition of land; this was first and foremost in their value system. In the peasant world, land gave men and women honor and standing. "If I could just buy three holds of land, it would be just like I have six holds. In share-cropping I had to work six holds to get the produce of three."[16] This or similar reasoning was usually given when I asked the emigrants about their original goals.

A return to the sending community and to the family was always part of the plan, but in practice things did not turn out this way. Of those who left, only about half returned; the rest remained permanently in the United States. From the point of view of the emigrants' original plans, it is not those who returned who needed to be explained, but rather those who settled permanently in America. Is it that the successful, more conservative ones returned to the village? Representatives of both types stayed and returned; division was not along these lines. Instead, it can be concluded from some of their life stories that among those who returned more considered that they had fulfilled their purpose for going. The majority of those who returned bought parcels of land in the village, some even as large as fifty or sixty holds, and immediately raised their social standing to that of wealthy peasant. Among those who remained in America for ten or fifteen years, three families were able to free themselves from hired work and open their own saloon or butcher shop. Some immigrant families succeeded in establishing sources of family income other than regular wage work by skills brought with them from the village. The larger savings — which allowed the migrant to buy twenty or more holds of land or to open a shop — came in every case from three sources: the husband worked in the mine, the wife kept boarders, and the family made and sold brandy (*pálinka*) to the boarders.[17] This multifaceted activity required family cooperation. The main forces in the family "enterprises" were always the wives, and success depended on their energy.

Among those who remained in America were those who admitted that it was primarily because they were ashamed to return home without money. Village opinion was fairly harsh on those who returned home empty-handed. The decision on whether to remain in America or to return to the village was influenced by developing family relations. A definite "yes" or "no" decision on whether to return home or not was formulated slowly, and the date of the return trip delayed.

A number of those who in the end decided not to return to the village had even bought land there. In some cases, only after repeated trips back and forth was a final decision made. Usually, it was fathers who returned to their wives and children in the village. In four cases, nuclear families were united in America, two of them after a number of transatlantic migrations.[18]

In general, those who had married and begun families in the United States stayed there permanently. There were quite a few of these people; of 259 emigrants, 148 were single and almost all had married in the United States. In those families in which one spouse was not from Szamosszeg, there was no longer a simple choice of returning "home." Yet, twelve of the couples married in America did actually return, bringing with them a total of thirty-four children born in the United States. But it also happened that parents who had sent their children back to the village with relatives (to be cared for by grandparents) in the end never returned themselves.

World War I cut the emigration in half. Having been unable to return home because of the war, the trend of the 1920s was more toward remigration than emigration. As the fears of war and revolution died down and emigration fever began to stir again, the United States closed its gates. Those who had come back from America but who had intended on returning now set their sights on Canada, and in 1927 a group of more than twenty set off together.[19] All had either been in America themselves or had close relatives who had gone, and so chain migration continued. Those who went to Canada went with the hope of sooner or later moving to the United States, and some succeeded. One couple lived illegally in Cleveland for more than a decade while their sons remained in the village.[20]

In the 1930s the possibility of immigrating to Canada became more difficult. At this time, though, children of emigrants who had themselves been born in the United States but raised in the village set off for America. Few were able to recall their previous experiences there; the majority of them had been sent back to the village when they were either infants or very young children. In a few cases they were forced to emigrate in the interest of family strategy. "You can go, so go! You can make money to build a house and buy land. You can help the family to be better off."[21]

Chain migration to America continued from 1946 to 1948, with the emigration of a few relatives of those who had left in the 1930s. Among the 1956 "refugees" were twelve young people from Szamosszeg, all but three left from the city to which they had previously gone from the village. Still, each of them had a close relative in either the United States or Canada.

After World War II, only one son of a wealthy peasant family and his family emigrated for political reasons, as a so-called "displaced person." He was a member of the intelligentsia, a college graduate who had been raised in the village but who lived in the city. His final destination was Australia.

Until the 1920s, in the majority of cases of chain migration the goal was not the reunification of a nuclear family in the United States. Family members who had previously emigrated did not always send a boat ticket or encourage other relatives to come. Those family members who had already gone would influence other relatives (usually brothers, sisters, or in-laws) to imitate their behavior more by their example. The existence of a relative at the receiving end of the trip was important not for their direct material assistance but rather for the help they could give in the new situation (e.g., in finding a job) and for psychological reasons, that is, "if they could do it, then so can I!"

The Transplanted Community

Robert Swierenga summarizes his evaluation of the new studies on immigration as follows: "The most remarkable finding of the new immigration studies is that migration customarily involved the transplanting of *communities* over time, rather than the uprooting of nuclear families and individuals. By the process of chain migration, particular Old World sending communities became linked to particular New World receiving communities. Migration was a rational process and the outcome was homogeneous ethnic communities, held together by shared familial, religious, and social bonds. Cultural maintenance and distinctiveness, not assimilation, was the end result. American society was, and remains, a pluralistic society."[22]

This is an example of how recent writings within the field strongly emphasize connection and continuity with the sending communities in the formulation of immigrant communities. Through chain migration, those who set off from the same place would, at first, settle in the same place in the United States, implying a bridge between the sending and the receiving communities. According to U.S. government sources, emigrants from Hungary located in industrial states. The 1910 census puts the largest groups of Hungarian immigrants in Cleveland and New York, and in a number of settlements in West Virginia, Pennsylvania, Ohio, New Jersey, and Illinois. The list of the branches of American-Hungarian fraternal organizations also contains the names of a few hundred Hungarian settlements. From these it appears that "Hungarian America" was in reality spread across a large area as industrial workers settled in small enclaves. Large and small colonies from the same sending community appear in records of Hungarian churches in America. Even so, it is not enough to answer the question of whether those from the same village tended to group together in the same place or, more specifically, tended to stay in the same place. An examination of this question is better approached from outside, from the sphere of the sending community where everybody started. Therefore, let us look at what happened to those who went from Szamosszeg.

The name of New Brunswick, a small city in New Jersey, has become rooted in the collective consciousness of the village, for it is there that Szamosszegeans settled. At the beginning of my research I also believed that I would be able to track down nearly everyone there. Answers given in a series of systematic interviews uncovered the fact that even from the beginning of emigration the town played an important role as a destination for Szamosszegeans. Its preeminence, however, only came about in the late 1920s. "In the beginning, almost everybody went to West Virginia—to Holden—to work in the mines" reported the old people in the village.[23] The development of this small mining site began in 1904 with the opening of the coal mine there. It was through the work of labor recruiting agents that the first Szamosszegeans, brothers, came to Holden from another mining settlement in Cheswick.[24]

At that time Holden consisted only of what those who had cleared the forest had left behind them—makeshift wooden shanties. Those who lived in the settlement did not have as many of the advantages of civilization as they had in the village from which they had emigrated. In Holden, not only was there no doctor, but there was also no midwife to assist in childbirth—the women had only each other. They had neither a church nor a priest who could baptize their children. For example, the K. children were a few years old by the time their fathers were finally able to have a priest brought in to perform their baptism. The early difficulties were particularly embittering and exhausting for the women who lived with their families in Holden. The Szamosszegeans packed themselves into boardinghouses and tried to stay together as neighbors. "They all lived there right next to each other. On Sunday morning, they had a worship service. At our place was a very long table which were everywhere in those old houses. After they sang, my father said a prayer and read from the Bible. That was the worship service."[25] They always gathered together if a new person from the village arrived in order to be able to hear news from the village. But they would also come together if one of them had an accident; the murder of one of the women caused a great panic. "Nobody went to work on that day."[26]

The men frequently tried to escape the bleakness of life by drinking: the women, however, rebelliously demanded the closing of the saloon which after its opening had become far and away the community's most popular meeting place. At the same time, though, the situation in Holden actually lessened the difficulty of the transition from the Old World way of life. People were able to continue their peasant farming as a supplement to their earnings in the mines. They planted gardens next to the company houses, kept animals, not just chickens but pigs as well, and in fact even grazed cows on the hillsides.[27]

The coal companies paid each worker according to the amount he produced. Because the companies did not want Szamosszegeans to master any of the more modern techniques of mining, they dug as they had back home—with great physical exertion in an unfamiliar workplace. Those accustomed to task-oriented farm work in the sunny fields now had to go underground and work monotonously under dangerous conditions. Some could keep their nerve and strength and would not compete with each other at work. Those who could do more work, and in this way make "good money," happily and boastfully collected their gold dollars, planned the departure date for their return trip, and succeeded in their purposes in the village. Those who were not capable of such great physical exertion and who became dissatisfied with the work migrated restlessly on, searching for better and easier possibilities. In this way, groupings of Szamosszegeans were formed in two other mining settlements in West Virginia: in Granttown, near Fairmont, and in Dobra, south of Charlestown. At first only one Szamosszegean went to Granttown from Holden along with a newly acquired friend. As another Szamosszegean explained, he also got tired of the hard coal *diggolás* and was getting on in Granttown, where the mining work seemed easier.[28] He invited the other Szamosszegeans from Holden and called his brother-in-law together with his wife from the village. Other relatives came after them.

Although it is not known who among those in Holden initiated the migration to Dobra, by World War I a number of Szamosszegean families lived there. In the course of alternating between the three mining sites, each family became more separated from the others, not following their friends but rather going to other mining settlements. The opening and closing of individual mines contributed to the fact that a few of the families moved from place to place almost constantly.

The West Virginia mining sites hardly differed in the living conditions they offered; the years spent there are remembered generally as a bitter and difficult period. Those born and raised there described the mining sites as boring and uncivilized places. "There weren't even any streets in Granttown. It looked like a ghost town. The house we lived in didn't even have an address. On the building was just a post-box with a number '78' on it."[29] "We didn't know what to do in Dobra, so I kept myself busy by learning how to crochet. For the girls it was hard to find work. For a while I did the washing-up for a family. I could hardly wait to get out of there. . . ."[30] In Dobra, the Szamosszegeans lived next door to each other in company houses. "We were able to keep small livestock. I had a goose, a hen and a chicken. I milked the cow and made cheese and cream. In the garden I grew tomatoes, red peppers and other vegetables."[31]

A permanent movement among the Szamosszegeans from the West Virginia mining sites began between 1916 and 1917. News of job opportunities at the expanding Ford plant attracted the younger generation to Detroit, and by the beginning of the 1920s a small group had already moved there. After a few years hardly any remained in Granttown or in Holden, while "Dobra . . . was completely abandoned by the Szamosszegeans."[32] As an explanation for this migration from the mining area, recollections cited a decline in miners' wages, frequent and long-lasting strikes, and continued unsuccessful struggles for unions. Remigration back to the village also had its effects. "I worked in Granttown from 1914 to 1924 [recalled J.P.]. The big strike was in 1921. We were on strike for eight months, and all the time the mine was closed and nobody worked. The people wanted the union but the company didn't. The Hungarians went on relief and got help from the union too. Over the course of eight months though we ate up almost everything. When the eight months were up, in November, we went back to work. Then we worked as usual until 1924. But there was another strike. 'Ah,' I said, 'I'm moving on.' And I went too—I went to New Brunswick. . . ."[33] Other Szamosszegeans went, too. The Szamosszeageans had their first experiences of workers' struggles in West Viriginia and encountered the company's cruel attitude toward the workers; during the strikes they were driven with their families from the company houses and had to live for months in tents.[34]

Conditions in West Virginia in the early 1920s were a key factor in the remigration of some back to Szamosszeg and further migration of others to find work in factories. The largest number went to New Brunswick to the Johnson and Johnson medical supplies factory. Others went to Detroit, Cleveland, and even Duquesne and McKeesport, Pennsylvania. A few, though, "disappeared" somewhere in Pennsylvania.[35] The transformation from emigrant peasants into miners and then workers in other branches of industry was not unique to the Szamosszegeans. As historical sources indicate, multitudes of immigrant Hungarian peasants followed this very same path.

Who were the first to arrive in New Brunswick and why they remained is unknown, but a few people from the village already lived there in 1903. New Brunswick became the most important center of settlement for girls from the village, who were attracted by job possibilities in the cigar factories. The employment of the Hungarian female work force increased so rapidly that eventually the foremen were either Hungarian or could communicate in Hungarian.[36] The Hungarian working women of the cigar factories made New Brunswick known in the West Virginia mining sites as well. From there, young unmarried men— and not just Szamosszegeans—came to New Brunswick to get married, taking their wives back with them to the mining sites. The register of the Hungarian Reformed Church in New Brunswick contains entries for fifty-three such marriages between 1906 and 1925 in which at least one spouse was from the village.[37] Of those marriages, only fourteen were between two Szamosszegeans, although in all the marriages both bride and groom were Hungarian. Although it was still considered important to marry with the same denomination, mixed marriages did occur and were the result of acquaintances made in America.

From the mid-1920s, more Szamosszegeans began to settle permanently in New Brunswick. Only a few had their own house in 1920, typically a two-family house with the downstairs rented out. Living together in larger groups as boarders at a Szamosszegean family's house was common before 1914, but from the mid-1920s on the practice began to die out. Those who owned their own house or who rented a separate flat lived with, at most, one or two friends or relatives, but the tendency was toward the establishment of nuclear households. In this way, Szamosszegeans began to become physically and geographically separated, and their neighbors gradually became non-Szamosszegeans and often not even Hungarians.

By the 1920s, as New Brunswick was only a small town, its Hungarian immigrant community of several thousand represented a significant group. Every Hungarian religious denomination had established its own church: Reformed, Roman Catholic, Greek Catholic, and Baptist; there was even a Hungarian synagogue. The Reformed church had already split: one group accepted the direct control of the church authorities in Hungary; the other was strongly affiliated to the Reformed church in the United States. Szamosszegeans could be found in both groups, a fact that shows that their ties with each other had become looser. At that same time, the control of the sending community over them was also becoming weaker. If they were in village groups at first, from the mid-1920s onward they became increasingly integrated as individuals into various Hungarian communities.

From the point of view of the sending village, besides the initial gathering together, the changing character and dispersion of the transplanted community was plainly obvious, particularly when one takes into account the Szamosszegeans who had emigrated to Canada in the 1920s. They were taken to Saskatchewan to do agricultural work;[38] from there most moved to Hamilton, Ontario, and the surrounding countryside, spreading out into the tobacco-growing areas.

The existence and persistence of the transplanted community in New Brunswick for a fairly long time was closely related to the continuous chain migration. In the 1930s the immigrant Szamosszegeans' children who had been "born in America and raised in the village" returned to New Brunswick. It was their destination in spite of the fact that they had been taken to the village from West Virginia and their closest relative lived somewhere else. Family ties and friendships with those from the village were, on the whole, important in the lives of those who had emigrated from Szamosszeg, although not with the same degree of intensity in every case. For decades, many would spend vacations visiting their most distant friends and relatives, however, personal relationships had become greatly weakened, even in the first generation. Surviving first-generation emigrants who were interviewed did not always name someone from the village as their best friend. A few of the Szamosszegean emigrants, however, were eager to keep track of how other emigrants and their children were getting on. These individuals supplied me with the most and the most valuable information; by the 1970s only a few remained who desired to maintain the quasi-norms of community solidarity.

The one event that still brings Szamosszegeans together as a group in New Brunswick is the death of someone from the village.[39] A "burial on foreign soil" still keeps alive feelings of solidarity in those who, in time and place, are losing contact with each other. One Szamosszegean expressed this as following: "I still have to go to the funeral of a Szamosszegean as long as my aunt Piroska is still alive, because

she expects me to. She said that as long as there is even one Szamosszegean among you he must go to the funeral."

Although detailed discussion is not possible, something should be
said about the lives of the children and granchildren of the Szamosszegeans, as well as something about their marriages. The children
of Szamosszegeans, with one exception did not marry each other. The
second generation generally married Hungarians, but more often than
expected marriages occurred with persons of other ethnic backgrounds. The granchildren of the emigrants, without exception, married someone who had no Hungarian background. Those who married
non-Hungarians would also not necessarily choose someone of the
same religious denomination. If any tendency appears in their marriages it is that they often married children of Central or East European immigrants: Poles, Italians, and Slovaks, although the third
generation married into almost every national group.[40]

Microanalysis has confirmed, reinforced, and, at the same time,
made all the more lifelike that characteristic of the overseas Hungarian
migration identified by macroanalytical research—its basically temporary character in intention at least. On the basis of information
obtained by microanalysis, we cannot say that those who stayed in
America were settlement migrants and those who returned were sojourners. Microanalysis is better at illustrating the different sorts of
movement back and forth, the fragmented families on two sides of
the Atlantic, and how temporary migration often turned into permanent migration.

Second, microanalysis opens up to investigation those aspects of
the unfolding migration that simply are not accessible through macroanalysis. For example, microanalysis shows how it was always those
chains of information, personal and primary, which played a role in
overseas migration. This channel of communication across the Atlantic
was between Szamosszegeans in America and Szamosszegeans in the
village. Face-to-face relationships also played an important part in
migration within the United States for Szamosszegeans, but in a modified way. Their newly made friendships became, as time went on,
more and more with non-Szamosszegean Hungarians who helped them
move from one place to another.

Through microanalysis it becomes possible to follow the trails of
emigrants and to note the strengths and limits of group cohesion as
well as the manifestations of rebellion against it. For example, at the
time of migration not only the population of the village of Szamosszeg
but also the surrounding area was entirely Reformed church. Village
marriage laws bound people to the denomination, and only rarely

was there a marriage with someone from a different village. Those who emigrated to America began to deviate from this and to violate these norms, and the second generation frequently—and the third generation consistently—entered into ethnically mixed marriages. This raises the question of ethnic homogeneity across generations. We must take into account the important differences between those ethnic groups with millions of members, for example, Poles and Italians, and those with only a few hundred thousand, such as Magyars, Slovenes, Slovaks, and Croats. The niche in the economic structure into which each immigrant group settled was an important factor which determined its ability to maintain its respective ethnic homogeneity. The migrant-worker life-style of Hungarians, at least until the mid-1920s, made their transplanted community amorphous and, as such, they mixed more quickly with other ethnic groups. This mixing can be assumed to have been more rapid than, for example, Swedish, German, or Danish peasants who settled in more isolated agricultural regions of the United States.[41]

Only by microanalysis can we measure the real distance traveled on the scale of mobility—the real changes in life-style—because we can observe the emigrants set against their cultural background, which is impossible to do from migration statistics alone. In this way we can see what changes occurred in the lives of the migrating generation and what industrialization entailed for them. To learn more about those changes, the people who lived through them are important sources for the researcher. The Szamosszegeans viewed the changes in their lives as follows: "For a long time it was very hard. Our children and especially our grandchildren would not believe what America was like when we started off here. We've experienced an awful lot of change—but today we can see that, after all, even if it was hard and painful, we made the right choice."

NOTES

1. Frank Thistlethwaite, "Migration from Europe Overseas in the Nineteenth and Twentieth Centuries," XIe Congrès International des Sciences Historiques, *Rapports* 5 (Uppsala, 1960): 32-60.

2. Julianna Puskás, *From Hungary to the United States, 1880-1914* (Budapest, 1982); Puskás, *Kivándorló Magyarok az Egyesült Államokban, 1880-1940* [Emigrant Hungarians in the United States, 1880-1940] (Budapest, 1982).

3. Between 1899 and 1913 the official number of Hungarian immigrants was 492,031. Of these, 314,547, or 63.9 percent, remigrated according to U.S. immigration statistics; see *Harvard Encyclopedia of American Ethnic Groups*, ed. Stephan Thernstrom (Cambridge, 1980), 1036. In Hungarian emigration

statistics, the percentage of remigration was about 33 percent during the same time. From this point of view the Hungarian statistics are the more deficient. "A magyar szent korona országainak kivándorlása és visszaván- dorlása, 1888-1913" [Emigration and remigration in the counties of the Hungarian sacred crown], *Magyar Statisztikai Közlemények* (Budapest, 1918), 36 (hereafter, *Hungarian Statistics*).

4. In the 14-44 age group, 48.3 percent of the men and 37.2 percent of the women were married, *Hungarian Statistics*, Table 49, 57.

5. Among the emigrants from Hungary, 66.1 percent were men, and 33.9 percent were women in the period from 1899 to 1913. During these years the percentage changed in the following way: from 1899-1904, 69.3 percent of the emigrants were men, 30.7 percent were women; from 1905-7, 70.3 percent were men, and 29.7 percent were women; from 1908-13, 59 percent were men, and 41 percent were women, *Hungarian Statistics*, 9.

6. The social composition of Dutch emigrants and English emigrants was strikingly differed as is apparent from the analyses of Robert Swierenga, "Dutch International Migration and Occupational Change: A Structural Analysis of Multinational Linked Files," in *Migration Across Time and Nations: Population Mobility in Historical Contexts*, ed. Ira A. Glazier and Luigi De Rosa (New York, 1986), 95-124; and Charlotte Erickson, "The Uses of Passenger Lists for the Study of British and Irish Emigrations," ibid., 318-35.

7. Kristian Hvidt, *Flugten til Amerika eller Drivekraefter i massutvandrigen fra Danmark 1868-1914* [The flight to America, or push factors in mass emigration from Denmark] (Odense, 1971); and *From Sweden to America: A History of the Migration*, ed. Harald Runblom and Hans Norman (Minneapolis, 1976).

8. Puskás, *From Hungary to the United States, 1880-1914*, 57 (map).

9. The collection *Magyarok az Egyesült államokban és Kanadában: Szamos- szegiek, Interjúk, levelek, fotök* [Hungarians in the United States and Canada: The Szamosszegeans, interviews, letters, photos], collection in possession of author.

10. I was able to travel to Holden, West Virginia; Cleveland; Detroit; Pittsburgh; and to Hamilton, Ontario.

11. In 1913, eighteen Szamosszegeans went to the United States in a group; the "guardian" was Izabella S., a remigrant who made her second trip. Interview with Borbála Sz., New Brunswick, 1983.

12. Interview with Ignac T., Szamosszeg, 1983.

13. Interview with Julianna and Borbála Sz., New Brunswick, 1984.

14. Interview with Gusztáv K., Detroit, 1983.

15. Puskás, *From Hungary to the United States, 1880-1914*, 57.

16. 1 hold equals 1.42 acres; interview with Gábor F., New Brunswick, 1984.

17. Interviews with Julianna S. and Borbála Sz., New Brunswick, 1984.

18. Interviews with families of Sándor K., Detroit, 1983 and Joseph P., New Brunswick, 1986.

238   JULIANNA PUSKAS

19. One member of the group which migrated to Canada, Gusztáv L., related this information about those who left at that time. Interview in Hamilton, Ontario, 1982.

20. After World War II, Mrs. O. wrote a dramatic letter in which she informed her son that they could not arrange for his immigration because they themselves were illegal immigrants; letter in author's collection.

21. The parents insisted on this and sent back their plans; for example, Irma B. in 1930 and two brothers who went away in 1937 and 1939, Ferenc P. and István P. When they left, they thought they would return to the village, however both remained permanently in America. During World War II, István fought in the Pacific against the Japanese. It would make a good novelette: the war story of the "American Soldier" who "only know a few words of English." Interviews with Irma B. and István P., New Brunswick, 1984 and 1986.

22. Robert P. Swierenga, "Ethnic History," *Ethnic Forum* 4 (Spring 1984): 4.

23. Interview with Ignac K. and Ignac T., Szamosszeg, 1983.

24. Interview with Gusztáv K., Detroit, 1983 and 1985. He recalled in vivid detail how they were taken by wagon from Huntington to Holden, West Virginia, and how the agent who took them disappeared during the first night. When he spoke of the shanties, I thought he was exaggerating, but when I obtained a picture of Holden from the Logan County newspaper, I realized what he said was true. In any case Holden developed quickly; see Walter R. Thurmond, *The Logan Coal Field of West Virginia* (Morgantown, 1964).

25. Interview with Gusztáv K.

26. Ibid.

27. Interviews with Victor B., son of a Szamosszegean emigrant, Ashland, Kentucky, 1985 and 1986, and Ilona K. and Antal Sz., Holden, West Virginia, 1986.

28. Interview with Gusztáv K., Detroit, 1983. *Diggolás* is an American-Hungarian colloquial expression meaning *to dig*.

29. Interview with Margit Sz., New Brunswick, 1985.

30. Interview with Piroska Gy., New Brunswick, 1985.

31. Interview with Julianna S., New Brunswick, 1984.

32. Interview with Gusztáv K., Detroit, 1983 and 1985.

33. Interview with Joseph P., New Brunswick, 1985.

34. Gusztáv K. and Bertalan K. recounted these events in detail in the course of their interviews, Detroit, 1983, and New Brunswick, 1984.

35. Gusztáv K. was the most migratory among those who came from the village. In 1904 he went to America as a young boy with his mother and thus was able to provide the most information about the "ancient history" of the Szamosszegeans in America. On six occasions he spoke for several hours, and in the course of these talks he gave some sort of information about almost everyone because he had met them in one place or another

during his travels. "Last time I saw him here" or "I met him there," "he disappeared," or "he died somewhere in Pennsylvania," was how he remembered those who had separated themselves from the group. Interviews with Gusztáv K., Detroit, 1984-86.

36. Interview with Piroska Gy., and Irma F., New Brunswick, 1984.

37. *A New Brunswicki Magyar Református Egyház anyakönyvei: 1905-töl* [Birth, marriage, death records of the Hungarian Reformed Church since 1905], New Brunswick.

38. Interview with Gusztáv L., Hamilton, Ontario, 1982.

39. Interview with István P., New Brunswick, 1986.

40. One has married a Korean and another a Hindu; a few of Christian background have married Jews.

41. Walter Kamphoefner has written that "rapid Americanization of the old immigrant groups such as the German was used as a stick with which to beat the allegedly less desirable new immigrants." Walter D. Kamphoefner: "The German Agricultural Frontier: Crucible or Cocoon," *Ethnic Forum* 4 (Spring 1984): 1-2, 21.

PART THREE

Emigration and Immigration: Two Case Studies

10

The Crossroad Province: Quebec's Place in International Migrations, 1870–1915

BRUNO RAMIREZ

Canada is one of the few Western countries that participated in the great migration movements of the nineteenth and twentieth centuries as both a receiving and a sending country, a double role that raises important conceptual and methodological issues that have received little or no attention by immigration historians. Yet, the implications are important for both the study of the international migration phenomenon and for the understanding of Canadian history. The constant arrival of European immigrants on the one hand, and the chronic out-migration of Canadians on the other, generated a mechanism of population exchange that accelerated the ethnocultural recomposition of Canada's population. If this mechanism is placed in its proper historical context characterized by fragile nation-building and acute ethnic tension between the two founding groups, it begins to be apparent how central the contribution of immigration history can be for a critical comprehension of this formative period of Canadian history.

In addition to being the province where the majority of French Canadians resided, Quebec was also the geoeconomic region par excellence that witnessed this double process of population outflow and inflow, and where the political and cultural repercussions of such a process became most acute. Moreover, during the historical period discussed in this chapter Quebec experienced the convulsions associated with such far-reaching socioeconomic processes as the industrial revolution and widespread urbanization. These developments are at the roots of the ongoing population movements that marked Quebec and — more than the movements of capital — contributed to inserting the province into the Atlantic economies.

Thus, although the relationship between immigration and economic development, between immigration and the dynamics of regional and international labor markets, is central to this discussion, it will go beyond the now-classic push-pull paradigm and adopt a perspective that sees immigration not as a mechanical response to an overarching economic rationality, but rather as the subtle interplay between economic and cultural factors. This perspective will then be applied more particularly to the Montreal region in an attempt to provide a case study of one North American city where immigration contributed to the formation and development of a segmented labor market.

After the massive arrival of immigrants from the British Isles during the pre-Confederation period, Quebec took on a new role in the movement of transatlantic migrations by becoming the destination for new migratory currents originating primarily from East Central and Southern Europe. These currents were part of the unprecedented transfers of populations and labor power that marked the history of Europe and North America from the late nineteenth century to the 1920s.[1]

In Quebec, Montreal soon became the great point of distribution of the new immigrant work force. As Canada's leading commercial center and hub of the country's transportation network, Montreal became the labor market where the first large contingents of immigrants were recruited and sent to the interior to meet the demand of railroad construction projects and the extractive industries. At the same time, Montreal and its immediate surroundings constituted Quebec's great pole of industrial development and the major region of population attraction in that vast process of urbanization that marked the province at the time.[2] Therefore, the new immigration wave satisfied the needs of two rapidly expanding labor markets. One was essentially seasonal in character and closely followed the evolution of the industrial geography at a regional and a national level. The other was tributary to the development of the manufacturing industry in the Montreal region and the expansion of an urban economy.[3] It was in the latter context that the phenomenon of labor-market segmentation became most visible.

No separate statistics of yearly immigrant entries to Quebec exist for the period under discussion, thus making accurate estimates impossible of the actual volume of immigrant population which, temporarily or not, occupied the province. A partial quantitative view can only be obtained from the decennial census statistics which specified the ethnic origin of the enumerated populations. Thus, the immigrant-ethnic population whose origins were other than French or British progressed from 26,000 in 1901 to about 158,000 in 1931, when more than four-fifths of that population was concentrated within the Montreal region, with Jews and Italians constituting the majority.[4]

The arrival and settlement of this immigrant population in the province's social and economic space occurred as Quebec was experiencing a massive exodus of its own population toward the United States (Table 10.1).[5] The demographic loss resulting from this population outflow reached such alarming levels that it became a major political issue. This apparent paradox of opening the door to immigration while at the same time enacting economic policies having the effect of driving thousands of French Canadians away from their motherland was viewed by French-Canadian elites as a deliberate attempt on the part of federal politicians to weaken the francophone community within the Confederation. As the volume of departures reached new heights, "colonization" and "repatriation" became the two *mots d'ordre* that the francophone elite tried to translate into measures to block the demographic hemorrhage, or at least to bring it within tolerable limits.[6]

The process of colonization of vacant land in the province's interior had evolved for generations as a response to the overpopulation and landlessness that had plagued many parishes in the nineteenth century. On some occasions, as in the 1850s, the phenomenon had taken on a continental dimension, with considerable numbers of French Canadians moving to the American midwestern frontier and settling on farmland there. But as wave upon wave of Quebecers left their parishes to sell their labor in the New England manufacturing centers, colonization (and the patriotic ideology that accompanied it) was promoted as the vehicle through which potential emigrants could be turned toward the province's own territory, where vast forests still awaited the "civilizing" ax and plow of French-Canadian settlers. Some of the mixed results of this policy have been analyzed skillfully by Robert LeBlanc.[7]

The repatriation crusade waged by the same elites to bring back to Quebec the French Canadians who had already immigrated to the United States was inconclusive.[8] The failure of this program was due not only to the lack of political will by those responsible for rendering it truly operational and attractive, but also the attitude of the immigrants themselves—to their reading of the existing options and their perceptions of their economic and social universe. Ultimately, their choices and strategies produced a peculiar ethnocultural geography in the northeastern portion of North America under the powerless eyes of politicians and ideologues.

The paradoxical character of this double process of population

Table 10.1. Estimates of Net Emigration to the United States from
Canada and Quebec, 1840-1940

Period	Canada		Quebec		Percent Quebec of Canada
	Thousands	Percent*	Thousands	Percent*	
1840-50	75	4.30	35	5.40	47
1850-60	150	7.00	70	7.80	47
1860-70	300	10.70	NA	NA	NA
1870-80	375	11.00	120	10.10	32
1880-90	450	11.30	150	11.30	33
1890-1900	425	9.70	140	9.60	33
1900-1910	325	6.40	100	6.00	31
1910-20	250	4.00	80	4.00	32
1920-30	450	6.00	130	5.60	29
1930-40	25	0.30	NA	NA	NA
1840-1940	2,800	—	900	—	32

Source: Yolande Lavoie, *L'émigration des Québécois aux Etats-Unis de 1840 à 1930* (Québec, 1979), p. 45.
* Decennial rates of net emigration as percentage of total Canadian and Quebec population.

inflow and outflow was only an apparent one; it was paradoxial only for those bent on seeing entries and exits to and from their province exclusively from a patriotic standpoint. The paradox did not exist because those migratory movements were engendered by precise local conditions and directed toward zones of development on the basis of choices and calculations that had little to do with political considerations.

The rapid expansion of industrial capitalism on the Quebecois landscape meant that the emergence of powerful poles of development was accompanied by the marginalization of given geoeconomic areas. Quebec thus participated in the growth of the international economic circuit both as a point of development and as a marginal socioeconomic area. The deepening of these regional disparities within a specific international labor context was at the origin of the double mechanism of population transfers. Why, then, did these regional disparities not produce a geographic redistribution of Quebec's own population, thus obviating the province from resorting massively to external sources of labor power?

In reality, a process of internal population redistribution did occur and constituted one of the central dynamics of the province's socioeconomic history, for example, the movement from the country to the city particularly of the rural population to the Montreal region.[9] But a parallel movement — the colonization movement — is also apparent in the opposite direction, not toward the city but toward the province's back county. Both in terms of the population involved and in terms of economic consequences the colonization movement did little to redress the problem of regional disparities.[10] Its immediate effect was certainly to alleviate the problem of surplus population, especially in some of the overcrowded parishes. In the long run, this movement did lead to the creation of new areas of settlement, which in time acquired socioeconomic stability and regional physiognomy. However, with the exception of the preindustrial period, colonization was a weak competitor of the emigration movement south of the border. It is not surprising therefore if one of Quebec's most important regions of colonization, the Saguenay, had reached a population from 1851 to 1901 barely above the French-Canadian population of a single New England manufacturing center such as Fall River or Lowell.[11]

In some regions of Quebec, colonization also delayed the exodus to the United States, a fact clearly revealed by the comparative study of population movements in two countries of emigration, Berthier and Rimouski. One can reconstitute these movements with a certain accuracy from the information contained in the yearly parish reports sent to the local diocese. The parish priest (when he did his job properly) reported, among other things, the number of families that had joined the parish in a given year, and also indicated the parishes from which they had come. He also reported the number of families leaving the parish and the parish of their destination. Berthier County was a long-settled region just beyond the immediate rural-agricultural belt surrounding Montreal, about sixty kilometers northeast of the city. The county had enjoyed a relatively early linkage to the regional and continental railroad network. The population movements from parish to parish, or from old and large parishes to newer parishes situated farther into the hinterland, appear to be minimal in Berthier County. Instead, a considerable number of families and young unmarried people were departing for the United States. In the course of the 1880s the population movement to and from the United States rose dramatically and maintained high levels through the 1890s; Berthier County clearly experienced an early integration of its population into the labor markets of New England.[12]

The scenario is quite different in Rimouski County, one of the largest counties in the northeast of the province, extending from the St. Lawrence to the province of New Brunswick. During the last third of the nineteenth century, with the exception of the parishes situated along the littoral, most of the county was a region of colonization.[13] During the 1870s and 1880s most of the population movements that have been reconstituted occurred from parish to parish within the same county or to neighboring counties. The departures of families toward the United States or Montreal were negligible. Around the late 1880s the geography of these population movements changed dramatically, and throughout the 1890s nearly all the departures reported were toward the United States.[14]

The attraction that the gigantic industrial machine south of the border exerted was too powerful to be resisted. But unless it is accounted for in strictly abstract terms, the pull effect which radiated northward from the American manufacturing centers must be viewed in the context of the concrete options that many rural Quebecers faced. More specifically, this pull effect had to be evaluated against the material difficulties and the economic prospects offered by colonization. The interaction of these two options—colonization and emigration—constitutes the most important distinctive feature in the history of the emigration movement from Quebec.

A rare account of the vicissitudes awaiting a *colon* wishing to settle in the virgin forests exists in the autobiography of Félix Albert.[15] A rural Quebecer raised in the Rimouski-Temiscuata region, Albert had experienced the backbreaking work of clearing forest land from the age of fourteen, when his father joined the colonization movement in the area. After establishing his own family, Albert continued in his work of turning wooded "desert" into fertile farmland. His life story as a *colon* during the 1860s and 1870s is a sequence of successes and disasters, most due to crop destructions caused by early frosts or lack of rain. When such crises hit, the only option for Albert, like most neighboring settlers, was to sell his labor in the timber industry somewhere in the surrounding regions. With no secure propsect in view for himself and his family, he decided to try his chance in Maine, where his wife had relatives. Albert's trip to Maine in a horse-drawn cart is one of the most moving sections of his autobiography. He spent the winter months in Maine and returned to his farm just in time for the growing season. But once again his crop was ruined, this time by wheat rust. In despair, Albert and his wife took the only other decision left; they packed and moved their whole family to Lowell, Massachusetts, and ultimately settled there.

The penetration of the railroad into the province's hinterland made odysseys such as Félix Albert experienced needless. As the nineteenth century moved toward a close, tens of rural counties were linked, one after the other, directly or indirectly, to the great urban and industrial poles of the American Northeast. A growing number of rural Quebecers who might have been caught in the dilemma of whether to colonize or emigrate viewed emigration as a better and more viable alternative. Among other things, the option contained a variety of possibilities. One could resort to it as a temporary strategy; one could move with the whole family; one could send one or more children of working age as a way of redressing the family economy; or temporary emigration could be seen as a sort of testing period, in the course of which a final strategy could be decided. One aspect that has yet to be analyzed is that, for many Quebecers, the immediacy of reward made emigration a better alternative to colonization. The immediate cash reward that the wage system provided accelerated the social time when prospects could be turned into concrete individual and family economic strategies. Those cash rewards were only one day of travel away for most rural Quebecers by the 1880s.

It is not surprising then if, during the two closing decades of the century when emigration to the United States took on the character of an exodus, all the possibilities that the emigration alternative foreshadowed turned into distinct patterns. In some cases, some patterns grew from long-established internal migratory practices adapted to the new industrial context. Many young Quebecers, for instance, who had already been part of the seasonal forestry industry, often long distances away from their parishes, had only to change routes and alternate seasonal work in their own district's farmlands with temporary work in New England factories.[16] In most such cases, the move toward the new labor markets proved to be a shorter one, and the monetary rewards more substantial.

Another pattern reflected a kind of family strategy that possibly was specific to the Quebec geoeconomic context: the migration of entire families and then their return, after an indefinite period, to their original parishes. Usually a pattern of temporary migration that precedes a movement of definitive emigration is associated with single men or women. What is significant about the case under discussion is not merely the temporary nature of the migration, but the fact that an entire family would be involved. In Berthier County we found this pattern was more pronounced in the early stage of the mass migration movement, particularly during the 1870s. The families that had practiced this pattern were headed by men in a wide spectrum of occupations, a pattern that closely reflected the county's occupational structure. Not surprisingly, therefore, the majority belonged to the two most important occupational groups: small farmers and laborers. These were not the typical families that went down to New England to fill the textile mills with children and women. Their main characteristic was the relatively small number of members within each family, with children well below the working age and mothers in many cases continuing child-bearing while sojourning in the United States.[17] It seems probable that for such migrant families (clearly a minority) which had to survive on a single salary and in a much more exacting living environment than they had left, emigration must have been far from the solution to their problems.

Francis Early's study on the working and living conditions of French Canadians in Lowell during the 1870s has shown that it was nearly impossible for a family to survive in a mill-town urban economy without the joint wages of various family members.[18] Even as late as 1908, when the living environment in the large New England textile centers had become less onerous and French Canadians had moved somewhat up the occupational ladder of that industry, the Dillingham Commission found that 40 percent of the family income in the average French-Canadian household came from the earnings of wife and children. French Canadians must have soon found out that if family emigration was to be viable it was essential to count on the earnings of various family members.[19]

It was common for families to put an end to their temporary migratory experience by not returning to their original parishes, but by prolonging their stay in the United States and finally settling there. Aggregate statistical estimates of this immigration movement over a long period show the overwhelming numerical preponderance of those who settled in the United States over those who returned to Quebec.[20] The fact that many Quebecer families must have first resorted to emigration as a temporary strategy may be deduced from a frequent practice observed in the study of Berthier County: farmers who kept their farm property while sojourning in the United States. This practice clearly reflected the farm's importance as an economic resource on which to fall back in view of a possible return and resettlement in one's own parish. In this context, therefore, the act of selling one's farm property in Quebec strongly suggests an economic strategy involving the decision to remain, and most likely settle, in the United States. Systematic review of all the transactions notarized in Berthier County during the period of mass emigration (1875-1905) allows us to single out all those cases in which one party to land-sale transaction resided in the United States. U.S. residents who sold their land in Quebec were the overwhelming majority compared to U.S. residents who bought land in Berthier County. The annual fluctuations in the volume of these land-sale transactions are shown in Figure 10.1 and

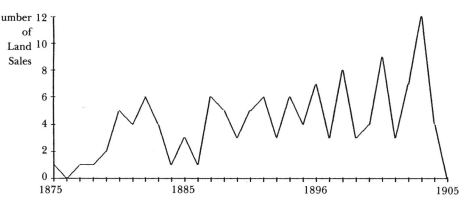

Figure 10.1. Annual Number of Land Sales by French Canadians
Residing in New England, Berthier County, Quebec, 1875-1905
Source: Bruno Ramirez and Jean Lamarre, "Du Québec vers les Etats-Unis: l'étude
des lieux d'origine," *Revue d'histoire de l'Amérique française* 38 (Winter 1985): 421.

reflect an overall trend toward increase until 1903. The signs of a
changing migratory pattern, from temporary to permanent, are apparent in this trend. And these signs seem to confirm the conclusion
of some scholars: by the 1890s the emigration movement from Quebec
had acquired a more stable character; Quebecers increasingly had
come to see emigration as a long-term strategy rather than as a temporary solution to immediate problems[21] Available statistical data do
not allow us to establish whether the Berthier County emigration
movement conformed to that overall provincial trend. But the persistence of land sales by former Berthier County residents, coupled
with the emergence of emigration networks linking that county to
various Rhode Island and Massachusetts locations, are important evidence that points to a stabilization of that emigration movement.

Our present attempts to reconstitute a number of such networks
from Berthier and Rimouski counties have not only revealed the
centrality of kinship in the migratory process—confirming conclusions reached by Tamara Hareven—but also seem to show that once
these networks reached a stage of consolidation, they tended to exert
a stabilizing influence on the emigration movement. They, for instance, facilitated the circulation of information regarding places of
destination, on the state of local labor markets, and on local socioeconomic conditions including such conflicts as prolonged strikes and
lockouts. Such information made it possible for a potential emigrant
to approach the decisions of when and whether to leave in more
realistic terms, greatly reducing the character of "adventure toward

the unknown" that emigration may have assumed thirty or forty years earlier.

When in 1899 the Boucher family put an end to a life of bare subsistence in a rural parish near Rimouski and moved to Fall River, for example, the decision to emigrate must have been based on concrete knowledge of the conditions at the other end of the trip and on the assurance of a certain degree of assistance forthcoming from relatives already settled in Fall River. Mr. Boucher had two cousins in Quebec who had sojourned in the United States "to make quick money." On the other side of the border, relatives "had been advertising" to the Bouchers the advantages of moving to Fall River. The day after they arrived in Fall River they could already lodge on their own, and three days later the school year started and three Boucher children could be placed in the local French-Canadian parish school. Elmire Boucher was only five at the time; when she reached fourteen in 1913, she began working in a local textile mill, starting at $7.77 a week.[22] In Montreal, European immigrant laborers were making the same money, if not less.

At about the same time that rural Quebec became solidly integrated into the labor markets of New England, Montreal entered a cycle of unprecedented industrial expansion and economic growth that provoked an internal migratory flow of Quebecers. However considerable this transfer of population proved to be, it was insufficient to meet the labor needs of the city; massive immigration of Europeans to the Quebec metropolis also occurred at this time. It is legitimate to inquire why Montreal did not attract more Quebecers and had to resort instead to external sources of labor. Part of the answer is implicit in the previous discussion of the spatial and temporal articulation of the emigration movement of Quebecers to the United States. Another part of the answer — much more difficult to supply conclusively — must be sought in the dynamics of the urban labor markets that characterized Montreal's economic development during that period. It would require a sectorial analysis of Montreal's urban economy during that phase of expansion to identify the occupational traits that the developing labor markets required, as well as the working and living conditions that the new jobs afforded. A parallel investigation should reconstitute the occupational profiles of those Quebecers who migrated to Montreal during the period and determine which labor markets they were attracted to and whether they competed with immigrant workers. Unfortunately this area of research has produced no significant historical investigation, and we are therefore forced to proceed with great caution. We can provide some answers—however partial they may be—by analyzing the urban unskilled labor market, the major destination for one of Montreal's most important European immigrant groups, the Italians.[23]

The economic and urban expansion that Montreal knew during the early twentieth century probably found its most visible expression in the construction industry. As the city limits were pushed farther to the North, East, and West, the construction of new roads, tunnels, canals, sewage systems and tramway lines proceeded relentlessly. At the same time, Montreal, as Canada's foremost industrial and commercial center, possessed an impressive network of commercial services linked largely to the system of fluvial and land transportation: a port that extended over several miles of the city's southern shore, several railway stations, and a large number of railroad yards, junctions, and entrepôts.

These two large sectors of the urban economy probably generated the greatest demand for general laborers. The fragmented available information about labor relations in these sectors points toward a highly precarious and unstable work environment marked by low salaries, seasonal fluctuations, and total lack of contractual protection. Moreover, especially in the large construction and excavation projects, laborers had to submit to dangerous and physically exacting tasks under an extremely rigid discipline. Not surprisingly, employment in this sector was plagued by chronically high turnover and periodic labor scarcity.

Most Italian immigrants who arrived in Montreal from the turn of the century onward were drawn into this labor market. Although Italian immigration to Quebec first followed a pattern of sojourning, this served primarily as a transitory labor market to which Italians turned according to immediate needs while waiting either to move to a more remunerative location or return to their home towns. However, as this immigration movement became one of permanent settlement, the labor market came to play a central role, making it possible for many Italian workers to realize the transition from sojourners to permanent residents. The workers endured these labor conditions for more or less lengthy periods of their working lives in the hope of more satisfactory situations.

This dual function of the unskilled labor market on the one hand serving the needs of an expanding urban economy, and on the other hand affecting the articulation of migratory phenomena, was also at work within the manufacturing sector. The Canadian Pacific Railway's Angus Works, "the world's largest railway shop," provides a major illustration. Built in 1904 over a 269-acre area in the east end of the city and with a labor force that fluctuated between four thousand and eight thousand, this industrial complex regrouped all the diverse operations necessary to manufacture engines, locomotives, and passenger and freight cars, as well as to repair and maintain them. During the ten-year period preceding World War I, thousands of Italian immigrants found work at Angus, and their employment experience confirms the precarious condition of general laborers and the dual function of the labor market.[24]

One of the most striking aspects of this labor scenario was the temporary nature of these workers' employment at the Canadian Pacific; Italian workers who made life-long careers at the CPR are virtually nonexistent. For the overhwhelming majority of these immigrants, working at CPR was a temporary experience that lasted only as long as they or the company did not see fit to terminate it. Detailed analysis of this aspect of the employment experience reveals several patterns. One is exemplified by those workers—the majority in this sample—who were hired only once and then disappeared from the company records. It is within this group that one finds the largest proportion of short employments. It seems probable that within this group a considerable number of sojourners entered the Montreal labor market for a limited period and then either moved on to other North American areas or back to their home towns. This pattern, in fact, is more predominant during the years when the phenomenon of sojourning was an important dimension of the Italian immigration movement.

Another pattern involved "repeat employment," that is, workers whom the company rehired a second time or even several times. Although a smaller group than the first, their number is far from negligible. Within this group one finds the largest proportion of Italian immigrants who settled in Montreal and became a permanent part of the city's labor force. Repeat employment, however, was also a reflection of a particular labor-market conjuncture marked by labor shortage or by greater employment opportunities. Thus, it is not surprising that this pattern was most frequent during the war years, when Italian immigrants residing in the city could afford choosing jobs and quitting them in pursuit of an optimal use of existing economic opportunites. Still another pattern was the seasonality of employment, with the largest volume of hirings and separations occurring from spring to fall; this suggests both a greater availability of Italian labor during those seasons and a greater demand for workers destined for jobs that the company expanded during those months.

Whether it fell into one or another of these patterns, clearly the employment experience of the majority of these workers was unstable and volatile. What is interesting to note, however, is that Italian workers were as much—if not more—responsible for the short duration of their jobs as was the CPR management. More than half the total number of separations involving Italians were initiated by the workers themselves; one-third were initiated by the company. Italian immigrants employed at the Angus Shops entered a labor universe marked by an increasingly diversified occupational structure, with jobs ranging from highly skilled to unskilled ones such as "laborer," "car washer," "car cleaner," and "general helper." Almost two out of three Italians who entered in the employ of the CPR did so by working at the latter kinds of jobs, no doubt the occupations with the highest degree of instability. The immigrants and the CPR encountered each other briefly, but nevertheless long enough to permit the CPR to replenish its supply of unskilled labor and the immigrants to gain a foothold in their search for more desirable employment. The scenario seems to fit perfectly the description of what labor economists term *labor-market segmentation.* The most sophisticated industrial-commercial complex in Canada was generating a constant demand for jobs whose performance only required physical strength and a willingness to submit to the dictates of some foreman or departmental boss. Italian immigrants met these requirements—out of necessity, or because nothing else was available at the moment, or because their lack of readily marketable skills precluded better jobs. Some stayed with the company a few weeks, others a few months.

Such mobility was as much a result of the company's occupational structure as it was a reflection of the workers' own economic strategies. Although in the CPR's work-flow scheme these unskilled tasks were integrated into the company's overall work process, workers performing those tasks very likely saw the barriers separating their jobs from better ones in other department or operations. Antonio Funicelli, who soon after his arrival in Montreal in 1913 held a general laborer's job for several months at the "Canadian Car," expressed his attitude toward such employment vividly. "They made us load pieces of scraps which were then sent to the foundry. The foreman called us all 'Joe.' "Hei, Joe, come here, you!' And then he ordered us: 'take this stuff over there, load this stuff on those trucks.' I remained there nine months—it was tough. I was not made for that kind of work; that was not work for artisans, but for *journaliers.*"[25]

If this held true for Funicelli, who came to Montreal to unite with his family and settle permanently, it held even truer for laborers who entered the employ of the CPR as "target migrants." For most of these workers, entering and exiting through these dead-end jobs was only remotely connected with considerations about career opportunities. Their decision was more likely linked to economic considerations whose temporal and spatial contexts transcended a specific CPR work site; it encompassed truncated family relationships and land-hungry Apennine villages. These workers' subsequent itineraries across Montreal work sites or through the Canadian and international highways of labor will probably never be known. The brief view that CPR records allow is clear enough to demonstrate the dynamics of unskilled labor mobility at work and to capture a moment in the working life of immigrants caught in the pursuit of a North American wage.

The labor-market segmentation thesis seems to be confirmed by a parallel investigation we pursued of the occupational structure in the various CPR's Montreal sites. This second sample was not limited to Italian workers, but included all workers independent of national origin. This investigation revealed a low presence of French Canadians in unskilled occupations and a heavy overrepresentation of immigrants, most of whom were from Southern and Eastern Europe.

If, therefore, we take one of Montreal's largest and occupationally diversified industrial-commercial complexes as being representative of the urban unskilled labor market of the period, we are led to believe that a segmentation process along ethnic lines was operative with the city's labor force. What enabled French-Canadian workers to shun the least desirable jobs available in the Montreal urban economy? Is it because Montreal tended to attract Quebecers who possessed skills that could be easily and quickly adapted to the metropolitan labor market? Or is it because French-Canadian unskilled laborers were concentrated in sectors of the urban economy other than those discussed? Only further research on the phenomenon of internal migration and on the dynamics of the urban labor markets can answer these questions. What clearly emerges from our research, however, is that, for many rural Quebecers without skills, Montreal offered a poor alternative to the more remunerative and diversified labor markets of New England, which they could join by inserting themselves into the widespread web of U.S.-bound emigration networks.

By the early twentieth century, Quebec had become a crossroads province, not only because it was sending off its own population while bringing in populations from distant countries but also because the metropolis that so many rural Quebecers bypassed in their migratory routes to the south increasingly became—for many European immigrants— the place to begin a new life. Five decades of emigration and immigration produced an ethnocultural configuration that would persist until sweeping socioeconomic transformations occurred after World War II. Montreal's multiethnic image contrasted sharply with rural Quebec where colonization and out-migration had contributed to preserve and perpetuate a cultural homogeneity that would make French Canada the leading example of twentieth-century folk society in North America. The traditional ethnic tensions between Canada's two "founding nations" would be compounded by the growing presence of European immigrant communities that would alter the urban texture of the Quebec metropolis and test Canadians' ability to gain access to the rank of a truly cosmopolitan society.

NOTES

This chapter grew out of two research projects presently in progress: "A Social History of the Italians of Montreal, 1870-1930," funded by the Canadian Ethnic Studies Program, Secretary of State, and "L'emigration des Canadiens français vers les Etats-Unis: analyse locale et comparée, 1870-1915," funded by the Social Sciences and Humanities Research Council of Canada. I am grateful to both agencies, as well as to Jean Lamarre, research assistant in the latter project.

1. Duncan M. McDougall, "Immigration to Canada, 1851-1920," *Canadian Journal of Economics and Political Science* 27 (February-November 1961): 162-75; Paul-André Linteau et al., *Histoire du Québec contemporain* (Montréal, 1979), chapters 2 and 3; Bruno Ramirez, "U.S. Industrialism and the Internationalisation of Labour: Two Case Studies," in *Essays from the Lowell Conference on Industrial History, 1984*, ed. Robert Weible (Lowell, in press). For immigration in the pre-Confederation period, see especially H. Clare Pentland, *Labour and Capital in Canada, 1650-1860* (Toronto, 1981); and Ronald Rudin, *The Forgotten Quebecers: A History of English-Speaking Quebec, 1759-1980* (Montréal, 1985).

2. Jean Hamelin and Yves Roby, *Histoire économique du Québec, 1851-1896* (Montréal, 1971); Fernand Harvey, *Révolution industrielle et travailleurs* (Montréal, 1978); Robert Armstrong, *Structure and Change: An Economic History of Quebec* (Toronto, 1984).

3. Donald Avery, *"Dangerous Foreigners": European Immigrant Workers and Labour Radicalism in Canada, 1896-1932* (Toronto, 1979); Robert Harney, "Montreal's King of Italian Labour: A Case Study of Padronismo," *Labour / Le Travail* 4 (1979): 57-84; Bruno Ramirez, *Les premiers Italiens de Montreal: l'origine de la Petite Italie du Quebec* (Montreal, 1984).

4. The most recent attempt at measuring the ethnic composition of Montreal's population in the nineteenth and twentieth centuries is Paul-André Linteau, "La montée du cosmopolitisme montréalais," *Questions de culture* 2 (1982): 23-54.

5. The standard works on the quantitative dimension of this emigration movement are: Gilles Paquet, "L'émigration des Canadiens français vers la Nouvelle Angleterre, 1870-1910: prises de vues quantitatives," *Recherches Sociographiques* 5 (September-December 1964): 319-70; Albert Faucher, "L'émigration des Canadiens français au XIXe siècle: position du problème et perspectives," *Recherches Sociographiques* 5 (September-December 1964): 277-317; Ralph D. Vicero, "The Immigration of French Canadians to New England, 1840-1900: A Geographical Analysis," Ph.D. dissertation, University of Wisconsin, 1968; Yolande Lavoie, *L'émigration des Canadiens aux Etats-Unis avant 1930: Mesure du phénomène* (Montréal, 1972). For a discussion on the particular problems posed by Canadian and American census statistics for the study of emigration, see Yolande Lavoie, "Les mouvements migratoires des Canadiens entre leur pays et les Etats-Unis au XIXe et au XXe siècles: étude quantitative," in *La population du Québec: étude rétrospective*, ed. Hubert Charbonneau (Montréal, 1973), 73-88.

6. "Rapport du comité nommé pour s'enquerir des causes de l'émigration du Canada aux Etats-Unis d'Amérique ou ailleurs, pour 1857," *Journaux de l'assemblée législative* 15, appendix 47; see also D. Aidan McQuillan, "Farm Size and Work Ethic: Measuring the Success of Immigrant Farmers on the American Grasslands," *Journal of Historical Geography* 4 (1978): 57-76.

7. Robert G. LeBlanc, "Colonisation et rapatriement au Lac Saint-Jean, 1895-1905," *Revue d'histoire de l'Amérique française* 38 (Winter 1985): 379-408.

8. Donald Chaput, "Some Repatriation Dilemmas," *Canadian Historical Review* 49 (1968): 400-412; Robert LeBlanc, "Regional Competition for Franco-American Repatriates," *Quebec Studies* 1 (1983): 110-29.

9. Linteau et al., *Histoire du Québec contemporain*, 409-27; Paul-André Linteau, *Maisonneuve, ou comment des promoteurs fabriquent une ville* (Montréal, 1981).

10. For a basic introduction to the historical literature on the colonization movement see Normand Séguin, ed., *Agriculture et colonization au Québec: Aspects Historiques* (Montréal, 1980); other important works include Normand Séguin, *La conquête du sol au XIXe siècle* (Québec, 1977); Gérard Bouchard, "Introduction à l'étude de la société saguenayenne aux XIXe et XXe siècles," *Revue d'histoire de L'Amérique française* 31 (June 1977): 3-27; Christian Morrisonneau, *La terre promise: le mythe du Nord québécois* (Montréal, 1978).

11. Christian Pouyez et al., *Les Saguenayens: introduction à l'histoire des populations du Saguenay* (Québec, 1983).

12. For a more detailed discussion of emigration from Berthier County that stresses methodological and archival problems see Bruno Ramirez and Jean Lamarre, "Du Québec vers les Etats-Unis: l'étude des lieux d'origine," *Revue d'histoire de l'Amérique française* 38 (Winter 1985): 409-22.

13. Arthur Buies, *Les Comtés de Rimouski, de Matane et de Témiscuata: exploration spéciale* (Québec, 1890); Marie-Ange Caron et al., *Mosaique Rimouskoise* (Rimouski, 1979); Guy Massicotte, "Rimouski et le Bas-Saint-

Laurent: identité culturelle et développement régional," *Questions de culture* 5 (1983): 35-60.

14. Bruno Ramirez and Jean Lamarre, "Emigration from Québec to the USA: The Study of the Places of Origin, 1870-1910," unpublished research report.

15. Félix Albert, *Histoire d'un enfant pauvre* (Nashua, N.H., 1909). For an excellent historical analysis of this autobiography see Frances Early, "The Rise and Fall of Félix Albert: Some Reflections on the Aspirations of Habitant Immigrants to Lowell, Massachusetts in the Late Nineteenth Century," in *The Quebec and Acadian Diaspora in North America*, ed. Raymond Breton and Pierre Savard (Toronto, 1982), 25-38.

16. For a thorough historical analysis of the forestry industry and work patterns in Quebec in the nineteenth century see Reneé Hardy and Normand Séguin, *Forête et société en Mauricie* (Montréal, 1984).

17. Sociodemographic profile based on the analysis of the manuscript census returns for the entire County of Berthier, 1871, 1881, 1891.

18. Frances H. Early, "French-Canadian Beginnings in an American Community: Lowell, Massachusetts, 1868-1886," Ph.D. dissertation, Concordia University, 1980, especially chapter 6.

19. For a detailed discussion of French Canadians working in the New England textile industry around 1908 see Bruno Ramirez, "A Socioeconomic Profile of the French-Canadian Labour Force in the New England Cotton Industry During the Progressive Era," *Labour/Le Travail* 11 (Spring 1983): 125-42. See also Tamara Hareven, *Family Time and Industrial Time: The Relationship Between the Family and Work in a New England Industrial Community* (Cambridge, 1982).

20. See Yolande Lavoie, *L'émigration des Québécois aux Etats-Unis, de 1840 à 1930* (Québec, 1979), especially 43-51.

21. Peter Haebler, "Habitants in Holyoke: The Development of the French-Canadian Community in a Massachusetts City, 1865-1910," Ph.D. dissertation, University of New Hampshire, 1976; Ramirez, "A Socioeconomic Profile"; Bruno Ramirez, "French-Canadian Immigrants in New England and their Geographical Mobility: Some Historical Hypotheses," unpublished manuscript, University of Montreal, 1983.

22. Oral interview, Department of History, University of Montreal, 1983; interview partially reproduced in Jacques Rouillard, *Ah les Etats!* (Montréal, 1985), 87-99.

23. The following section draws substantially from three studies: Bruno Ramirez, "Brief Encounters: Italian Immigrant Workers and the CPR, 1900-1930," *Labour/Le Travail* 17 (Spring 1986): 9-27; Bruno Ramirez, "Operai senza una 'causa' ? I manovali italiani a Montreal, 1900-1930," *Studi Emigrazione / Etudes migrations* 22 (March 1985): 98-111; and Ramirez, *Les premiers Italiens de Montreal.*

24. The data on which the following analysis is based come from the Canadian Pacific Railway, "Employees Pension Plan Records," CPR Montreal

Office. Our sample of Italian immigrants working at the CPR-Montreal from 1900 to 1930 included 773 such cases—two-thirds of which involved the Angus Works. Omer Lavallée, CPR archivist and Walter Gregory, head of the Pension and Actuarial Services graciously allowed me to consult this source.

    25. Oral interview, Montreal 1983; reproduced in Ramirez, *Les premiers Italiens de Montreal*, 125-30.

11

Emigration from an Area of Intense Industrial Development: The Case of Northwestern Italy

FRANCO RAMELLA

Emigration from northwestern Italy presents a case study of particular interest within the general context of Italian emigration. The three regions of the area — Piedmont, Lombardy, and Liguria — were the most developed in the whole country. Between the end of the nineteenth century and the beginning of the twentieth, this large area (with a population of approximately 9.5 million, slightly more than one-fifth of the country's total population) was subjected to an intense process of industrialization. In 1911 the percentage of the population employed in secondary activities in the three regions amounted to 9.6 percent, compared to 3 percent in the rest of Italy. This proportion was similar to that of such central Western European countries as Belgium (10.1 percent) and Switzerland (12 percent), both highly industrialized small nations.[1]

In the absence of detailed studies, little is yet known of emigration from these regions. The problem has been generally neglected by Italian historians, who are inclined to construct global explanatory models based almost exclusively on flows from the country's less developed regions.[2] Emphasizing connections between migrations and a contraction or lack of locally available resources, these models prove sorely inadequate when applied to population movements from northwestern Italy that, on the contrary, developed in an economic context characterized by processes of structural changes which increased local resources.

The case study of the Northwest, moreover, seems to be paradoxical: the regions were areas of emigration toward other countries as well as areas of immigration from inside Italy itself as industry attracted labor. This paradox is particularly interesting for historians concerned with emigration because it suggests a different perspective.

It is necessary to shift emphasis away from the push factors—external and impersonal—that *force* people to migrate and focus attention instead on the strategies of the emigrants as social actors who actually *choose* to migrate.

Foreign migration from northwestern Italy was important both in numerical terms and in relation to the other two large geographical areas into which the country is generally divided with reference to emigration: the Northeast and the Center, considered together, and the South, including the islands of Sicily and Sardinia. State statistical data on expatriates were first collected in Italy in 1876. Between that year and World War II, emigrants from the northwestern regions totaled more than four million. In the entire period the average annual ratio of emigrants in relation to the population, divided into the three geographical areas, was as follows: first, the Northeast and Center with an annual average of 6.08 expatriates per thousand inhabitants; second, the South and the islands with 5.38, and third the Northwest with 4.72 (Table 11.1). Contrary to widespread and mistaken opinion, these data show that the modern mass migration was largely present in the *whole* country—independent of agrarian structures and of the existence of industrial activities—even if there were considerable differences from one district to another within each of the three geographical areas. Consequently, migration was not correlated to the one factor of backward economic conditions and underdevelopment.

The Mezzogiorno—the peninsula south of Rome—is regarded as the principal exporter of Italian emigrants, however state statistical data show that this idea is false. The peasants and artisans who left the South and the islands did indeed number in the millions, but the greatest flow of emigrants came from the Northeast and the Center, primarily due to the contributions of the northeastern regions of Veneto and Friuli. In the entire period the average annual rate of emigrants per thousand inhabitants from the Northwest was not markedly different from those of the other two geographical areas. In absolute terms it accounted for approximately 23 percent of Italian emigration between 1876 and World War II.[3]

Dividing the period into subperiods the general picture is as shown in Table 11.1. Migration from northwestern Italy was more regular than from the other two geographical areas. During the first years of statistical surveys, the highest Italian migration was from the Northwest. In this area the initial ratio of emigrants per thousand inhabitants remained at the same level until 1900. On the other hand, these first twenty-five years saw an ever-increasing number of people leaving the Northeast and Center, as well as the South and the islands, where the

Table 11.1. Average Emigrants per Thousand Inhabitants in Italy (1876-1940)

	1876-80	1881-90	1891-1900	1901-10	1911-13	1914-20	1921-30	1931-40	1876-1940
Northwest*	6.64	7.46	6.02	12.60	15.91	6.90	6.93	1.60	4.72
Northeast and Center†	4.71	7.87	12.94	17.98	20.73	5.12	6.67	1.69	6.08
South and Sicily and Sardinia‡	1.27	4.35	7.64	21.65	23.18	10.03	5.71	1.22	5.38

Source: Ercole Sori, *L'emigrazione italiana dall'Unità alla seconda guerra mondiale* (Bologna 1979), 23.

* Piedmont, Lombardy, and Liguria.

† Veneto, Friuli, Emilia, Tuscany, Umbria, Marche, and Latium.

‡ Abruzzi, Molise, Campania, Puglia, Basilicata, Calabria, Sicily, and Sardinia.

initial rate had been lower. In the first decade of the twentieth century, emigrants from the Northwest doubled, and their number continued to increase in the years immediately following. In the same period there occurred the mass exodus from the Mezzogiorno, while in the Northeast and Center the increase in emigration that began during the last decade of the nineteenth century continued to rise. The percentage of expatriates fell in all parts of the country during World War I. In the 1920s emigration returned to its initial level in the Northwest, which again had the highest migration rate in the nation. It fell steadily in this area during the 1930s, as in the rest of Italy, due to the anti-emigration policy of Fascism.[4]

Considering migration from the Northwest in the entire period, two important aspects can be emphasized. First, migration in the area was already widely developed at the time the government began to collect data. Second, migration not only continued, but also actually increased in the years of the most intense industrial growth between 1900 and 1913. These years also saw rapid urbanization in the three northwestern regions, but internal migration which determined the demographic growth of the cities did not replace foreign migration. Both movements overlapped and coexisted with waves of immigration from other regions of Italy. In those years, therefore, the regions of the Northwest offer an extremely dynamic picture characterized by considerable population mobility.

Given the marked process of industrialization by then under way, this is hardly surprising. What remains to be explained are specific population movements denoting preference for foreign employment opportunities over those local industry could offer. The hypothesis that emigration abroad continued and widened because industrial development was unable to absorb all the labor force does not supply satisfactory answers. The questions posed by the situation are much more complex than historians have usually made it appear.

At the turn of the century, when foreign migration from northwestern Italy took on massive proportions—within the explosion of the "great emigration" in the whole country—it appears as a strongly heterogeneous population movement. The types of migrants involved were very different, the lengths of moves were different, and there were many different countries of destination. The migration was extremely complex, and included skilled and unskilled workers, artisans and peasants, men and women; temporary, seasonal, and permanent migrants; and people who moved toward one particular foreign country and those who moved from one country to another. Migration was predominantly continental, primarily to France and Switzerland which border these regions, but it was also directed to North and South America and even, in fewer numbers, to the European colonies of Africa.

Three distinct, if closely overlapping, types of flows in this composite movement may be isolated for analytical purposes. They can be distinguished on the basis of socioeconomic characteristics prevailing in the communities of origin. The first type of flow developed in the mountain communities, both in the Alps of Piedmont and Lombardy—which form an arc that borders the country—and in the Apennines that cross Liguria. This migration flow is rooted in ancient tradition. Agricultural resources in these communities was never entirely sufficient to support the population; the soil was poor, and agricultural holdings were extremely fragmented. The only large properties were the common lands belonging to the community. Composed primarily of grazing lands and woods, these were exploited by the residents as an adjunct to their small estates.

The disparity between the scarcity of local resources and the needs of the population was bridged by migration, still prevalently temporary and seasonal at the turn of the century. Such migration furnished incomes complementary to the meager incomes earned from bare subsistence farming. In family budgets, money earned working in cities and villages inside or outside state borders did not constitute a substitution for—but an addition to—livelihoods gained locally. Thus, migration could be considered an integral part of people's lives; it structured the family and social organization of the community in which it developed.

Some people migrated in winter—when agricultural work was slow— and returned to the village of residence in summer to work their own fields. These migrants performed various jobs according to their areas of origin and destination. They were laborers or peddlers, and also tumblers, laundresses, porters, or waiters, as in the case of the winter tourist localities on the French Riviera. Such migration may be considered analogous to the better-known *golondrinas* (swallows), the farm laborers who took advantage of the difference in seasons in the two hemispheres by traveling to South America between November and May for the wheat harvest and then returning home at the beginning of summer in Europe for agricultural work in the Italian countryside.[5]

A more characteristic emigration from many parts of the northwestern mountainous areas, however, was that of skilled workers such as masons, stonecutters, and pavers. Contrary to the emigration discussed previously, which involved both men and women, this type was highly sex-selective. All of these emigrants were males whose working life began at the age of twelve or thirteen with adult relatives or other men of the community. Learning the trade intertwined with learning the rules of behavior in distant and foreign labor markets because these workers were able to exercise their trade only outside the small and often isolated communities in which they were born.

Construction and public works emigrants generally left their villages at the beginning of spring and returned at the end of fall. The seasonal nature of their emigration was due to technical reasons; cold weather drastically reduced work during the winter. These workers too were all small landowners in their villages of origin. During the men's absence the agricultural tasks were assigned exclusively to the women of the village. A strict division of labor between the sexes characterized family organization in such communities.

The second type of migration flow involved the rural communities in the fertile plains and hills. Although emigration to foreign countries was not unknown in these communities, its dramatic surge seems to be closely related to the "great agricultural crisis" which heavily affected the social equilibrium of Italian rural areas from the 1880s and is also commonly cited as a primary economic cause of peasant emigration from the Italian South. The agricultural crisis was triggered by the fall in prices that resulted from the internationalization of markets.

Typical of the agriculture of the northwestern regions was the presence of two sectors: one capitalistic and capital-intensive, the other peasant and labor-intensive. The latter sector was the more adversely affected by falling prices. Its representative social group was composed of small peasant landowners and tenants who produced for the market—a numerically significant class widespread in the northwestern countryside. Less affected, on the other hand, were two areas: large capitalistic agricultural concerns (better equipped to meet the challenge of international competition) and subsistence agriculture (whose relation to the market was on a very small scale because the majority of its production was destined for auto-consumption).

This qualification is important because it underlines the need to analyze the social structure of rural areas in order to formulate the problem of emigrant selection. The question, Who left? is rich in implications. In the past, the emphasis on push factors gave strength to the idea that the population emigrating from the countryside was socially undifferentiated. More recently, the reexamination of this approach has permitted the vigorous reformulation of the crucial problem of selection in emigration. American scholars in particular have viewed self-selection by emigrants as a consequence of a natural inclination toward innovation and change.[6] Indeed, this view rests on a highly ambiguous concept—the idea that emigration occurred as a result of a biological-cultural selection. Various scholars have focused attention on the ideological nature of this interpretation. It assumes that individuals more suited to the New World would emigrate, whereas those who remained would be less naturally gifted.[7] This interpretation discourages, by rendering superfluous, historical analyses of the migratory phenomenon's causes, its rhythms and the various ways in which it developed, as well as the social milieu in which emigrants matured their choices.

Emigration is by definition selective, but the selection in fact is social. It is in this direction that research needs to be deepened. Mass rural emigration from the Northwest during the great agricultural crisis which affected small market-dependent peasant landowners was the expression of a reaction to ongoing processes of proletarianization.

The third type of migration flow stemmed from the changes brought about by industrial take-off in traditionally protoindustrial areas. Situated primarily in northwestern regions of Piedmont and Lombardy, these areas were the site of longstanding industries, principally textiles. They were rural industries located in the countryside, thus the term *protoindustries*.[8] During the nineteenth century, both before and after the political unification of the country in 1861, these protoindustries developed slowly yet steadily, a growth that contributed to creating the conditions necessary for the take-off which occurred at the end of the century when the new heavy-industry sectors concentrated in the big cities.

The evolution of rural industries during the nineteenth century represented the specific and original manner in which Italy prepared its own industrial revolution as a latecomer located on the periphery of the great industrial nations dominating the international market. Two fundamental characteristics of the evolution are relevant. First, rural industries constituted an economic system in which modern forms of production were combined with cottage workshops. Consequently, even small producers were of great relevance. Their activity was not necessarily in competition with that of industry; often it was complementary in that it filled in phases of factory production that were barely mechanized or not mechanized at all. In other cases small producers covered local markets that industry either did not care to serve or was unable to serve.

The second characteristic concerns the type of labor force employed in production. Because such industries were located in rural areas, the labor force consisted almost exclusively of workers who maintained a relationship with farming. They alternated industrial and agricultural work and so were factory workers and farmers at the same time. Because the areas where these rural industries developed suffered from overpopulation, peasant families allowed some members to be involved in producing industrial goods as long as their involvement did not mean abandoning agricultural activities.

At the end of the nineteenth century when all the processes generating the industrial take-off had matured, the social consequences in these areas were significant. The completion of mechanization and the appearance of new technologies, the concentration of production and industry's greater aggressiveness in the markets, the decline in old manufacturing processes and the development of new ones—the combination of all these factors—produced severe disruptions and consistently affected social groups of protoindustrial workers. These groups included both small producers, whose main resources lay in protoindustry, and rural cultivators who supplemented work on family farms with protoindustrial income.

Of these three migration flows—which were actually intertwined and overlapped—the first, from poor mountain communities, accounts for a large portion of total migration from northwestern Italy throughout the whole period. It formed by far the largest contingent in the first years of statistical surveys and continued to expand in the following decades. At the turn of the century it still had the traditional characteristics of seasonal and temporary emigration, even if the number of permanent migrants had increased. In spite of this increase, mountainous areas continued to be densely populated, at least until the 1920s. This phenomenon can only be explained in relation to the conservative character of the emigration, its essential function in reproduction of the local social structure. Far from stimulating an uncontrolled exodus from the communities of origin, temporary emigration actually tended to check wider movements out of the area for a long time.

This migration flow was not only restricted to this area of Italy; the phenomenon was also widespread in many other mountainous parts of Italy and Europe.[9] It gave rise both to foreign migrations and to internal migrations, as in France.[10] One of the characteristics of the migration flow was its recurrence in time within economic, social, and political contexts that were very different. Migration, as part of a wider population mobility, is not an exclusive feature of the era of industrialization, as many authors have stressed.[11] In the nineteenth and twentieth centuries, modern migration developed in relation to structural changes which marked the development of capitalism on a world scale, but at the same time it presented characteristics whose origins can be found in previous eras. Many of the internal social mechanisms that seem typical of modern migration are in fact surprisingly analogous to those observed in the Europe of the ancien régime.[12]

Mass migration from Italy at the turn of the century has generally been considered as a devastating social trauma. Scholars have often emphasized the aspects of rupture represented by the explosion of the "great emigration."[13] Seeing the phenomenon in a long-term historical perspective suggests instead a different approach. Let us consider the problem of the emigration at the turn of the century in rural northwestern Italy, both in the areas of commercialized agricultural production and in those where agricultural activities— either subsistence- or market-oriented—were flanked by protoindustry.

The problem can be confronted by isolating as a field of analysis the traditional social strategies of the peasant and protoindustrial families. The question is whether mass migration denoted a radical change in traditional social strategies in these areas, or whether it was simply the continuation of patterns of behavior carried over from the past.

To answer the question it is useful to refer to the animated debate that has gone on for years over the study of peasant and protoindustrial families in modern Europe.[14] Recent studies suggest the importance of shifting the emphasis from the family considered as a co-resident domestic group sharing the same physical space to the family as a unit of income and consumption. This new direction of analysis uncovers a fundamental characteristic of the social behavior of peasant and protoindustrial families in their complex processes of income formation. A wide range of complementary activities which could vary during the life-cycles of family members contributed to the formation of total family income. The goal was to minimize dependence on any one source of income and so reduce vulnerability to periodic crises. At the same time, it was a way of enlarging opportunities for the whole family and so led to an improvement in social position.[15]

In the case of the protoindustrial families, the complementarity of agricultural income with wages was a clear example of this behavior pattern. In other cases more directly of interest, some members of peasant families moved from their communities temporarily in order to earn a wage that could be added to general family income. For example, in the 1800s in northwestern rural areas, daughters were sent to the city to work as servants, only to return home once they reached the age of marriage.[16] Sons were also sent away to work temporarily as manual workers in public construction such as irrigation canals, roads, and railways. Many other examples could be cited. All of these cases expressed family strategies aimed at exploiting the opportunities offered by a range of resources. These resources could be present in the community or, more often, outside of it. Within this picture, the temporary migration of one or more members of a family was not only foreseen but also decided upon, upheld, and encouraged by the whole group, a behavior pattern that increased during crises.

Considered from this point of view, emigration at the turn of the century was not a rupture—imposed or voluntary—with respect to the traditional social strategies. On the contrary, it was the consequence and the extension of these strategies in a new economic context. Despite appearances, a fundamental aspect of continuity was apparent with respect to the past in social behavior expressed through mass emigration. For this reason too, the emigration conceived and carried out within the tradition foresaw the return of the migrant.

Return migration was important in the northwestern area as in the whole country. It is well known that Italy, among European countries that underwent mass emigration in the nineteenth and twentieth centuries, registered the highest number of temporary emigrants. The phenomenon's analysis has fundamental implications for the study of emigration, as Thistlethwaite indicated in his suggestion for a new approach.[17] For a long time, the predominant idea was that emigration essentially consisted of a move of individuals from one point to another in the world, a "once and once only" phenomenon. This tendency was favored by the data available to scholars,[18] data that measured emigration on the basis of the difference among successive censuses, thereby taking into consideration only net increases and not the turnover of emigrants resulting from temporary migration. This tendency contributed to a neglect of the complexity of emigrants' social strategies. Their influence on determining the moves could explain return migration.

The idea that emigration is a once and once only phenomenon has also favored the tendency to consider return migration as a sign of failure. In fact, provided the family strategies had not been replaced, it was the sign of the achievement of the goals which prompted departure.[19] Return migration led to investment in the community of origin of earnings and savings made abroad. Although the idea that emigration permitted and resulted in processes of social mobility only in the host countries is widespread, the consequences of return migration represented a process of social mobility in the village of origin. Emigration could then also constitute a much more than secondary factor for remodeling social stratification in the community that gave rise to it.

Of course, in the actual choices of each migrant, emigration could from the beginning also represent the desire to settle in new places permanently. Even when this was not the case, expectations and traditional strategies at departure could change and result in new behavior patterns when the migrants lived in a new urban space. This is an important aspect of the history of emigration, that is, the sociocultural changes migrants experienced in the host society. It implies the need to study the social experience of migrants and focus on the interaction among individuals and specific social spaces in which they lived. In Italy's northwestern rural communities between the end of the nineteenth century and the beginning of the twentieth, prevailing cultural norms did not consider emigration to be deviant behavior. Rural culture did not consider physical separation of individuals as necessarily leading to a break in social ties or a weakened cohesion of the family unit, the kin, or the social group.

One of the conclusions emerging from this analysis is that the question of propensity to migrate at the time of the "great Italian emigration" may be viewed in a new perspective. The propensity to migrate was a much more widespread behavior pattern than has commonly been recognized. This hypothesis helps to explain the extraordinary population movements abroad that Italy experienced in its modern history. As is evident in the case of the Northwest, emigration cannot be attributed only to the strength of push factors because of growing local resources in the area.

Having decided to migrate, how did the choice of destination take place? The question is important because in the case of northwestern Italy there were both foreign and internal migrations—long- and short-distance moves to places very different from a cultural point of view. Emigration was a way to exploit resources outside the community of origin. In order to emigrate, people needed information on existing opportunities and access to these opportunities. Information, however, was not unlimited, nor were the possibilities to take up known opportunities. Both information and actual possibilities depended on individual social relationships; by standing between the individual and social reality, social relationships determined individual perceptions of social reality.[20] In small northwestern Italian communities at the turn of the century the social relationships in which the emigrants were involved were those family, kin, or social group and based on interwoven common interests and the alliances of recriprocal obligations.

In this sense the tradition of foreign emigration preceding the "great emigration" could have had a decisive influence; the unbroken relationship between those who emigrated and those who remained provided channels through which a continuous flow of information reached a geographical area extending far beyond the borders of any given region. The role of social ties in determining the direction of emigration is well known, but in this case the role was so prominent that it virtually nullified geographical and cultural distance in evaluating the destination to be reached.

On these premises we may also formulate some hypotheses on the function of social ties in emigration, not only as sources of information about opportunities but also as social channels that guaranteed access to resources. A particular case to consider is that of the emigration of masons from the Piedmont mountains to France between 1880 and World War I.[21] For these migrants, France was a long-standing destination, however in the second half of the 1800s, in relation to the strong development of public and private building there, the movement increased considerably. The social group of Piedmontese masons created a quasi-monopoly on the construction market, which was founded on the close and interwoven relationships that tied migrant masons together and to the contractors who came from the same villages. Their common origin guaranteed access to opportunities and control by the social group. It constituted a powerful pull factor on the emigration of certain Piedmontese villages to the French areas.

The problem also arose for the unskilled workers; the search for work through interpersonal relations was not a marginal aspect of emigration.[22] As studies of ethnicity show, it could lead to the creation of niches partially controlled by a social group with significant effects on the directions of emigration flows.[23] Between skilled and unskilled workers, however, an interesting difference could exist which requires more careful consideration. Skilled workers seemed to follow structured and determined circuits of mobility based on the geographical location of the specific resources on which they depended to carry out their trade. Unskilled workers, instead, drew on widespread and territorially dispersed unspecific resources. Thus they could be more mobile and sensitive to a wider range of opportunities. Compared with skilled workers, they had less protection from workers' organizations but fewer constraints in the trades they practiced. They were thus more available to adapt to changes in the labor market by moving from one job to another inside or outside of factory work.

The subject of emigration considered essentially as a phenomenon of geographical mobility and dealt with from the point of view of the areas of departure and the social and cultural backgrounds of the emigrants in all of its ramifications extends beyond the scope of this analysis.

NOTES

This chapter uses some of the results obtained from a research on foreign emigration from Biellese, an industrial district in northwestern Italy. The research was promoted and sponsored by Fondazione Sella and Banca Sella, Biella, Italy.

1. Luciano Cafagna, "Italy 1830-1914," in *The Fontana Economic History of Europe: The Emergences of Industrial Societies,* ed. Carlo M. Cipolla (London, 1973), 1:279-328.

2. See, for example, Anna Maria Martellone, "Italian Mass Emigration to the United States, 1876-1930: A Historical Survey," in *Perspectives in American History,* ed. Bernard Baylin, Donald Fleming, and Stephan Thernstrom (Cambridge, 1984), 1:379-423.

3. Luigi Favero and Graziano Tassello, "Cent'anni di emigrazione italiana," in *Un secolo di emigrazione italiana: 1876-1976,* ed. Gianfausto Rosoli (Rome, 1978), 9-60.

4. The rate of emigration from the South and the islands in the 1920s was considerably affected by the immigration policy of the United States, which had received the greatest number of emigrants from this area in the preceding years. The rate of emigration from the Northeast and Center was affected by a postwar decrease toward Central Europe which traditionally was one of the most important destinations from the area. Too, statistical data from the 1920s and 1930s obviously did not include illegal migration, which, for example was considerable toward France in that period. See Franco Ramella, "Biografia di un operaio antifascista: Ipotesi di ricerca per una storia sociale dell'emigrazione politica" in *Les Italiens en France de 1914 à 1940,* ed. Pierre Milza (Rome, 1986).

5. E. J. T. Collins, "Offerta e domanda di mano d'opera agricola in Europa dal 1800 al 1880" in *Agricoltura e sviluppo economico: Gli aspetti storici,* ed. E. L. Jones and S. J. Woolf (Turin, 1973).

6. Some useful considerations are in Sean Wilentz, "On Working-class Culture in the United States," *Mezzosecolo* 5 (1985): 27-42.

7. See Giovanni Levi, "A proposito del libro di Massimo Livi Bacci," *Inchiesta* 45 (1980): 1-4.

8. Alain Dewerpe, *L'industrie aux champs: Essai sur la proto-industrialisation en Italie du Nord (1800-1880)* (Rome, 1985).

9. See Jean-Pierre Raison, "Migrazione," in *Enciclopedia Einaudi* (Turin, 1984), 9:285-311.

10. Abel Poitrineau, *Les migrations montagnardes en France* (Paris, 1983).

11. See Charles Tilly, "Migration in Modern European History," in *Human Migration: Patterns and Policies*, ed. William H. McNeill and Ruth S. Adams (Bloomington, 1978), 48-72.

12. Tilly, "Migration in Modern European History."

13. Ercole Sori, *L'emigrazione italiana dall'Unità alla Seconda Guerra Mondiale* (Bologna, 1979).

14. Richard Wall, Jean Robin, and Peter Laslett, eds., *Family Forms in Historic Europe* (Cambridge, 1983).

15. See the very interesting issues developed by Giovanni Levi in his important criticism of *Family Forms in Historic Europe*; Giovanni Levi, *"La famiglia nel mutamento," Passato e Presente* 7 (1985).

16. Joan W. Scott and Louise Tilly, "Lavoro femminile e famiglia nell'Europa del XIX secolo," in *La famiglia nella storia*, ed. Charles E. Rosenberg (Turin, 1978), 185-227.

17. Frank Thistlethwaite, "Migration from Europe Overseas in the Nineteenth and Twentieth Centuries," in *Population Movements in Modern European History*, ed. Herbert Moller (New York, 1964), 73-92.

18. J. A. Jackson, "Migration-Editorial Introduction," in *Migration*, ed. Jackson (Cambridge, 1969), 1-10.

19. Maurizio Gribaudi, "Stratégies migratoires et mobilité relative entre village et ville," in *Population*, ed. Hervé Le Bras (Paris, 1985), 387-411.

20. See Bruce Kapferer, "Introduction," in *Transaction and Meaning: Directions in the Anthropology of Exchange and Symbolic Behavior*, ed. Kapferer (Philadelphia, 1976).

21. Franco Ramella, "Il Biellese nella grande emigrazione di fine Ottocento," in Franco Ramella, Chiara Ottaviano, and Marco Neiretti, *L'emigrazione biellese fra Ottocento e Novecento* (Milan, 1986).

22. See, for example, John Bodnar, Roger Simon, and Michael P. Weber, *Lives of Their Own: Blacks, Italians and Poles in Pittsburgh, 1900-1960* (Urbana, 1982).

23. Abner Cohen, "Introduction," in *Urban Ethnicity*, ed. Cohen (London, 1974).

PART FOUR

Return Migration

12

Return Migrations: Theoretical and Research Agenda

EWA MORAWSKA

Voluminous research, accumulated since the 1960s on mass migrations between Europe and the United States during the second half of the nineteenth and early twentieth centuries, has significantly modified the once-dominant conceptions about immigration and the process of the newcomers' adjustment to the new environment. Two themes in particular have had the most impact. One is the emphasis on broadly conceived structural determinants—time, location, and the economic and political conditions—of the processes involved in the emigrants' movement from their home country and of their subsequent adaption to the receiving society. The second is the focus of the collectivist, that is, socially embedded and group-sustained, rather than "self-made" or individualistic, strategies used by the emigrants, starting with the migration process itself and continuing through incorporation into the economic and social systems of the host society.[1]

Several reassessments have also been made regarding return migrations. First the realization has grown that the flow of people from Europe to America was not an abrupt one-step transplantation of previously sedentary village and town residents, but rather was part of extensive labor migrations of shorter or longer duration and distance that began well before the migrants reached the United States. Second, even emigration to distant America was not exclusively a unidirectional movement, but had a back and forth, "transilient" or circular character. Close to one-fourth of the Slovaks residing in Western Pennsylvania at the beginning of the century reported previous visits to the United States; similar proportions were found among the South Slavs and the Italians; and the historical studies of American labor migrations of Polish peasants report 20 to 30 percent of such multiple entries.[2] Third, a considerably greater proportion than was earlier assumed of turn-of-the-century immigrants to the United States returned to their home countries: no less than 35 percent of the Poles,

277

Serbs, Croats, and Slovenes; 40 percent of the Greeks; and about 50 percent of the southern Italians, Magyars, and Slovaks from the northeastern part of Austro-Hungary. Recent investigations indicate that over 20 percent of the Jews returned during the period between 1880 and 1900, even though their mass migration from Eastern Europe at the turn of the century was prompted as much by increasing political persecution as by adverse economic conditions, and the majority of them had come with their families and intended to remain permanently.[3] A fourth reappraisal concerns reasons for return of the immigrants. Whereas earlier interpretations focused on fluctuations in the American economy, more recent studies have suggested that additional factors of a personal and, in particular, social nature, played an important role in patterning this process.[4] A fifth and final reassessment has been the recognition that the immigrants' original intentions of staying only temporarily in America—while certainly important in accounting for both the high return rates and the circular character of the migrations between the receiving and sending societies—are insufficient explanations for repatriation and are not a constant but a variable affected by the economic, social, and political developments taking place on both sides of the Atlantic.[5]

With these reassessments has come an increased recognition of the need to place the interpretation of return migrations within a more coherent theoretical focus providing a general framework for the existing typologies of reemigration that usually treat only its partial and specific aspects. The factors most commonly analyzed have been the emigrants' motivations for leaving and coming back to the home country; their length of stay in the host society and their success or failure there before return; the frequency and character of back and forth movement; and the impact of returnees on their home environment.[6] The most common treatments of return migration in the literature are still reports on the statistics of the outflow of particular groups over time.[7] Results of recent accumulated research have made clear the need to move beyond such studies toward a more comprehensive and more specific analysis of the "dynamic conjunctions" of the conditions aiding and impeding reemigration.

What follows is such a general theoretical framework and an outline of an agenda for empirical research that would help to advance understanding of return migration.

In the classical theories of human migrations, international population movements are interpreted in terms of push and pull demographic and economic forces that induce people to move from the sending societies, which have a surplus of population, little capital, and underemployment, to the receiving ones where labor is scarce and wages are higher. This model focuses on individual actions resulting from a rational economic calculation of the costs and benefits of migration. In a newer, modified version of this approach, individual decisions in generating and sustaining migrations are seen as important, but are placed within the context of structural forces from both the pull and push sides of the process. The most recent theories on international migrations have further reconceptualized this problem by recasting the unit of analysis, from separate countries-societies linked by one-way movement of people following favorable economic conditions to a single extended system consisting of a dominant center and a dependent periphery forming a supraregional network of back and forth exchanges of technology, capital, and labor. Rather than focusing on the decisions and actions of individuals, this approach emphasizes broad structural determinants of the transfer of labor within the global economic system of which it is viewed as a component.[8] The global system model has until now been applied mostly in sociological research on immigration, which deals predominantly with current population movement into the United States from third-world countries.[9] It should also be tested in historical studies of past European migrations to and from America.

During the last third of the nineteenth century, the traditional local economies of the "peripheral" agricultural societies of Southern and Eastern Europe were increasingly absorbed into the orbit of the West European and North American "centers" of the expanding capitalist system. Profound structural imbalances and dislocations set in motion millions of people in search of wages from Russian, Polish, Hungarian, Slovak, Greek, and Italian towns and countryside. Most of the current historical research on these migrations has been conducted in a modified push and pull conceptual framework that acknowledges the impact of broader socioeconomic forces operating within the sending and receiving societies.[10] Evidence of multidirectional flow of population within and outside of Europe in the nineteenth and early twentieth centuries, and of the nature of labor migrations to America as part of this movement, indicates that elements of the global system model should be applicable to the interpretation of return migrations from the United States. In addition to the economic and demographic arguments (circular flow of people providing the labor force for the economies on both sides of the ocean), there is also a sociological one, suggesting that the interpretation of labor migrations between Europe and America may gain in theoretical breadth by applying the extended system approach.

The wage-seeking journeys of migrant laborers were not an individual movement, but a collective one. The social networks created in this process played significant roles in channeling, building up, and then sustaining these ventures out of the villages. Particularly important were networks of information about prospective employment. "[Rural] laborers," remarked F. Bujak on the basis of his studies of the migration movement in several villages in the Austrian section of Poland conducted at the beginning of the century, "constitute among themselves a kind of employment agency, remaining in constant contact with each other either personally or through correspondence. . . . From one or a few [who had gone earlier] they receive . . . information about the [employment] prospects in a given area, so that most often they leave with a conviction that even though they do not have work contracts, they will find jobs in the course of a few days."[11] In Babica, a village in the same region, the first emigrant (not a native Babican and a socially peripheral member of the community) left for America in 1883 because he lost the court suit against his neighbor about a cow. He settled in Detroit. After three years he returned and then in 1888 went back to Detroit, where he already had employment contacts, taking with him a group of five relatives and neighbors. After that, more Babicans followed so that by 1900 seventeen of them were in Detroit.[12]

The immigrant press in America, the press in the sending societies, and correspondence (between 1900 and 1906 alone, more than three million letters from the United States arrived in Europe) also carried information about the current economic and labor conditions. "The most effective method of distributing immigrant labor in the United States . . . is the mail service," concluded a report on Southern and Eastern Europeans in American factories prepared for the U.S. Bureau of Labor at the beginning of the century.[13]

With thousands of immigrants arriving and returning in ongoing overseas traffic, and with intensely circulated correspondence, personal messages, and money orders, close ties were maintained between those in America and those left behind in Europe. For a long time, the emigrants sent home remittances; at the beginning of the century, Southern and Eastern European laborers in the United States were capable of saving 60 to 70 percent of their monthly earnings for transfer home. In only six years, from 1900 to 1906, the total amount of money sent to Russia and Austro-Hungary was $69 million. To take just one country and one year as an illustration, in 1902, Polish emigrants sent to the Austrian section of Poland $3.5 million in American money orders and an additional sum of nearly $4 million was brought in by the returnees. American money orders for about $3.5 million went to the Russian section of Poland (this sum does not count smaller bills commonly enclosed in letters, nor the sums brought home by the returning emigrants).[14] This "lower-circuit" international capital, sent into European villages from those working in the United States and carried in by the returnees, can be construed as yet another dimension of the incorporation of the periphery into the extended transatlantic economic system linking the European countryside with the American urban-industrial centers.

As social networks of information, travel, and employment assistance directed the increasing flow of immigrants to places where the original colonies of settlers had formed, the village communities were partially reestablished in American cities. "We have here now the second Babica" wrote an immigrant from Detroit in his letter home to Galicia. Emigrants from nearby Maszkienice concentrated in four places: Chicago, and Pleasant, Sommerset, and Pittsburgh in Pennsylvania. In Pittsburgh, 150 emigrants from neighboring Moczarka settled and worked together in the same factory. More than 80 percent of the 174 people from Kurzyny in Galicia who left for America between 1890 and 1914 lived in St. Louis, Oil City, and Youngstown, and most emigrants from the village of Skrzypne settled in Chicago. Podgaje, split by a long-standing feud between two groups over the local pasture, transplanted this division across the Atlantic: the "left side" of the village, following its own social network, migrated to Elizabeth, New Jersey; the "right side" followed a different route to Detroit.[15]

As long as they remained sojourners and had not yet resolved to settle in America for good, the emigrants continued long-distance management of their European farms and households, either through repeated visits or through correspondence and messages sent back and forth with traveling friends and relatives. "Now dear husband," Jozefa Pawiak from Galica informed her husband in America, "I write to you for advice, what to do with this house which is for sale. . . . Now people, give for it 530 *renski*. It seems to me too expensive, but if you order so, I won't buy." And an immigrant from Massachusetts to his mother in Congress, Poland: "Tell me how was the weather, the crops, and how big the harvest. . . . Buy potatoes, and you may buy a pig." And another emigrant to his family at home: "Wojtek wants to return [to the village], but he does not have much [to come] with. When we get work [i.e., save some money], we'll both come back in the fall. [So now] tell me whether you left clover in the fields and whether you plowed . . . buy rye how[ever] much you need.

... And those plum trees that we planted in the spring [tell me] whether they all have taken root or some withered. Nothing more of interest I have to say. . . ." "You went with piglets to Rzeszow and Niebylec" wrote a husband temporarily in Detroit to his wife at home, "but you did not sell them did you? Because I know every movement in the village." And in a follow-up letter, he commented on some unpleasant gossip he heard about his wife from someone who just arrived: "Every movement in Babica I know, because I live here among the Babicans, and I hope it is not all true [what I have been told about you]."[16]

These sustained networks of communication and social control extended both "forward" from the emigrants' place of origin in Europe to the United States and "backward" from America in a homebound direction, and paralleled the two-way population flow, which in part they serviced and in part they created. Evidence of these networks further substantiates the interpretation of the overseas migrations within the framework of the "global system" of interrelated parts.

While a historical global system provides the structural inducements for population movements and delineates the geographical, economic, and social space within which people migrate, it is at the level of local surroundings that they define their purposes, make decisions, and undertake actions. The remainder of this chapter points out some directions for empirical research should be added to those pursued thus far to broaden our knowledge of the conditions, character, and consequences of return migrations. Unfortunately, research may prove difficult if not impossible in many areas that seem especially deserving of investigation. In the case of written records, sources are few, incomplete, or unreliable (particularly in Eastern Europe as well as in many of the local settings in the United States). In the case of oral histories, the generations of actors-witnesses of the migrations have already passed away or are now disappearing. The effort is nevertheless worth trying, even if the outcome will be only partially satisfactory.

It has been demonstrated that particularly in the late nineteenth and early twentieth centuries, the general volume of returns varied significantly with both cyclical and seasonal fluctuations in the American economy. Little systematic research exists about the effects of immigrant groups' differential concentration in particular industries in the United States (characterized by different types and rhythms of production) on the rates and patterns of reemigration. According to turn-of-the-century descriptive sources, the annual outflow of Italian laborers, who were heavily concentrated in the railroad and construction industries, regularly increased in the fall and winter when work in these industries slowed. Likewise, contemporary observers noted that the Slavs employed in the Pennsylvania steel industry tended to leave the country during the slack months in the mills.[17] Unfortunately, the U.S. returns statistics classified reemigrants only by ethnicity and not by type of employment. A correlation between the two can be estimated indirectly by calculating gross measures of concentration of particular immigrant groups in specific industries and relating them to return rates. More information might be gathered in particular cities from local industrial and labor statistics and from content analysis of local American and immigrant newspapers. In particular, the foreign-language newspapers, a historical source still underexplored but difficult to "access" without sufficient linguistic skills, could provide interesting insights into the local situations; many regularly reported on fluctuations in the local industries and labor markets and on the reactions of immigrant laborers.

At the other end of the global system, economic conditions in the emigrants' home countries also varied by region and were subject to seasonal fluctuations. For example, it has been found that the proportions of returnees to Slovakia at the beginning of this century varied considerably among particular counties with different demographic profiles, landholding composition, local tax levies, and abundance of annual harvest.[18] This avenue of research should be pursued further. To gain a better grasp of the factors contributing to and differentiating the rates and directions of reemigration, more systematic research is needed, both on economic conditions in regions and localities in Europe to which emigrants returned and on the information about these conditions that reached potential repatriates in America. Such information was brought in and disseminated by new immigrants arriving in this country at the turn of the century, but most of these people have died. Immigrants' letters and, in particular, the immigrant press, which regularly reported news of the economic situation at home (often specifically for the local districts) could be used to gain insight into the problem.

Economic considerations were not the only ones that influenced immigrant departures from America; rather they played against other factors of a personal and social nature. As time went by and more and more immigrants arrived (including increased numbers of women), more families were reunited or founded in this country. Ethnic communities were formed and expanded, providing a firmer social environment for permanent settlement. A study of return migrations of Germans during the second half of the nineteenth century found an inverse relationship between the length of time immigrants spent in the United States and the number of visits to the home country (the latter an indication of the strength of their "animus revertendi"). A similar investigation of a homebound movement among Southern and Eastern Europeans during the decade preceding World War I reported lower reemigration rates for groups in which greater proportions of immigrants came to join relatives, that is, those who had established family networks in this country.[19] Other studies of Slovaks and Yugoslavs have pointed to an active involvement of ethnic organizations in the issue of immigrants' repatriation.[20] Time, as well as regional and group variation in the degree of social embeddedness in kinship and community networks in America, most likely significantly influenced both the rates and the patterns of return. This important aspect of reemigration has until now been studied very little.[21]

The immigrant communities that formed in American cities differed in age, size, density of residential concentration, gender, household composition, and institutional completeness—factors that jointly accounted for the dynamic of social embeddedness as a condition for permanent settlement. Because the U.S. statistics contain no passenger lists for repatriates (similar to those for the arriving immigrants) that registered their residence in the United States, and because this information was not recorded at the European ports where they disembarked, only studies of local immigrant communities in different American cities could help to evaluate the impact of social embeddedness on return migrations. Data could be gathered from census material, local group histories, foreign-language newspapers, and other sources such as immigrant letters and memoirs. The aim would be to arrive at some reasonable estimates of immigrant return rates from different American cities and to relate them to the indicators or conditions of social embeddedness in the ethnic communities of these localities.

Another problem to pursue further in empirical research is that of the immigrants' intentions of returning home. Such were indeed the original plans of the majority of Southern and Eastern Europeans who arrived in America at the turn of the century (this was much less true for the earlier immigrants from Germany, Ireland, and Scandanavia).[22] The traditional explanation for reemigration—"They returned because they intended to do so from the beginning"—is not sufficient. The majority of migrant laborers from Southern and Eastern Europe originally planned to go back, but only about one-third eventually returned. People's plans and intentions change as they encounter new and different situations, and often they are pulled by contradictory impulses and desires. The immigrants' experience in America was no different in this regard; perhaps their transplantation and the need to confront and cope with changes and changing situations in the new environment even intensified the volatility of their subjective states of mind. A Slovenian immigrant wrote in a diary in 1903 as, somewhat unexpectedly for himself, he decided after two years in Pennsylvania to move to Michigan in search of better employment: "During the journey I remembered the promise I had given Mother upon my departure for America: 'We shall see one another in two years.' I felt ashamed. It was absurd! [Time passed and] instead of returning home, I was traveling in the opposite direction, more than a thousand miles away, at the other end of America."[23]

Extension of their stay in America by emigrants who were torn between a desire to save more money here and to return to commitments at home in Europe often caused painful conflicts with those awaiting them there. A young man from Philadelphia wrote to his fiancée in Poland to inform her of his intention to prolong his stay in America for another year beyond the promised two. "Dear Walcia, I wrote you, my dear, in answer to your letter . . . if you don't come [here] and don't wait for me longer it means that you will not be mine, because I will not return sooner than perhaps on the next holiday of Easter, by no means can I sooner. And you write that you will wait only till autumn, and so one disagrees with the other. Therefore, I request you, answer me, what will become of us. . . ."[24] And from a husband in Glassport, Pennsylvania, to his wife waiting in Europe: "I received your two letters, and in both of them I heard nothing else but if I would come back. You see, my dear treasure, although you write to me that I love money better than you, nevertheless you see that I love you and the money . . . because when we have a great deal of money then we fill ourselves up by eating and drinking, and when we dress up, then it will be pleasant to look at each other. . . . So you see, I want to work [here] for some time yet."[25] The process and various determinants of these shifts and evolutions of the emigrants' attitudes toward repatriation have thus far been studied very little. This area of research seems particularly promising because a wealth of suitable and unexplored sources exists for such analysis, such as immigrant letters, diaries, memoirs, foreign-language newspapers, and the surviving immigrants themselves.[26]

Now that the numerical volume of reemigration for particular groups and particular periods of time has been reasonably estimated, it would be useful to know more about the demographic, family, and socioeconomic profiles of emigrants returning to different regions and localities in Europe. Although they are fragmentary and difficult to compare because of different variables used in the analyses, some studies have been conducted of the characteristics of German repatriates in the nineteenth century, and of the Italian, Croatian, and Polish returnees in the present one.[27] One may hope that similar investigations at both the aggregate and local community levels will be undertaken for these and other groups.

Another interesting issue deserving more research attention is the problem of different reemigrant cultural types and of the subsequent adjustment of the returnees in their home countries. Existing classifications of return migrations, which specify various types of reemigrants according to their original goals in migrating, their success or failure in the host society as the motivation for returning, and their economic and social behavior following reentry into the home environment (see note 6), can provide a conceptual base for such empirical studies. Fine-grained ethnographic investigations such as that conducted by Julianna Puskás in Szamosszeg, a village in Hungary that sent to and received from America a number of its residents during the period of mass migrations at the turn of the century, are more suitable for this purpose.[28] Even more rewarding would be a combination in one study of the demographic-economic analysis with ethnographic-cultural investigation.

In recent years, the impact of repatriation on the sending societies has attracted considerable attention in the literature on mass migrations to America during the second half of the nineteenth and the beginning of the twentieth centuries. For instance, data on the considerable financial resources brought home by the German returnees in the late nineteenth century have been used as evidence against a popular thesis in American immigration historiography, that "repatriation [was] a sign of failure."[29] A study of the remittances sent to and brought from the United States by Yugoslav emigrants shows that while they did play a role in maintaining the value of the dinar on international markets and in improving the country's balance of foreign payments, no significant modernization of the economic structure of the southern Slavic lands resulted from the influx of American dollars, most of which were privately consumed through the improvement of the material standards of reemigrants and their families.[30] Similar results have been reported concerning the impact of emigrants' American savings in Poland.[31] Studies of the Slovak and Italian repatriates usually point to the conservative character of this reemigration, in that the returnees did not serve as agents of change (whether economic or cultural) but, having never really absorbed new values and attitudes during their sojourn in America, became reintegrated into the traditional way of life in their home environment.[32] Two recent studies of repatriates in Yugoslavia and in Sicily have arrived at different conclusions, however, regarding their "radicalizing" political influence on local compatriots.[33]

All these observations raise important questions for further research. In particular, two general problems seem worthy of investigation. One, to be studied at a macro-level on the basis of aggregate national data and within a theoretical framework of the "global system," is the impact of capital sent and brought home by the emigrants on the overall economic transformation and development of the sending societies. The second, for microanalysis in community settings, concerns the character and extent of attitudinal and behavioral changes returning emigrants introduced into the local societies and cultures. Such studies should investigate the impact of reemigrants on their home surroundings depending, on the one hand, on the length of their stay in the United States and the extent and type of contact with the American society, and, on the other, on the character of the environment in which they settled upon returning to Europe. The last postulate about empirical research on return migrations concerns not its theme, but its character, that is, comparison. Most studies of reemigration deal with only one group, one country treated generally, or one particular locality. Because these studies are conceptualized differently and address different questions, systematic comparisons of their results are often difficult. Research on return migrations would profit considerably from comparative projects focusing on the investigation of one immigrant group studied in different local settings in the United States or originating from different places in the home countries, or on investigations of a few selected nationality groups with different characteristics (time of arrival in the United States, residential and occupational concentration, and degree of social embeddedness in kinship and community networks in America). Finally, a revival of sociological studies of immigration (and reemigration), due to the influx in the last decades of a large new wave of immigrants from Hispanic America and Asia, offers an opportunity to undertake comparative studies of the old groups from the past and the new ones from the postwar period.[34]

NOTES

1. For a review of recent reassessments in the historical and sociological literature on immigration, see Ewa Morawska, "The Sociology and Histo-

riography of Immigration," in *Immigration Reconsidered: History, Sociology, and Politics*, ed. Virginia Yans-McLaughlin (New York, 1990), 187-241.

2. U.S. Immigration Commission, *Abstract Reports*, 2 vols. (Washington, D.C., 1911); Monika Glettler, "Slovak Return Migration from the U.S. to Hungary Before the First World War," paper presented at the conference "A Century of European Migrations, 1830-1930: Comparative Perspectives," Wayzata, Minnesota, November 6-9, 1986; Ewa Morawska, *For Bread with Butter: Life-Worlds of East Central Europeans in Johnstown, Pennsylvania, 1890-1940* (New York, 1985), 39.

3. J. G. Gould, "European Inter-Continental Emigration, 1815-1914: Patterns and Causes," *Journal of European Economic History* 8 (1979): 593-681; and Gould, "European Inter-Continental Emigration: The Road Home, Return Migration from the United States," *Journal of European Economic History* 9 (1980): 41-113; Jonathan Sarna, "The Myth of No Return: Jewish Return Migration to Eastern Europe, 1891-1914," *American Jewish History* 71 (1981): 256-69.

4. For classical interpretations, see Brinley Thomas, *Migration and Economic Growth: A Study of Great Britain and the Atlantic Economy* (London, 1973); Thomas, "Migration: Economic Aspects," in *International Encyclopaedia of Social Sciences*, ed. David I. Sills (Glencoe, 1968), 292-300; and Thomas, "Economic Factors in International Migration," in *Population Growth and Economic Development in the Third World*, ed. Leon Tabah (Liege, 1975), 441-72; Frank Thistlethwaite, "Migration from Europe Overseas in the Nineteenth and Twentieth Centuries," XIe Congrès Internationale des Sciences Historiques, *Rapports* (Uppsala, 1960), 5:32-60; and Charlotte Erickson *American Industry and the European Immigrant* (Cambridge, 1957). For a general overview of the reassessments in this regard, see Dirk Hoerder, "Immigration and the Working Class: The Reemigration Factor," *International Labor and Working Class History* 21 (1982): 28-41. For a discussion of social factors involved in repatriation, see Ewa Morawska, "Sociological Ambivalence: The Case of East European Peasant Immigrant-Workers in America, 1880s-1930s," *Qualitative Sociology* 10 (1987): 225-51; and Ronald Rothbat, "The Mobilization of Immigrant Workers: Labor, Family Formation, and Protest in Three American Industries, 1880-1920," Ph.D. dissertation, University of California at Berkeley, 1988.

5. See, for example, Ivan Cizmič, "South Slavic Return Migration, 1880-1939: Economic, Social, and Political Consequences," paper presented at the conference "A Century of European Migrations, 1830-1930: Comparative Perspectives," Wayzata, Minnesota, November 6-9, 1986; Walter Kamphoefner, "The Volume and Composition of German-American Return Migrations," 293-305 in this volume; Glettler, "Slovak Return Migration"; and Rothbar, "The Mobilization of Immigrant Workers."

6. For a general review of this topic, see Hoerder, "Immigration and the Working Class"; and Hoerder, ed., *Labor Migration in the Atlantic Economies* (Westport, 1985) which contains several useful discussions of the types of

return migrations; Thistlethwaite, "Migration from Europe Overseas"; Theodore Lianos et al., "Flows of Greek Out-Migration and Return-Migration," *International Migration* 13 (1975): 119-33; Lars-Goran Tederbrand, "Reemigration from America to Sweden," in *From Sweden to America: A History of the Migration*, ed. Harald Runblom and Hans Norman (Minneapolis, 1976), 201-28; Russel King, "Return Migration: A Neglected Aspect of Population Geography," *Area* 10 (1978): 175-82; Francesco Cerase, "A Study of Italian Migrants Returning from the USA," *International Migration Review* 1 (1967): 67-74; Cerase, "From Italy to the United States and Back: Returned Migrants, Conservative or Innovative?" Ph.D. dissertation, Columbia University, 1971; Cerase, "Expectations and Reality: A Case Study of Return Migration from the United States to Southern Italy," *International Migration Review* 8 (1974): 245-62; Dino Cinel, "The Seasonal Emigration of Italians in the Nineteenth Century: From Internal to International Destinations," *Journal of Ethnic Studies* 19 (1982): 43-68; Frances Krajlic, "Croatian Migration to and from the United States Between 1900 and 1914," Ph.D. dissertation, New York University, 1975; George Gilkey, "The United States and Italy: Migration and Repatriation," *Journal of Developing Areas* 2 (1967): 23-35; and Glettler, "Slovak Return Migration."

7. For the classical push and pull interpretations of international migrations, see Harry Jerome, *Migration and Business Cycles* (New York, 1926); Brinley Thomas, *International Migration and Economic Development* (Paris, 1961); Thomas, *Migration and Economic Growth*; Michael Piore, *Birds of Passage* (New York, 1979); Gould, "European Inter-Continental Emigration"; and Jeffrey Williamson, "Migration to the New World: Long-Term Influences and Impact," *Explorations in Economic History* 11 (1974): 357-91.

8. See, for example, Mary Kritz et al., eds., *Global Trends in Migration* (New York, 1981); William Petersen, "International Migration," *Annual Review of Sociology* 4 (1978): 533-75; Alejandro Portes, "Migration and Underdevelopment," *Politics and Society* 8 (1978): 1-49; and Charles Wood, "Equilibrium and Historical-Structural Perspectives on Migration," *International Migration Review* 16 (1982): 298-319.

9. Compare Kritz et al., *Global Trends in Migration*; Alejandro Portes and Robert Bach, *Latin Journey: Cuban and Mexican Immigrants in the United States* (Berkeley, 1985); Lucie Cheng and Edna Bonacich, eds., *Labor Migration under Capitalism* (Berkeley, 1984); Saskia Sassen-Knoob, "The Internationalization of the Labor Force," *Studies in Comparative International Development* 4 (1980): 3-26; and Sassen-Knoob, "The International Circulation of Resources and Development: The Case of Migrant Labor," *Development and Change* 9 (1978): 509-47.

10. See, for example, Ivan Berend and Gyorgi Ranki, *The European Periphery and Industrialization, 1780-1914* (New York, 1982); Hoerder, ed., *Labor Migration in the Atlantic Economies*; Hoerder, "International Labor Markets and Community Building by Migrant Workers in the Atlantic Economies," 78-100 in this volume; and John Bodnar, *The Transplanted: A History of*

Immigrants in Urban America (Bloomington, 1985). For an interpretation of the turn-of-the-century Polish labor migrations within the "global system" framework, see Ewa Morawska, "Labor Migrations of Poles in the Atlantic World-Economy, 1880-1914," *Comparative Studies in Society and History* 31 (April 1989): 237-72.

11. Franciszek Bujak, *Maszkienice.Wieś Powiatu Brzeskiego:Rozwój od R.1900 do R.1911* (Krakow, 1914), 93-94.

12. Krystyna Duda-Dziewierz, *Wieś Malopolska a Emigracja Amerykańska.Studium Wsi Babica Pow.Rzeszowskiego* (Warsaw, 1938), 23-28.

13. Frank Sheridan, "Italian, Slavic, and Hungarian Unskilled Immigrant Laborers in the United States," *Bulletin of the Bureau of Labor* (September 1907): 407-8.

14. Sheridan, "Italian, Slavic, and Hungarian Unskilled Immigrant Laborers," 475-97; Emily Greene Balch, *Our Slavic Fellow Citizens* (New York, 1969), 471-73; Wladyslaw Grabski, *Materyaly w Sprawie Wlosciańskiej* (Warsaw, 1907), 3: 91; Jozef Okolowicz, *Wychodźstwo i Osadnictwo Polskie Przed Wojną Światową* (Warsaw, 1920), 280.

15. Duda-Dziewierz, *Wieś Malopolska a Emigracja Amerykańska*, 57; Bujak, *Maszkienice*, 87-88; Bujak, *Zmiaca.Wieś Powiatu Limanowskiego:Stosunki Gospodarcze i Spoleczne* (Krakow, 1903), 100; Franciszek Gusciora, *Trzy Kurzyny.Wsie Powiatu Niskiego* (Warsaw, 1929), 74; Maria Gliwicowna, *Drogi Emigracji* (Warsaw, 1937), 507-9.

16. William Thomas and Florian Znaniecki, *The Polish Peasant in Europe and America* (New York, 1927), 2: 300; Witold Kula et al., eds., *Listy Emigrantów z Brazylii i Stanów Zjednoczonych* (Warsaw, 1973), introduction, 57; Duda-Dziewierz, *Wieś Malopolska a Emigracja Amerykańska*, 61, 95.

17. Sheridan, "Italian, Slavic and Hungarian Unskilled Immigrant Laborers"; U.S. Immigration Commission, *Reports: Immigrants in Industries* (Washington, D.C., 1911); Margaret Byington, *Homestead: The Households of a Mill Town* (Pittsburgh, 1975); Peter Roberts, "The New Pittsburghers," *Charities and the Commons*, January 2, 1909; John Fitch, "Wage Earners of Pittsburgh," *Charities and the Commons*, March 6, 1909; Donna Gabaccia, *Militants and Migrants: Rural Sicilians Become American Workers* (New Brunswick, 1988); Rothbat, "The Mobilization of Immigrant Workers."

18. Glettler, "Slovak Return Migration."

19. Kamphoefner, "The Volume and Composition of German-American Return Migration"; Rothbat, "The Mobilization of Immigrant Workers."

20. Cizmic, "South Slavic Return Migration, 1880-1939"; Glettler, "Slovak Return Migration."

21. Rothbat's dissertation, "The Mobilization of Immigrant Workers," provides interesting insights into this problem; see also the sociological research on contemporary immigrants in the United States: Rosemarie Rogers, ed., *Guests Come to Stay* (Boulder, 1985); Robert Bach, "Emigration from the Spanish-Speaking Carribean," in *U.S. Immigration and Refugee Policy*, ed. Mary Kritz (Lexington, Mass., 1983); Harley Browning and Nestor Rodrigues,

"The Migration of Mexican Indocumentados as a Settlement Process: Implications for Work," in *Hispanics in the U.S. Economy*, ed. George Borjas and Marta Tienda (New York, 1985); and Douglas Massey et al., *Return to Aztlan: The Social Process of International Migration from Western Mexico* (Berkeley, 1988).

22. Julianna Puskás, *From Hungary to the United States, 1880-1914* (Budapest, 1982); *Emigration from Northern, Central and Southern Europe* (Krakow, 1983); Mark Stolarik, *Slovak Migration from Europe to North America, 1870-1918* (Cleveland, 1980); Branko Colakovic, *Yugoslav Migrations to America* (San Francisco, 1973); Morawska, *For Bread with Butter*; Cerase, "A Study of Italian Migrants Returning from the U.S.A."; Kamphoefner, "The Volume and Composition of German-American Return Migration"; Kerby A. Miller, *Emigrants and Exiles: Ireland and the Irish Exodus to North America* (Oxford, 1985); Lars-Goran Tedebrand, "Reemigration from America to Sweden," in *Labor Migration in the Atlantic Economies*, ed. Hoerder, 357-80; Keijo Virtanen, "Finnish Migrants (1860-1930) in the Overseas Return Movement," in *Labor Migration in the Atlantic Economies*, ed. Hoerder, 381-98.

23. Ivan Molek, *Slovene Immigrant History, 1900-1950: Autobiographical Sketches by Ivan Molek* (Dover, 1979), 52.

24. Thomas and Znaniecki, *The Polish Peasant in Europe and America*, 2:245.

25. Ibid., 2:338.

26. Rothbat, in "The Mobilization of Immigrant Workers," attempts an interesting analysis of the "evolving intentions" of immigrants based on the emigrants' letters from Thomas and Znaniecki, *The Polish Peasant*; see also Morawska, "Sociological Ambivalence."

27. Kamphoefner, "The Volume and Composition of German-American Return Migration"; Betty Caroli, *Italian Repatriates from the United States, 1900-1914* (Staten Island, 1973); Cerase, "A Study of Italian Migrants Returning from the U.S.A."; Krajlic, "Croatian Migration to and from the United States"; Adam Walaszek, "Return Migration from the U.S.A. to Poland," in *The Politics of Return: International Return Migration*, ed. Donald Kubat (New York, 1984), 213-21.

28. Julianna Puskás, "Hungarian Overseas Migration: A Microanalysis," 221-36 in this volume.

29. Kamphoefner, "The Volume and Composition of German-American Return Migration."

30. Cizmic, "South Slavic Return Migration, 1880-1939."

31. Morawska, "Labor Migrations of Poles in the Atlantic World-Economy, 1880-1914."

32. See, for instance, Francesco Cerase, "Expectations and Reality: A Case Study of Return Migrants from the U.S. to Southern Italy," *International Migration Review* 8 (1974): 245-62; Cerase, "From Italy to the United States and Back: Returned Migrants, Conservative or Innovative?"; Cinel, "The Seasonal Emigration of Italians," and *Stumbling into Modernity: The Impact of*

American Savings on the Southern Italian Economy (in press); Joseph Lopreato, *Peasants No More: Social Class and Social Change in an Underdeveloped Society* (San Francisco, 1967), esp. 211-23; and Glettler, "Slovak Return Migration."

33. Cizmic, "South Slavic Return Migration, 1880-1939"; Gabaccia, *Militants and Migrants,* chapter 8.

34. For a comparative review of recent findings in the historical and sociological research on old and new immigrant groups in the United States, see Morawska, "The Sociology and Historiography of Immigration."

13

The Volume and Composition of German-American Return Migration

WALTER D. KAMPHOEFNER

One of the important new impulses which Frank Thistlethwaite's 1960 essay contributed to migration studies was a renewed focus on return migration. The fact that about one-third of all immigrants on the eve of World War I returned to their homelands certainly should give pause to those viewing America as the land of unlimited possibilities. Welcome as this corrective was, it went too far, or was taken too far by other scholars who failed to read the small print. Thistlethwaite's statement, after all, was based on American data beginning in 1907.[1] There is no reason to simply project this figure backward into the nineteenth century, when the speed, cost, and comfort of transatlantic travel were much less favorable. Moreover, the same statistics that reveal these heavy repatriation rates also show substantial differences among various ethnic groups (although not a simple old versus new immigrant dichotomy as the racist interpretations of the U.S. Immigration Commission would have it). For German immigrants in particular, twentieth-century statistics on repatriation have little to say to the period of mass immigration during the nineteenth century. The volume of German immigration fell so drastically after the panic and depression of 1893 that there is no reason to assume much continuity in its composition. Only by developing statistical materials from this earlier period can we hope to gain insight into the extent of return migration during the era of German mass immigration.

As difficult as it might be to establish the volume of German repatriation, more challenging yet is the question of its composition. Without this sort of information, however, one can say little about the significance of the return flow. The simple equation of *Emigration and Disenchantment,* as the title of one book on the subject would have it, does not necessarily hold. This is particularly true in cases where immigration from the outset was intended to be temporary, for example the transatlantic labor migration that was prevalent with many new immigration groups. Most of the studies of return migration have concentrated on these groups, but it is doubtful that they had much in common with German return migration. The groups that were most similar, both structurally and culturally, were the Scandinavians, for whom some studies of repatriation have also been conducted.[2]

Estimates of Return Migration Volume

Several attempts have been made to estimate return migration before 1900 from Europe as a whole (Table 13.1), but the only previous estimate of German return migration is an attempt by Günter Moltmann on the basis of passenger records from the port of Hamburg.[3] These figures do not distinguish between Germans and non-Germans, but few of the latter traveled via Hamburg before 1880. A more serious flaw is the failure to distinguish between permanent migrants and temporary travelers. Records exist of the number of Americans returning from Germany via Hamburg, and Moltmann assumes that they crossed eastbound in the same year and subtracts their numbers from the passengers in both directions to arrive at the figures for calculating the ratio of eastbound to westbound passengers, the presumed return migration rate.

Harry Jerome, dealing with overseas migrants as a group, has calculated the annual ratio of arriving male immigrants to departing male steerage passengers since 1870. The figures in Table 13.1 were aggregated by decades, but the annual ups and downs of the Moltmann and the Jerome series (not shown here) also parallel one another closely. From about 1883 on, however, Jerome's figures, encompassing all immigrants including increasing numbers of remigration-prone Italians, show considerably higher absolute levels than Moltmann's figures dealing with Germans alone.

The U.S. Immigration Commission report included figures comparing gross immigration from Europe by decade with net increase in the number of European immigrants present in successive censuses. Such figures do not, of course, reflect return migration alone, for they leave out the variable of mortality. This is not a constant but increases over time as the immigrant cohort ages, and as the size of the resident group increases relative to the amount of in-migration.

The most sophisticated calculations of net return migration by decade were constructed by Simon Kuznets and Ernest Rubin, who used life-table techniques to calculate the degree to which both the immigrants resident at the beginning of the decade and those who arrived during the next ten years would be depleted by mortality. By

Table 13.1. Return Migration Rates by Decade and Ethnicity
(as Percent of Immigration during Same Period)

	German Return Migration Rate (Moltmann)	Returning Male Steerage Passengers as Percent of Male Immigration (Jerome)	Difference between Net and Gross Gain from Immigration during Census Interval (U.S. Imm. Comm.)	Estimated Return Migration Rate (Kuznets-Rubin)	Calculations Based on Kuznets-Rubin Mortality Rates			
					German	Irish	British	Scandinavian
1850s	6.6[a]		22.7	(7.2)[e]	11.9	5.6	30.3	[g]
1860s	18.4[b]		45.2	(1.6)[e]	13.7	[f]	48.1	[g]
1870s	22.3	24.7	64.5	24.3	14.6	18.9	43.4	[f]
1880s	14.2	22.1	51.9	18.8	12.0	35.7	31.4	7.1
1890s	16.9[c]	26.3[d]	76.1	38.6				

Sources: Günter Moltmann, "American-German Return Migration in the Nineteenth and Early Twentieth Centuries," *Central European History* 13 (1980): 378-92; Harry Jerome, *Migration and Business Cycles* (New York, 1926), 105; U.S. Immigration Commission *Reports* (Washington, 1911), 1:123-24; Simon Kuznets and Ernest Rubin, *Immigration and the Foreign Born* (New York, 1954), 45. Additional calculations based on Kuznet-Rubin and statistics of U.S. Immigration and foreign population in *Harvard Encyclopedia of American Ethnic Groups*, ed. Stephan Thernstrom (Cambridge, 1980), 1047-52.

[a] Excluding 1851-54.
[b] Excluding 1863-66.
[c] 1891-92 only.
[d] Excluding 1896-97.
[e] Assuming .8183 survival of census population and .958 survival of immigrants during decade.
[f] No calculation possible; actual increase exceeds expected increase allowing for mortality.
[g] No calculation possible; actual increase exceeds sum of previous census population and gross immigration without allowing for mortality.

comparing the actual to the expected increase in immigrant population between two successive censuses, they arrive at an indirect estimate of the return migration rate for each decade beginning with the 1870s.

These same techniques can also be applied to earlier decades or individual immigrant groups if one is willing to assume fairly constant mortality rates across time and ethnicity. I calculated the figures for the 1850s and 1860s, using the same rates of mortality as obtained in the 1870s.[4] I also applied the Kuznets-Rubin formula to individual ethnic groups, using the same mortality rates for all nationalities and applying the 1870 rates also for earlier decades. Table 13.1 presents the results that obtained for Germans, Irish, British, and Scandinavians.[5] It is immediately obvious that striking contrasts exist; the question is whether they arise from difference in return migration or problems of the data. In the Scandinavian case the data are clearly at fault: in both the 1850s and the 1860s, the sum of the initial census population and the total recorded immigration over the decade adds up to less than the census population at the end of the decade without making any allowances for mortality. Two factors appear to have caused serious discrepancies. Many Scandinavians,[6] and to a lesser extent, Irish,[7] traveling on British ships were enumerated as British, and immigration via land from Canada went virtually unrecorded, so that the inflow and thus also the return flow was underestimated. In the case of the British, the first factor would inflate and the second deflate immigration figures. In the case of the Scandinavians and Irish, both would contribute to an underestimation of the numbers coming in, and thus also the volume of return migration.

Of all the ethnic groups, one should be on safest ground estimating the return migration of Germans. They had by 1880 replaced the Irish as the largest immigrant group, comprising over one-fourth of the total. Moreover, they fell about midway on the most important variable affecting mortality: less concentrated in big cities than the Irish and more so than British or particularly Scandinavians. Only a negligible portion of Germans arrived via Canada. The calculations for the 1850s and 1860s are based on minimum estimates of mortality (rates from the 1870s) and thus maximum estimates of return migration.[8]

For immigrants as a whole, there is at least a rough degree of correspondence in all the estimates in Table 13.1. The depression decades of the 1870s and 1890s show higher rates of return migration than the other decades regardless of the estimation method used. The figures derived for Germans from the Kuznets-Rubin method of calculation square reasonably well with Moltmann's estimates. However, accurate as these calculations may be in determining the relative volume of eastbound traffic, the question remains whether this can necessarily be equated with return migration.

One way to assess the magnitude of the problem is to draw upon repatriation figures from the German side. Authorities from the port of Bremen reported one return migrant for every thirty-two emigrants in 1854 and one for every eleven in 1855, or reduced to percentages, about 3 and 9 percent respectively. Moltmann's figures for the same two years are 4.8 and 11.3 percent, parallel, but about two points higher. Greater insight into the magnitude of this problem is gained by looking at statistics from the German side at the state level rather than at the ports. During the mid-nineteenth century, several German states kept figures on return migration or immigration from America, most of the latter being returning emigrants.[9] These figures agree closely with one another from the 1850s on, but contrast rather sharply with Moltmann's figures. While the latter show return migration rates of 6.6 percent for the 1850s and 18.4 percent for the 1860s, the German statistics hover around 2 percent. Figures for earlier periods are even lower, consistently under 1 percent. That too, would make sense, for it was only during the 1850s that steam travel on the ocean was becoming common. So we are faced with quite a discrepancy to be resolved.

It is possible but improbable that German authorities simply overlooked a large proportion of return migrants.[10] One factor that should inspire confidence in the German figures is that a half-dozen sovereign states enumerated immigrants from America according to their own rules and procedures, but reached repatriation rates that run closely parallel. Another reassuring factor is that higher remigration rates from other destinations appear in these statistics. The same Prussian statistics that show return rates from North America averaging 1.3 percent in the 1860s give remigration rates from Australia and South America nearly three times as high, around 3.5 percent.[11] The Oldenburg statistics also record emigration to and immigration from "other European states." Such emigration averaged fewer than ten persons annually for the first years, then jumped to 115 in 1858, 143 the next year, and 77 in 1860 before falling off again to practically nothing. Immigration followed an identical pattern with two years' lag. From a previous high of three, it jumped to twenty-three in 1860, forty-three the next year, and then two years with seventeen returnees interrupted by a year with none. Here one sees a classic case of return migration as disillusionment. As an official statistician explained, "This was the trek to Hungary, which soon came to an end because of disappointed expectations of the emigrants." Similarly, the jump in immigration "was caused by the return of many who in the previous years had emigrated to Hungary." All told, the remigration rate from Europe during the 1850s came to 29 percent; that from America, barely 0.5 percent.[12] If the one was registered by officials, why not the other? The parallel case of emigration should provide some hints about the degree of efficiency in the German registry of population movements. By calculating the difference between population gain (or loss) between successive censuses on the one hand, and the surplus of births over deaths during the same time period on the other, one can arrive at an indirect estimate of net migration and see how this comports with official emigration figures over the same period. For the states of Bavaria, Baden, and Prussia during the mid-nineteenth century, actual emigration exceeded officially recorded levels (including some clandestine emigration) by at most 50 percent.[13]

However, unrecorded emigration is not strictly comparable with unrecorded immigration. For the former to take place, one must only escape official notice for one day; for the latter, every day. German states in the nineteenth century and to the present register the place of residence of all their inhabitants.[14] Even if one were to assume an undernumeration of return migration equal to that of emigration, repatriation rates in the 1850s would still be below 4 percent, or less than half of Moltmann's figure.

What have Moltmann's calculations, plausible as they appear at first glance, failed to take into account? A clue is given by a local official who compiled the migration statistics from Iburg and obviously kept his eyes peeled for return migrants, in whom his superiors were apparently vitally interested: "Nobody returned this year [1843], although several persons came back to this region for a short time, in some cases to take up capital that was left behind, in others to arrange for the emigration of family members who had remained here."[15] Moltmann does subtract eastbound "Americans" from both the emigration and immigration totals, but it is not clear what proportion of visiting German Americans end up under that rubric. The most reasonable assumption is, only those who were naturalized, that is to say, those who had spent at least five years in America. In terms of the preceding quotation, it is doubtful that many emigrants would have waited that long before liquidating their holdings or picking up their family. From my unsystematic observations, especially in immigrant letters, it appears that visits to the homeland came either in the first few years after arrival in America, often to seek a wife or conduct family members to the New World, or in retirement age.

The latter category doubtless increased substantially during the course of the century and cannot have been very important before the Civil War. In any case, a perusal of several thousand immigrant letters suggests that for every case of repatriation, there were four or five visits in the old homeland.

The Kuznets-Rubin figures are plagued by similar problems; here too, German Americans or other immigrants on temporary visits back home are treated as return migrants unless they were American citizens. Furthermore, there is the problem of Europeans on temporary visits to the United States. Estimates place this no higher than 2 percent of all arriving aliens, an insignificant amount at first glance, but if return migration is at 10 percent, then 20 percent of it consisted in reality of European travelers. After 1868, American statistics apparently exclude such temporary travelers from the immigration figures on which the Kuznets-Rubin estimates are based, but Moltmann's "return migrants" through the entire period include such Germans on business or vacations in the United States.[16] The distortions due to temporary travelers probably become worse over time as speed and comfort of travel increased, and explain why Moltmann's figures in later decades become higher than those derived from the Kuznets-Rubin method. Jerome's figures are subject to similar problems to the extent that temporary visitors traveled steerage. His westbound figures include only immigrants, whereas his eastbound figures include all steerage passengers, visitors as well as repatriates. Moreover, Jerome deals only with males, who were more prone to return than females. One reason, then, for the general agreement between Moltmann's and other estimates of return migration is that they suffer from similar problems of data contamination.[17]

From the turn of the century on, more information on return migration becomes available from the American side (Table 13.2). The ranking of Germans among the main old immigration groups varies according to the period examined. Over the whole periods from 1908 to 1924, only the Irish ranked lower than Germans, but in part this reflects the obstacles to repatriation during World War I and the catastrophic economic situation that encouraged emigration from the early Weimar Republic. If one focuses on the period before migration was affected by war and economic disaster, Germans (whether defined by "race" or by country of last and future residence) show the highest return migration rates of all the groups considered here. Other indicators, however, suggest that this pattern may have been recent. The volume of German immigration dropped markedly with the Panic of 1893 and the ensuing depression. While Germans were

Table 13.2. Indicators of Return Migration from America, by Ethnic Group

	German	Irish	English	Scottish	Swedish	All
All Immigrants:						
Return migration as proportion of immigration, 1908-24	13.7	8.9	19.3[a]		15.4[b]	
Return migration as proportion of immigration, 1908-14	18.1	8.7	12.7	11.2	11.2	
Departures as proportion of admissions, by race, 1908-10	21	7	14	10	14[b]	32
Proportion of arriving immigrants, 1899-1910, previously in U.S.	11.5	18.3	25.4	20.2	14.8	12.4
U.S. Immigration Commission Survey, Male Immigrants Employed in Industry:						
Proportions of husbands with wife residing abroad	4.3	1.2	3.4	3.2	2.9	22.7
Proportion reporting visits abroad by years of residence in U.S.:						
under 5 years	5.6	4.0	9.8	12.2	4.8	8.7
5-9 years	12.1	12.4	32.2	32.0	18.7	20.0
10 years or more	10.3	15.5	32.2	30.9	19.9	23.5
Proportion naturalized, men aged 21 and above, resident 10 years or more in U.S.	81.5	80.0	67.0	79.6	87.6	56.9

Sources: Taken or calculated from Thomas Archdeacon, *Becoming American: An Ethnic History* (New York, 1983), 139; Imre Ferenczi, ed., *International Migrations* (New York, 1929), 1: 390-92, 436-40; U.S. Immigration Commission, *Reports* (Washington, 1911), 1:104, 113, 459-61, 488.

[a] All British and British-Canadians.
[b] All Scandinavians.

far and above the largest immigrant group in the 1880s, their number of new arrivals during the first decade of the twentieth century was only one-quarter of that in the 1880s, although no other group suffered a decline of more than one-half. There is good reason to suspect that this changed volume also brought with it a changed composition. For example, the proportion of immigrants arriving since 1899 who had been in the United States previously was lower for Germans than for any other "old stock" group. Similarly, among immigrants in the industries investigated by the Dillingham Commission, the propensity of Germans to have made visits back home—the lowest of any ethnic group—was actually lower for those who had been residents for longer than ten years than for newcomers, another hint at a recent shift in migratory behavior. German industrial workers were slightly more likely to have a wife residing abroad than was the case with the other ethnic groups, but the rate was very low in all cases. To the extent that naturalization rates indicate an intention to settle permanently, Germans also show considerable evidence of stability. Only Scandinavians showed higher naturalization rates; the Irish and Scots were in the same range, but the English level was decidedly lower. Taken together, these indicators give little reason to believe that Germans had above-average repatriation rates during the era of mass immigration in the nineteenth century.

Structure of Return Migration

The structure of return migration is perhaps a more elusive issue than the volume of the migration. Sources on the American side provide practically nothing, and in the case of Germans there is neither the possibility of oral history as with more recent new immigration groups nor the rich population register sources of the Scandinavians.[18] One of the few alternatives to literary sources with an elite bias are aggregate-level statistics, where they exist. Fortunately, such statistics on return migration were collected at least for short periods by the states of Bavaria and Württemberg. Although not on the individual level, they are broken down enough to provide hints about the makeup of return migration.[19] To the extent one can generalize from this limited base, German repatriates appear to have much in common with their Scandinavian counterparts.[20]

Males generally were overrepresented in overseas migrations, but even more so among returnees. This held true for both of the German states with data from the late 1850s. Both emigration statistics from Württemberg in the early 1850s and American statistics on German immigrants from the same period show a female proportion of 41 percent, but women made up only about 23 percent of the returnees to Württemberg during the same period. In the officially registered Bavarian emigration from 1856 to 1858, males were even a slight minority at 47 percent, but three of five return migrants were men. This is very similar to Swedish repatriates, whose male proportion was three-fourths in the 1880s and two-thirds in the 1890s.

In terms of family status, the makeup of the return migration was especially characterized by the scarcity of single women: 5 percent or fewer of the total among both Bavarians and Württembergers. One reason for this was that with the more favorable sex ratio among Germans in America compared to back home, few women stayed single for long in the New World. The decrease in single women was compensated among Bavarians by an increase in returning families, while in Württemberg the proportion of single men increased substantially. Although there is no direct information on age structure, it appears that many who returned as families had only recently been married. Statistics on both emigrants and repatriates provide a breakdown between parents and children, making it possible to calculate average family size.[21] While Bavarian emigrants registered nearly three children per couple, return migrants barely exceeded one child on average. The figure for Württemberg was slightly higher, 1.4 children per repatriate family, but still considerably lower than the 3.5 children per emigrant family. Most of the families among Swedish repatriates also had been recently formed; the age group from fifteen to nineteen had an extremely low representation among return migrants.

Such figures might comport with either repatriation after a short stay in America or a retirement in the homeland after the children had grown up and started on their own. But in the 1850s, the number of German Americans who would have reached retirement age was relatively small. Bavarian statistics contain another measure that adds weight to the assertion that most people who returned did so after relatively short sojourns: the number of people naturalized. Assuming that this figure applies only to adult males, one arrives at a naturalization rate of only about one-third, representing the minimum proportion that had spent at least five years in the United States. Here again, the German figure agrees very closely with Swedish figures showing that only 29 percent of return migrants had stayed five years or longer.

As with Scandinavians, there were no consistent patterns concerning regional distribution of return migration. With Bavarians, the Palatinate showed consistently heavier rates of return than other parts of the kingdom. Because this area also had far and above the highest per-capita emigration rates, there might have been a relationship between the two. But the difference was partly illusory, because migration from the Palatinate had been underway longer and clandestine emigration was less perfectly registered than in the rest of Bavaria, so that the population at risk was in fact greater than the statistics would indicate. A more plausible factor is better access to transportation routes in the Palatinate, which borders the west bank of the Rhine, than in the rest of Bavaria farther eastward and off the main water routes. Another hint in the same direction is return migration to Hannover, which was highest for the district on the North Sea coast, especially the hinterland of Bremen. For the two short periods when information is available for Württemberg, there is no consistent ranking of the four districts' return migration rates. Of course, one cannot tell from these statistics whether people returned to the same places they had left, but Swedish figures showing about 80 percent of repatriates returned to their parish of origin suggests that it is safe to assume so.

Several other social indicators present more difficulties of interpretation. Bavarian authorities posed the question of how many return migrants had emigrated without permission. Upon first glance, these figures might suggest a picture of repatriates as rebels and eternal malcontents. While statistics show about 20 percent of all emigrants leaving clandestinely, among returnees the average was around one-third, and in one year exceeded 60 percent. But if we assume that the bulk of returnees had emigrated as single males (those most prone to emigrate clandestinely), the discrepancy becomes considerably smaller. And in any event, since clandestine emigration was imperfectly registered, the true figure was higher than 20 percent. For two years of the 1850s, statistics from Württemberg provide another social indicator, religion. One might expect that the dominant religious group, in this case Protestants, would be more likely to return home than religious minorities. Instead, the confessional makeup of the groups traveling in each direction was strikingly similar, especially considering the small numbers of returnees involved.[22]

One of the most controversial aspects of return migration is what it means in terms of immigrant success or satisfaction. At first glance, repatriation might appear as a sign of disillusionment, the retreat of the America-weary. However, this need not be so, particularly if the migration was intended to be temporary in the first place. In such a case, return might signify that the person has found what he (and in

most cases, it was a "he") was looking for, while remaining in America
might suggest failure to attain one's goals.[23]

Perhaps the most interesting aspect of the statistics from Bavaria
and Württemberg are their figures on the financial resources of return
migrants. At least in the case of male emigrants, they strongly contradict the interpretation of return migration as failure. Return migrants from Bavaria in the aggregate showed double or more the
economic resources of emigrants during the same time period (Table
13.3). When the data are broken down by subgroups, both returning
families and single males maintain their advantage over emigrants in
the same categories. The exception is the few single women who
returned home; initially less well-off than male emigrants and largely
restricted on the American job market to domestic service, they were
at an even greater disadvantage when they returned. In two out of
the three years and on an overall average, female repatriates returned
with less money than they had left with.

The Württemberg figures overlap in time with the Bavarian ones,
and again show return migrants as having about twice the financial
resources of emigrants, with one exception. Returnees in 1858 appeared to have been near destitution. This figure gains some plau-
sibility in that the Panic of 1857 struck in the fall, primarily affecting
migration the next year, and 1858 showed one of the highest levels
of return migration recorded in Württemberg during that era. It was
also the year in which Bavarian returnees showed the smallest advantage over emigrants. One might object that such aggregate mean
figures could be inflated by a few extreme cases, but in Bavaria the
advantages of return migrants still hold across all family categories
except single women. Similarly, the Württemberg data for 1856 and
1857 was broken down among the four districts of the kingdom,
resulting in subgroups of fewer than twenty persons, or in some cases
fewer than ten. But also at this level, in seven of the eight subgroups
return migrants still showed a two-to-one financial advantage over
emigrants.

If anything, the gap was even larger because of two factors. First,
any clandestine emigrants overlooked in the tabulation undoubtedly
clustered toward the bottom end of the economic scale—the fewer
resources one had, the greater the chances of slipping away unno-
ticed.[24] Second, statistics on emigrants' resources included money that
had to be paid for ship passage, while return migrants had their
journey and their expenses behind them.[25]

Moltmann concludes his article by stating, "Historians are only at

Table 13.3. Financial Resources of Emigrants and Return Migrants*

Year	Emigrants to North America	Immigrants from North America
Bavaria:		
1856	190	471
1857	193	632
1858	139	282
Württemberg:		
1856	215	456
1857	189	910
1858	438	26
1859	427	701
1860	386	754
1861	232	979
1862	260	1719

Sources: Calculated from Hauptstaatsarchiv Stuttgart, Innenministerium, E 146, Bü. 1818; *Württembergisches Jahrbuch* (1856), 2:151-89; (1857), 2:1-39.
* All numbers in guilders (1 guilder = 41 cents).

the beginning of an analysis of the American-German return migration patterns."[26] This chapter has done little to change that; if anything, it has raised as many questions as it has answered, although it has posed serious doubts about equating remigration with disillusionment. But it has also pointed up several promising avenues for further research. As early as 1931, Walter Willcox asserted that there was "no important or promising field of American immigration statistics so little worked as the attempt to relate the immigration statistics to the foreign born statistics."[27] As the rudimentary calculations herein demonstrate, this still remains a promising field, one where the application of more sophisticated demographic measures and a combination of American, Canadian, and European data might provide some firmer footing in what remains a statistical swamp. A second approach that could bring large dividends would be to develop individual-level investigations of the occupational and social makeup of return migrants. This could be done where the material behind state-level statistics such as those cited above is still extant, or it might be undertaken on the basis of passenger lists at the ports. In either case, in conjunction with indexed U.S. census material, it could shed light on the crucial issue of how much of the return traffic was really return migration and which social and occupational groups were most prone to repatriation.

NOTES

For a German version of this chapter with additional tabular material, see "Umfang und Zusammensetzung der deutsch-amerikanischen Rückwanderung," *Amerikastudien / American Studies* 33 (1988): 291-307.

1. Frank Thistlethwaite, "Migration from Europe Overseas in the Nineteenth and Twentieth Centuries," XIe Congrès Internationales des Sciences Historiques, *Rapports* (Uppsala, 1960), 5:38, 58 n. 35.

2. A good critical overview of literature on return migration is provided by Dirk Hoerder, "Immigration and the Working Class: The Remigration Factor," *International Labor and Working Class History* 21 (1982): 28-41. Wilbur H. Shepperson, *Emigration and Disenchantment: Portraits of Englishmen Repatriated from the United States* (Norman, 1965), is, as Hoerder points out, "almost useless to historians of the working class," dealing with an exceptional group of only seventy-five repatriates, most of whom published autobiographies. Alfred Vagts, *Deutsch-Amerikanische Rückwanderung* (Heidelberg, 1960), is plagued by similar unrepresentatitveness. Dirk Hoerder, ed., *Labor Migration in the Atlantic Economies* (Westport, 1985), contains several useful chapters on return migration, in particular Lars-Göran Tedebrand, "Remigration from America to Sweden" (357-80) and Keijo Virtanen, "Finnish Migrants (1860-1930) in the Overseas Return Movement" (381-98).

3. Günter Moltmann, "American-German Return Migration in the Nineteenth and Early Twentieth Centuries," *Central European History* 13 (1980): 378-92; Harry Jerome, *Migration and Business Cycles* (New York, 1926), 105; U.S. Immigration Commission, *Reports* (Washington, 1911), 1:123-24; Simon Kuznets and Ernest Rubin, *Immigration and the Foreign Born* (New York, 1954), 45. A good German case study, but unfortunately dealing with an atypical area in the North Sea islands, is Gerhard Kortum, "Migrationstheoretische und bevölkerungsgeographische Probleme der nordfriesischen Amerikarückwanderung," in *Die deutsche und skandinavische Amerikaauswanderung im 19. und 20. Jahrhundert,* ed. Kai Detlev Sievers (Neumünster, 1981), 111-201.

4. Kuznets and Rubin's calculations dealt with males and females separately, however, a breakdown by sex is not available for individual ethnic groups or earlier decades, so I used aggregate figures calculated from their findings instead. The survival rate of the 1870 cohort was .8183; this figure was applied to the 1850 and 1860 cohorts as well. The mortality of persons immigrating during the 1870s came to 4.2 percent of the gross immigration, so a survival rate of .958 was applied to the immigrating cohorts of earlier decades. Ideally, the mortality rate should be calculated as a proportion of *net* immigration, but since this is an unknown quantity in the 1850s and 1860s, the ratio to gross immigration had to be used instead. In any case, the most crucial variable affecting the calculated remigration rate is the survival of the population from the previous census, not the survival of immigrants arriving during the current decade.

5. For the 1850s, 1860s, and 1870s, the same survival rates were applied

as in note 4: .8183 of the census population from the previous decade, and .958 of the decade's immigration. For the 1880s, the rates were .7966 and .958.

6. Runblom and Norman, *From Sweden to America*, 179-81, 197. Swedish emigration statistics (117-18) also provide an independent check on American immigration figures; for the decade of the 1860s, the former are about twice as large as the latter. Exact comparisons are impossible because the Swedes used calendar years, the Americans, fiscal years ending June 30. Some Scandinavians probably were included in German as well as British immigration figures.

7. According to records from the European side, Irish migration to the United States was 75,000 higher during the 1850s and 250,000 higher during the 1860s than the American figures indicate. Applying the same mortality rates used in Table 13.1 to these figures yields a return migration rate of 12.5 percent for the 1850s and 18.0 percent for the 1860s. This probably exaggerates return migration, for Irish mortality was doubtless higher than for other immigrants. It does indicate, however, that there were serious problems with American records. Kerby A. Miller, *Emigrants and Exiles: Ireland and the Irish Exodus to North America* (Oxford, 1985), 569, 291-92, 316-19.

8. There are several reasons to assume higher mortality and thus lower repatriation than appears in Table 13.1. The 1850s probably represented the peak of mortality rates in urban America. In Massachusetts, the only state with halfway reliable death registration, mortality was nearly 10 percent higher in 1855 than in the decade of the 1870s. Warren S. Thompson and P. K. Whelpton, *Population Trends in the United States* (New York, 1933), 229-31. For 1855, there were 21.4 average annual deaths per thousand population; for 1868-82, 19.57; the depression years of 1873-77 had a higher mortality rate than the years before or after. See also the discussion and tables in Yasukichi Yasuba, *Birth Rates of the White Population in the United States, 1800-1860* (Baltimore, 1962), 86-89. The proportion of all German immigrants living in America's eight biggest cities dropped from 29.6 percent in 1850 to 24.8 percent in 1870; Walter Kamphoefner, *The Westfalians: From Germany to Missouri* (Princeton, 1987), Table 3.3. For what they are worth, calculations from mortality figures in the 1850 U.S. Census show that Germans and particularly Irish had higher mortality rates than other whites, and that the death rate was especially high in cities.

9. Sources on return migration or immigration from America: Staatsarchiv Osnabrück, Rep 350 Iburg, Nr. 5030. *Zur Statistik des Königreichs Hannover*, 9:159-63; 11:90-95. The source itself does not directly enumerate returnees from America, but rather the number of immigrants from America, other European states, and other German states respectively, plus a summary statistic on the total number of returnees among them. An upper boundary on the number of returnees from America could be established by assuming that it could not exceed the total number of returnees, nor the

total number of incoming Americans. Many who were not returnees may have been their American-born children. *Statistische Nachrichten über das Grossherzogtum Oldenburg* 9 (1867): 164-77; *Beiträge zur Statistik des Königreichs Bayern* 1 (1850): 194-97; 3 (1854): 322-23; 8 (1859): 240-41; 11 (1863): 16; *Württembergisches Jahrbuch*, 1848-70; T. Böddicker, "Die Einwanderung und Auswanderung des preussischen Staates," *Preussische Statistik* 26 (1874): ix-xvii; Vagts, *Deutsch-Amerikanische Rückwanderung*, 20-21. Comments in several of these sources indicated that most of the immigrating Americans were return German emigrants. In *Germany and the Emigration, 1816-1885* (Cambridge, 1964), 173, Mack Walker states that 1854 saw the first significant return migration since 1817, about 5 percent of the emigration for that year.

10. At least a small piece of information from the American side suggests that German return migration rates remained very low even in the latter part of the century when transportation conditions were more favorable. Among the ten thousand requests for aid processed by the German Society of Chicago from 1883 to 1908, there were only about 210 instances of people requesting help to return to Germany, or about 8.4 per year. If we project from Chicago's share of German Americans nationally, we arrive at a figure of about 140 subsidized repatriates annually. Germans in Chicago made up about 6 percent of the national total. If the Chicago figures were projected nationally and expressed as a proportion of total immigration from 1884 to 1908, the rate of people requesting return assistance would only be 0.22 percent. In fact, return migration was no doubt heavier from this bustling transportation hub with many new arrivals than from most rural areas. Of course, this figure only includes those too poor to return home on their own, but it does cast doubt on the thesis equating repatriation with impoverishment and disillusionment. John B. Jentz and Hartmut Keil, "From Immigrants to Urban Workers: Chicago's German Poor in the Gilded Age and Progressive Era, 1883-1908," *Vierteljahresschrift für Sozial- und Wirtschaftsgeschichte* 68 (1981): 57-61, 83-84.

11. There are also Prussian statistics for the period after 1871 which record American immigration or return migration from America. Even more than for figures from before 1871, these conflict with Moltmann's return migration rates. Here, however, it is the German statistics that are responsible. Prussians no longer automatically lost their citizenship when they emigrated; instead, this took place only after ten years' residence outside the country, or through a formal request for an emigration permit. But an ever-smaller proportion took this formal step before leaving, only 30 percent in 1872, and 20 percent or less by the mid-1870s. In some cases this may have reflected indecision about whether to emigrate permanently, but more often simply the desire to avoid needless formalities. "Der Erwerb und Verlust der Reichs- und Staatsangehörigkeit," *Zeitschrift des Königlichen Preussischen Statistischen Bureaus* (1874 through 1887). See especially the discussions of the statistics in the 1881 and 1882 volumes. The naturalization and re-

naturalization procedures were instituted by a law passed by the North German Confederacy on June 1, 1870, and the Reich law of April 22, 1871. Even if one were to project (on the basis of Swedish statistics from the 1880s) that only 3.5 percent of the repatriates had been in America for the ten years necessary to lose their citizenship, and assuming that Prussians made up about half of all German emigration, one would still arrive at only about 4,400 return migrants per year, fewer than one-third of Moltmann's figure.

12. *Statistische Nachrichten über das Grossherzogtum Oldenburg* 9 (1867): 164-77, 286.

13. Bavarian census officials made such a calculation for all the triennial census periods from 1834 to 1861. Overall, the deficit came to over fifty thousand, but almost all of this was restricted to the exclave of the Palatinate, lying west of the Rhine. There the actual emigration was 50 percent higher than the official figure, while for Bavaria as a whole it was only 25 percent higher. *Beiträge zur Statistik des Königreichs Bayern* 13 (1865): 25-27. Similarly, for the state of Baden between the censuses of 1852 and 1855, the migration deficit (the difference between net natural processes and recorded overseas migration) came to just 50 percent of the latter. *Beiträge zur Statistik der inneren Verwaltung des Grossherzogtums Baden* 5 (1857): 1-35. From 1868 to 1871, the number of Prussians emigrating via Hamburg and Bremen alone exceeded by 18 percent the officially registered Prussian emigration. In addition, a substantial number, particularly from the Rhineland, emigrated by other ports such as Havre, Antwerp, and Rotterdam. About 40 percent of the emigration registered in official statistics was clandestine as well. *Zeitschrift des Königlichen Preussischen Statistischen Bureaus* (1875): 40-42. In the cases of Bavaria and Baden, some of the deficits probably resulted not from overseas migration but in net migration losses to other German states, but Prussia probably gained in the process.

14. In the city of Duisburg from 1871 to 1891, the number of persons cited for violations of registration laws ranged from 0.9 to 5.4 percent of the annual volume of migration, according to James Jackson, "Migration and Urbanization in the Ruhr Valley, 1850-1900," Ph.D. dissertation, University of Minnesota, 1980, Table A-1.

15. Staatsarchiv Osnabrück, Rep. 350 Iburg, Nr. 5030, p. 361; on p. 283 another official made a similar remark with his 1841 report: an emigrant who had left in 1838 had come back, but planned to return to American the next year.

16. Kuznets and Rubin, *Immigration and the Foreign Born*, 54, state that they included all migrants, temporary or permanent, in their calculations, but their statement appears to be slightly erroneous in that American arrival statistics after 1868 exclude temporary European travelers. See the discussion on American immigration statistics in Imre Ferenczi, ed., *International Migrations* (New York, 1929), 1:374-76. The proportion of transient visitors among incoming aliens was estimated at 2 percent in Ferenczi (648), and 1 ⅔ percent in Edward Young, *Special Report on Immigration* (Washington, 1872),

xii-xix. The latter source also includes a table (xxiii) presenting a comparative statement of immigration and emigration from July 1866 to December 1870, showing a proportion of net emigration 8.5 percent of net immigration.

17. Of course, not all returnees traveled steerage, and there were some visitors among steerage passengers as well. But eastbound steerage passengers outnumbered return migrants by 13.2 percent in 1908 and 1909, the first years information on both was available. Jerome, *Migration and Business Cycles,* 103.

18. For example, Theodore Saloutos, *They Remember America* (Berkeley, 1956), dealing with Greek repatriates.

19. Statistics herein were taken or calculated from *Württembergisches Jahrbuch* (1856), 2: 151-89; (1857), 2: 1-39, and for Bavaria from archival material in Hauptstaatsarchiv Stuttgart, Innenministerium, E 146, Bü. 1818. This archive is in Württemberg rather than Bavaria; no complete set of this material appears to have survived in Bavaria, although the Hauptstaatsarchiv in Munich does have the 1857 data under MInn 43339-43343. The material encompasses calendar years 1856 and 1857 and fiscal year 1857-58, presumably from the fourth quarter of the former through the third quarter of the latter. These tables are clearly labeled as return migration from North America. Although the time periods covered do not correspond exactly with those in the published Bavarian statistics, it appears that the latter slightly undernumerated immigrants from North America.

20. Comparisons herein are based on Tedebrand, "Remigration from America to Sweden," and Virtanen, "Finnish Overseas Return Migration."

21. Statistics give only the number of adults and of children traveling in families, but not the number of families nor a breakdown of adults by sex. In calculating family size and male naturalization rates, it was assumed that one-half of the family adults were male and one-half female, and that all families had two parents. Odd numbers of adults show that this was obviously not always the case, but probably the discrepancy was not great and would affect migrants in both directions equally.

22. For 1856 and 1857, confessional makeup of emigrants/return migrants was as follows: Protestant, 81.9/82.5 percent; Catholic, 16.6/15.5 percent; and Jewish, 1.1/1.9 percent. Total number of return migrants was 103.

23. Peter Marschalck, *Deutsche Überseewanderung im 19. Jahrhundert* (Stuttgart, 1971), 52-71, posits a category of "economic-speculative" emigration with the goal of return.

24. Wolfgang v. Hippel, *Auswanderung aus Südwestdeutschland: Studien zur Württembergischen Auswanderung und Auswanderungspolitik im 19. und 20. Jahrhundert* (Stuttgart, 1984), 142, assumes that clandestine emigrants were more likely to be young, male, and single, usually had fewer financial resources, and were disproportionally attracted to North America compared to officially registered emigrants.

25. Württemberg was among the states that expressly stated "inclusive

of travel costs"; Prussia even included a similar statement on the printed forms on which emigration permits were issued; for more detail, see Kamphoefner, *The Westfalians*, 46-47, note 9.

26. Moltmann, "German-American Return Migration," 392.

27. Walter Willcox, ed., *International Migrations* (New York, 1931), 2:90, as cited in Kuznets and Rubin, *Immigration and the Foreign Born*, 10.

PART FIVE

Ideologies and Migrants

14

Socialist Immigrants from Germany and the Transfer of Socialist Ideology and Workers' Culture

HARTMUT KEIL

Historians of German immigration have long been interested in the transfer of ideas that took place during the course of mass emigration from Germany to the United States during the nineteenth century. They have focused on European jacobinism and socialism, two radical traditions. European jacobinism or radical republicanism, was a product of the Enlightenment, of the French Revolution, and of subsequent efforts by social movements in various European countries to undo the post-Napoleonic repressive political order. Of the two uprisings in Germany resulting from such efforts, the failed revolution of 1848-49 caused the exodus of many of its participants to the United States. As is well known—because this group of emigrants has been studied in detail—intellectuals and artisans stimulated the flowering of German-American political and cultural institutions in the 1850s, becoming ardent opponents of slavery and fighting for its abolishment in the Civil War.[1]

Radical republicanism was replaced by socialism at the moment of its greatest triumph, however. Along with the resumed mass immigration after the war, German socialism was transferred to the United States at the same time that the German Social Democracy began to expand in unprecedented ways. Often having participated in the emerging movement at home, immigrant workers tried to transplant its ideas and institutions to their adopted country. Historians of immigration, labor, and American political institutions have claimed that socialist ideology was an alien, marginal, even un-American doctrine that remained isolated from the mainstream of the emerging American labor movement, whereas the former European republicanism was easily reconciled with American political traditions.[2]

Of course, historical developments were more complex and social

315

and political movements in reality were interrelated rather than so neatly isolated as this brief characterization of the two radical traditions seems to suggest. For example, the German-American labor movement appeared even before the Civil War, when the utopian communist Wilhelm Weitling and the Marxian socialist Joseph Weydemeyer, among others, published labor papers and organized workers in the East and Midwest. Likewise, radical republicanism did not disappear overnight at the end of the Civil War, but continued to exert an ideological and institutional influence well beyond the 1860s.

This chapter seeks to evaluate the scope of socialist immigration from Germany. I will point out the interrelatedness of the two political emigrations by analyzing underlying continuities in the transition from the first to the second. I will also describe the mechanisms of transfer of socialist ideology and culture, including the dialectical relationship between the numerical growth and ideological development of the German Social Democracy, continuing socialist immigration into the United States, and the emergence of a distinct German-American labor movement and workers' culture. I will also indicate how modifications in the American context set the stage for the gradual adaptation of German socialism as well as workers' culture to an increasingly multiethnic American working class.

The Scope of Socialist Immigration from Germany

Because of its very nature as ideological transfer, socialist immigration cannot be quantified with any degree of accuracy. A typology of migrations, including ideological and political factors caused by threat or expulsion, suggests group migration and permanent settlement only for religious groups, whereas political (individual or mass) emigration is seen as backward-oriented, that is, such emigrants are expected to return home.[3] Analysis of the emigration from Germany in 1848 has shown, however, that motivations for emigration were complex and that a high degree of speculation is involved in trying to separate socioeconomic motives from personal and political ones.[4]

In the case of socialist immigration, we therefore stand on solid ground only with respect to professed socialists known to have been active in the German labor movement before coming to the United States. These certainly numbered in the hundreds or even thousands, but what about the mass of immigrants who, of course, were not asked to register their political beliefs upon entering the country? In the absence of reliable statistics, wild guesses have been offered on various occasions. Thus, after the passage of the antisocialist law of 1878 in the German Reich, the American press carried the news that a mass exodus of socialists was imminent; there were even rumors that Bismarck's administration encouraged such emigration in order to rid the Reich of malcontents and revolutionaries.[5] American authorities and politicians were worried enough to seek new legislation to keep such persons off U.S. shores, and tried to get expert opinion to substantiate suspicions of high numbers of this group of political immigrants. Appearing before a congressional committee in 1888, Johann Most denied, however, that large numbers of radicals had emigrated from Germany.[6]

In the absence of reliable statistics we have to use other sources for an informed guess, for example, knowledge of the origins and the social composition of mass emigration as well as of the composition of the German-American labor force, fragmentary indicators of actual socialist immigration, and the character of German-American labor organizations.

German mass emigration in the nineteenth century was triggered by social upheavals caused by agrarian reforms and industrialization.[7] Their uneven and regionally deferred impact established the well-known pattern of gradual change of the areas of emigration. Until the middle of the century, the southwestern states predominated, whereas afterward the northeastern and eastern regions of Prussia took the lead. This development has been interpreted as evidence of the predominantly agrarian composition of the German emigration. Mass emigration originated from regions, then, which because of their economic structure were largely unaffected by the emerging Social Democracy, as an article in the *Neue Zeit,* the intellectual organ of the German socialists, maintained.[8]

However, substantial numbers of artisans emigrated in the earlier as well as the later period. Although "the data concerning social composition, especially with regard to the occupational status of the German emigrants, are even less complete than those concerning demographic structure,"[9] artisans accounted for somewhat fewer than 30 percent of emigrants from Baden between 1840 and 1855 and for about 40 percent of emigrants from Hesse between 1845 and 1847, while in general the proportion of emigrants from the southwest who had agricultural backgrounds declined after 1860.[10] Emigration statistics for the port of Hamburg from 1871 to 1894 also indicate the increasing importance of industrial workers and "workers" in general departing from there, although the latter category hides real occupational backgrounds that probably include a high proportion of agricultural laborers.[11]

On the other hand, regions such as west and central Germany, with mixed economies that included trades, handicrafts and industries, also supplied a "relatively high number of emigrants."[12] Thus emigrants from Saxony, one of the early industrial regions in Germany and a stronghold of the socialist party, tended to come from declining trades and handicrafts. The desolate state of the home and textile industries caused thousands of weavers to emigrate.[13] American consuls in other areas of Germany also continually pointed out the relationship between depressed industrial conditions and the emigration of workers.[14] The exact extent of the relationship cannot be gauged from such incomplete documentation, although it is noteworthy that emigration from agrarian regions tended to decline compared to that from urban-industrial areas during the second half of the nineteenth century. Taken with the fact that more than 70 percent (about 3.5 million) of German immigration in the nineteenth century occurred from the end of the Civil War until 1900, we have to assume a continuously rising number of artisans and skilled and industrial workers among this group.

The urban concentration and the occupational distribution of the German-American work force corroborate such a conclusion. Even at mid-century the proportion of Germans who settled in large cities was more than three times that of the total American population[15] (Table 14.1). This percentage kept increasing with each decennial census.[16] Whereas the total population in the larger urban areas seems to have remained relatively constant from 1870 to 1890, the German population in those areas increased by 8.4 points. This growth coincides with contemporary mass immigration from Germany, other than during the depression years from 1873 to 1877.

The occupational pattern confirms the importance of industrial employment among German immigrants (Table 14.2). The rough division into sectors of the economy that the census introduced in 1870 is the only available basis of comparison for the United States as a whole. Of the two most important sectors, industry (fluctuating around 35 percent) clearly had the lead over agriculture, although this lead decreased from 1870 to 1890. The proportion of the work force in agriculture increased significantly in the 1870s while that in industry declined slightly. Because of certain inconsistencies in the census categories, however, the figures for industry underrepresent the actual work force employed there. Thus a significant proportion of unskilled laborers included under "services" was employed in industry as well as in trade and commerce.

Artisans and skilled workers, however, were the most important

Table 14.1. Urbanization 1850-1900: German Immigrants Compared
to Total U.S. Population*

Population Group	1850	1860	1870	1880	1890	1900
Total U.S. population	23.2	31.4	39.8	50.2	62.9	76.0
Total urban population in cities of more than 5,000	3.2	5.6	8.8	12.5	19.8	27.3
Total German immigrant population	0.6	1.3	1.7	2.0	2.8	2.7
Total population in the largest cities (%)	10.4	9.7	18.8	15.5	18.4	25.9
Total German immigrant population in the largest cities (%)	36.4	38.3	39.3	39.3	47.7	50.2
Number of cities included†	38	43	50	50	124	160
Population	>15,200	>20,000‡	>26,000	>35,000	>25,000	>25,000

Sources: 1850: J. D. B. DeBow, *Statistical View of the United States . . . being a Compendium of the Seventh Census* (Washington, 1854), 123; 1860: U.S. Census Office, *Statistics of the United States in 1860* (Washington, 1866), lvii f.; 1870: *Ninth Census, Population and Social Statistics* (Washington, 1872), 386-89; 1880: *Tenth Census, Population* (Washington, 1883), 538; 1890: *Eleventh Census, Population*, pt. 1 (Washington, 1895), 670-77; 1900: *Twelfth Census, Population*, pt. 1 (Washington, 1901), clxxvi; U.S. Department of Commerce, Bureau of the Census, *Historical Statistics of the United States: Colonial Times to 1957* (Washington, 1960), 8, 14.
* Population numbers in millions.
† The criterion for cities included when referring to the German population is obscure. Twelve cities with a population under 15,200 were included, whereas twelve cities with higher population figures were excluded, among them Brooklyn, Buffalo, Rochester, Utica, Pittsburgh, and San Francisco. Several of those cities had a high proportion of German immigrants.
‡ Including two cities with a population below 20,000.

group in the industrial work force in this connection because they formed the backbone of trade unions as well as the emerging Socialist party in Germany. In fact, they also contributed large numbers of immigrants to the United States, as is apparent from the numerical profile of the thirteen most important occupations of German immigrant workers other than laborers (Table 14.3). In each of the three census years (1870, 1880, and 1890), these trades consistently comprised about 60 percent of the German-American industrial work force. Traditional crafts in building, food processing, furniture, and the metal industry predominated, but differences in patterns of de-

320   HARTMUT KEIL

Table 14.2. Occupational Structure of German Immigrants, 1870-90

Sector of		1880			1890		
Economy	1870	Men	Women	Total	Men	Women	Total
Agriculture	26.8	30.5	3.2	28.4	29.9	7.8	27.5
Agricultural laborers	6.8			4.7	5.9	0.7	5.3
Professions	2.1	1.8	3.0	1.9	2.1	2.2	2.1
Service	20.8	15.9	59.6	19.3	17.7	60.9	22.4
Unskilled laborers	11.5	11.9	0.8	11.1	11.5	0.8	10.4
Trade and transportation	13.4	15.5	6.2	14.8	14.9	5.7	13.9
Industry	36.9	36.3	28.1	35.6	35.4	23.4	34.1
Total %	100.0	100.0	100.0	100.0	100.0	100.0	100.0

Sources: *Compendium of the Ninth Census 1870* (Washington, 1872), 604-15; *Tenth Census 1880, Population*, pt. 1 (Washington, 1883), 752-59; *Eleventh Census 1890, Population*, pt. 2 (Washington, 1895), cxlvi.

velopment occurred between 1870 and 1890. Whereas baking, butchering, and brewing expanded enormously in absolute terms, and the building trades in particular profited from the mass immigration of the 1880s, other crafts such as shoemaking and furniture-making declined, although cabinetmaking remained one of the most heavily German trades in 1890. A decline also occurred in other woodworking crafts such as in coopering and wagon-making. In contrast, the increase of German workers in the metal industry was enormous. The occupation of machinist ranked seventeenth for German workers in 1870; two decades later it had advanced to ninth place. Crafts threatened by industrialization apparently still held their own because of the constant replenishment of their ranks by new immigrants who tried to escape from the pressure of social dislocation and occupational degradation in the German Reich.

We may conclude from such circumstantial evidence that a considerable number of immigrants adhered to socialist convictions and remained socialist supporters or at least sympathizers after settling in the United States. Such support dating back to the time before emigration became a matter of public record on certain rare occasions. A letter written in 1885 from Lawrence, Massachusetts, mentions heavy migration from the seventeenth election district in Saxony, and a correspondent from Albany points out that recent immigrant workers

Table 14.3. Most Frequent Occupations of German Immigrant Workers, 1870, 1880, 1890 (According to Ranking of Occupations in 1890)

Occupation	1870 Number	Rank	Percent	1880 Number	Rank	Percent	1890 Number	Rank	Percent
Carpenter	29,704	2	9.6	30,388	2	8.8	50,501	1	10.7
Tailor	33,200	1	10.8	31,506	1	9.1	36,351	2	7.7
Shoemaker	28,226	3	9.2	27,512	3	7.9	27,978	3	5.9
Butcher	13,227	5	4.3	18,166	4	5.2	24,402	4	5.1
Baker	10,863	8	3.5	15,031	6	4.3	23,529	5	5.0
Blacksmith	14,012	4	4.5	15,129	5	4.4	19,745	6	4.2
Mason	11,606	7	3.8	11,857	8	3.4	19,043	7	4.0
Painter	6,736	15	2.2	10,251	10	3.0	18,862	8	4.0
Machinist	5,016	17	1.6	8,206	15	2.4	16,441	9	3.5
Cigarmaker*	9,292	9	3.0	11,529	9	3.3	14,316	10	3.0
Ironworker†	8,164	12	2.6	9,303	13	2.7	13,547	11	2.9
Brewer‡	6,780	13	2.2	9,910	12	2.9	13,174	12	2.8
Cabinetmaker	11,798	6	3.8	13,275	7	3.8	12,240	13	2.6
Total German Immigrant Workers (%)			61.1			61.2			61.4

Sources: *Compendium of the Ninth Census 1870* (Washington, 1872), 608-15; *Tenth Census 1880: Population*, pt. 2 (Washington, 1897), 486-89.

* 1870 and 1880: cigarmakers; 1890: tobacco workers and cigarmakers.

† Iron and steel workers; four different occupations listed in 1870.

‡ Brewers and maltsters.

Ranking of other occupations not listed: 1870: coopers, 10; miners, 11; tile workers, 14; wagon-makers, 16; 1880: miners, 11; coopers, 14.

from Saxony voiced radical ideas.[17] Wilhelm Liebknecht, on his tour through the industrial districts of New England in 1886, encountered many weavers from Saxony. In 1899 Julius Vahlteich, on a speaking tour in New England, also met workers from Saxony, who knew him from his work as editor of the *Freie Presse* in Chemnitz, Saxony's largest industrial city.[18] A large share of skilled workers from such trades as cigarmaking, brewing, baking, printing, and furniture making also left urban-industrial strongholds of the Social Democracy in Germany for the United States. Thus tobacco workers from the Hamburg area, many of whom were members of the General German Workers' Association and later of the German Socialist Labor party, decided to emigrate because of the depressed condition of their trade, despite repeated warnings by the respective unions in the United States about scarce employment opportunities.[19] Evidence of socialist sympathies was especially strong when occasion arose to support the labor movement back in Germany. Then many more workers than the relatively small group of party members answered the calls to provide financial support for election drives, strikes, and victims of natural disasters.[20]

It was on the organizational level, though, that evidence of socialist activists who had immigrated from Germany is most conclusive. The membership of both the International Workingmen's Association and the Socialist Labor party (SLP) was overwhelmingly made up of German immigrants, as the often-voiced complaints about the foreignness of these labor organizations make abundantly clear. Thus more than eight-tenths of SLP members in New York City between 1878 and 1881 had German names.[21] Not only were labor unions often founded by socialists, but there were also heavy concentrations of socialists in those very unions whose trades were dominated by, or had a large membership of, German workers, for example, the International Furniture Workers Union, the Bakers and Confectioners' Union, the Metal Workers Union, and the Cigarmakers Union.[22] What is more, the conflicts that arose in several unions in the late 1870s concerning ideological orientations were caused by recent immigrants from Germany who tried to uphold socialist principles rigorously. Thus the Progressive Cigarmakers Union was dominated by recent immigrant cigarmakers from the Hamburg area.[23]

The problem of continued socialist emigration from Germany therefore was important enough for the Social Democratic party to discuss thoroughly and take a clear position about. It became especially urgent after passage of the antisocialist law in 1878, when a wave of despair threatened to drive party and union members out of Germany in large numbers.[24] Socialists on both sides of the Atlantic tried to prevent such an exodus, keeping to the established principle that "social grievances cannot be eliminated by mass emigration" which only served as a "safety valve against the revolution" in Germany.[25] The labor press published thorough and realistic information on work and living conditions in the United States, warning against exaggerated expectations.[26] German-American socialists were asked to use their private correspondence to plead for restraint of emigration.[27] Although the party press and the party's leaders kept pointing out the risks of emigration, insisting that members should make such a decision only after the most careful deliberations, these warnings apparently were not heeded sufficiently.[28] Farewell notices of socialists leaving Germany for America continued to be published in the *Sozialdemokrat,* the party organ printed in Zurich, the major European center of communication in the 1880s. They were the proverbial tip of the iceberg, for most socialists who left did so without public announcement.[29] A serious confrontation occurred in 1881, when two prominent party leaders decided to emigrate. One of them, F. W. Fritzsche, had toured the United States only a few months earlier in the party's interest. The other was Julius Vahlteich, Ferdinand Lassalle's former secretary and a socialist deputy in the German Parliament. Their emigration came as a surprise to the party, and the *Sozialdemokrat* did not hesitate to condemn their move as a "cowardly act" by leaders who in difficult times had a special responsibility.[30] In an effort to discourage members from leaving Germany, Wilhelm Liebknecht coined the famous dictum, "Our America is in Germany!"[31]

Official party policy differed from the actual behavior of individuals, who often had no other choice but to emigrate. Petty harassment by police and legal authorities, outright discrimination in the work place, and bleak prospects of economic betterment were the breeding grounds for such a decision. Even in cases of forced political exile, a complex range of motivations, including the threat of economic ruin, is evident in those who emigrated, as in the post-1848 emigration. Although the practice of discriminating against labor organizations and socialist workers predated the time when the antisocialist law was in effect in the German Reich (1878-90), the period witnessed the clearest instances that can be documented of politically motivated emigration of socialists. The government on several occasions used a clause in the infamous law authorizing the expulsion of party and union members when a "state of siege," that is, a state of emergency, had been declared over a large urban area. Of the hundreds of socialists from Berlin, Hamburg, and Leipzig who were forced to leave their homes and work, at least one-fourth emigrated to the United States, either in groups or individually.[32]

A case study of this group of exiled socialists yields significant clues on the importance of individual immigrants in the transfer of ideology.[33] First, their occupations mirror the socioeconomic base from which the Social Democracy drew its membership (Table 14.4). More than 70 percent of all exiled and emigrated socialists belonged to the working class, and a negligible portion of these were unskilled laborers. Cigarmakers contributed 20 percent; other representative skilled trades were cabinetmakers, masons, shoemakers, and weavers, printers, tailors, basket makers, and machinists. In addition, a large proportion of the self-employed were master artisans and saloon keepers. Half of the saloon keepers had once been skilled workers; they assumed important functions in the party's communicative network, as had others whose trades had been intimately connected with the production and distribution of the socialist press including typesetters, printers, editors, shipping clerks, and press dealers. Twenty persons in occupations unrelated to the printing trade had even worked as distributors of the party press as a sideline.

By exiling these socialists, the German government intended of course to destroy the labor movement's infrastructure, at least on the local level. Therefore it banned persons who had carried out more or less important party functions. As a consequence, these exiled socialists were an experienced group whose loss was dearly felt (Table 14.5). Although information is fragmentary (none was available for more than one-fifth of these persons), it shows that more than two-thirds of them served the party actively in local elections and support committees, in official party and union functions, as organizers, and as press agents. Others had been delegates to regional or national labor conventions and candidates or deputies for regional or national parliaments.

Was this transplanted potential of experienced persons actually introduced into the German-American labor movement? It seems as if many socialists who had been active in Germany and who upon their arrival were taken care of by the SLP and other labor organizations soon became alienated.[34] (Table 14.5). They joined the large group of "drop-outs," those "many thousands of the oldest, more experienced, and theoretically clear comrades holding themselves aloof" whose inactivity was again and again deplored in the German-American labor press.[35] On the other hand, almost half of those exiled socialists became active in the labor movement, although the functions took on a different importance. Since the SLP was hardly ever rep-

Table 14.4. All Exiled Socialists Compared to Those Who Emigrated to the U.S. (According to Occupational Groups)

Occupational Group	Exiled Socialists in U.S. (Absolute Numbers)	Percent	All Exiled Socialists* (Absolute Numbers)	Percent
All Workers:	135	70.7	608	76.3
Food and provisions	40	20.9	126	15.8
Woodworking	15	7.8	103	12.9
Construction workers	15	7.8	85	10.7
Metal workers	12	6.3	68	8.5
Printing and publishing	13	6.8	61	7.7
Leather workers	13	6.8	61	7.7
Textile workers	17	8.9	51	6.4
Other skilled workers	7	3.7	25	3.1
Unskilled workers	3	1.6	28	3.5
Salaried Employees	3	1.6	14	1.8
All Self-Employed:	47	24.6	142	17.8
Merchants and dealers	21	11.0	69	8.7
Master artisans and other self-employed	26	13.6	73	9.2
Professions	6	3.1	33	4.1
Total	191	100.0	797	100.0

Sources: Ignaz Auer, *Nach Zehn Jahren. Materialien und Glossen zur Geschichte des Sozialistengesetzes*, vol. 2 (London, 1889); *New Yorker Volks-Zeitung*, 1878-90; *Chicagoer Arbeiter-Zeitung* and *Vorbote*, 1878-90; *Sozialist*, 1885-90; Heinzpeter Thümmler, *Sozialistengesetz §28. Ausweisungen und Ausgewiesene 1878-1890* (Berlin, 1979); Georg Eckert, *100 Jahre Braunschweiger Sozialdemokratie. I. Teil: Von den Anfängen bis zum Jahre 1890* (Bad Godesberg, 1965); Ernst Heilmann, *Geschichte der Arbeiterbewegung in Chemnitz und im Erzgebirge* (Chemnitz, 1912); Emil Kloth, *Geschichte des Deutschen Buchbinderverbandes und seiner Vorläufer*, 2 vols. (Berlin, 1910, 1913); Theodor Müller, *Geschichte der Breslauer Sozialdemokratie* (Berlin, 1925); Recording Secretary's Book, SAP Section "New York," Tamiment Institute, Bobst Library, New York University.
* From: Thümmler, Table 17: Die Strucktur der Ausgewiesenen nach Berufsgruppen und Ausweisungsgebieten, p. 156.

resented in a state assembly, no one held such a position. Only one person actually ran for such an office, and few were delegates to party and union conventions, perhaps because of the language barrier. Therefore, the grass-roots level became more important in the United

Table 14.5. Functions of Emigrated Exiles in German Labor Movement
and in German-American Labor Movement*

Function	German Labor Movement		German-American Labor Movement	
	Number	Percent	Number	Percent
Local Level:	99	51.8	75	39.3
Official (general)	24	12.6	33	17.3
Election, assistance committee	13	6.8	16	8.4
Agitation	19	9.9	13	6.8
Press distribution	33	17.3	7	3.7
Press publication	7	5.2	6	3.1
Delegate, member of regional, state, and national conventions	23	12.0	13	6.8
Deputy in state or national, parliament resp. candidate for state and congressional elections	8	4.2	1	0.5
Spy	3	1.6	2	1.0
Party member	17	8.9	6	3.1
No information	41	21.5	94	49.3
Total	191	100.0	191	100.0

Source: See Table 14.4
* If an individual held several positions, only the highest-ranking function was taken
into account; thus local-level functions of a member of parliament were not included.

States than in Germany. The socialists had to prove themselves in
routine duties such as heading party sections and educational and
agitational work, whereas press and publishing were of lesser dimension and confined to few persons in the United States.

Contrary to the common behavioral pattern of political exiles, the
majority of these socialists chose to stay in the United States. Only
ten of the group of 191 listed in Table 14.4 appear to have gone
back to Germany, although initially more may have had intended to
return. Their reluctance to leave New York City for other regions
and small industrial towns where party sections badly lacked experienced leadership may have been indicative of their ambivalence.
Most either came with their families or had them brought over afterward with funds raised by auxiliary committees of the SLP.[36] Their

determination to settle permanently is best documented by the fact that most applied for citizenship soon after arrival.[37]

There is conclusive evidence then that mass immigration from Germany provided a strong contingent of skilled industrial workers who sympathized with the German Social Democracy and formed a sizeable potential of supporters for the emergent labor movements in American industrial cities. The experienced leadership of socialist exiles, however, was indispensable in founding a variety of labor organizations, thereby supplying the necessary institutional base for a German-American labor movement.

The Transfer of Institutions and Culture

The institutional and cultural transfer of socialism was connected intimately with German mass immigration. That coincidence had important repercussions on the mechanisms of transfer, that is, on its direction and reception, on its duration, and even on its content.

First, an intricate communications network developed between socialist movements in Germany and those in the United States.[38] The network was not balanced evenly because from its beginning the German Social Democracy, as progenitor of the German-American socialist movement and as the theoretically most advanced and electorally most successful socialist party, assumed the role of a shining example to be emulated. It was therefore essential to remain informed of the development of theory, tactics, and organization in the parent party and to receive guidelines for action. However, the communications network also served other more practical and individual needs.

Basically, three channels of communication were used: private correspondence between leading socialists in which official matters and background developments were discussed; personal exchanges through visits of socialist leaders and other individuals; and the labor press (party, trade union, and local daily and weekly papers). The latter clearly was the most important of the three because it was widely circulated and covered a broad spectrum of needs, serving both the rank-and-file and the leadership as well as outsiders who wished to be informed of the goings-on in the labor movement.

The extent to which labor papers were read and information exchanged among them on both sides of the Atlantic is remarkable. As early as 1874 the Chicago *Vorbote* advertised seventeen German-language labor papers published in Germany and other European countries.[39] The German-American labor press quoted the German *De-*

mokratisches Wochenblatt and its successors *Volksstaat* and *Vorwärts* as well
as local socialist papers as the main sources for European labor events.
Several papers, for example, the *Arbeiter-Union* and the *New Yorker
Volks-Zeitung,* also hired such prominent socialist leaders as Wilhelm
Liebknecht or Julius Vahlteich as regular correspondents for Germany.[40] Official announcements, proceedings of party and union conventions, and important new theoretical and political publications
were often reported verbatim or serialized. After 1878, when the
publication of socialist papers was forbidden in the German Reich,
the flow was reversed in favor of the more numerous German-American labor publications. The editors of the *Sozialdemokrat* received all
German-language labor papers from the United States and exploited
them thoroughly for pertinent information.

Both in Europe and America, the German-language labor press
also served individuals who had more practical concerns, as documented by short notices, appeals, and advertisements in the *Sozialdemokrat* specifically addressed to, or inserted by, persons wanting to
emigrate. Comrades publicly announced their intention, were in turn
bidden farewell by those staying behind, and recommended to socialists in the New World.[41] Countless receipts of money sent by individuals and organizations from prominent and obscure places in the
United States and information on the condition of work in specific
trades and cities are testimony to the extent of this international
network of communication, practical help, and solidarity.[42]

The practice of mutually exchanging and using information from
all available sources was founded not only upon an underlying ideological agreement but also on common experiences and personal
contacts and friendships in Germany. With few exceptions, German-
American labor papers were edited by journalists who had learned
their job in Germany; some were recruited while still there because
of a shortage of qualified people in the United States. In the late
1870s and early 1880s, the increased emigration of journalists who
had lost their jobs when labor papers had been banned in Germany
created an oversupply in the United States.[43] Voluntary and forced
transatlantic job mobility among journalists thus tended to reinforce
the continuity of perspective of the German-American labor papers
and the flow of information between them and their sister publications
in Europe.

For the process of institution-building, the German-American labor
movement leaned heavily on the German example, imitating both
organizational structures and functions. In order to become accepted,
new associations could not operate in a vacuum of pure socialist theory,

however, but had to be responsive to the needs of immigrant workers. Ideological transfer was therefore tied closely into the actual practice of establishing and maintaining working-class institutions. Their functional context was immigrant neighborhoods, that is, in addition to the usual lower-class social setting also known in Germany, workers were part of an alien ethnic culture. Ethnic-cultural overtones tended to have considerably more weight within the German-American working class than within the German working class, especially in conflicts with other immigrant groups and with the dominant culture. When socialist institutions had to contend with class and cultural issues at the same time, socialist principles sometimes were neglected for concerns that touched upon everyday life. Thus the associational life flourishing in these immigrant working-class neighborhoods should not be approached simply from an ideological perspective, but must also be understood for its social functions.

This associational network of German immigrant neighborhoods cannot be analyzed thoroughly in this chater.[44] Instead, two examples of institutions that reached beyond individual neighborhoods — the Socialist party and press — will be discussed to demonstrate how organizational structures were transferred from Germany. Immigrant socialists admired the German Social Democracy, above all for its quick electoral growth since the mid-1870s, which was taken as proof that its theoretical position was also the most advanced of its time. They were proud that it was in Germany, "the center of Europe," the "recognized cradle of modern science," where the "communistic science was put to the severe test of proving its inner validity" and that it had "obviously passed it." The international socialist movement had thereby "found an intellectual center" in Germany.[45]

Given this perspective, the unification of Lassalleans and Marxists at the Gotha congress in 1875 was also seen as a model to be followed quickly. The various German socialist groups had secured a foothold in the United States. Now the attempts at unification were closely watched by German-American socialists who welcomed them as an incentive to similar efforts of their own. In April 1875 the Chicago *Vorbote* published an article demanding the unification of the three existing factions — the International Workingmen's Association, the Labor Party of Illinois, and the Social Democratic Workingmen's Party of North America — by pointing to the expected unification of the two wings of the German labor movement and by explicitly suggesting that the example be copied.[46] When unity was accomplished seven weeks later at the Gotha congress, the *Vorbote*'s editor pleaded for a similar move in an editorial. He sought to underscore the necessity for such a step by quoting from a private letter from Wilhelm Lieb-knecht: "Now it is to be hoped that in America, too, unification will be accomplished, putting an end to the itching for special alliances. You only need the good will of those who are sincere in their con-victions. In Germany the obstacles were certainly larger than over there. And yet we succeeded. Where there is a will there is a way."[47] In an appeal issued by a "Unification Committee of the Two Socialist Factions in Chicago" on July 11 the German example was referred to again.[48] The Workingmen's Party of the United States emerged one year later at Philadelphia as a result of these efforts.

The party's organizational structure as well as its goals and tactics reflected its orientation toward the German party. For several years political actionists gained the upper hand, advocating participation in elections as the right path to recognition and growth. They clearly tried to emulate the German strategy, ignoring warnings by experi-enced Internationalists against premature political action and instead insisting that institutions, liberties, and rights granted in the American political system had to be used. The party also adopted the principle of centralization, placing the ultimate power in the national conven-tion and creating a strong national executive controlled by a board of appeals. Its goals consisted of principles and demands almost iden-tical with those of the German party.[49]

The German-American labor press also built on the experience of German parent institutions. Although the first German-language labor papers in the United States date from the 1840s and 1850s, greater demand arose after the Civil War, along with the rapid increase of the German industrial labor force.[50] As in the German Reich, a period of hectic organizational activity beginning in the late 1860s resulted in the establishment of new papers. When Section 1 of the Interna-tional Workingmen's Association founded the *Arbeiterzeitung* in 1873, it adopted a cooperative organizational structure, including a gov-erning and a control board elected by the members.[51] Other labor papers followed suit; continuity on the personnel level facilitated the institutional transfer. When the Social Democratic Workingmen's Party of North America decided in 1874 to publish a paper, the *Social-Demokrat,* it also established the Social Democratic Cooperative Print-ing Association, which party members could join by acquiring a share worth $5.[52] In this case the similarity to the structure of the publishing house of the General German Workingmen's Association is obvious; even the name of its paper was copied. It was especially the Eisenach (Marxist) wing of the labor movement in Germany, however, which used the cooperative for its press. The statutes of the *Volksstaat,* the paper of the Social Democratic Labor party since 1869, were basically adopted by the Chicago *Vorbote* association five years later. Founded on a cooperative basis and owned and controlled by the members, it was administered by a press committee of six, three trustees, and a managing director.[53] Typically, the discussions on the structure of the party press at the unity congresses at Gotha in 1875 and at Philadelphia in 1876 were almost identical.[54]

The preceding examples of institutional transfer could be multiplied. Thus a variety of other secondary associations as well as specific forms, contents, and enactments of German working-class culture were also initially transferred from Germany: for example, lodges, insurance and benefit societies, educational clubs and schools, singing and theater societies, typical forms of celebration and leisure, and a viable radical literary tradition used in a communal context for cultivating common ideological identification and class solidarity.[55] However, even after the initial transfer, the continued vitality of working-class institutions and culture depended largely on uninterrupted migration of skilled workers and socialists from Germany and on the intimate interrelationship with the German Social Democracy. Organizational, ideological, and cultural traditions were thus maintained by an intricate network of migration, personal communication, and institutional imitation.

Adaptation to American Society

For all their ties with the country of origin, German-American socialists did not remain isolated from other groups in the American labor movement or from American life in general. Several factors contributed to the gradual adaptation of these immigrant socialists and their institutions to American society. Of course, German socialism was not transplanted into a vacuum, but continued to be nourished by the demographic, technological, and social upheaval engendered by American industrialization that was structurally similar to the changes occurring in Germany or, for that matter, in any industrializing country. It was therefore not simply the experience in their country of origin before immigration that brought forth workers with socialist beliefs; conditions in American industrial centers were also increasingly conducive to such political convictions. As the nineteenth century progressed, the American labor movement, including its radical wing, integrated more workers with diverse backgrounds. These workers had either grown up in agrarian economies abroad and first came into contact with industrial society after emigrating or had been born in America and received their industrial training and experience in American industry. The latter group of workers included, for instance, children of German immigrants, who lacked first-hand knowledge of the traditional socialist culture brought over by their parents. They knew its modifications only in the American context.

Mass immigration from Germany came to an end with the onset of the depression in 1893. When German immigration rose again after the turn of the century, its composition had changed considerably, consisting of white-collar employees and single industrial workers often seeking employment for a limited period before returning home. Since the German labor movement was now firmly embedded in German society as a powerful alternative institution of the working class, socialists indeed tended to hold out on this "battleground" instead of emigrating to the United States in large numbers.[56] The German-American labor movement lacked the steady replenishment of its ranks that had been so important for the maintenance of close cultural and ideological ties.

As a result of these diverse influences and developments, German-American socialism gradually changed its demographic base. The German ethnic and cultural impact, so dominant for a whole generation, gradually began to weaken as the close connection between ideology and cultural traditions began to dissolve. The internationalist stance of socialism favored this process because socialist ideology had always argued for transcending national barriers and for class solidarity. German-American socialists also greeted this development because they had long labored for the "Americanization" of the movement. In order for this to happen the predominance of German immigrants had to be diminished and their ethnic and cultural isolation overcome. To many German-American socialists, the founding of the Socialist party in 1901 accomplished this long-aspired goal; the venerated Julius Vahlteich reported as one of the most significant aspects of the Socialist Unity Congress at Indianapolis the fact that young Americans had dominated the discussions and proven their substantial organizational skills.[57] This new American membership base of the Socialist party was worth pointing out to European fellow socialists in order to assure them that the American party was no longer just a party of immigrants.[58]

NOTES

1. See Carl Wittke, *Refugees of Revolution: The German Forty-Eighters in America* (Philadelphia, 1952); Wittke, "The German Forty-Eighters in Amer-

ica: A Centennial Appraisal," *American Historical Review* 53 (1948): 711-25; A. E. Zucker, ed., *The Forty-Eighters: Political Refugees of the German Revolution of 1848* (New York, 1950); Bruce C. Levine, "Free Soil, Free Labor, and *Freimänner:* German Chicago in the Civil War Era," in *German Workers in Industrial Chicago, 1850-1910: A Comparative Perspective,* ed. Hartmut Keil and John B. Jentz (DeKalb, 1983), 162-82; Bruce C. Levine, "In the Heat of Two Revolutions: The Forging of German-American Radicalism," in *"Struggle a Hard Battle": Essays on Working-Class Immigrants,* ed. Dirk Hoerder (DeKalb, 1986), 19-45; Ernest Bruncken, *German Political Refugees in the United States During the Period from 1815-1860* (San Francisco, 1960); Eitel Wolf Dobert, *Deutsche Demokraten in Amerika: Die '48er und ihre Schriften* (Göttingen, 1958); Wilhelm Hense-Jensen and Ernest Bruncken, *Wisconsin's Deutsch-Amerikaner, bis zum Schluss des Neunzehnten Jahrhunderts,* 2 vols. (Milwaukee, 1900-1902); and Hanni M. Holzman, "The German Forty-Eighters and the Socialists in Milwaukee: A Social Psychological Study of Assimilation," M.A. thesis, University of Wisconsin, 1948.

2. For examples of respective interpretations see Daniel Bell, *Marxian Socialism in the United States* (Princeton, 1967); William M. Dick, *Labor and Socialism in America: The Gompers Era* (Port Washington, 1972); Gerald N. Grob, *Workers and Utopia: A Study of Ideological Conflict in the American Labor Movement, 1865-1900* (Evanston, 1961); Stuart B. Kaufman, *Samuel Gompers and the Origins of the American Federation of Labor, 1884-1896* (Westport, 1973); Aileen S. Kraditor, *The Radical Persuasion, 1890-1917* (Baton Rouge, 1981); John H. M. Laslett and Seymour M. Lipset, eds., *Failure of a Dream? Essays in the History of American Socialism* (Garden City, 1974); Selig Perlman, *A Theory of the Labor Movement* (New York, 1928); Howard Quint, *The Forging of American Socialism: Origins of the Modern Movement* (Indianapolis, 1964); August Sartorius von Waltershausen, *Der moderne Sozialismus in den Vereinigten Staaten von Amerika* (Berlin, 1890); John R. Commons et al., *History of the Labour Movement in the United States,* vol. 2 (New York, 1918); Gerald Rosenblum, *Immigrant Workers: Their Impact on American Labor Radicalism* (New York, 1973); and David Saposs, *Left Wing Unionism: A Study of Radical Policies and Tactics* (New York, 1926).

3. Wolfgang Köllman and Peter Marschalck, "German Emigration to the United States," *Perspectives in American History* 7 (1973): 502f.

4. Mack Walker, *Germany and the Emigration 1816-1885* (Cambridge, 1964), 153ff.; cf. also Peter Marschalck, *Deutsche Überseewanderung im 19. Jahrundert. Ein Beitrag zur soziologischen Theorie der Bevölkerung* (Stuttgart, 1973).

5. "German Socialism in America," *North American Review* 128 (April and May 1879): 372-77, 481-92; cf. also the reaction to that article in the *New Yorker Volks-Zeitung,* March 20, 23, 1879 (cited hereafter as *NYVZ*).

6. "Testimony of Johann Most," *Testimony Taken by the Select Committee of the House of Representatives to Inquire into the Alleged Violation of the Laws Prohibiting the Importation of Contract Laborers, Paupers, Convicts, and other Classes,* U.S. Congress, House of Representatives, 50th Cong., 1st sess., misc. doc. no. 572 (Washington, 1888), 246-53.

7. For overviews see Köllmann and Marschalck, "German Emigration"; Walker, *Germany and the Emigration*; Marschalck, *Deutsche Überseewanderung*; and Klaus J. Bade, "German Emigration to the United States and Continental Immigration to Germany in the Late Nineteenth and Early Twentieth Centuries," *Central European History* 13 (December 1980): 348-77.

8. "Die deutsche Auswanderung," *Neue Zeit* 3 (1885): 253-57; cf. also the commentary to this article in *NYVZ*, June 20, 1885.

9. Köllmann and Marschalck, "German Emigration," 530. Not until 1899 did the official statistics of the German Reich begin to include such information. Only fragmentary evidence exists on the German states for the years before 1871. Since the mid-1850s occupations were recorded for those emigrating via Hamburg, and from 1890 for those departing from Bremen. American immigration statistics included information on occupation by nationality beginning in the 1870s, but its categories were of little value for German occupational characteristics; cf. Marschalck, *Deutsche Überseewanderung*, 77, and Mönckmeier, *Die deutsche überseeische Auswanderung*, 151.

10. Köllmann and Marschalck, "German Emigration," 530f.

11. Mönckmeier, *Die deutsche überseeische Auswanderung*, 164.

12. Köllmann and Marschalck, "German Emigration," 535.

13. *NYVZ*, December 4, 1881; for emigration from Saxony see Hildegard Rosenthal, *Die Auswanderung aus Sachsen im 19. Jahrhundert (1815-1871)* Stuttgart, 1931).

14. See, for example, U.S. Congress, House, *Consular Reports on the State of Labor in Europe*, 46th Cong., 1st sess., House Executive Documents 5 (Washington, 1878); and U.S. Congress, House, *Reports of Diplomatic and Consular Officers Concerning Emigration from Europe to the United States . . .*, 50th Cong., 1st sess., misc. doc. no. 572, pt. 2 (Washington, 1889).

15. The definition of "large cities" is not consistent here because the Census, which provided the only available figures, changed the base number for the population.

16. The numbers given by the Census of 1880 suggest that the percentage remained steady in the 1870s and that the total urban population declined by more than three percentage points. However, this seeming stagnation was the result of a change of the population base for large cities from twenty-six thousand inhabitants at the Census of 1870 to thirty-five thousand inhabitants ten years later. In 1890, the base was returned to nearly the previous figure.

17. *NYVZ*, September 13, 1885; another correspondent from Buffalo also reported "the arrival of German immigrant socialists," *NYVZ*, June 20, 1885.

18. Wilhelm Liebknecht, *Ein Blick in die Neue Welt* (Stuttgart, 1887), 103f.; Julius Vahlteich to Motteler, November 25, 1899, in Motteler Papers, 121/6, International Institute of Social History, Amsterdam. For other evidence on socialist immigrants in different occupations see Georg Eckert, *100 Jahre Braunschweiger Sozialdemokratie. I. Teil: Von den Anfängen bis zum Jahre 1890* (Bad Godesberg, 1965); *NYVZ*, September 28, 1881, December 4, 1881,

September 13, 1885; *Sozialdemokrat,* November 2, 1882; *Chicagoer Arbeiter-Zeitung,* January 24, 1888. The Congress of the German Social Democrats at Copenhagen in 1883 also dealt with the issue, see *Sozialdemokrat,* April 12, 1883.

19. Cf. Walter Frisch, *Die Organisationsbestrebungen in der deutschen Tabakindustrie* (Leipzig, 1903); Dorothee Schneider-Liebersohn, "Gewerkschaft und Gemeinschaft. Drei deutsche Gewerkschaften in New York 1875-1900," dissertation, Munich 1983, 69ff.; Heinrich Laufenberg, *Geschichte der Arbeiterbewegung in Hamburg, Altona und Umgebung* (Hamburg, 1931), 2:214; *Sozialdemokrat,* December 12, 1880. See also the remark made in the Detroit *Der arme Teufel* on the occasion of the Labor Day Parade: "Who carried the red flag? The cigarmakers. . . . Although one cannot say that all social democrats are cigarmakers, one is almost justified in claiming that all cigarmakers are social democrats," September 11, 1886, 324. Cf. also *Sozialdemokrat,* November 10, 1881; January 21, February 13, and March 2, 1882; March 23, April 5, May 10, and May 17, 1883; August 14 and November 27, 1884; August 27, 1885; March 5 and June 17, 1886; April 27, 1889.

20. Dirk Hoerder and Hartmut Keil, "The American Case and German Social Democracy at the Turn of the Twentieth Century, 1878-1907," in *Pourquoi n'y a-t'il pas de socialisme aux États-Unis?* ed. Jean Heffer and Jeanine Roret (Paris, 1988), 141-65; Hartmut Keil, "Deutsche sozialistische Einwanderer in den USA im letzten Drittel des 19. Jahrhunderts. Lebensweise und Organisation im Spannungsfeld von Tradition und Integration," ms., Munich, 1985, 255-302.

21. Analysis of membership lists of SLP New York; nationality was not given, but it can be assumed that most persons with German names had immigrated; Socialist Party Collection, Tamiment Institute, Bobst Library, New York University. This finding is consistent with the general observation on the predominance of Germans in the SLP in the secondary literature.

22. For overviews of the organizational activities of German socialists, see Philip S. Foner and Brewster Chamberlin, eds., *Friedrich A. Sorge's Labor Movement in the United States: A History of the American Working Class from Colonial Times to 1890* (Westport, 1977); Hermann Schlüter, *Die Anfänge der deutschen Arbeiterbewegung in Amerika* (Stuttgart, 1907); and Schlüter, *Die Internationale in Amerika: Ein Beitrag zur Geschichte der Arbeiterbewegung in den Vereinigten Staaten* (Chicago, 1918). For the role of women in the socialist movement, cf. Mari Jo Buhle, *Women and American Socialism, 1870-1920* (Urbana, 1981).

23. Cf. Schneider-Liebersohn, "Gewerkschaft und Gemeinschaft," 69ff. Several exiled socialists who were cigarmakers from the Hamburg area became leaders in the union, see the Progressive Cigarmakers' journal *Progress* (1882-85).

24. Cf. *NYVZ,* December 16, 18, 1878; January 6, February 24, April 1, May 1, 1879; *Chicagoer Arbeiter-Zeitung,* June 4, 1879; *Philadelphia Tageblatt,* December 14, 1878.

25. *Volksstaat,* January 4, May 17, August 22, 1873; *NYVZ,* July 1, 1881; cf. also August 10, 1880, April 25, July 10, 1881. The *Sozialdemokrat* joined in with this evaluation of the "emigration fever," which "we must deplore and fight," February 13, 1881.

26. *NYVZ,* January 20, 1881; *Sozialdemokrat,* February 13, August 18, 1881.

27. *NYVZ,* January 20, July 1, 1881.

28. *NYVZ,* October 9, 26, 1878; April 19, 1889; *Philadelphia Tageblatt,* December 1, 1880; *Chicagoer Arbeiter-Zeitung,* January 24, 1888.

29. Cf. Hoerder and Keil, "The American Case," 145.

30. *Sozialdemokrat,* June 19, 26, July 21, 1881; *NYVZ,* June 27, July 4, 6, 1881; see also editorial "Gegen die Ausreisserei," *Sozialdemokrat,* October 13, 1888.

31. *Sozialdemokrat,* January 16, February 20, June 19, August 11, September 1, October 13, 1881; also *NYVZ,* August 13, 1885; *Philadelphia Tageblatt,* December 1, 1880; *Sozialist,* February 19, 1887. See also the statement by the National Executive of the SLP: "Emigration of German socialists should not be encouraged for if there was ever a time when they should be at their post it is now," *Socialist* (Chicago), January 4, 1879; see also December 21, 1878.

32. See Heinzpeter Thümmler, *Sozialistengesetz §28. Ausweisungen und Ausgewiesene 1878-1890* (Berlin, 1979); Ignaz Auer, *Nach zehn Jahren. Material und Glossen zur Geschichte des Sozialistengesetzes* (London, 1889); Helga Berndt, "Die auf Grund des Sozialistengesetzes zwischen 1881 und 1890 Ausgewiesenen aus Leipzig und Umgegend. Eine Studie zur sozialen Struktur der deutschen Arbeiterklasse und Arbeiterbewegung," dissertation, Humboldt University, Berlin, 1972.

33. Keil, "Deutsche sozialistische Einwanderer," 126-84.

34. The German Social Democracy on the occasion of the tenth anniversary of the antisocialist law asked exiles to answer a questionnaire giving details of the circumstances and the consequences of their being driven into exile. The SLP cooperated in this venture, publishing the questionnaire in its paper *Sozialist* on December 24, 1887. The information received was published in Auer, *Nach zehn Jahren.*

35. For example, in *NYVZ,* October 12, 1889; *Sozialist,* January 15, April 30, August 6, September 3, 1887; January 7, July 21, 28, August 4, 1888; March 8, 1890; cf. also Gretch to Eichle, Evansville, November 19, 1889, box 3; Brown in Boston to Emil Kreis, July 26, 1883, Box 6, SLP Papers, State Historical Society of Wisconsin, Madison.

36. *NYVZ,* August 1, October 1, 1881; March 1, 1882; August 13, 1882, April 3, 1887; Keil, "Deutsche sozialistische Einwanderer," 168f.

37. See Hartmut Keil, "An Ambivalent Identity: The Attitude of German Socialist Immigrants toward American Political Institutions and American Citizenship," in *In the Shadow of the Statue of Liberty,* ed. Marianne Debouzy (Saint-Denis, 1988), 247-63.

38. See Hoerder and Keil, "The American Case."

39. *Vorbote*, May 30, 1874; such advertisements often appeared in the German-language labor press.

40. Wilhelm Liebknect regularly wrote for the *Arbeiter-Union* from April 1869 to September 1870, Julius Vahlteich for the *New Yorker Volks-Zeitung* before his emigration to the United States in 1881.

41. See Hoerder and Keil, "The American Case."

42. See, for example, *Sozialdemokrat*, November 10, 1881; January 23, February 13, March 2, 1882; March 23, April 5, May 10, 17, 1883; August 14, November 27, 1884; August 27, 1885; March 5, June 17, 1886; April 27, 1889; cf. also Hoerder and Keil, "The American Case."

43. In an interview in mid-October 1878, two journalists who had just arrived in New York from Germany voiced their opinion that, in case of passage of the antisocialist bill, "of course many of our editors and journalists will lose their means of existence. A goodly number of them will probably emigrate to America," *NYVZ*, October 16, 1878.

44. For examples see Schneider-Liebersohn, "Gewerkschaft und Gemeinschaft"; Kathleen Neils Conzen, *Immigrant Milwaukee, 1836-1860: Accommodation and Continuity in a Frontier City* (Cambridge, 1976); Agnes Bretting, *Soziale Probleme deutscher Einwanderer in New York City 1800-1860* (Wiesbaden, 1981); Christiane Harzig, "Chicago's German North Side, 1880-1900: The Structure of a Gilded Age Ethnic Neighborhood," in *German Workers*, ed. Keil and Jentz, 127-44; and Hartmut Keil, "Einwandererviertel und amerikanische Gesellschaft. Zur Integration deutscher Einwanderer in die amerikanische städtisch-industrielle Umwelt des ausgehenden 19. Jahrhunderts am Beispiel Chicagos," *Archiv für Socialgeschichte* 24 (1984): 45-87.

45. Adolf Douai in *Vorbote*, June 15, 1878. Such praise was reiterated in countless variations, see, for example, *NYVZ*, November 16, 1881, June 7, 1885, when the German Social Democracy was named the "guiding star of the European and American working classes" and the "trailblazer for all the other movements in other countries."

46. Jakob Winnen, "Die Aufgabe der verschiedenen Arbeiter-Organisationen in der Jetztzeit," *Vorbote*, April 3, 1875.

47. Quoted by Conrad Conzett in *Vorbote*, July 10, 1875.

48. "Aufruf an alle Mitglieder der IAA, sozial-demokratischen Arbeiter-Partei von Nord-Amerika und der Arbeiterpartei von Illinois zur Gründung einer neuen, einheitlichen sozialistischen Arbeiterorganisation von Amerika," dated Chicago, July 13, 1875, in: *Vorbote*, July 17, 1875.

49. Keil, "Deutsche sozialistische Einwanderer," 324-41.

50. For overviews see Carl Wittke, *The German Language Press in America* (New York, 1973); William F. Kamman, *Socialism in German American Literature* (Philadelphia, 1917); and Schlüter, *Anfänge*. For more details see Keil, "Deutsche sozialistische Einwanderer," 316-21.

51. "Konstitution des Verwaltungsrathes der 'Arbeiter-Zeitung,'" Papers of the International Workingmen's Association, Reel 1, misc., State Historical Society of Wisconsin, Madison.

52. *Vorbote,* July 18, 1874.

53. Renate Kiesewetter, "Die Institution der deutsch-amerikanischen Arbeiterpresse in Chicago: Zur Geschichte des 'Vorboten' und der 'Chicagoer Arbeiterzeitung,' 1874-1886," in *Glimpses of the German-American Radical Press,* ed. Dirk Hoerder (Bremen, 1985), 186-90.

54. Renate Kiesewetter, "German-American Labor Press: The *Vorbote* and the *Chicagoer Arbeiterzeitung,*" in *German Workers Culture in the United States 1850 to 1920,* ed. Hartmut Keil (Washington, 1988), 137-55.

55. For analyses see Hartmut Keil and Heinz Ickstadt, "Elemente einer deutschen Arbeiterkultur in Chicago zwischen 1880 und 1890," *Geschichte und Gesellschaft* 5 (1979): 103-24; Heinz Ickstadt and Klaus Ensslen, "German Working-Class Culture in Chicago: Continuity and Change in the Decade from 1900 to 1910," in *German Workers,* ed. Keil and Jentz, 236-52. For an example of the communal context in which German-American working-class culture flourished, see the collection of documents in *German Workers in Chicago: A Documentary History of Working-Class Culture from 1850 to World War I,* ed. Hartmut Keil and John B. Jentz (Urbana, 1988). For an analysis of German working-class culture see Vernon L. Lidtke, *The Alternative Culture: Socialist Labor in Imperial Germany* (New York, 1985).

56. A phrase used as early as 1873, see *Volksstaat,* May 17, August 22, 1873.

57. "Der Einigungskongress der amerikanischen Sozialisten in Indianapolis," *Neue Zeit* 19 (1900-1901): 663-66.

58. Alexander Jonas to Morris Hillquit, June 23, 1904, Morris Hillquit Papers, Correspondence, box 1, State Historical Society of Wisconsin, Madison.

15

Emigration as Exile: Cultural Hegemony in Post-Famine Ireland

KERBY A. MILLER

Until quite recently, the interpretation of emigration which enjoyed greatest legitimacy in Irish Catholic society was that of emigration as exile, as involuntary expatriation obliged by forces beyond individual choice or control, sometimes by fate or destiny, but usually by the operations or consequences of "British misrule" or "landlord tyranny." However, this interpretation was not literally credible. British imperialism certainly influenced Ireland's economic development, and the exile label was appropriate for Irish political rebels, transported felons, and perhaps even evicted tenants, as in the Great Famine of 1845-50. Nevertheless, the vast majority of Irish Catholic emigrants left home for essentially mundane reasons similar or identical to those which produced mass migration from other European countries: the decline of cottage industries, crop failures, falling agricultural prices, the exigencies of impartible inheritance and the dowry system, and the increasing redundancy of petty farmers and agricultural laborers brought about by the consolidation of holdings, the conversion of tillage to pasture, and the introduction of labor-saving farm machinery. In short, the processes of modern agrarian and industrial capitalism were primarily responsible for Irish emigration. Moreover, many of the most compelling, immediate causes of emigration were generated within the Irish Catholic community, especially during the post-Famine era (from the 1850s through the 1920s) when most departures occurred, and it is problematic how much suffering and emigration among the rural lower classes (laborers, smallholders, farmers' noninheriting children) were really more attributable to profit-maximization among Catholic commercial farmers and rural parents, generally, than to the machinations of Protestant landlords or British officials.[1]

Nor is this to say that Irish emigrants invariably characterized themselves as unwilling exiles—as in their personal letters and memoirs—although some certainly did so. Among those who remained in Ireland or who had not yet emigrated there were alternative conceptualizations of emigration, as opportunity or even escape, which contradicted the unhappy, compulsory connotations of exile. However, popular interpretations of complex social realities are often inconsistent or contradictory, and although the Irish at home and abroad *individually* employed the exile motif occasionally and situationally, they expressed it *collectively* with great regularity in their songs, poems, speeches, sermons, and newspapers. Moreover, the fact that it was utilized so often and so successfully in the appeals of Irish and Irish-American nationalists and clerics indicates that the hearts and purses of ordinary Irish people on both sides of the Atlantic were almost instinctively receptive to the imagery of political banishment.[2]

Cultural Hegemony in Post-Famine Ireland

A useful framework for understanding the prevalence of the notion that emigration was exile is provided by the theory of cultural hegemony of Antonio Gramsci, as elaborated by Raymond Williams.[3] According to Gramsci, every individual has a "spontaneous philosophy," embodied in language, religion, conventional wisdom, and empirical knowledge, that usually contains profound discrepancies between inherited or externally received notions and those implicit in everyday actions, experiences, and social position. This "contradictory consciousness," often producing political passivity or paralysis, is the result of the processes of "cultural hegemony" by which a ruling class disseminates its values; it does this through a variety of institutional means and through pervasive cultural expressions that reflect the society's economic "base" or governing social processes, for example, industrial capitalism. Although the ruling class could exercise authority through "political" coercion, in a capitalist society it more commonly creates a hegemony ("intellectual and moral leadership") through such agencies of "civil" society's "ideological superstructure" as religion, selective historical tradition, formal education, the organization of work and family life, political parties, trade unions, and other ostensibly "voluntary" organizations. Of course, the "political" and "civil" realms are analytically rather than actually distinct. Gramsci defined the nature of power in contemporary society as "hegemony armoured by coercion"; however, the function of hegemony is to produce among the masses a *spontaneous* consent to what another scholar calls "the values, norms, perceptions, beliefs, sentiments, and prejudices that support and define the existing distribution of goods, the institutions that decide how this distribution occurs, and the permissible range of disagreement about those processes." In other words, what Raymond Williams has termed the "dominant" culture so saturates a given society that its norms and values seem to be "commonsensical"—organized, experienced, and ratified through popular participation in the processes which generate them.[4]

Williams also points out that the dominant or hegemonic culture is neither static nor monolithic. It reflects the dynamism, fluidity, and diversity of society's governing processes, institutions, and classes (which can themselves exhibit contradictory consciousness), and furthermore, it also interacts with potential "counter-hegemonies"—that is, with "alternative" or "oppositional" cultures that reflect "deviant" practices, experiences, and norms. Williams defines these other cultures as either "residual" or "emergent." Residual values are holdovers from previously dominant social formations (e.g., feudal or preindustrial), whereas emergent cultures express new meanings rooted in actual, contemporary experiences and that reflect the embryonic self-consciousness of new classes (such as the proletariat) and social realities and practices not yet recognized by the dominant culture. The dominant culture usually incorporates certain aspects of the residual and emergent alternatives, thereby reducing their potential opposition. This means that the process of cultural hegemony is "open at both ends."[5]

According to Gramsci, it is primarily society's intellectuals who perform the historic task or function of articulating the hegemonic culture and incorporating or reconciling its potential oppositions. In Gramsci's view, every ruling class, as it advances to power, creates its own "organic" intellectuals. Hence, the needs of the capitalist entrepreneur give rise to the engineer, the scientist, the economist, the journalist, and others who "explain" and express those needs or "hegemonic imperatives" in contemporary and "materialistic" ways. Also, before a class can exercise hegemony over its rivals and subordinates, it must confront and assimilate what Gramsci calls the "traditional" intellectuals—for example, ecclesiastics and lawyers—that is, the organic intellectuals of previously dominant social formations, whose "residual" wisdom, adapted to contemporary conditions, can invest the new hegemonic culture with an apparently timeless and even "spiritual" authority in the consciousness of the subordinate classes. Although Gramsci's distinction between organic and traditional intellectuals is somewhat artificial and vague, the point is that, together, they articulate the ideology of the ruling classes in ways that not only incorporate elements of residual and emergent cultures, but in the process also facilitate the creation of ideological blocs or transcendent political alliances (for example, between the bourgeoisie and, say, the church, skilled trade unions, or farmers, versus the industrial proletariat) which themselves disseminate the dominant culture and generate popular consent.

Before examining how cultural hegemony theory can illuminate the origins and functions of the Irish perception of emigration as exile, it is necessary to describe briefly some salient features of post-Famine Irish Catholic society. That society was overwhelmingly rural. As late as 1911, two-thirds of Ireland's population lived on farms or in villages and towns containing fewer than two thousand inhabitants. More than two-thirds of Irish farms enclosed fewer than thirty acres, and nearly half contained less than fifteen acres. These were family farms on the "peasant model," characterized by "a subsistence economy, where production for the market [was] not the dominating purpose of production." In addition, about one-third of those employed in agriculture were landless laborers and farm servants.[6]

However, despite Catholic Ireland's relative "backwardness," from the late eighteenth century it was a society in rapid transition to agrarian capitalism. British demands for Irish foodstuffs generated greater profits from market production and greater financial pressures by landlords through higher rents and estate rationalization, to which tenants and subtenants responded by producing more grain and, especially, livestock for British consumption. Well before the Great Famine of 1845-50, contemporaries noted the emergence of a prosperous Catholic bourgeoisie, based on a partnership between urban businessmen and professionals on one hand and large commercial or "strong farmers" — primarily rich graziers — on the other. Simultaneously, Catholic Ireland's commercial growth stimulated a comparable increase in the wealth, infrastructure, and influence of the Irish Catholic church, largely financed and staffed by the donations and the offspring of the Catholic middle classes.[7]

Ironically, the tragedy of the Great Famine enabled the Catholic bourgeoisie and the church to consolidate their socioeconomic position and moral authority. The deaths and departures of nearly three million people during the Famine and its immediate aftermath (1845-55) ravaged the subsistence sector of Irish society (landless laborers, cottiers, and smallholders), broke the hitherto-fierce resistance of peasant-dominated secret agrarian societies to the commercialization and consolidation of agriculture, and enabled the middle classes to gain greater influence over a relatively more affluent, literate, and shrunken populace. During the post-Famine period, the ranks of small farmers and, especially, cottiers and farm laborers continued to shrink, largely through emigration (more than four million departures from 1856 to 1921) as industrial and rural employment steadily declined and as middling and small farmers abandoned the once common custom of partible inheritance in favor of impartible inheritance, which consigned most farmers' children to the emigrant ships. Religious strictures increasingly reinforced bourgeois norms, as Catholic church leaders such as Paul Cardinal Cullen promulgated a "devotional revolution" which conformed Catholic countryfolk, formerly lax in religious observance or fidelity to clerical authority, to Roman prescriptions of belief and practice.[8]

Finally, it is important to remember that before the Anglo-Irish war of 1919-21 and the subsequent creation of the Irish Free State, Catholic Ireland was not a nation-state. Legally, since 1800 Ireland had been an integral and equal member of the United Kingdom, but historically and economically it was a British colony, established by conquest and maintained ultimately by force. England's conquest had imposed a "Protestant Ascendancy" led by a handful of landlords who owned 90 percent of Irish soil. Although Catholics constituted about 80 percent of Ireland's inhabitants, until 1829 they were subject to a variety of politically and economically disabling Penal Laws, and until 1869 the Protestant Church of Ireland was the legally established religion. Even after those dates, the Ascendancy remained disproportionately powerful until the Land War of 1879-82 and the subsequent rise of the Home Rule movement obliged the British government to dismantle Irish landlordism and democratize Irish politics. However, the Irish economy was so thoroughly integrated to British capitalism that even the achievement of independence for southern Ireland in 1921 was, in economic terms at least, merely nominal.[9]

With respect to the theory of cultural hegemony, the position of the Catholic bourgeoisie was greatly complicated by Ireland's colonial status. Looking at the United Kingdom as a whole, the Irish middle class could be seen as merely a regional component of a ruling British bourgeoisie instead of a dominant or potentially dominant class in its own right. In that view, what might be called the Catholic bourgeoisie's hegemonic imperatives toward its subordinate classes (the peasantry and the urban and rural proletariat) would be virtually identical to the imperatives of the British governing classes. From an all-U.K. perspective, the dominant Irish Catholic subculture could be classed as a regional variant of the dominant British culture, especially with respect to values reinforcing capitalist institutions and processes, such as private property, free competition, and individual acquisitiveness, as well as in regard to certain notions of style or taste emanating from the English metropolis. Indeed, in some respects Catholic Ireland's dominant culture was extremely emulative or, as critics charged, "West British."

However, the unequal development of southern Ireland's agrarian economy in its dependent relationship to English industrial and finance capitalism, coupled with Catholic resentments against Irish political inferiority at Westminster and the Protestant Ascendancy at home, inspired much of the Catholic middle class to seek regional self-government or even total independence as a means of becoming a "national" rather than a colonial ruling class. The Catholic bourgeoisie had to supplant British/Protestant hegemony over Irish civil society before it could challenge British domination: it had to generate what was, to use Gramsci's terms, an emergent, nationalist counter-hegemony in order to achieve autonomy from its British/Protestant opponents and to secure support from allies, primarily within Irish Catholic society but also among the Irish emigrants abroad. The success or failure of these external and internal "projects" of the Catholic middle class were inextricably related. The attainment of political independence from Britain was contingent on the achievement of internal hegemony and the mobilization of the Irish masses behind the nationalists' program—despite the fact that that program entailed the creation of an Irish bourgeois state governed by the same processes and classes which were primarily responsible for lower-class Catholic immigration and emigration. Conversely, as long as Ireland remained a political colony, the Catholic middle class lacked the authority to order Irish society and incorporate its values throughout the ideological superstructure.[10]

The processes through which the Catholic middle class "made itself" were necessarily complex and subtle. That class began to emerge as a self-conscious entity in the relatively prosperous late eighteenth century, led by urban merchants and professionals whose ideas and ambitions, shaped by capitalism, were distinct from those of the old Catholic gentry and the Gaelic peasantry alike. Initially, in the 1770s and 1780s, the Catholic middle class desired only the creation of economic and political conditions which would promote their interests within the British constitution: repeal of the Penal Laws, equal economic opportunities, and equal political rights for propertied Catholics. Inspired by the success of the French Revolution, some middle-class Catholics joined with like-minded Protestants in the Society of United Irishmen, whose efforts to create an independent, nonsectarian Irish republic were crushed in 1798. However, most members of the

Catholic middle class distrusted the radical egalitarianism and anti-clericalism of French republicanism and welcomed both the defeat of the United Irishmen and the subsequent Act of Union in 1800, which seemed to presage the granting of full Catholic rights by the British government. Unfortunately, between 1800 and 1829 the Westminster parliament disappointed Catholic hopes. Moreover, the effects of the post-Napoleonic War depression not only gave added urgency to Catholics' desire for economic and political equality, but also convinced many that only repeal of the Act of Union and creation of a new, popularly elected (hence, Catholic-dominated) Irish legislature would enable them to protect and promote their interests. During the pre-Famine period (1815-44) what Gramsci would call the organic intellectuals of the Catholic bourgeoisie, especially lawyers like Daniel O'Connell, borrowed the theories of Adam Smith, William Godwin, and other British political economists to explain their economic position and political ambitions and to justify successive political campaigns for Catholic Emancipation and repeal of the union.[11]

The political notions shared by most rural Catholics differed greatly from the liberal ideals of their putative leaders. Usually illiterate and often Irish-speakers, Catholic artisans, smallholders, and, especially, cottiers and laborers were intensely parochial, their sense of Irish identity bound to specific localities or to tribal traditions and hatreds rather than to bourgeois concepts of nationalism. For leaders, Irish-speaking peasants and members of the secret agrarian societies generally preferred men of their own class or even paternalistic landlords rather than middle-class townsmen and wealthy graziers whom they regarded as half-Anglicized snobs, who eulogized capitalist progress and ignored its consequences for the exploited masses. When such men thought in political terms, they oscillated between visions of a pastoral Gaelic commonwealth and the radical, half-assimilated ideals of the French Revolution and the United Irishmen. Thus, to mobilize and control these potential allies, the Catholic middle class had to broaden its ideological appeal. The fragmented and transitional nature of Catholic society, and the precarious social position of the middle class itself, demanded that the nationalist counter-hegemony incorporate a range of values and symbols that in more "advanced" capitalist societies would be characterized as residual or premodern. It did so in at least three major ways.

First, early in the nineteenth century, under the leadership of Daniel O'Connell, the middle class formed a nationalist alliance with the Irish Catholic church. It assimilated the church's traditional intellectuals, who gave a "spiritual" substance and legitimacy to the political goals of the middle class, and gained access to Catholic society's most elaborate and pervasive institutional infrastructure— including temperance societies and confraternities, as well as parish churches. In return, the church assumed a "patriotic" stature in popular opinion, and also gained influence over the course and content of Catholic nationalism—plus the opportunity to assume predominance in any future Irish government. Because the Catholic clergy's ideal Irish society was organic and authoritarian, guided by religion instead of the marketplace or popular opinion, the alliance between middle-class nationalists and the church created an uneasy ideological synthesis that historians have termed "Catholic liberalism."[12]

Second, the Catholic bourgeoisie mobilized the land hunger of the lower classes in the nationalist crusade. This was a delicate and complicated process because middle-class graziers and other strong farmers, although sharing the peasants' resentments against landlordism, high rents, and evictions, held divergent attitudes toward agrarian capitalism and the sanctity of private property. It was no wonder that middle-class Catholic nationalists were unwilling to raise the rallying cry—"the land for the people"—until after the Great Famine, mass emigration, and the Catholic church's devotional revolution had reduced and tamed the lower classes. Driven by peasant land hunger and led hesitantly by bourgeois nationalists and clerics, the Land War of 1879-82 initiated legal changes which, by 1920, virtually abolished landlordism and enabled Irish tenants to own their farms. However, although the successful agitation against landlords provided an enormous stimulous to the penultimate phase of middle-class nationalism, the Home Rule movement, the creation of a so-called peasant proprietorship only ratified the inequitable distribution of Irish soil among the Catholic population. Many land-poor smallholders, landless laborers, and farmers' noninheriting sons remained bitterly frustrated, but the Catholic bourgeoisie vehemently rejected more radical schemes for the redistribution or the nationalization of Irish land, as proposed by the peasant-born leader of the Land War Michael Davitt, or by the Dubin socialist James Connolly.[13]

In a sense, the Catholic middle class's alliances with the church and the peasants' desire for land only incorporated within the nationalist bloc the social and cultural tensions caused by rapid commercialization. And so, third, the Catholic middle class had to resolve or obscure those tensions by broadening its hegemonic culture further to incorporate other notions embedded in traditional Irish Catholic culture.

Origins and Functions of the Exile Motif

The popular belief that all Irish emigration was involuntary exile, tantamount to political banishment, was an integral and residual element of the Irish Catholic worldview or—in Gramsci's terms— spontaneous philosophy. Because that belief contradicted or obscured emigration's actual causes, rooted in the dynamics and inequalities of agrarian capitalism, it epitomized the contradictory popular consciousness produced or at least deepened by the processes of cultural hegemony.

Ultimately, the notion of emigration as exile was one expression of a native Irish culture which had been dominant before the Norman conquest and, especially, the sixteenth- and seventeenth-century English conquests, but which remained vigorous in post-conquest Catholic society, particularly among the peasantry. Long before the Norman invasion of 1169, Gaelic poets commonly employed the Irish word *deoraí* (literally, exile) to describe anyone who left Ireland for any reason. Given the impacts of the later, more thorough English/ Protestant conquests and confiscations, it was natural that seventeenth- and eighteenth-century Irish bards applied *deoraí* and similar terms to the fates of banished Catholic chieftains and their expatriated adherents—thereby providing seemingly apposite models for subsequent, ordinary emigrants.[14]

However, the idea that emigration was communal necessity and tragedy rather than, say, individual opportunity was more than a literary device. It was a reflection of a pervasive cultural system which tended to devalue individual action, ambition, and the assumption of personal responsibility—especially when actions, such as emigration, seemed innovative and threatening to customary patterns of behavior and thought which enjoined, by example and precept, passive, communal and precapitalist values such as continuity, conformity, and duty. This value system or worldview was incorporated in the secular, religious, and linguistic aspects of traditional Gaelic society, and although conquests and confiscations largely destroyed the classes which had dominated that society, substantial continuities between pre- and post-conquest ways of life still validated many elements of that system, especially among the masses of impoverished and, often, Irish-speaking Catholics.[15]

In terms of the secular aspects of pre- and post-conquest Catholic society, both practically and ideally that society had been and remained hierarchical, communal, familial, and customary—and each emphasis, as expressed through land tenure systems, farming practices, and traditional proverbs, for example, diminished individual responsibility and importance in relation to society and its governing institutions. Likewise, the religious expressions of Irish society reinforced the temporal constraints and sacralized their emphases on obedience to collective authority. This was true of both peasant religion, with its belief in fairies and "predictive celebrations," and the more formal religious system imposed through the Catholic church's devotional revolution. Too, the Irish language makes sharp distinctions between active and passive states of being, and, in comparison to English, classifies a much broader range of phenomena into an area in which action and self-assertion are inappropriate. Thus, the most common way for an Irish-speaker to describe emigration has been *dob éigan dom imeacht go Meirice*: "I had to go to America"—or, more precisely, "going to America was a necessity for me"—an impersonal interpretation entirely consistent with the use of *deoraí* to designate emigrant, as one subject to imposed pressures, and likewise consistent with the selective historical traditions of Irish rebellion and banishment.[16]

On one level, it is arguable that both the interpretation of emigration as exile and the residual or precapitalist value system which supported that interpretation remained part of the popular consciousness in post-Famine Ireland because of the structural contradictions and psychological tensions which characterized a society in swift but uneven transition. Although contemporaries sometimes decried the rationalization or "Anglicization" of rural values which accompanied agrarian-capitalist development, and complained that some culturally deracinated Irish youths no longer viewed emigration sorrowfully, the expatriate imagery and many aspects of its corroboratory worldview still seemed applicable to certain social realities which were "explainable" in premodern terms. As a result of the uneven impact of commercialization, many traditional institutions, task orientations, and even linguistic patterns (in Hiberno-English as well as the vanishing Irish language) lasted well into the twentieth century. Moreover, not only did the influence of externally imposed authorities (Protestant landlords, British officials) long remain potent, but within Catholic Ireland the disappearance of secret agrarian societies, increased clerical authority, the marginalization of farm laborers and farmers' noninheriting children, and the enmeshing of smallholders in webs of debt also may have reduced, rather than widened, the scope of responsible choice most rural dwellers enjoyed. Thus, some aspects of Irish development may not have promoted more individualistic or independent outlooks, but instead enjoined continued or even in-creased dependence on and deference to familial obligations, patron-client ties, and communal authorities in order to ensure survival and status.[17]

However, although mitigated, socioeconomic and cultural changes in post-Famine Ireland were great, even traumatic, especially in the western districts which produced a disproportionately large share of Irish emigrants from 1856 through 1921. But those very innovations, so pregnant with social disruption and demoralization, encouraged greater popular reliance on residual outlooks and "explanations" which could relieve the tensions consequent on rapid transition—producing in the process a deeply contradictory consciousness with respect to new social realities. In order to ensure social and psychological equi-librium, especially among subordinate social groups, changes had to be interpreted in customary, comforting ways. Thus, whereas most post-Famine Irish responded "rationally" to new economic exigencies or opportunities (e.g., by adopting impartible inheritance or by em-igrating), they often fell back on traditional cultural categories ("it was a necessity. . . .") to justify, exculpate, or obscure causation and accountability—sometimes, as in the case of emigration, projecting responsibility for change on uncontrollable and/or "alien" forces. Hence, they could square traditional values and customary, communal sanctions with the actual practice of new, "freer" actions implicit in agrarian capitalism, cloaking the rising tide of individual calculation in the assumed anonymity of explanatory strategies which assuaged psychological and social tensions.[18]

Such compromises between tradition and innovation may have been psychological necessities. However, the precise forms of such ideo-logical adjustments—such as the fiction that all emigration was bas-ically political exile—were largely determined by Catholic Ireland's middle classes. They generated a new, dominant culture which in-corporated such residual outlooks in a symbiotic relationship with the social and psychological needs of the subordinate classes. The archaic *deoraí* tradition remained vibrant in the Irish-speaking western coun-ties, but its formalized expression throughout the commercialized, English-speaking Ireland of the post-Famine era served as an instru-ment of cultural hegemony for the social classes which had emerged preeminent from the wreckage of pre-Famine society and which found it essential to explain their social position in traditional terms which could inhibit resentment from subordinates and potential allies who felt disadvantaged by the socioeconomic and cultural discontinuities caused by the Famine and capitalist development.

In the post-Famine period the hegemonic culture of the Catholic bourgeoisie was incorporated primarily through three media: the Catholic church, which dominated Catholic education as well as religious life; Irish nationalist movements, which shaped popular political consciousness; and, most intimately, the strong-farmer *type* of rural family (the "stem family"), characterized by impartible inheritance, the dowry system, postponed marriage, and capital accumulation. All three institutions reflected the recent *embourgeoisement* of Catholic society—adopted by or imposed on peasant farmers and laborers from models of "proper" religious, political and socioeconomic behavior enjoined by middle-class townspeople, clerics, and farmers. To a degree, all three upset or challenged traditional peasant practices and outlooks—sometimes to people's obvious disadvantage, as in the case of farmers' disinherited children—yet all demanded absolute conformity and proscribed deviations as familial ingratitude, religious apostasy, or even national treason.[19]

The success of the Catholic bourgeoisie's complementary projects (cultural hegemony and political domination) depended on the articulation of its values through these and other media in order to contain intracommunal conflicts, mobilize the masses, and win regional self-government or Irish independence. Consequently, the Catholic bourgeoisie's hegemonic culture had to incorporate the residual imagery of emigration as exile because the bourgeoisie itself shared major responsibility for mass lower-class emigration: generally, through the processes of agrarian capitalism; particularly, through the operations of the stem family; and, some critics charged, because of the Catholic church's stifling impact on social life and personal expression. The remainder of this chapter focuses on political and clerical ideals concerning emigration, but, with regard to the rural family, the notion of emigration forced by fate or British oppression, rather than economic calculation, was vital in mitigating potentially explosive conflicts between parents and offspring and between inheriting and noninheriting children. However, just as the intrafamilial tensions and resolutions respecting emigration were much more complex than that brief statement suggests, so also did the Catholic bourgeoisie's political and clerical spokesmen have to balance middle-class interests and peasant and proletarian sensibilities. In the process, they often produced messages which, in their inconsistency, both mirrored and exacerbated the contradictory popular consciousness.[20]

Emigration and the Contradictions of Catholic Nationalism

Given the impact of capitalism on Irish society, it was predictable that a few Catholic leaders regarded emigration "rationally," openly acknowledging that many people's "irredeemable poverty" or laudable ambition made at least some emigration "absolutely necessary" or even "natural" and praiseworthy. For example, many priests viewed their parishioners' departures with resignation or even with favor. However, both the hegemonic imperatives of the Catholic bourgeoisie and the traditions and prejudices of the masses determined that emigration had to be interpreted communally and symbolically, in political and religious contexts. On one hand, Catholic spokesmen often eulogized the accomplishments of the "Irish Race" overseas, and clergy were especially prone to describe the exodus as "divine destiny" and the emigrants as "holy missionaries" for the Catholic faith. On the other hand, negative characterizations of emigration predominated, and after the Great Famine most clerics and nationalists united in condemning it. For Ireland as a whole emigration was described as tragic because it deprived the society of its young men and women, its "bone and sinew," and so threatened ultimate depopulation. Likewise, critics charged that emigration was tragic and potentially dangerous for the emigrants themselves. Catholic clerics, in particular, espoused this argument: at midcentury they emphasized primarily the hazards of the voyage and the poverty and physical dangers which awaited poor emigrants in the New World, but later they broadened their attack and stigmatized the United States itself as a vicious, materialistic, "godless" society which corrupted the emigrants' morals and destroyed their faith. According to such priests as Peter O'Leary, Joseph Guinan, and Patrick Sheehan, America was an "unnatural land" where innocent Irish youths would be "dragged down to shame and crime," and they urged their listeners "to save their souls in Holy Ireland rather than . . . hazard them for this world's goods among American heretics."[21]

Although agreeing that emigration was lamentable, nationalists and clergymen were inconsistent in assigning blame for its prevalence. Some charged that the emigrants themselves were culpable, either because they were too naive to resist the blandishments of ticket brokers, relatives overseas, or "returned Yanks," or, more harshly, because they were "coward[s]," "sordid churl[s]," and "lucre-loving wretch[es]," as the nationalist poet and agitator Fanny Parnell charged in 1880, or "traitor[s] to the Irish State" and "deserters who have left their posts," as Patrick Pearse, the leader of the 1916 Easter Rebellion, later claimed. Nevertheless, it was much more common to blame emigration on landlordism and British oppression and to characterize the emigrants as sorrowing, vengeful "exiles." According to priests such as Guinan and Thomas Burke, the emigrants were victims of religious and political persecution, while the Irish abroad were purportedly consumed with a passionate "love for Ireland" and a desire to "breathe once more the peat-scented air of their native valleys." Likewise, nearly all nationalist politicians characterized the exodus as a "reluctant emigration" which would cease only when Ireland was self-governing or independent and able to provide employment and prosperity for her citizens at home. "Ireland has resources to feed five times her population," Pearse asserted; hence, "a free Ireland would not, and could not, have hunger in her fertile vales and squalor in her cities."[22]

Contradictory attributions of blame for emigration reflected the Catholic bourgeoisie's torturous efforts to reconcile traditional social ideals and their own hegemonic imperatives with new social realities which violated those ideals and yet, paradoxically, both sustained and threatened their authority over the Catholic masses. Save in the context of wholesale emigration by the dispossessed and disinherited, bourgeois ascendancy over rural Ireland could not have been achieved without immeasurably greater tension and conflict within Catholic society. Many Catholic spokesmen were conscious of the fact that only the massive, lower-class exodus had created the relatively commercialized Ireland which had been a precondition for the success of disciplined nationalist movements and of the church's devotional revolution. Lower-class emigration had enabled the comparatively conflict-free consolidation of many strong farmers' and graziers' holdings, and those affluent groups and their shopkeeper allies were vital support sources for institutionalized piety and patriotism. Similarly, emigration stabilized the family farm, helped preclude overt social and generational strife over land, and prevented the subdivision, pauperization, and subterranean agrarian violence which had characterized the pre-Famine decades. In addition, Catholic leaders understood that emigration brought specific material benefits to key components of the bourgeoisie. For instance, publicans and shopkeepers—proverbially vociferous nationalists—profited from the sale of passage tickets, while much of the £1 million in annual remittances from the Irish in America found its way to the retailers' coffers and the priests' collection boxes. More crucially, clerics and nationalists relied heavily on Irish-Americans' loyalty and contributions to finance church-building, political agitation, and, ultimately, successful insurrection at home. Thus, Catholic spokesmen had good reasons to praise the emigrants and rationalize the exodus as the "Divine Mission of the Irish Race."[23]

However, Irish nationalists had to denounce emigration, for emigration, and popular opposition to it and its causes, threatened to undermine the dual projects of the Catholic bourgeoisie. Symbolically, emigration connoted depopulation, and since the early nineteenth century, when British economists urged wholesale removal of Ireland's "surplus" inhabitants, the issue of Irish population had been charged with politics and emotion. In that context, both the Famine clearances and more recent evictions of Irish tenants, as during the Land War of 1879-82, made the equation of emigration with planned "extermination" seem logical, if ahistorical. Practically, emigration endangered nationalists' hopes for Ireland's future and their efforts to oppose British authority and anglicizing influences. For example, the nationalists' proposed rejuvenation of Ireland's economy seemed threatened by the drain of potential entrepreneurs, workers, and consumers. More important, many leaders feared that mass departures were undermining Catholic Ireland's religious and political bulwarks by either eroding church membership or providing a safety valve for discontent which otherwise could be mobilized against British rule. Thus, in 1920 during the Irish War of Independence, the minister of defense for the Dáil, the nationalists' alternative government, issued a manifesto warning that the British administration was attempting to stimulate more emigration and thereby weaken the nationalist struggle: "The young men of Ireland must stand fast," he demanded, for "[t]o leave their country at this supreme crisis would be nothing less than base desertion in the face of the enemy." Catholic leaders were also apprehensive lest emigration deprive them of political and religious influence over the emigrants, especially those who left home for "selfish," materialistic reasons. Lay nationalists feared the emigrants "were casting off all allegiance to the motherland," while churchmen were concerned about the dangers of apostasy or "spiritual ruin" overseas.[24]

Hence, their self-assumed roles as Ireland's champions obliged the Catholic bourgeoisie's spokesmen to denounce emigration. As Bishop George Butler of Limerick put it in 1864 in a letter to fellow churchmen, "The depopulation of our Country is progressing at an awful pace and *we must not appear to be taking it too easy.*" Such opposition was usually sincere, and many of post-Famine Ireland's most prominent men had spent time abroad, witnessed emigrant poverty, and returned home determined to oppose the exodus. Nevertheless, Bishop Butler's private remark, made in response to the rumblings of lower-class discontent, revealed the profound difficulties faced by the Catholic bourgeoisie. Middle-class nationalists had to address emigration and its socioeconomic causes because those issues, rather than political abstractions, were the ones which most concerned the disadvantaged elements of Irish society whose mass support the nationalists wanted and needed. Grass-roots pressures forced nationalists to link the political goals of the bourgeoisie to the practical grievances and aspirations of the masses—specifically, to promises of fundamental socioeconomic changes which would obviate the need for mass emigration.[25]

Nationalists were successful in forging that link. Historical research indicates that nationalism's fiercest partisans were members of precisely those groups most threatened by economic displacement and the necessity of emigration. However, the social issues which mobilized landless laborers, farmers' noninheriting sons, and urban workers were potentially dangerous. If thwarted in their aspirations by their leaders' concessions to British authority or indigenous bourgeois interests, lower-class nationalists might disrupt Catholic unity, assault middle-class "patriots," or switch allegiance to schismatic varieties of nationalism opposed by dominant sectors of the bourgeoisie, as during the Irish Civil War of 1922-23. Whereas mass emigration among the subordinate classes would vitiate nationalist movements, their continued presence in Ireland threatened to break or divert those movements. The dilemma was clearly stated during the Irish War of Independence, when the Dáil's defense minister urged Ireland's sons to "stand fast," while its minister of agriculture warned that, if they did, in their land hunger they would "swarm . . . onto the land" belonging to Catholic graziers and strong farmers, thus alienating key segments of the bourgeoisie from the national struggle.[26]

The source of their dilemma was that most Catholic leaders had little or no inclination to take the radical measures necessary to restructure Irish society and so halt emigration. They had risen to the top of an Irish Catholic society whose very shape and stability depended to a large degree on emigration's continuance; the success of their complementary projects, their very affluence and authority, derived ultimately from socioeconomic systems and institutions which might not survive if emigration ceased. Consequently, with very few exceptions such as Michael Davitt, no post-Famine politicans advocated or implemented measures sufficient to stop emigration once they had achieved national prominence. For example, in the face of grazier opposition, Charles Stewart Parnell, leader of the Home Rule movement from 1880 through 1890, retreated from his suggestion that western smallholders colonize the rich north Leinster grasslands; and after 1921 the political successors of Arthur Griffith, founder of Sinn Féin, eschewed the protective tariffs which he had urged to create industrial employment. Likewise, the publicans, traders, and strong farmers who led nationalist movements at the parish level were staunchly opposed to the peasants' dream of land redistribution, to Davitt's scheme of land nationalization, to James Connolly's and James Larkin's socialism—indeed, even to tariffs and cooperative enter-prises—in short, to any fundamental changes in a social system which had institutionalized lower-class emigration.[27]

"Holy Ireland": The Creation of a Hegemonic Culture

Caught between their poor followers' demands that they support radical measures to halt emigration and their own aversion to such steps, bourgeois nationalists and churchmen had to formulate broad, ideological "explanations" of emigration, in spiritual and residual terms, which would ignore or obscure post-Famine Ireland's real social processes and conflicts. As a result, their interpretations of emigration were integrally related to their idealization of a mythical "holy Ireland" which could be defended against external assault and internal schism, thus ensuring the success of the bougeoisie's twin projects. The "holy Ireland" ideal had emerged in the early nineteenth century, but after the Famine it became more elaborate and pervasive and assumed a profoundly anti-modernist thrust. After 1850 the growing influence of the Catholic church on Irish society, the Papacy's own crusade against modernism, and the sentimentalism pervading much Victorian culture all reinforced and romanticized Irish opposition to the allegedly "British" influences transforming Catholic society. In response, middle-class Catholics conceptualized a fortress Hibernia, an ideal and purportedly "traditional" Irish society antithetical to their negative images of England (and America) and to the modern and purportedly "alien" tendencies within Ireland itself. According to Catholic leaders, especially churchmen, Irish Catholics were su-perior to the English and other Protestants because of their relative indifference to material success and other false gods of urban-indus-trial societies. Because of such unworldliness, allegedly the Irish were profoundly conservative, content to live simple lives at home under clerical guidance and in harmony with family, neighbors, and natural environment. The ideal society for such folk was static, organic, and paternalistic: a divinely-ordered, hierarchical community devoid of internal conflicts, insulated by faith and patriotism from potential "contamination." To ensure such stability and continuity, the economy of "holy Ireland" needed to remain overwhelmingly agricultural and, supposedly, pre-capitalist, based on the peasant family—the devout and paternal microcosm of the larger corporate society. Lay and cler-ical nationalists played variations on these themes, but all save a few radicals such as Davitt and Connolly conceptualized an ideally unchanging social order which, in theory, could support all Ireland's people in frugal comfort at home. Sometimes their rhetoric implied that this model society was still in the process of creation, at other times indicated that it was already in being. In either case its perceived enemies — British oppression, landlordism, Protestantism, secularism, and socialism — were legion, and so "holy Ireland" needed constant, vigorous defense. Consequently, the church made assiduous efforts to shape Catholic minds by controlling education; it supported Irish self-government as a means to insulate the faithful from pernicious English laws and anglicizing influences; and, despite the bishops' usual concern for property rights, it espoused agrarian reforms designed to root the "peasantry" in the soil and so secure "holy Ireland's" social and moral foundation.[28]

Within this conceptual framework, nationalists and clerics could both oppose emigration and condemn the emigrants themselves. Although the notion of a divinely ordered Irish society could reinforce churchmen's sometime boast that its pious emigrants were furthering God's work overseas, the more prevalent imagery of "holy Ireland" struggling against the forces of evil implied that mass departures constituted an intolerable weakening of its ranks. In addition, the very ideal of "holy Ireland" made emigration seem highly inappropriate, if not treacherous. If, as many Catholic spokesmen claimed by the 1890s, the ideal Irish society was already in being, then continued emigration indicated that subtle, subversive forces were at work internally. Because Catholic leaders had already created most or all of the conditions and institutions which purportedly obviated emigration's continued necessity, then by the logic of their vision any departures which still occurred implied the emigrants' self-willed or self-deluded repudiation of the organic nation-as-family and their violation of the sacralized peasant ethos on which the nation was supposedly based. After all, even if America did still offer superior material advantages (which many Catholic spokesmen were no longer willing to admit), Irish Catholics by definition were allegedly too selfless and unworldly to succumb to such lures. Hence, the emigrants must be either "fools" or "traitors," and devout nationalists such as Patrick Pearse stigmatized them as both.[29]

The ideology of "holy Ireland" imperfectly reflected only some residual aspects of post-Famine society's complex realities, and in the sense that it ignored, obscured, or denied the real and often ruthless aspects of Irish capitalism, the concept was at best an appealing illusion, at worst a pious fraud. Not only did those who propagated the concept fail to use their influence to make reality match the dream of an organic society capable of sustaining all its people, but even conceptually the notion of "holy Ireland" was grievously flawed with respect to emigration. To a degree, it was merely a rhetorical cloak, woven of medieval dogmas and Victorian pieties, masking a petty bourgeois society whose vaunted stability and sacralized family farm both mandated and depended on constant emigration. The concept not only ignored Irish Protestants, but also failed to make concessions to the need for Irish cities and industries as outlets for the countryside's "surplus" population: Ireland must remain rural, churchmen demanded, for urbanization and industrialization connoted secularism, social fragmentation, and the "black devil of Socialism." In light of such anomolies, Catholic spokesmen's demands that emigrants not desert "the holy peace of home" for the fleshpots of America smacked of willful blindness, if not overt hyprocrisy.[30]

However, the hegemonic imperatives of the Catholic bourgeoisie — and the sensibilities of the masses — demanded that the "holy Ireland" concept be further elaborated with respect to emigration. For if the real social processes which were "explained" or masked by the dominant culture were in fact the primary causes of mass emigration, then how could "holy Ireland's" champions explain the continuing waves of departures without either admitting their own culpability or ineffectiveness or exposing the concept's inadequacies — and without thereby alienating the lower classes and the emigrants from the society left behind? To be sure, nationalists and clerics could redouble their denunciations of the emigrants as fools and traitors, but such epithets violated realities too obviously and threatened to embitter the emigrants toward "holy Ireland" and its guardians. Or, they could resort to the old religious rationalization "that God in his inscrutable wisdom . . . had intended and used the Irish race to carry Catholicism to the ends of the earth," but, as one proletarian critic shrewdly perceived, "The Irishman who accepts this teaching cannot any longer lay the misfortunes of his country upon the shoulders of the British government." Thus, in order to secure the twin projects of the Catholic bougeoisie, the capstone of the dominant culture had to remain the oldest and most residual "explanation" of all — that emigration was "exile" forced by British oppression.[31]

Conclusion

The interpretation of emigration as exile implied no criticism of "holy Ireland" or its spokesmen. It postponed embarrassing socioeconomic questions until after self-government or independence was won, and, in the meantime, it deflected the emigrants' "fierce rage and fury" against the British "misgovernment" which purportedly obliged emigration from an island allegedly "capable of supporting twice its present population." Nor did that interpretation imply criticism of the emigrants themselves, for in terms of the dominant culture they were merely "victims" whose assiduously cultivated love for their homeland and hatred for England would inspire their unceasing devotion and donations to "holy Ireland's" staunch defenders: the Irish and Irish-American nationalists and clerics who promised that emigration would cease when "holy Ireland" was free from English rule.[32]

The socialist James Connolly and others voiced dissent from both the dominant Catholic culture and its facile "explanations" of emigration, and many emigrants themselves were too ambitious, realistic, or alienated to conceptualize their departures in prescribed ways. Nevertheless, the flood of remittances and donations from America indicates that many, if not most, Catholic Irish emigrants adhered to the dominant culture and remained emotionally or at least publically loyal to the society which had expelled them. In part, this was because the concept of emigration as exile was both deeply rooted in Irish tradition and constantly reinforced by contemporary conflicts with Protestant landlords, bigoted Orangemen, and British officials, thus corroborating "official" Catholic rhetoric. However, since the fundamental causes of most post-Famine emigration stemmed from the dynamics and structures of Catholic society itself, it is doubtful whether the archaic notion of emigration as exile would have remained credible had the notion and the "holy Ireland" imagery not been seemingly natural and logical expressions of a still-extant, traditional worldview which condemned innovation and individualism while externalizing responsibility for unsettling change. Not only did "holy Ireland" seem to be at least a partly valid metaphor for a society still locally centered on family farm and parish church, but more crucially, it was a systematic expression of what a people in rapid social and cultural transition desperately wanted and needed to believe was still entirely true about their society and themselves. Emigration as exile's ultimate appeal lay in its symbolic resolution of the discrepancies between the reality of social fragmentation and exploitation and the ideal of an organic, harmonious, self-sustaining community. If England could be blamed for emigration's causes, for the inability of "holy Ireland" to support all her children, then both the emigrants and those who profited by their departures could be absolved of culpability, while the consequent resentments against England could reinforce the outlooks and allegiances which held Catholic Ireland together in the face of the disintegrative and potentially demoralizing or alienating effects of commercialization and anglicization.[33]

Thus, the residual culture of the Catholic masses, their needs for continuity and reassurance, and the hegemonic imperatives of the Catholic bourgeoisie and its nationalist and clerical spokesmen all converged to create a hegemonic culture and a contradictory popular consciousness which controlled and obscured the discontinuities and conflicts within Irish Catholic society. In 1887 a traveler asked a farm laborer in County Tipperary, a region ravaged prior to the Famine by fierce conflicts between peasants and graziers, whether he and his exploited fellow workers now subscribed to the bougeois-defined and led nationalist movement. The man replied that although the laborers "hate the farmers, . . . *they love Ireland, and they all stand together for the country.*" And, mystified by an imagery which reflected peasant traditions and both mitigated and externalized their resentments, such men usually blamed England when they emigrated in search of the dignity and decent wages denied them by the "pathriotic" graziers and shopkeepers of "holy Ireland."[34]

NOTES

1. For a fuller exposition of many points in this chapter and for more complete citations, see Kerby A. Miller, *Emigrants and Exiles: Ireland and the Irish Exodus to North America* (New York, 1985), especially 427-92, and 102-30 on the interpretation of emigration as exile; Kerby A. Miller, with Bruce D. Boling, and David N. Doyle, "Emigrants and Exiles: Irish Cultures and Irish Emigration to North America," *Irish Historical Studies* 22 (September 1980): 97-126. On the causes of emigration during the pre-Famine, Famine, and post-Famine periods, see William Forbes Adams, *Ireland and Irish Emigration to the New World, from 1815 to the Famine* (New Haven, 1932); Oliver MacDonagh, "The Irish Famine Emigration to the United States," *Perspectives in American History* 10 (1976): 357-448; and Arnold Schrier, *Ireland and the American Emigration, 1850-1900* (Minneapolis, 1958); also see relevant chapters of Miller, *Emigrants and Exiles*.

2. For contrasting interpretations of Irish emigration, see Kerby A. Miller and Bruce D. Boling, "Golden Streets, Bitter Tears: The Irish Image of America During the Era of Mass Migration," *Journal of American Ethnic History* 10 (Fall 1990-Winter 1991): 16-35. On Irish-American nationalism, see Thomas N. Brown, *Irish-American Nationalism, 1870-1890* (Philadelphia, 1966), and William L. Joyce, *Editors and Ethnicity: A History of the Irish-American Press, 1848-1883* (New York, 1976).

3. Unless otherwise cited, the material in this and two following paragraphs are derived from Antonio Gramsci, *The Modern Prince and Other*

Writings (New York, 1957); Quentin Hoare and Geoffrey Nowell Smith, eds., *Selections from the Prison Notebooks of Antonio Gramsci* (New York, 1971); and Raymond Williams, "Base and Superstructure in Marxist Cultural Theory," *New Left Review* 82 (November-December 1983): 3-16.

4. Joseph V. Femia,*Gramsci's Political Thought: Hegemony, Consciousness, and the Revolutionary Process* (Oxford, 1981), 28; T. J. Jackson Lears, "The Concept of Cultural Hegemony: Problems and Possibilities," *American Historical Review* 90 (June 1985): 569.

5. Lears, "Concept of Cultural Hegemony," 571-73.

6. Miller, *Emigrants and Exiles*, 380-83, 430; Damian F. Hannan, "Peasant Models and the Understanding of Social and Cultural Change in Rural Ireland," in *Irish Studies 2: Ireland—Land, Politics and People*, ed. P. J. Drudy (Cambridge, 1982), 142-44, 146. The best general study of Irish economic development is Louis M. Cullen, *An Economic History of Ireland since 1660* (London, 1972). I have excluded consideration herein of the Protestant-dominated, urban-industrial counties of Ulster (later, Northern Ireland) as a sociocultural system distinct from "southern" or "Catholic" Ireland.

7. Cullen, *An Economic History*, 50-133 and *The Emergence of Modern Ireland, 1600-1900* (London, 1981). On the Irish Catholic church before the Famine, see Sean J. Connolly, *Priests and People in Pre-Famine Ireland, 1780-1845* (Dublin, 1982).

8. On post-Famine Irish economy and society, see Cullen, *Economic History*, 134-70; and Joseph Lee, *The Modernization of Irish Society, 1848-1918* (Dublin, 1973). On the causes of post-Famine emigration, see Miller, *Emigrants and Exiles*, 353-426. On secret agrarian societies and violence, see Samuel Clark and James S. Donnelly, Jr., eds., *Irish Peasants: Violence and Political Unrest, 1780-1914* (Madison, 1983). On the Irish Catholic church after the Famine, see Emmet Larkin, "The Devotional Revolution in Ireland, 1850-75," *American Historical Review* 77 (June 1972): 625-52.

9. The best one-volume studies of Irish political history are Tom Garvin, *The Evolution of Irish Nationalist Politics* (Dublin, 1981); and, for the post-Famine period, F. S. L. Lyons, *Ireland since the Famine* (London, 1971).

10. On the development of Irish nationalism, see Garvin, *Evolution of Irish Nationalist Politics*; D. George Boyce, *Nationalism in Ireland* (Baltimore, 1982); Michael Hechter, *Internal Colonialism: The Celtic Fringe in British National Development, 1536-1966* (Berkeley, 1975); and E. Strauss, *Irish Nationalism and British Democracy* (London, 1951).

11. Garvin, *Evolution of Irish Nationalist Politics*, 14-52. The best study of late-eighteenth-century Irish nationalism is Marianne Elliott, *Partners in Revolution: The United Irishmen and France* (New Haven, 1982). On O'Connell, see Fergus O'Ferrall, *Daniel O'Connell* (Dublin, 1981).

12. On Irish peasant *mentalité*, see the essays by Paul E. W. Roberts and James S. Donnelly, Jr., in *Irish Peasants*, ed. Clark and Donnelly, 64-139; and Miller, *Emigrants and Exiles*, 60-130. On O'Connell, the church, and "Catholic liberalism," see Fergus O'Ferrall, *Catholic Emancipation: Daniel O'Connell and the Birth of Irish Democracy* (Dublin, 1985).

13. On post-Famine Irish politics, see Garvin, *Evolution of Irish Nationalist Politics*, 53-134; also, Paul Bew, *Land and the National Question, 1858-82* (Dublin, 1979); and David S. Jones, "Agrarian Capitalism and Rural Social Development in Ireland," Ph.D. thesis, Queen's University of Belfast, 1977. On Davitt and Connolly, see Theodore W. Moody, *Davitt and Irish Revolution, 1846-1882* (Oxford, 1982); and C. Desmond Greaves, *The Life and Times of James Connolly* (New York, 1961).

14. Miller, *Emigrants and Exiles*, 103-7. I am grateful to Bruce D. Boling for information on the Irish language contained in this and the following paragraphs.

15. Ibid., 107-14; the primary and secondary sources which informed the analysis summarized in this and the following paragraph are voluminous; for full citations, see notes 9-35, ibid., 597-600.

16. Ibid., 114-21.

17. For complaints of emigrant "disloyalty," see George R. C. Keep, "Some Irish Opinions on Population and Emigration, 1851-1901," *Irish Ecclesiastical Record*, 5th ser., 84 (1954): 377-86. Both Garvin *Evolution of Irish Nationalist Politics*, and David Fitzpatrick, *Politics and Irish Life, 1913-1921* (Dublin, 1977), stress continuities between pre- and post-Famine Irish political culture, in contrast to Lee, *Modernization of Irish Society*; see also Miller, *Emigrants and Exiles*, 427-35.

18. On social and cultural tensions in post-Famine Ireland, especially in the western counties, see ibid., 469-92.

19. The classic study of the Irish rural family is Conrad M. Arensberg and Solon T. Kimball, *Family and Community in Ireland*, 2d ed. (Cambridge, 1968).

20. On emigration and the Irish family, see Kerby A. Miller, "Paddy's Paradox: Emigration and America in Irish Imagination and Rhetoric," in *Distant Magnets: Migrants' Views of Opportunities in America and Europe*, ed. Dirk Hoerder (in press).

21. One churchman's favorable views on emigration are in Walter McDonald, *Reminiscences of a Maynooth Professor* (London, 1925), 221-23; also see Oliver MacDonagh, "Irish Emigration to the United States . . . ," in *The Great Famine: Studies in Irish History*, eds. Robert Dudley Edwards and T. Desmond Williams (New York, 1957), 300-301; Thomas N. Burke, *Lectures on Faith and Fatherland* (London, n.d.), 212-13; and M. O'Connor, "The Destiny of the Irish Race," *Irish Ecclesiastical Record* 1 (November 1864): 79. For negative views on emigration, see Keep, "Some Irish Opinions," 377-81; J. O'Hanlon, *Irish Emigrants' Guide to the United States* (Boston, 1851), 10-13; P. O'Leary, *Sgothbhualadh*, trans. Bruce D. Boling (Dublin, 1907), 107-9; Joseph Guinan, *Scenes and Sketches of an Irish Parish* (Dublin, 1906), 43-45, 118-19; and Patrick Sheehan, "The Effect of Emigration on the Irish Church," *Irish Ecclesiastical Record*, 3d ser., 3 (1882): 602-15.

22. O'Leary, *Sgothbhualadh*; Guinan, *Scenes and Sketches*; Burke, *Lectures on Faith*, 228-31; R. F. Foster, *Charles Stewart Parnell: The Man and His Family*

(Atlantic Highlands, 1979), 323-25; Patrick O'Farrell, "Emigrant Attitudes and Behaviour as a Source for Irish History," *Historical Studies* 10 (Dublin, 1976), 114-16; A. M. Sullivan, "Why Send More Irish out of Ireland?" *Nineteenth Century* 14 (July 1883): 131-44; Ruth Dudley Edwards, *Patrick Pearse: The Triumph of Failure* (London, 1977), 78-79, 183.

23. One Irish nationalist who admitted the "salutary" effects of the Famine and agrarian capitalism on Irish society and culture was A. M. Sullivan, *New Ireland: Political Sketches and Personal Reminiscences*, 2 vols. (London, 1878). On post-Famine remittances and donations, see Schrier, *Ireland and the American Immigration*, 103-28, 167-68; and Miller, *Emigrants and Exiles*, 458-59.

24. For British comments on Irish population and emigration, see R. D. Collison Black, *Economic Thought and the Irish Question* (London, 1960). For typical Irish responses, see Schrier, *Ireland and the American Immigration*, 45-65; Sullivan, "Why Send?," 131-44; Sheehan, "The Effect of Emigration," 613; Guinan, *Scenes and Sketches*, 54-55; and O'Farrell, "Emigrant Attitudes and Behaviour," 115, 128-29.

25. Bishop Butler citation courtesy of Emmet Larkin. For evidence of lower-class political consciousness, see Bernard Becker, *Disturbed Ireland* (London, 1882), 85-86; and Guardian of the Poor, *The Irish Peasant: A Sociological Study* (London, 1892), 14.

26. On post-Famine nationalism and its adherents, see Garvin, *Evolution of Irish Nationalist Politics*, 53-134; R. V. Comerford, *The Fenians in Context: Irish Politics and Society, 1848-82* (Dublin, 1985); Bew, *Land and the National Question;* Fitzpatrick, *Politics and Irish Life;* and E. Rumpf and A. C. Hepburn, *Nationalism and Socialism in Twentieth-Century Ireland* (New York, 1977). Quotation from David Fitzpatrick, "Class, Family, and Rural Unrest in Nineteenth-Century Ireland," in *Irish Studies 2*, ed. Drudy, 48-49.

27. On Parnell, see F. S. L. Lyons, "The Economic Ideas of Parnell," *Historical Studies* 2 (London, 1959), 67-73; and Paul Bew, *C. S. Parnell* (Dublin, 1980), 49. On Griffith and his successors, see Richard P. Davis, *Arthur Griffith and Non-Violent Sinn Féin* (Dublin, 1974), 127-44; and Terence Brown, *Ireland: A Social and Cultural History, 1922-1979* (London, 1981), 15-16. On local elites, see especially Líam Kennedy, "The Early Response of the Irish Catholic Clergy to the Co-operative Movement," *Irish Historical Studies* 21 (March 1978): 55-74, and "Farmers, Traders, and Agricultural Politics in Pre-Independence Ireland," in *Irish Peasants*, ed. Clark and Donnelly, 339-73.

28. In general, see Patrick O'Farrell, *Ireland's English Question: Anglo-Irish Relations, 1534-1970* (New York, 1971), 189-241; and Tom Garvin, "Priests and Patriots: Irish Separatism and Fear of the Modern, 1890-1914," *Irish Historical Studies* 25 (May 1986): 67-81. For more complete citations, see Miller, *Emigrants and Exiles*, 636, notes 137-38.

29. Edwards, *Patrick Pearse.*

30. O'Farrell, *Ireland's English Question*, 270-71; J. A. MacMahon, "The

Catholic Clergy and the Social Question in Ireland," *Studies* 70 (1981): 263-86; Emmet Larkin, "Socialism and Catholicism in Ireland," *Church History* 30 (1964): 462-83; Guinan, *Scenes and Sketches*, 43.

31. Greaves, *Life and Times of James Connolly*, 52.

32. Guinan, *Scenes and Sketches*, 46.

33. On Connolly, see Owen Dudley Edwards and Bernard Ransom, eds., *James Connolly: Selected Political Writings* (New York, 1974), 363-64.

34. William Henry Hurlbert, *Ireland under Coercion*, 2d ed. (Edinburgh, 1888), 2:257. No attempt has been made herein to place Ireland's emigration and hegemonic culture in comparative European perspective or to make more than passing references to the Irish situation in North America. Whether Gramsci's model can be applied to other European societies and their emigrations—for example, to those of Poland or Italy, as suggested by several participants in the Spring Hill symposium—is an issue awaiting study. For an application of hegemony theory to the formation of ethnic culture among Irish Americans, see Kerby A. Miller, "Class, Culture, and Immigrant Group Identity in the United States: The Case of Irish-American Ethnicity," in *Immigration Reconsidered: History, Sociology, and Politics*, ed. Virginia Yans-McLaughlin (New York, 1990).

16

Companies as Caretakers: Paternalism, Welfare Capitalism, and Immigrants in the Lake Superior Mining Region

ARNOLD R. ALANEN

Virtually all resource-based regions of the United States, and many manufacturing enterprises developed before the 1930s, have experienced various forms of paternalism or welfare capitalism. Paternalism, a situation whereby an authority treats those under its control in a "fatherly" way—especially by regulating conduct and deportment, and providing for the needs of such individuals—tended to be much more prevalent in America during the nineteenth century. Welfare capitalism, a somewhat more sophisticated form of corporate largesse that emerged at the turn of the century, has been termed by Stuart Brandes as "any service provided for the comfort or improvement of employees which was neither a necessity of the industry nor required by law."[1]

The Lake Superior mining region of northern Michigan, Wisconsin, and Minnesota provides an excellent laboratory for assessing the impact that corporate "caretakers" and their programs had upon local employees and residents. When copper-mining activities commenced in northern Michigan during the mid-1840s, the area was totally remote from America's cities and agricultural areas, and the subsequent evolution of the entire Lake Superior region also occurred in a relatively isolated setting. Because large population centers and their employment opportunities were situated a considerable distance from the region, the singular role of the corporation as either demagogue or benefactor (or some combination thereof) was present for many years.

Given these conditions and situations, the primary purpose of this chapter will be to explore the role that paternalism and welfare capitalism played in the lives of immigrants who resided and worked in one of America's foremost mining regions. Because other investigators have reported that programs based upon concepts of paternalism or welfare capitalism often ignored the needs of the foreign born, it can be asked whether this practice also was true in the Lake Superior mining region, an area where European immigrants formed such a significant proportion of the total population spectrum for several decades.

A secondary objective of this study is to demonstrate that in addition to the archival documents and information typically used in immigration research, other sources can be employed to explore the relationships that existed among corporations, communities, and the foreign-born population. Examples of such items, according to Alan Trachtenberg in his review of Anthony F. C. Wallace's pathbreaking study, *Rockdale: The Growth of an American Village in the Early Industrial Revolution,* include prints and photographs, account books and work records, oral histories, and even the building details of structures such as bell towers which can reveal work concepts while disguising functional realities. To use such sources, Trachtenberg has noted, requires "a new sense of what a historical document is."[2] This study of the Lake Superior region has relied upon maps, community plans and plats, architectural drawings, and photographs to establish the physical settlement context, while social and economic conditions have been assessed by employing such commonly used primary sources as census data, company records, government reports, and newspaper accounts.[3]

Paternalism and Welfare Capitalism in America

The concept of corporate-sponsored paternalism, or *welfare capitalism* as it was termed by the late-nineteenth and early-twentieth centuries, was neither limited to North America nor to immigrants alone. The origins of paternalism and welfare in the Western world can be traced to medieval Europe, when landlords provided accommodations and protection for their serfs. Such provision, of course, were accompanied by a definite quid pro quo: in exchange for a basic level of sustenance and security, a peasant was bound to the landlord virtually for life and served as a regular source of labor for the maintenance and success of the manorial estate. Later in the nineteenth century, various European industrialists such as the Krupp family in Germany and Titus Salt, the Cadbury brothers, and the Lever brothers in England also would provide examples of relatively enlightened, albeit tightly controlled, communities for workers and their families.[4]

In the United States the practice of corporate paternalism—especially via the provision of company-sponsored housing and communities—became evident in the 1790s and early 1800s when accommodations were provided for families and young women employed in New England's emerging textile manufacturing industry. Although the nature and extent of the provisions would not be equaled in later nineteenth-century examples, the idea of supplying company housing and other services accompanied the development of America's industrial frontiers from the anthracite coal fields of Appalachia to the mining camps of the Rocky Mountain region.[5] The degree of corporate control generally was greatest in the most isolated enclaves, where a shortage or even a complete lack of services and facilities required that the employer provide for all the needs of workers and their families. Unfortunately, such practices often led to excess, with the employer not only dominating the workplace, but also regulating the employee's economic resources and individual behavior via the company store and corporate police forces.[6]

As is well known, immigrants were employed in many nineteenth-century industries, with their distinctive skills often giving some American enterprises a unique ethnic identity. The Welsh, for example, were noted for their concentration in anthracite coal mining and tin-plate manufacturing; the Scots in bituminous coal mining; the Cornish in lead and copper ore mining; the English in iron, steel, and textiles; and the Germans in various traditional crafts. While immigrants did play an important role in certain occupations, American industry, by and large, was not directly involved in recruiting large numbers of Europeans to places of employment—even though the U.S. Congress authorized the importation of contract laborers from 1864 to 1885. "Industry itself did not organize the immigrant labor market," Charlotte Erickson has stated, "nor did it provide constructive measures for dealing with abuses."[7]

By the late 1800s, the requirements of American industry had begun to shift dramatically. Rather than relying primarily upon the craft skills of workers, most of whom came from Northern and Western Europe or were born in America, the demand for unskilled and ordinary laborers began to increase appreciably. It was at this time, too, that the primary source of overseas arrivals shifted away from the "old immigration" heartland to the "new immigration" areas of Southern and Eastern Europe.[8] As large numbers of Italians, Poles, South Slavs, and other immigrants poured into this country's industrial and mining centers to pursue the menial, poorly paid, and often dangerous jobs that were waiting to be filled, American capitalists and corporate executives began to modify their approaches to corporate paternalism.

These new attitudes were based upon the notion that paternalism, with its often-heavy-handed approach to labor-management relations, was considered outmoded and in need of specific change. In addition, prominent social scientists such as William Howe Tolman began to call for a more scientific approach to corporate benevolence by American industry. After organizing the Get-Together Club in New York City in 1894, Tolman joined with the Protestant minister Josiah Strong and several business executives to form the League for Social Service (later named the American Institute of Social Services). Recommending a more comprehensive approach to "industrial betterment," the members of these organizations advocated many improvements, including the building of model villages for workers and their families. In addition to the League for Social Services, the National Civic Federation was developed in the early 1900s by various industrialists such as Mark Hanna, Andrew Carnegie, and Elbert Gary; the federation soon coined the term *welfare work* to identify the new approaches to corporate benevolence that it was recommending. The programs were viewed as ways to divert labor strikes and violence and to forestall certain reform movements—factory inspections, safety standards, limits on hours of work, women and children in the workplace, and so forth—that were being promulgated by some governmental and consumer groups during the Progressive era.[9]

As also had been the case with the earlier paternalistic offerings, the most important purpose of the welfare programs was to attract and keep skilled workers. Because emphasis was given to the most highly trained employees, who generally were white, native-born Americans or members of established European groups, they received many more benefits and services than did recent immigrants and blacks. Nevertheless, workers of all classes and backgrounds were affected to some extent by the welfare offerings. David Montgomery has noted that of the three major managerial reforms instituted in America during the early twentieth century—corporate welfare, the professionalization of personnel management, and scientific management (i.e., Taylorism)—only the former affected immigrants to any extent.[10] As mentioned earlier, over the span of many decades a significant proportion of workers and residents throughout the Lake Superior region were of foreign origin; therefore, corporate paternalism and welfare could not ignore the immigrant completely.

The Region

In the Lake Superior mining region, the exploitation of mineral resources, the emergence of permanent settlements, and the origins of corporate paternalism can be traced back to the mid-1840s. Copper ore began to be mined in Michigan's Upper Peninsula in 1844; and the first iron ore was mined on the Marquette Range of Michigan in 1846, although full-scale development would not occur until 1855 following the construction of a canal and lock at Sault Ste. Marie along the Michigan-Ontario border. The iron ore mining frontier then proceeded to move westward, with the Menominee Range in Michigan (1877), the Gogebic Range in Michigan and Wisconsin (1884), and the three Minnesota ranges—the Vermilion (1884), Mesabi (1892), and Cuyuna (1911)—entering the shipping ranks (Figure 16.1).

Given that both copper and iron ore mining occurred in the region and the initial development of the different ranges spanned a period of more than sixty years, some variety obviously was found in the total array of corporate provisions offered to workers. When mining commenced on Michigan's Copper Range (known colloquially as the "Copper Country") during the 1840s, the region was a complete wilderness. The formative aspects of mining development in such a frontier area obviously were accomplished only under extreme hardship and duress, but by the 1850s increased investment from financiers headquartered in New England and the eastern United States provided the necessary capital for a steady flow of people and materials into the region, as well as the means for exporting copper ore to eastern markets. To develop and maintain such linkages with the populated areas of the United States demanded considerable planning and management by the investors and their on-site representatives. An 1862 account summarized the problems associated with such significant distance constraints: "In no other country on the globe has the slow, tedious and heavy business of regular mining at great depths in the rock been attempted, on a large scale, without the aid of a *resident population* and where all the food necessary for the sustenance of the laborers, as well as all the numberless supplies . . . must be transported for a thousand miles, — and where the parties that control the practical operations of exploitation, resided fifteen hundred miles away—only making hurried visits to the country during a few weeks of the summer."[11] Indeed, the seeds for what would evolve into one of the nation's most completely controlled systems of paternalism were planted during these formative years of development when the Copper Range was so far removed from the mainstream of American settlement and economic activity.[12]

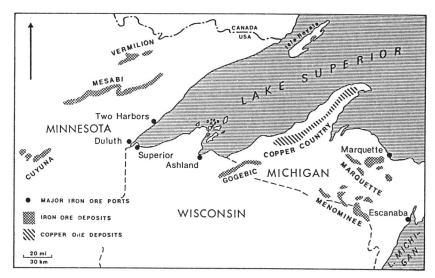

Figure 16.1. Ore-producing districts of the Lake Superior mining region. Following the initial development of Michigan's Copper Range or "Copper Country" in the mid-1840s, the subsequent exploration of six iron ore ranges occurred elsewhere in Michigan, Wisconsin, and Minnesota.

When compared to the copper producing district, nineteenth-century versions of corporate paternalism were not quite as evident on the iron ore mining ranges, but many of the miners and their families still lived in company-built housing and in communities controlled by corporations. One of the major reasons for the difference was that early iron ore mining activities in Michigan during the 1850s, 1860s, and 1870s were not nearly as well financed as operations in the copper production district. Minnesota's Vermillion Range, where iron ore mining began in the early 1880s, did display some early vestiges of classical paternalism, but the entire iron ore industry of the Lake Superior region experienced a dramatic transition following the national financial panic of 1893. Many small, undercapitalized companies suffered bankruptcy and were taken over by a few large corporations with vertically integrated mining, transportation, and steel-making operations and facilities. This period of corporate take-over and merger also corresponded with the ideas of welfare capitalism that began to be espoused in the leading business suites of America. Thus, most programs of corporate benevolence in the iron ore producing districts of the Lake Superior mining region were touted as examples of corporate welfare rather than as paternalistic ventures.[13]

Immigrants as Miners: Michigan's Copper Range

Once it was confirmed in the mid-1840s that possibilities existed to mine and process the copper deposits of northern Michigan, every-thing necessary for the development of settlements—including the people themselves—had to be imported into the region. Virtually immediately, the labor force was dominated by immigrants. In 1850, just a half decade after the first copper ore had been shipped from the region, close to 70 percent of the more than 1,200 residents who lived in the few incipient communities were of immigrant origin; and in 1860 immigrants comprised 65 percent of the Copper Country's eleven thousand inhabitants. Given the mining experience they had previously acquired in their native Cornwall and in other areas of the United States, individuals of English background predominated in the occupational hierarchy; in addition, an ability to speak the lingua franca of the New World helped immeasurably in their immediate movement into key positions as captains and skilled miners. The Ger-mans filled a variety of positions, ranging from mining to trades and crafts, while the Irish traditionally served as mining laborers and trammers (the trammers pushed loaded ore cars up the mine shaft to its mouth). The French Canadians, the fourth major group, seldom worked below ground but often served as woodcutters and lumber-jacks on the surface.[14]

The ethnic character of the Copper Range began to change during the late Civil War period when the U.S. Congress enacted legislation to legalize the importation of contract laborers from foreign countries. Although this act had relatively little impact upon overall immigration patterns, Charlotte Erickson has termed the efforts undertaken in Michigan's copper-producing district during 1864-65 as one of the more ambitious labor recruitment schemes ever developed and pur-sued in the United States. When veteran miners began to leave north-ern Michigan during the Civil War era to join the Union Army, local firms formed the Association of Mining Companies to recruit expe-rienced miners from Norway and Sweden. By July 1864, advertise-ments were appearing in Stockholm newspapers, and in June of that year more than 250 people were bound for the mines of Michigan. In the spring of 1865 some 150 miners (plus women and children) departed from northern Norway for Michigan; included in this group were several Finns who had moved to Norway previously to work in that country's copper mines. Although many Scandinavians broke their labor contracts for various reason—to secure enlistment bonuses by serving in the Union Army, to join their immigrant colleagues in nearby states, or to leave the stony and marginal land of northern Michigan that was unsuitable for agriculture — the nucleus for a small Norwegian and Swedish settlement was established at this time. More important, the few Finns who disembarked at Hancock, Michigan, were joined by growing numbers of their Old World compatriots; by the mid-1890s, the Finns had become the largest immigrant group in the Copper Country.[15]

As larger numbers of Eastern and Southern Europeans began to immigrate to the United States by the 1890s, a certain proportion found their way to northern Michigan's copper mines. The manuscript schedules for the 1910 federal census, which for the first time provide information on the mother tongue of foreign-born individuals then residing in the United States, offer considerable insight to the actual diversity of immigrant groups found on the Copper Range (Figure 16.2). The Finns were by far the largest single ethnic community in the district, followed by two "old immigrant" groups: the British and French Canadians. By this time South Slavs — especially Croatians and Slovenians — from the Austro-Hungarian Empire appeared in increasing numbers. Indeed, Calumet, Michigan, emerged as the largest Croatian mining settlement in the United States prior to 1914, while the city also served as a major economic and cultural center for large numbers of Slovenians. During the early twentieth century Italians also emerged as a significant foreign-born group in the Copper Country.[16]

Immigrants as Miners: The Iron Ore Ranges

The major development of the iron ore ranges occurred after copper mining already was well established in the Lake Superior region. Although underground iron ore mining required some skilled employees — especially in supervisory roles — significant numbers of unskilled laborers could be employed in a variety of positions. (Later, when large-scale, open-pit mining was established on Minnesota's Mesabi Range, much larger numbers of unskilled workers could be hired.) In 1880, for instance, Michigan's Marquette Range was the only iron ore producing area with an established production record. By this time Canadians formed the largest foreign-born group on the Marquette, followed by the Swedes and Irish; smaller numbers of English, German, Norwegian, and Finnish immigrants also were evident.[17]

Twenty years later, in 1900, all of the iron ore districts in the region, except for Minnesota's Cuyuna Range, were shipping raw materials to eastern steel mills. When considered as a group, the five

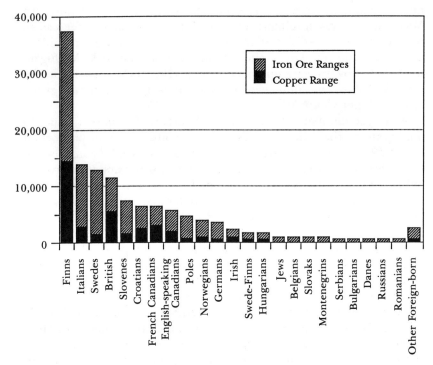

Figure 16.2. Foreign-Born Population of the Lake Superior Mining Region, 1910*

Ethnic affiliation determined by using country of birth and mother tongue listings noted in the 1910 federal population census.

producing ranges embraced a wide variety of immigrant groups. As also was true on the Copper Range, Finns predominated, followed by Swedes, the British, and Canadians. South Slavs (listed as Austrians in the census) and Italians also were evident in increasing numbers. Over the next ten years the Finnish population grew appreciably, and by 1910 their numbers exceeded each of the two next groups, the Swedes and Italians, by almost three times (Figure 16.2). They were followed by the Slovenians, British, Poles, English-speaking Canadians, Croatians, French Canadians, Norwegians, and Germans, as well as smaller representations of Irish, Swede-Finn, Jewish, Belgian, Slovak-ian, Montenegrin, Serbian, Bulgarian, Danish, Russian, and Romanian immigrants. Nowhere was the array of ethnic enclaves more tellingly displayed than on Minnesota's Mesabi Range, where some twenty-five nationality groups were represented, by far, the greatest diversity of immigrants to be found in any non-metropolitan area of the state.[18]

Paternalism on the Copper Range

Despite the wilderness that mid-nineteenth-century copper mining entrepreneurs encountered in northern Michigan, their invest-ments—be it of a financial, moral, or esthetic nature—quickly in-troduced a system of regularized order to the region. Gridded streets were platted, rows of uniform houses were built, and clearings for gardens and marginal agricultural operations were developed. Ac-companying these efforts to build orderly physical environments were the programs intended to direct social behavior. Although hundreds of companies were organized for the purpose of locating and mining the elusive copper ore of the region, no more than seventy-five firms invested large amounts of capital in mining operations and community development, and only a score or so ever realized a profit. Never-theless, a few large corporations such as the Calumet and Hecla Mining Company and the Quincy Mining Company dominated the area and provided an array of paternalistic offerings that affected a majority of laborers.[19]

Such programs, according to corporation apologists, not only as-sisted the workers and residents, but also benefited the stockholders: "[They] reap advantages . . . ," stated an 1875 account, "for the higher the moral and intellectual standard of a workingman, the better he is able to give a just return in labor for the wages he receives."[20] The perceived relationship that existed between an orderly landscape and community and a well-behaved (and productive) miner also clearly was spelled out in an 1856 issue of the *Mining Magazine*:

> How pleasant it is to see taste and comfort consulted in the arrange-ment of our mining locations, or villages, as these locations must become where the mine is a productive one. We would like to see the agents, in laying out village or location lots, leave a reasonable garden plot to each house. Every family might have from 25 to 150 feet for garden and yard to make their homes attractive to themselves and others. We believe that stockholders by consulting the home comfort of their workmen, are consulting their own interests in the long run. Men who have spent long hours several hundred feet below the reach of sunshine must have recreation. And many who now become dis-orderly would not frequent the bar-room if they had a garden to cultivate or a comfortable house to bring themselves about.[21]

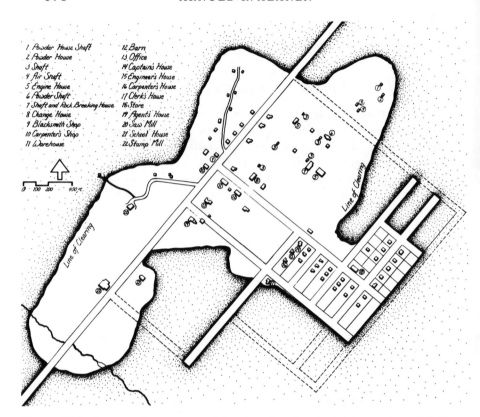

Figure 16.3. Layout of a copper mining location developed in northern Michigan by the Amygdaloid Mining Company, 1866. Shortly after a scattering of buildings had emerged at an early mine site (upper left), companies such as the Amygdaloid sought to carve out orderly, gridlike plats from the surrounding wilderness (lower right). (From Amygdaloid Mining Company of Lake Superior, *Report of the Directors to the Stockholders, June 6, 1866*, Philadelphia: J. B. Chandler, 1866).

Orderly physical layouts, of course, did not necessarily translate into the most attractive environments. While tightly organized settlements may have reduced the feeling of isolation and suggested a sense of security for residents, monotonous and rigid organizational patterns generally emerged upon the landscape (Figure 16.3). Mining supervisors and their families lived in large and comfortable dwellings, but the majority of inhabitants lived in housing that reflected the basic uniformity of the ground plans. Nevertheless, subtle differences in architectural details could reflect the position of individual workers in the corporate hierarchy (Figure 16.4). A change in the pitch of a roof line, the existence or lack of a porch or dormer, and the size

Figure 16.4. Company housing on the Copper Range of Michigan, early 1940s. Built during the late 1800s and early 1900s, company houses continued to shelter residents well into the twentieth century. Smaller houses, such as the saltbox units in the foreground, generally were rented to miners and skilled laborers, while larger two-story dwelling units usually accommodated higher-paid foremen, shift bosses, and clerks. (Farm Security Administration Collection, Library of Congress)

and number of windows often distinguished foremen and skilled employees from common laborers and recent immigrants.[22]

Although design esthetics may have been of little interest to the companies, one investigator has stated that the mining firms "created a stark aestheticism of their own" in the process of developing communities. Early observers, nonetheless, were prone to point out the "well-regulated appearance" of the villages, where uniformity contrasted "strangely with wild and romantic surroundings"; or to comment on the substantial buildings, "arranged in orderly rows, whose neatness and regularity have not so much of the picturesque, but bespeak far healthier conditions than that mingling of the squalid and romantic which characterizes other mining camps." Other observers were even more pragmatic in their interpretations of the layouts: "The buildings [of the Fulton Mine] are judiciously located," stated an 1854 report, "with a proper regard to sanitary precautions, and prevent the spread of conflagration."[23]

Immigrant impressions of company housing and communities are difficult to find, although some early Finnish settlers did distinguish between the small, squat, and dull log structures, sometimes arranged in a helter-skelter pattern on the land, and the frame dwellings that reportedly were larger and better constructed, designed, and painted. "Life here is clean and quiet," claimed a Finnish copper miner in 1881. "The way of existence is rural, and the Finns always appear to be working around their houses." When Scandinavians were being recruited to the region during the Civil War era, one of the companies built an enclave—termed "Swedetown"—situated one mile away from its other residential communities. When the recruits failed to remain in the region, their actions were tersely summarized in the following manner: "There are thirty good log houses, and the people could have lived very comfortably, had they possessed the usual industry of their nation (i.e., Sweden)."[24]

The companies exerted considerable leverage over employees via management of the housing supply. Workers who lived in company housing had to secure permission before their lease could be transferred to someone else, and eviction could occur with no more than fifteen days' notice. Similar regulations governed the ground leases, a provision that made the social critic Graham Taylor question "the mental comfort of people who thus build their own homes on ground from which the company has absolute power to force their removal at almost any time." During a major strike in 1913 and 1914 it was reported that the companies would seek to eliminate the Finns—the most active participants in the confrontation—by cancelling their leases. Even though the threat was carried out only to a limited extent, some years later a U.S. Department of Labor investigator determined that at least some company rental agents continued to discriminate against Finns, who were believed to lack company loyalty and supported socialism.[25]

An array of medical, educational, spiritual, and recreational programs also was provided in the copper district. A version of the Cornish "bal" system, whereby the miner paid a monthly sum to the company (generally $1 for married men and 50 cents for unmarried) in exchange for medical services, was quickly introduced to the Copper Country and subsequently spread to other mining regions of the United States. Some companies also built hospitals and employed doctors for varying periods of time. By 1914, the Calumet and Hecla Company reported that it provided or supported the following for its employees: an armory, ten school buildings, a YMCA, a library with thirty-five thousand volumes, bowling alleys, a bath house, and an indoor swimming pool; in addition, thirty churches received subsidies from the company. Other offerings included the distribution of free fuel to needy persons and the provision of free garbage collection, reduced electrical rates, summer band concerts, and medical, life insurance, and pension programs. Also provided was an employee relief fund (one of the earliest in the nation when formed in 1877), which offered some financial assistance to disabled miners and to the families of laborers who were killed while working.[26]

Despite gestures of corporate largesse such as the relief programs, immigrants often found it necessary to develop their own benevolent societies. The rate of mining accidents in the Copper Country was somewhat lower than in other similar regions of the United States, but at least 1,400 men met untimely deaths in the district between 1885 and 1920, and thousands more were injured. During this thirty-five-year period, 80 percent of the victims were foreign born. Company safety programs, often undertaken with the prodding of newly formed governmental agencies, succeeded in reducing the figure after 1915, although immigrant deaths generally failed to generate significant public outcries.[27]

The 1913-14 strike marks the longest and most bitter labor-management confrontation ever experienced in the Copper Country. Calling for better wages and improved safety and working conditions, the strikers (the majority of whom were immigrants) ended their walkout after ten months, primarily because of hunger, privation, and the nonconciliatory attitudes of the companies. Although the companies apparently "won," the seemingly successful paternalism that had existed for much of the nineteenth century no longer was acceptable by the early 1900s. Nevertheless, the companies failed to recognize this fact even after the strike, and emphasized efficiency and output over improved labor-management relations. It was obvious that even benevolent paternalism could work only if the employees agreed with the system; when the workers actively objected in the twentieth century, the copper mining companies did not modify their practices or agree to share control, but proceeded to adopt even harsher measures and standards.[28]

Welfare Capitalism on the Iron Ore Ranges

Unlike the copper mining companies, most firms operating on the iron ore ranges in the nineteenth century did not have such ready resources of capital available for employee assistance programs. Thus, the early development of communities was characterized by their unkempt appearance and lack of sanitary provisions. Ishpeming, Michigan, was depicted in 1874 as having wooden buildings, "mostly low, and set directly over what has been swamp, without drainings whatever, the water from the mines going into the main swamp." Some years later residents of Virginia,. Minnesota, were informed that they should clean up the "rottenness and filth which abounds on the main street of the city," while the primary thoroughfare in Eveleth, Minnesota, was portrayed as "a solid row of large boarding, tenement and bath houses, with little or no open space between the buildings, nearly all over crowded, with a number of home laundries in the block, and a row of cow sheds and much used privies on the high ground adjoining the alley."[29]

An early plat for Ishpeming illustrates the conditions that residents encountered on a daily basis in such communities (Figure 16.5). The townsite, built upon a marshy area that was filled in with mining spoils, displayed a compact grid that contained very small lots; the houses, therefore, virtually butted up against each other, and allowed very little space, light, or air to penetrate between them. Just outside the townsite were several small enclaves — "locations" — under complete control of the mining companies. Eventually mining firms throughout the region would lay out and organize their locations along rigid and highly structured lines, but during the formative years of these settlements — when they often were inhabited almost exclusively by immigrants — the houses were described as being "all in a jumble" and appearing "as if they had just been poured out of something into a heap."[30]

Company housing and basic medical services also were provided by the iron-mining companies, but it was not until consolidations had occurred in the mining and steel-making industry after 1893 that sufficient funds were available to support a more complete array of employee programs in the region. Since these developments occurred at the same time that the concept of welfare capitalism was emerging in America, most of the programs were touted as examples of the new philosophy.

Welfare capitalism, both in theory and practice, was initially introduced to the iron ore producing areas of the Lake Superior region in the late 1890s by William G. Mather, president of the Cleveland-Cliffs Iron Company. Mather actually began to explore the possibilities of corporate welfare after a Cleveland-Cliffs official visited several manufacturing towns in England, Germany, and Sweden and noted that the design of housing and factories was "far-ahead" of anything in the United States.[31]

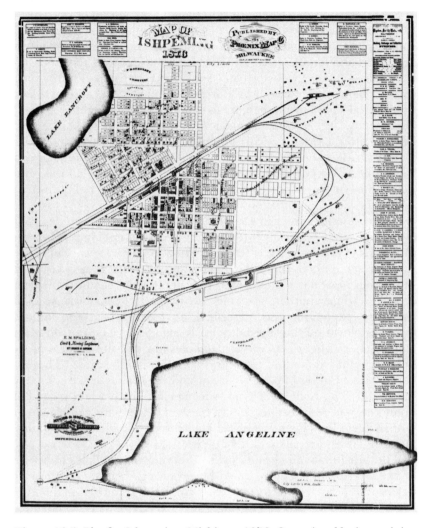

Figure 16.5. Plat for Ishpeming, Michigan, 1876. Constricted by iron mining activities that virtually surrounded the townsite, and built over a marshy area, Ishpeming's layout displayed the compact organizational pattern that characterized the vast majority of mining towns in the Lake Superior region. Adjacent to the townsite were several "locations" that included a single winding street flanked by housing situated on lots of varying shape and dimension. Later company locations would be platted in rigid grid patterns. (Michigan State Archives, Lansing)

Safety was one area where corporation officials saw an obvious need to increase instruction and vigilance, for an injured or dead miner could hardly contribute to the profit-making enterprise. Immigrants received considerable attention because it was claimed that such individuals — especially Eastern and Southern Europeans — were dying or were being injured in disproportionate numbers because of a lack of technical skills and an inability to communicate in English. "[They] have hands," H. N. Casson caustically announced in 1909, "but no heads." After accidents occurred, investigating committees and juries almost always exonerated the companies of any liability and placed the blame squarely on the shoulders of the laborers. As a local Minnesota newspaper reported in 1909, accidents occurred "through carelessness or ignorance on the part of the employees."[32]

When described in local accounts, immigrant deaths were depicted graphically and generally without sentiment or apology. Although hundreds of reports were written, a perusal of only a few is necessary to understand their tone. An immigrant iron ore miner killed in Minnesota in 1893, for example, reportedly was "cut in two by an ore car," while another, who met his death in 1905 because of a dynamite explosion, was described as having "the top of his head . . . blown off and the body badly mangled." The remains of a Slavic miner, caught between a metal elevator and the timbers of an underground excavation, were portrayed in literal detail: "The top part of his head was taken off clean and his brains scattered about the shaft." The body of a Finn who met his death when rocks fell upon him was described as being "crushed beyond any semblance to human form and his remains . . . brought up the shaft in a gunny sack."[33]

The price that immigrants paid in serving the mining enterprise of Minnesota is tellingly revealed by reviewing the listing of mining deaths that occurred during the early twentieth century. For the five-year period from July 1906 through June 1910, a total of 425 fatalities occurred in the state's mines — 5.62 for every thousand employees. Whereas immigrants constituted 75 percent of the total mining work force at this time, they suffered close to 90 percent of all the fatalities. Because of the significant number of Finns, Italians, Slovenes, and Croatians who were engaged in mining, almost three-fourths of all the accidental deaths occurred among members of these groups. No group, however, had a higher fatality rate than the Montenegrins. From 1906 to 1910, the average annual fatality rate for Montenegrins in Minnesota was three deaths per hundred employees. The Poles, with a fatality rate of 1.2 deaths per hundred workers, experienced the second worst record, followed by the Italians (0.8 per hundred), the Finns (0.7 per hundred), and the Slovenians and Croations (0.6 per hundred).[34]

As more safety measures were introduced during the next five-year periods (1911-15), the number of fatalities decreased (from 425 to 255), even though the work force grew larger; the overall fatality rate, for example, declined from 5.62 during the 1906-10 interim to 2.64 deaths per thousand employees over the subsequent five-year period. The improvement, claimed Minnesota governmental officials in 1916, was due to "safety first" measures, improved first aid, and the general corporate welfare movement. Although the fatality figures continued to fall over subsequent years, safety improvements could not prevent the region's worst mining tragedy from occurring in 1924. The accident resulted in the deaths of forty-two miners (most of Finnish and South Slav descent), who were drowned or buried by mud when a lake flooded their underground shaft.[35]

Another provision for laborers recommended by many corporate welfare advocates throughout the nation was the development of model villages. Such communities generally demonstrated better planning features and a larger number of amenities for residents. In the Lake Superior region, once again it was William G. Mather of the Cleveland-Cliffs Iron Company who led the way in promoting this aspect of welfare capitalism. Mather commissioned Warren H. Manning, a nationally known landscape architect from Cambridge, Massachusetts, to plan the development of a model village on the Marquette Range in 1906. The plan that Manning prepared for the new town, Gwinn, featured a public commons and the protection of the nearby landscape to insure that residents would be no more than a ten-minute walk from the river and woodland environments. Areas also were reserved for a hospital, a community building, schools and playgrounds, stores, hotels, churches, and for the Finns, special sauna accommodations. In addition, house purchase plans were available for employees who had sufficient funds to make a down payment and to meet monthly payment obligations. The residential areas, however, were differentiated both economically and socially: only mining supervisors and managers were allowed to live in the larger and more attractive residences, and efforts reportedly were made "to split up the various nationalities in order to make congenial living conditions."[36]

At the same time that plans for Gwinn were on the drawing board, officials at the Oliver Iron Mining Company (a subsidiary of the U.S. Steel Corporation) also sponsored the development of a model village on Minnesota's Mesabi Range. This town, Coleraine, was envisioned as serving the needs of dependable and carefully selected employees who would work in a recently opened area along the mining frontier. By creating a mining town "utopia," U.S. Steel officials also hoped to establish a more favorable image for a corporation that was experiencing problems with its public image. The plan for Coleraine exhibited features of the "City Beautiful," a planning movement that defined many of the civic improvement programs recommended and undertaken for large urban centers in America during the late 1800s and early 1900s. For Coleraine, the planning approach was dubbed the "Village Beautiful," which meant that the model village was to be replete with parks, formal gardens, parkways, and boulevards (Figure 16.6).[37]

Potential commercial operators were screened to determine if they demonstrated sufficient qualities of "citizenship" before being allowed to establish a business in Coleraine; reportedly this was done to insure that the community would be populated by "stable, virile men who have the interest of their own town at heart." In addition, corporation officials exercised strict selection procedures in an effort to populate Coleraine with a majority of American-born citizens and immigrants from Northern and Western Europe. The results of the policy were evident immediately, for by 1910 almost 70 percent of the residents had been born in the United States, while another 25 percent were from Canada and the countries of Western and Northern Europe. (Figures for Minnesota's entire mining region were 40 percent and 15 percent, respectively.) Only some 5 percent of Coleraine's residents were from Eastern and Southern Europe, even though immigrants from these areas of the Old World comprised 45 percent of the total mining town population in Minnesota. The most striking contrast between Coleraine and the Iron Range of Minnesota, however, was provided by the Finnish population. Finns formed close to 30 percent of the total resident population in the region by 1910, but fewer than 2 percent of Coleraine's inhabitants had been born in Finland. The Finns were especially ostracized at this time; only three years earlier they had played a visible role as leaders and participants in the 1907 Mesabi Range strike, a major conflict that colored labor-management relations for many years thereafter. In addition to blacklisting Finns who were perceived to have supported the strike and the recognition of labor organizations such as the Western Federation of Miners and the Industrial Workers of the World (IWW), mining companies attempted to reduce the concentration of foreign ethnic groups in some

Figure 16.6. Overview of Coleraine, Minnesota, 1918. Unlike most of the speculatively built settlements such as Ishpeming, Michigan, and Hibbing, Minnesota, which developed very rapidly throughout the region, the model village of Coleraine was carefully planned by the Oliver Iron Mining Company in 1906. Substantial buildings were constructed, and parks and boulevards graced the townsite. Early applicants for housing, however, were carefully screened by company officials to limit the number of Eastern and Southern Europeans who could reside in the settlement. (Itasca County Historical Society, Grand Rapids, Minn.)

communities. Nowhere else was this policy implemented to a greater extent than in the model village of Coleraine.[38]

In addition to building a few model villages, corporate welfare programs on the iron-producing ranges sought to improve residential and social conditions in existing communities. Visiting nurse programs were initiated; recreational facilities, electric lights, graded streets, paved sidewalks, and water and sewer systems were provided; and garden and community beautification programs were sponsored (Figure 16.7). Many of these efforts grew out of the "mutuality" or "employee representation" plans that began to be developed by various companies just before the 1920s. These plans, which actually were company unions or work councils, provided a forum whereby workers supposedly could bring any problems and grievances to the attention of their employers, for example, the treatment of employees, working conditions and equipment, medical concerns, and residential or living accommodations.[39] In describing the latter issue, officials of the Oliver Iron Mining Company noted how employees (and their

Figure 16.7. The garden of a South Slav family residing in a Minnesota mining settlement, ca. 1917. Most mining companies encouraged employees to plant and maintain gardens to reduce food costs, to improve the appearance of surrounding environments, and to keep idle hands occupied. Since most immigrants owned one or two cows, an array of small barns, out buildings, and haystacks also dotted the immediate landscape. (Iron Range Research Center, Chisholm, Minn.)

wives) were giving more importance to the improvement of residential milieux: "Employees are demanding something more than mere houses to live in. They want running water . . . they want baths and toilets. They insist that the outside toilet is unsanitary and inconvenient. They want their wives to have conveniences that twenty years ago, most of them did not think of because they were not in common use."[40]

Another provision stressed by corporation executives during the formative years of welfare capitalism on the iron ore ranges was the improvement of medical services. While basic medical programs had been available since the early years of mining activity, visiting nurse programs expanded the array of offerings and reached a greater number of inhabitants. The nurses, for example, not only attended the sick, but also provided instruction in hygiene and domestic science and helped families with their financial, marital, and personal problems. Dealing with immigrant groups often posed difficulties for these American-born women. One nurse noted that it was not possible to devote all her attention to the ill, for even healthy families could cause serious problems whenever neighborhood feuds erupted between three or four nationality groups. Another small immigrant community divided into two parts by railroad tracks was claimed to be constantly "at war" by a college-age social worker. She observed that because of tedium and boredom, women on each side of the tracks would throw shoes, clubs, tin cans, and pieces of cord wood at one another for as many as five hours per day. Such problems taxed the abilities of even the best trained nurse, as revealed by the comments of another health provider: "To work here requires infinite patience. In such cases one must be prepared to turn seamstress, dietitian, sanitarian, home demonstrator, gardener, yes, even mechanic, and in these things can a worker demonstrate the results of kindliness and win her way for further health work, something the entire neighborhood has in common."[41]

While the programs did provide certain improvements in the health, welfare, and living conditions of employees and their families, there was no doubting the regulatory criteria that accompanied such largesse. The Oliver Company's mutality plan, for example, stated that an employee could be dismissed for insubordination, creating disorder or confusion among workers by agitation, soliciting membership while at work or on community property, serving as a member of an organization that promoted violence or anarchy, and incapacity. After the plan had been in operation for just over half a year, Oliver Company officials in 1918 reported that through certain unknown processes or reasoning, some workers were asking for "rights" or "seniority." The officials proceeded to inform their employees that if seniority were recognized, the jobs would quickly be filled by mediocre men. Appealing to their masculinity, the officials sought to convince the employees that if they were not able to keep up with their colleagues, then they should take a "back seat" to them. Somewhat later, relieved Oliver Company executives were pleased to report that the men had agreed with this line of reasoning.[42]

Conclusion and Aftermath

The question that still can be asked is whether the early paternalistic offerings and the later welfare programs benefited the immigrant worker to any great extent. Again, it is important to note that evidence from other mining areas of America indicates how often immigrants were ignored.

Because housing was the most common provision offered to mining employees through the Lake Superior region, an assessment of the quantity and quality of residential units provides important insight to this question. The most complete information on housing in the Copper Counry comes from 1913 and 1914, a period when governmental investigations focused upon strike-related conditions in the region. The surveys revealed that of the close to fourteen thousand individuals who were employed in copper-mining activities, the companies rented out more than 3,300 houses to their workers, and land was leased for an additional 1,750 units. Many single men also were accommodated in boarding houses. Overall, it has been estimated that one-half to two-thirds of the total copper mining work force resided in company houses or on company land. The housing and other services, however, were provided in a clearly hierarchical manner. Managers, supervisors, and the most highly valued and paid employees received all of their benefits without cost; besides housing, these services included free medical treatment and fuel, as well as labor, horses, and wagons for household use.[43]

Housing data for areas of Minnesota are even more complete, and provide insight into the practice of welfare capitalism. Information from the 1910 census for seventy-eight company-controlled enclaves (i.e., mining camps and locations) reveals that immigrants formed a population majority in some three-fourths of the settlements, while American-born residents predominated in the remaining one-fourth. Even though large numbers of immigrants obviously were housed in many of these small company communities, definite differences existed in housing quality and in the level of services provided. The residences constructed for persons born in the United States were larger and better built than those which accommodated immigrants; and married individuals employed as mining superintendents, captains, foremen, bosses, and clerks also secured a company house more readily than did common laborers. By 1918, almost 70 percent of the Oliver Iron Mining Company's supervisory and professional employees were located in company-supplied housing. For skilled laborers who were married (this group included immigrants from Northern and Western Europe, as well as persons born in America), the figure was 44 percent. Of the unskilled workers, only 12 percent were housed; many of the latter individuals might have lived in a corporate community, but they often built their own house or shanty on land leased from the company or else they acquired a "squatter's license" for this right.[44]

Pension and profit-sharing programs also were open to employees throughout the iron ore mining districts, but unmarried immigrant workers often were excluded—especially if they were considered to be itinerant laborers. A Mesabi Range missionary-social worker described the existence of these single men in the following manner: "Immigrant men live here, the shacks crowded to the doors. Night and day shift men alternate in occupying the bunks, and bread and meat and beer is the standard meal." The local saloon keeper, the observer reported, often served as the immigrant male's banker, ticket agent, and sole friend.[45]

While paternalistic offerings and corporate welfare might have reached a larger number of immigrant workers in the Lake Superior mining region than was true in other areas of the United States, there is no doubt that it was American-born employees (and a smaller number of selected immigrants) who benefited the most. Also, paternalism and corporate welfare placed strict restrictions upon individual and group rights; such constraints were anachronistic approaches to labor organization and management in a nation built upon democratic principles. The effect, Rowland Berthoff has stated, was to impose the employer's "conception of system and order upon his employees."[46]

In essence, it was the unskilled immigrant who suffered most under such a system. Not only were these individuals subject to discrimination, constant exposure to death and injury, and the ever-present possibility of unemployment, but they also did not have access to the majority of corporate welfare programs. It was not until the passage of New Deal legislation in the 1930s such as the National Labor Relations (Wagner) Act, which ended employee representation plans and corporate welfare programs and eventually replaced them with collective bargaining agreements, that more complete protection was provided for all workers. Ironically, by the time such provisions were put into place during the 1940s, relatively few immigrants remained in the work force of the Lake Superior region. It was their descendants who would benefit most from the new legislation and practices.

NOTES

1. Stuart D. Brandes, *American Welfare Capitalism, 1880-1940* (Chicago, 1976), 5, 6.

2. A. Trachtenberg, "Machines Come to America," *New York Times Book Review,* January 21, 1979, p. 32; Anthony F. C. Wallace, *Rockdale: The Growth on an American Village in the Early Industrial Revolution* (New York, 1978). For one study of photographic research used to study urban ethnic history, see Deborah L. Miller, "Minneapolis Picture Album, 1870-1935: Images of Norwegians in the City," *Norwegian-American Studies* 31 (1986): 131-62.

3. An earlier study also probed some of the sources that are available when undertaking research on mining towns and regions; Arnold R. Alanen,

"Documenting the Physical and Social Characteristics of Mining and Resource-Based Communities," *Bulletin. Association for Preservation Technology* 11, no. 4 (1979): 49-68.

4. Leiffur Magnusson, "Company Housing," and Horace B. Davis, "Company Towns," in *Encyclopedia of the Social Sciences* 4 (New York, 1931), 115-22; Norman Newton, *Design on the Land: The Development of Landscape Architecture* (Cambridge, 1971), 447-53.

5. Magnusson, "Company Housing," 115-16; also see John S. Garner, *The Model Company Town: Urban Design Through Private Enterprise in Nineteenth-Century New England* (Amherst, 1984).

6. It was not, however, an isolated company town that drew the greatest amount of public attention to the excesses of corporate paternalism, but rather, Pullman, Illinois, an industrial suburb of Chicago which received this dubious honor. Developed by sleeping-car magnate George M. Pullman in the early 1880s, the community was a tightly controlled fiefdom that mirrored the elitist attitudes of its founder. Following a bitter strike and confrontation in 1894, caused in no small part by the onerous control George Pullman exerted over his employees—both in the shop and community— the Illinois supreme court ordered that the community be sold to outside bidders. With this action, America's most infamous example of company town organization came to an end. See Stanley Buder, *Pullman: An Experiment in Industrial Order and Community Planning, 1840-1930* (New York, 1967).

7. David Brody, "Labor," in *Harvard Encyclopedia of American Ethnic Groups*, ed. Stephan Thernstrom (Cambridge, 1980), 609; Charlotte Erickson, *American Industry and the European Immigrant, 1860-1885* (Cambridge, 1957), vii.

8. Brody, "Labor," 609.

9. William H. Tolman, *Social Engineering: A Record of Things Done by American Industrialists Employing Upwards to One and One-half Million People* (New York, 1909), iii; Brandes, *American Welfare Capitalism*, 21,23; Gwendolyn Wright, *Building the Dream: A Social History of Housing in America* (Cambridge, 1983), 177-82.

10. Wright, *Building the Dream*, 184; David Montgomery, "Immigrant Workers and Managerial Reform," in *Immigration in Industrial America, 1850-1920*, ed. Richard L. Erlich (Charlottesville, 1977), 96-98.

11. *Mining Gazette* (Houghton, Mich.), July 26, 1862, p. 4.

12. Vernon H. Jensen, in his study of labor relations in the American metal industry, made the following comment about Michigan's Copper Country: "No more completely controlled paternalism has ever existed in this country," *Heritage of Conflict: Labor Relations in the Nonferrous Metal Industries Up to 1930* (Ithaca, 1950), 273.

13. Henry R. Mussey, "Combination in the Mining Industry: A Study of Concentration in Lake Superior Iron Ore Production," in *Studies in History, Economics and Public Law* 23 (New York, 1905), 23; David A. Walker, *Iron Frontier: The Discovery and Early Development of Minnesota's Three Ranges* (St. Paul, 1979), 127; Arnold R. Alanen, "The Planning of Company Com-

munities in the Lake Superior Mining Region," *Journal of the American Planning Association* 45 (July 1979): 264.

14. Information on the ethnic and occupational backgrounds of early Copper Range residents has been derived from the original manuscript schedules for the federal population censuses of 1850 and 1860.

15. Erickson, *American Industry and the European Immigrant*, 43-44, 48, 215; Arnold R. Alanen, "The Norwegian Connection: Early Emigration from Arctic Norway to the American Midwest," *Finnish Americana* 6 (1984-85): 30-31.

16. "Croats," and Rudolph M. Susel, "Slovenes," both items in *Harvard Encyclopedia*, ed. Thernstrom, 251, 931; the data for immigrant groups have been derived from the manuscript schedules for the federal population census of 1910.

17. Manuscript schedules for the federal population census of 1880.

18. Manuscript schedules for the federal population censuses of 1900 and 1910; Arnold R. Alanen, "Years of Change on the Iron Range," in *Minnesota in a Century of Change: The State and Its People since 1900*, ed. Clifford E. Clark, Jr. (St. Paul, 1989), 177.

19. Larry D. Lankton, "Paternalism and Social Control in the Lake Superior Copper Mines, 1845-1913," *Upper Midwest History* 5 (1985): 1-2.

20. *Portage Lake Mining Gazette*, August 25, 1875, p. 3.

21. "Cliff Mine," *Mining Magazine* 7 (1856): 311.

22. Alanen, "Documenting the Physical and Social Characteristics," 53-54.

23. Sarah McNear, *Quincy Mining Company: Housing and Community Services, ca. 1860-1931*, report prepared for Historic American Engineering Record (HAER) Ml-2. (Washington, ca. 1979), 521; *Portage Lake Mining Gazette*, October 28, 1865, p. 2; T. A. Rickard, *The Copper Mines of Lake Superior* (New York, 1905), 20; *Mining Magazine* 3 (November-December 1854): 554.

24. *Amerikan Suomalainen Lehti* (Calumet, Mich.), July 11, 1879, p. 2; August 29, 1879, p. 1; August 26, 1881, p. 2; *Portage Lake Mining Gazette*, December 1864, p. 2.

25. U.S. Secretary of Labor, *Strike in the Copper District of Michigan: Letter from the Secretary of Labor Transmitting in Response to a Senate Resolution of January 29, 1914: A Report in Regard to the Strike of Mine Workers in the Michigan Copper District which Began on July 23, 1913*, Senate Document no. 381, serial 6575, 63d Cong., 2d sess. (Washington, 1914), 117-120; Graham R. Taylor, "The Clash in the Copper Country," *Survey* 31 (November 1, 1913): 135; "The Proposed Elimination of the Finns," *Engineering and Mining Journal* 97 (May 2, 1914): 920; Leiffur Magnusson, *Housing by Employers in the United States*, U.S. Bureau of Labor Statistics, bulletin no. 263, Miscellaneous Series (Washington, 1920), 38.

26. Brandes, *American Welfare Capitalism*, 93; Lankton, "Paternalism and Social Control," 5, 11-12; U.S. Secretary of Labor, *Strike in the Copper District*, 34-35, 125-26.

27. *Portage Lake Mining Gazette,* July 22, 1886, p. 3; Larry Lankton, "Died in the Mines," *Michigan History* 67 (November-December 1983), 33-34, 40-41.

28. Alanen, "The Planning of Company Communities," 264; Lankton, "Paternalism and Social Control," 13-14.

29. *Weekly Agitator* (Ishpeming, Mich.), September 5, 1874, p. 1; *Virginia Enterprise* (Virginia, Minn.), May 24, 1901, p. 6; *Mining News* (Eveleth, Minn.), January 25, 1908, p. 1.

30. Interview with Joe Jagunich, September 12, 1983, conducted by David Perry, on file with Iron Range Research Center, Chisholm, Minnesota; Marguerite Lains, "Six Weeks on the Range, 1928," daily vacation bible school reports, W. J. Bell Papers, Minnesota Historical Society, St. Paul.

31. William G. Mather, "Some Observations on the Principle of Benefit Funds and Their Place in the Lake Superior Mining District," *Proceedings of the Lake Superior Mining Institute* 5 (August 1898): 12; *Iron Ore* (Ishpeming, Mich.), September 29, 1928, p. 1.

32. Herbert N. G. Casson, *The Romance of Steel: The Story of a Thousand Millionaires* (New York, 1907), 252, 253; *Virginia Enterprise,* April 30, 1909, p. 4.

33. *Mesaba Range* (Biwabik and Merritt, Minn.), August 17, 1893, p. 4; *Virginia Enterprise,* September 8, 1905, p. 1; *Hibbing News* (Hibbing, Minn.), February 1, 1902, p. 1; *Hibbing Sentinel* (Hibbing, Minn.), June 16,1894, p. 1.

34. Accident data for 1906-10 have been derived from the following sources: Bureau of Labor, *Tenth Biennial Report of the Bureau of Labor of the State of Minnesota, 1905-1906* (Minneapolis, 1907); Bureau of Labor, Industries and Commerce, *Eleventh Biennial Report of the Bureau of Labor, Industries and Commerce of the State of Minnesota, 1907-1908* (Minneapolis, 1909); and *Twelfth Biennial Report of the Bureau of Labor, Industries and Commerce of the State of Minnesota, 1909-1910* (n.p., ca. 1910).

35. Accident data for 1911-15 are from the following: Bureau of Labor, Industries and Commerce, *Thirteenth Biennial Report of the Bureau of Labor, Industries and Commerce of the State of Minnesota, 1911-1912* (n.p., ca. 1912); Department of Labor and Industries, *Fourteenth Biennial Report of the Department of Labor and Industries of the State of Minnesota, 1913-1914* (Minneapolis, ca. 1914); and *Fifteenth Biennial Report of the Department of Labor and Industries of the State of Minnesota, 1915-1916* (Minneapolis, 1916); *Crosby Courier* (Crosby, Minn.), February 8, 1924, p. 1.

36. Warren H. Manning, "Villages and Homes for Working Men," *Western Architect* 16 (August 1910): 85; Oglebay, Norton and Company, *Housing Report for Oglebay, Norton and Company Mining Properties* (Ironwood, 1921).

37. *Duluth News-Tribune,* June 9, 1907, p. 4; Donald L. Boese, *John C. Greenway and the Opening of the Western Mesabi* (Bovey, Minn., 1975), 85-112.

38. *Duluth News-Tribune,* June 9, 1907, p. 4; John Syrjamaki, "Mesabi Communities: A Study of Their Development," Ph.D. dissertation, Yale

University, 1940, 127; U.S. Immigration Commission, *Reports of the Immigration Commission: Immigrants in Industries*, parts 17 and 18, Senate Document no. 633, serial 5677, 61st Cong., 2d sess. (Washington, 1911), 336. The figures for Coleraine have been derived from the original manuscript schedules for the federal population census of 1910.

39. Oliver Iron Mining Company Adopts Labor Co-operation Policy," *Engineering and Mining Journal* 105 (July 29, 1918): 1166; Brandes, *American Welfare Capitalism*, 120.

40. "First Report of Mutuality Department Covering the Period Beginning May 22, 1918 and Ending December 31, 1918, Inclusive. Virginia: Oliver Iron Mining Company, March 14, 1919," in Oliver Iron Mining Company (OIMC) Records, J. S. Steel, comp., Minnesota Historical Society, St. Paul.

41. Alma B. Brown to Rentecost Mitchell, "Monthly Report of Visiting Nurse—October, Nov. 16, 1928," in Oliver Iron Mining Company Papers; "Report of Agusta Jokich from July 14 to Aug. 1, 1919," in daily vacation bible school reports, Bell Papers.

42. *Engineering and Mining Journal* 105 (July 29, 1918): 1166; "First Report of Mutuality Department," OIMC Records.

43. Lankton, "Paternalism and Social Control," 3, 4, 16.

44. Assistant to the Vice President, Oliver Iron Mining Company, to W. J. Olcott, "Housing Conditions Minnesota Ranges, June 25, 1918," OIMC Records; Arnold R. Alanen, "The 'Locations': Company Communities on Minnesota's Iron Ranges," *Minnesota History* 48 (Fall 1982): 97. Figures for ethnic groups have been derived from the original manuscript schedules for the federal population census of 1910.

45. William J. Bell, "The Range Parish, Presbyterian, Mountain Iron, Minn." (ca. 1917), Bell Papers.

46. Rowland Berthoff, *An Unsettled People: Social Order and Disorder in American History* (New York, 1971), 337.

Contributors

ARNOLD R. ALANEN is a professor in the Department of Landscape Architecture and School of Natural Resources at the University of Wisconsin-Madison. A geographer, his research and teaching activities in the field of landscape history have led him to explorations of immigrant culture (especially among Finns) and the study of isolated, resource-based communities in the American Midwest. He is the co-author of *Main Street Ready-Made: The New Deal Community of Greendale, Wisconsin* and contributed one of the chapters for a volume on the twentieth-century history of Minnesota. He is writing a book about the immigrant communities of Minnesota's Iron Range.

JUNE GRANATIR ALEXANDER teaches courses on Slavic immigration and ethnic groups in the United States for the Department of Russian and East European Studies at the University of Cincinnati. Her major publications include *The Immigrant Church and Community: Pittsburgh's Slovak Catholics and Lutherans, 1880-1915*, "Diversity within Unity: Regionalism and Social Relationships Among Slovaks in Pre-World War I Pittsburgh," and "Staying Together: Chain Migration and Patterns of Slovak Settlement in Pittsburgh Prior to World War I." Her research focuses on immigrants and ethnic groups during the Great Depression.

JON GJERDE is associate professor of history at the University of California, Berkeley. Among his publications are *From Peasants to Farmers: The Migration from Balestrand, Norway to the Upper Middle West*, "Conflict and Community: A Case Study of the Immigrant Church in the United States," and "Patterns of Migration to and Demographic Adaptation within Rural Ethnic American Communities." He is working on a book-length study of the ethnically segmented migration to and settlement of the rural Midwest.

DIRK HOERDER teaches North American social history at the University of Bremen and is coordinator of the International Labor Migration Project. His publications include a three-volume bibliography of the immigrant labor press in the United States and Canada and *Labor Migration in the Atlantic Economies*. Together with Leslie Page Moch he is preparing a summary of research: *Migration: A Frame of Reference*.

WALTER D. KAMPHOEFNER is associate professor of history at Texas A & M University, where he teaches immigration history, urban history, and quantitative methods. He is author of *The Westfalians: From Germany to Missouri* and has co-edited a collection of immigrant letters (with Wolfgang Helbich and Ulrike Sommer), *Briefe aus Amerika: Deutsche Auswanderer schreiben aus der Neuen Welt, 1830-1930.* His research centers on a collaborative transatlantic project to collect and edit German immigrant letters.

HARTMUT KEIL teaches American social and cultural history at the American Studies Department of the University of Munich in Germany. His research interests and publications include political ideologies and labor and immigration. For several years he was the director of the Chicago Project on German immigrant workers to that city. Numerous articles and several books have come out of that project, including *German Workers in Chicago: A Documentary History of Working-Class Culture from 1850 to World War I*, edited with John B. Jentz, and an edition of essays, *German Workers' Culture in the United States 1850 to 1920*. He is presently engaged in a study on the presentation of Germany in American television news.

REINO KERO teaches American history and economic and social history at the University of Turku. Among his major publications are *Migration from Finland to North America in the Years between the United States Civil War and the First World War, The Finns in North America: Destinations and Composition of Immigrant Societies in North America before World War I*, and *Intiaanien Amerikka*. He has been conducting research on hunting as a profession in nineteenth-century Africa.

ODD S. LOVOLL is a professor of Norwegian and history at St. Olaf College, Northfield, Minnesota and is editor of the publications of the Norwegian-American Historical Association. His research focuses on Norwegian migration and settlement in the United States. His most recent major work is *A Century of Urban Life: The Norwegians in Chicago*, and he is also preparing a contemporary history of Norwegian Americans.

RUSSELL R. MENARD is professor of history at the University of Minnesota. A specialist in early American history and American social history, he is the author of *The Economy of British America, 1607-1789* (with John McCusker), *Economy and Society in Early Colonial Maryland*, and *Robert Cole's World: Agriculture and Society in Early Maryland* (with Lois Carr and Lorena Walsh). Along with Steven Ruggles, he is directing a project funded by the National Institutes of Health to construct a large public-use sample of the 1880 U.S. Census of Population.

KERBY A. MILLER is professor of history at the University of Missouri, Columbia, where he teaches U.S. urban and immigration history as well as modern Irish history. His most notable publication is *Emigrants and Exiles: Ireland and the Irish Exodus to North America*. He is editing a collection of Irish immigrants' letters and memoirs from the colonial period to the present.

EVA MORAWSKA teaches in the Sociology Department at the University of Pennsylvania. She is the author of several articles on immigration and ethnicity in the United States and a historical-sociological study: *For Bread with*

Butter: Life-World of the East Central Europeans in Johnstown, Pennsylvania, 1890-1940. She is at work on a book titled *Insecure Prosperity: Jews in Small-town Industrial America, 1880-1940.*

JULIANNA PUSKÁS is a scientific advisor at the Institute of History of the Hungarian Academy of Sciences in Budapest. Since the 1970s she has published numerous papers on overseas migration concerning Hungary and ethnic problems of Magyars. Her book *From Hungary to the United States, 1880-1914* appeared the same year (1982) as the more comprehensive work *Kivandorlo magyorok az Egyesult Allamokba, 1880-1940.* She is preparing a monograph on Hungarian migrants and their experiences in the United States and conducting research on Hungarians in Cleveland for the project "Conflict and Cooperation: Comparative Research on the East-European Migratory Experience, 1830s-1930s."

FRANCO RAMELLA is associate professor of history at the University of Turin, where he teaches contemporary history with emphasis on the nineteenth and twentieth centuries. Among his publications are *Terra e telai.* Together with Samuel L. Baily, he has edited *One Family, Two Worlds: An Italian Family's Correspondence Across the Atlantic, 1901-1922.* More recently he has been studying internal and external migration and strategies of social mobility in northern Italy from 1880 to 1920.

BRUNO RAMIREZ is professor of history at the University of Montreal. A specialist in labor and immigration history in North America, he is the author of *When Workers Fight: The Politics of Industrial Relations in the Progressive Era, Les premiers Italiens de Montreal, La vida social en Angloamerica,* and *On the Move: French-Canadian and Italian Migrants in the North Atlantic Economy, 1860-1914.* He is working on a research project on comparative labor and ethnic history of the United States and Canada.

SUZANNE M. SINKE is a doctoral candidate in immigration history at the University of Minnesota. She is currently editor of the *Austrian Studies Newsletter.* Her dissertation, in progress, examines Dutch immigrant women in the United States in the period from 1880 to 1920. She is the author of several articles on immigrant women, including "Children, Church, and Sickbed? The Lives of Dutch-American Women," in *Papers from the Fourth Interdisciplinary Conference on Netherlandic Studies* edited by Margriet Lacy, and "A Historiography of Immigrant Women in the Nineteenth and Early Twentieth Centuries."

ROBERT P. SWIERENGA is professor of history at Kent State University, where his areas of specialization are immigration, economics, business history, and quantitative methodology. His recent publications include *The Dutch in America: Immigration, Settlement, and Cultural Change,* and he is completing two manuscripts, one on Dutch Jewish immigrants in the nineteenth century and a second general study of Dutch immigration to the United States.

FRANK THISTLETHWAITE is emeritus professor and founding vice-chancellor (president) of the University of East Anglia. He is also Honorary Fellow of St. John's College, Cambridge, where he lives. His field of study is American history, with an emphasis on Anglo-American social and economic relations and the history of European migration. Among his major publications are *The Great Experiment: An Introduction to the History of the American People*, *America and the Atlantic Community*, and *Dorset Pilgrims: The Story of West County Puritans Who Went to New England in the 17th Century*. He is working on the history of a family of Lancashire cotton manufacturers.

RUDOLPH J. VECOLI is professor of history and director of the Immigration History Research Center at the University of Minnesota. His publications include " 'Free Country': The American Republic Viewed by the Italian Left, 1880-1920," in *In the Shadow of the Statue of Liberty: Immigrants, Workers and Citizens in the American Republic 1880-1920* edited by Marianne Debouzy, " 'Primo Maggio' in the United States: An Invented Tradition of the Italian Anarchists," in *May Day Celebrations* edited by Andrea Panaccione, and (with others) "The Invention of Ethnicity: A Perspective from the U.S.A." He is at work on a history of the role of Italian immigrants in radical labor movements in the United States.